Foundations of Comparative Law

JCL Studies in Comparative Law

Editors
Professor William E. Butler
Professor Michael Palmer

A series dedicated to classic works in the field of comparative law, commonly with a modern introduction, contemporary monographs, and collected essays by leading and rising scholars:

No. 1: Constitutional Courts: A Comparative Study. Edited by Andrew Harding and Peter Leyland (2009). ISBN 978-0-854-900633

No. 2: Mixed Legal Systems at New Frontiers. Edited by Esin Örücü (2010). ISBN: 978-0854-900701

No. 3: Building the Civilization of Arbitration. Edited by Thomas E. Carbonneau and Angelica M. Sinopole (2010). ISBN: 978-0854-900688

No. 4: Foundations of Comparative Law: Methods and Typologies. Edited by W. E. Butler, O. V. Kresin, and Iu. S. Shemshuchenko (2011). ISBN: 978-0854-900923

No. 5: Global Wrongs and Private Law Remedies and Procedures edited by Stathis Banakas (2011). ISBN: 978-0854-900916

JCL Studies in Comparative Law

Foundations of Comparative Law
Methods and Typologies

Edited by

W. E. Butler
O. V. Kresin
Iu. S. Shemshuchenko

Wildy, Simmonds & Hill Publishing

Foundations of Comparative Law. Methods and Typologies

British Library Cataloguing-in-Publication Data:
A catalogue record for this book is available from The British Library

ISBN 9780854900923

First published in 2011 by
Wildy, Simmonds & Hill Publishing
58 Carey Street, London WC2A 2JB
England

CONTENTS

Introduction 1
- O. V. Kresin and Iu. S. Shemshuchenko

Applied Comparative Law and Periodization

The Place of Ukraine on the Legal Map of the World 4
- W. E. Butler

The Periodization of Comparative Law: In Search of an Acceptable Model 13
- O. V. Kresin

Typologies and Method

Typologies of Modern Legal Systems of the World 36
- L. A. Luts

Legal Systems of the Modern World: Problems of Identification 53
- V. V. Oksamytnyi

Comparative Law Hermeneutics: Cognitive Possibilities 84
- M. A. Damirli

Functionalism and the Development of Comparative Law Cognition 92
- A. V. Tkachenko

Systemic Considerations

Comparative Law and the Integrating Role of International Law 110
- Iu. A. Tikhomirov

Comparative Legal Research in an Era of Globalization 123
- Kh. N. Bekhruz

Unified Potential of Comparative Law as a Science and Instructional Discipline 141
- A. Iu. Salomatin

Legal System: State, Region, World? 159
- O. F. Skakun

Legal Theory and Comparison

The Concepts of "Jus" and "Lex": Historical and Legal Linguistic Aspects 189
- R. A. Romashov
Philosophical Problems of Legal Comparativistics 207
- A. D. Tikhomirov
Social Naturalism as a Methodological Principle of Comparative Law and Legal Globalistics 234
- A. N. Kostenko

On European Comparative Law

Classification of European Systems of Private Law 255
- E. O. Kharitonov and O. I. Kharitonova
Convergence of Romano-Germanic and Anglo-Saxon Law 276
- M. N. Marchenko

Legal Systems and Religion

Religious Legal Systems: Features and Classification 304
- D. V. Lukianov
Canon Law in the Modern Legal System of Society 318
- A. S. Smykalin and V. P. Motrevich
Confessional Law and the Subject of Comparative Research 326
- S. O. Shaliapin

Review Article

Renaissance of Slavonic Law? 331
- W. E. Butler

Bibliography

Publications of Ukrainian Association of Comparative Law 337
- W. E. Butler

Index of Names 347

Introduction

O. V. KRESIN* AND IU. S. SHEMSHUCHENKO**

The present issue of *The Journal of Comparative Law* is devoted principally to articles based on public lectures and master classes given during the past four years (2007 to 2010 inclusive) at the international symposia styled "Comparative Law Days". These have been held in various cities of Ukraine under the auspices of the V. M. Koretskiy Institute of State and Law, National Academy of Sciences of Ukraine and the Ukrainian Association of Comparative Law, with other partners. The authors chosen for publication here originate in Russia or Ukraine or otherwise specialize in the legal systems of countries which are members of the Commonwealth of Independent States (CIS).

The organizers of the "Comparative Law Days" from the very outset assumed the ambitious task of drawing the attention of jurists, including law students, in the post-Soviet jurisdictions to comparative law as an instrument for better understanding their own and foreign legal traditions, in identifying the common, the special, and the unique in processes of legal development, and in pursuing law reform of national and other legal systems. It was also hoped that these Forums would bring comparative law specialists together on a professional and social basis, encourage a greater awareness of comparative law as an "interest group" in its own right, further the cause of comparative law in institutions of higher legal education and specialist publications, bring comparative law from its present marginal status in law faculties to the center of attention and concern, promote the formation of chairs of law specialized in comparative

* кандидат юридических наук, Docent. Senior Research Associate, V. M. Koretskiy Institute of State and Law, National Academy of Sciences of Ukraine; Learned Secretary, Ukrainian Association of Comparative Law: Associate, International Academy of Comparative Law.

** доктор юридических наук, Professor, Academician. Director, V. M. Koretskiy Institute of State and Law, National Academy of Sciences of Ukraine, Foreign Member, Russian Academy of Sciences; President, Ukrainian Association of Comparative Law; Associate, International Academy of Comparative Law.

legal studies, institutionalize comparative law as a recognized specialization for law students at postgraduate levels, and encourage the preparation of dissertations for lower and higher doctorates.

The "Comparative Law Days" are unique in post-Soviet legal space. There is nothing like them elsewhere in the countries who are members of the Commonwealth of Independent States nor, so far as we are aware, elsewhere in Europe or North America. The Forum, normally extending over a four-day period, consists of a variety of lectures, master classes, seminars, round tables, plenary meetings, specialist groups, and presentations.[1] Some amount to collective "brain storming" on a selected topic; others discuss approaches to teaching and research methodologies; others simply pursue new ideas.

The initial Forum was the occasion for establishing the Ukrainian Association of Comparative Law (UACL). The activities of the UACL are reported on the sole website in the CIS devoted to comparative law (www.comparativelaw.org.ua) in three languages: English, Russian, and Ukrainian. Documents of the UACL, programs of past and future seminars, announcements and press releases, photographs of Forums and other occasions, brief accounts of books, journals, and other publications presented at Forums appear there. Collected materials of each seminar have been published in book form. The Open Lectures appear in a special series of booklets called the "Academy of Comparative Law" (there are twenty-three to date) in either Ukrainian or Russian. Those whose primary language is English are translated into, as a rule, Ukrainian (W. E. Butler, Ugo Mattei, Akmal Saidov). A full Bibliography will be found herein below.

The UACL publishes its own journal in Russian, Ukrainian, and Greek twice yearly entitled "Comparative Law Studies" (October 2005-) and is issuing a series of substantial books under the general title "Encyclopedia of Comparative Law". Five volumes have appeared to date, as well as extra-series titles.

The "Comparative Law Days" have been held in various cities of Ukraine: Kiev, Simferopol, Odessa, Ivano-Frankivsk. The UACL has been fortunate to involve a number of co-organizers and co-sponsors of the Forums. They may vary from one year to the next, depending upon where the Forum is held. Collaborators in the Forums have included: the Institute of State and Law, National Academy of Sciences of Ukraine; Tauride National University, Kiev University of Law, Kiev National University,

[1] "Presentations" are literally that: an author or editor makes a brief presentation about his new book or new journal, replies to questions from the audience (some of whom may make public remarks supportive or critical of the new publication), distributes publicity material, and otherwise generates interest in the publication.

Ukrainian legal newspapers and law publishers, the National OSCE Projects Coordinator, the American Bar Association Rule-of-Law Initiative in Ukraine, the CMS Reich-Rohrwig Hainz TOV law firm, among others. Attendance from throughout the world in 2010 reached over 300.

The authors collectively express their gratitude to Academician W. E. Butler, who has translated all of the articles herein.

The Place of Ukraine on the Legal Map of the World

W. E. BUTLER*

This article serves the dual function of introducing the materials which follow and sharing some of my own observations concerning the development of comparative legal studies in Ukraine, Russia, and other countries of the CIS. So far as the present writer is aware, the present collection of materials is the first and most comprehensive of its kind[1] in the English language for more than a quarter century, when the Direct Link between University College London and the Institute of State and Law of the then USSR Academy of Sciences produced a series of bilateral comparative law seminars and colloquia that flourished for nearly a decade. Those seminars included participants from throughout the United Kingdom and several of the union republics of the USSR, including Ukraine.

For a time it appeared that comparative law proper would find its footing in Central Asia, particularly Tashkent. Ultimately, in the post-Soviet era Ukraine has proved to be the catalyst for the renaissance of comparative law in the former Soviet Union. A rare combination of energy, organizational skills, broad intellectual horizons, handsome support from colleagues throughout Ukraine, and a thirst for new intellectual adventures have made Ukraine the most active center for comparative legal activities in Europe, with nothing known to me in the western hemisphere, Asia, Africa, or the Near East to rival it.

* John Edward Fowler Distinguished Professor of Law, Pennsylvania State University: Emeritus Professor of Comparative Law, University College London; Foreign Member, National Academy of Sciences of Ukraine, Associate Member, International Academy of Comparative Law

1 W. E. Butler and V. N. Kudriavtsev (eds.), *Comparative Law and Legal System: Historical and Socio-Legal Perspectives* (1985). On the reaction at the time to the papers delivered at this colloquium, see J. Henderson, "The Problems of Comparative Law", *Russian Law: Theory and Practice*, no. 2 (2010), p. 112.

It will become immediately evident from these materials that the concept of "families of legal systems" has acquired an exceptional foothold in the countries of the Commonwealth of Independent States. René David's thesis apparently struck an immediate chord in the former Soviet Union. Whether this is because he identified socialist law as an autonomous family of legal systems, or because he personally knew many of the senior generation of Soviet comparatists (French academic relations with Soviet institutions of higher education were closer during the 1960-70s than elsewhere in Europe), or partly reflected the contacts made in Strasbourg at the Academy of Comparative Law, or otherwise, remains to be determined. His *Les Grands Systèmes de droit contemporain* (1964; 11th ed.; 2002) was translated into the Russian language in the 1970s and has gone through several editions, each reprinted several times, and sold tens of thousands of copies. At least three generations of Ukrainian and Russian law students have been, and continue to be, brought up on David. Zweigert and Kötz came along later, but the Russian translation of their treatise has been no less popular than David's and attracted Ukrainian and Russian comparatists with its treatment of "legal style".

David and Zweigert/Kötz offered an intellectual oasis where thirst was chronic and the intellectual tradition of "classification" deeply rooted. The most influential Ukrainian, Russian, and Uzbek figures in modern comparative legal studies all continue the David and Zweigert/Kötz approach with their own emendations, as most of the essays herein will demonstrate. Interest exists among the rising generation of Ukrainian and Russian comparatists in other methodologies being discussed in western circles – as the essays herein likewise demonstrate – but these are still little known and have no larger audience through the teaching of comparative law.

If Ukraine for the moment has become the venue of choice for comparative law dialogue, Russia remains the principal actor in the production of detailed studies of individual foreign legal systems or aspects thereof. Most of the leading specialists in English, Islamic, Japanese, Chinese, Hindu, Latin American, African, Australian, United States, Canadian, European Union, German, French, Italian, Spanish, Scandinavian, Roman, and canon law are to be found in Russia and, within Russia, the great majority are associated with Moscow institutions. The reasons lie primarily in the Soviet era and the allocation of resources, including financial and personnel, for the development of legal specialists. The imbalances that resulted in personnel distribution will require substantial efforts from Ukraine to match the formidable resources of the Russian Federation in foreign law.

* * *

Comparative legal studies are these days a domain in which many methodologies are being used or explored in addition to the comparative method itself. Some go far beyond the agenda of comparative law which preoccupied the interwar and early postwar generations of comparatists.[2] For some comparatists the utility of classifying legal systems by types, genres, classifications, geography, traditions, and the like is passé. Apart from pedagogical purposes, where such classifications can raise instructive questions and produce useful insights about how to analyze differences and similarities between legal systems and to identify the factors that one considers to be helpful or even decisive in determining their essential features, what objective truth does such a discussion produce? Whatever light doctrinal comparative legal writings may shed on these matters, what practical value or implications do any conclusions drawn actually have other than being intellectually stimulating? Does it actually matter to which "family"[3] or families[4] one ascribes a legal system?

In international treaties or arbitration clauses, of course, from time to time one finds references to the "principal legal systems of the world" as a criterion for representation on international judicial tribunals[5] or even arbitral tribunals. Where such criteria exist, it is not clear that they are rigorously adhered to; for example, if it is correct to say that the Russian and other CIS legal systems are part of the Romano-Germanic legal tradition, should it follow that these countries should compete for electing individuals to the International Court of Justice together with other continental European jurisdictions, or even those of Latin America, China, and Japan? Or does "principal legal systems" have reference in practice to a combination of geographical representation and status as a great or influential power?[6] The public record, so far as the present writer can

[2] H. C. Gutteridge, *Comparative Law: An Introduction to the Comparative Method of Legal Study and Research* (2d ed.; 1949).

[3] O. F. Skakun, Общее сравнительное правоведение [General Comparative Law] (Kiev, 2008).

[4] See V. I. Lafitskii, Сравнительное правоведение в образах права [Comparative Jurisprudence in Images of Law] (2010), I, p. 274. Lafitskii observes that there is no reason why one legal system cannot belong to two or more families of legal systems.

[5] The Statute of the International Court of Justice requires (Article 9) that persons elected to the Court should individually possess the qualifications required and that in the "… body as a whole the representation of the main forms of civilization and of the principal legal systems of the world should be assured". The Statute of the International Tribunal for the Law of the Sea (Article 2[2]) provides that "In the Tribunal as a whole the representation of the principal legal systems of the world and equitable geographical distribution shall be assured".

[6] In the case of the International Tribunal for the Law of the Sea the Statute plainly draws a distinction between equitable geographical distribution and the principal legal systems of

determine, does not begin to suggest that countries in exercising their right to choose, by election or appointment, representatives for international tribunals or organizations have evidenced the slightest interest in the writings or classifications of comparative lawyers in this respect.

However, from time to time classifications of legal systems have been deployed in judicial or arbitral adjudication to influence or determine the outcome of a proceeding. In one recent proceeding whose results remain confidential to the parties it was maintained that an alleged "gap" in Ukrainian law could be filled from another legal system of the Romano-Germanic "family" on the basis of the analogy of law [аналогия права].

The parameters of the considerations here differ from the debate about whether judges in national legal systems should have recourse to foreign law for guidance when domestic authority points towards an outcome that would be inappropriate or unjust or where domestic authority seems to offer no clear answer.[7] Here a post-socialist legal system (Ukraine) with a new Civil Code and professed intention to effect a transition to a market economy while retaining in the interim a major State sector in industrial production deliberately avoids legislative formulas or judicial practice which would extent the liability of entrepreneurs to what in Anglo-American law are known as "economic torts". The resistance takes the form of doctrinal gloss on the Civil Code which confines the general provisions on delicts to situations where physical harm or damage is caused and the absence of any judicial practice to the contrary. There exists, in other words, overwhelming opposition to extending the general provisions on delict to economic torts, although the wording of the relevant legislation, on its face, would not appear to compel such a reading.

When matters of this nature arise in foreign courts, especially Anglo-American courts where there is a developed body of legislation and precedent that supports the existence of economic torts, there is a natural inclination for British and American counsel to read Ukrainian legislation as though it did extend to economic torts and to assume that fact situations brought to them by Ukrainian or other CIS clients fit neatly into this category. Their task is to formulate the allegations of delict in Anglo-American style, place them within the language of Ukrainian legislation, and when they discover that Ukrainian legislation is understood differently, to persuade the court or arbitral tribunal to find a way to "introduce" economic delicts by way of interpretation into Ukrainian law. The court or arbitral tribunal is, in effect, being invited to "make" Ukrainian law.

---

the world. See note 5 above.

[7] See Thomas H. Bingham, *Widening Horizons: The Influence of Comparative Law and International Law on Domestic Law* (2010), p. 8.

One approach ventured in this direction draws upon the classifications of legal families. Whether Ukraine is now, or always has been, or never will be, a member of the Romano-Germanic family of legal systems is a source of considerable debate within Ukrainian legal circles. Opinions are divided, not surprisingly. But that debate is being conducted on both sides at a high level of abstraction, neither side appreciating that the conclusions reached may have implications for the outcome of matters in litigation.

The details of the arguments on both sides are of considerable interest for comparative lawyers. We set out one example below, but certain distinctive features of the matter should be noted at the outset. First, in this case counsel for the Plaintiff is initiating and advancing the argument that the arbitrators or judges should reach out for relevant foreign experience and precedent. The arbitrators or judges are not themselves looking to non-Ukrainian sources in what otherwise is concededly a matter for Ukrainian law because they confront a situation where the outcome would be unjust or where domestic authority offers no answer. Ukrainian jurisprudence and practice do offer an answer and an outcome: there is no case for recovering damages as a result of economic delicts. That, for the moment, is the preferred outcome in Ukraine when such situations arise. The proposition that recourse to a foreign court or arbitral tribunal with non-Ukrainian judges and arbitrators may produce a result under applicable Ukrainian law that is antithetical to Ukrainian law and practice by applying "comparative law" analysis will understandably not be welcomed in Ukraine.

A CASE IN POINT

Facts. The essential facts, appropriately disguised to protect the identity of the parties, were as follows. A Ukrainian company had for several years sold its entire output of a highly specialized product exclusively through a European middleman, which in turn sold the entire output to a British company. After several years of doing business in this manner, the Ukrainian company approached the British company about doing business directly and eliminating the role of the middleman, thereby avoiding the cost of the middleman and increasing its profits. Negotiations were entered into by the Ukrainian and British companies in full knowledge that the Ukrainian company was bound by its contract with the middleman. After negotiations, the Ukrainian and British companies concluded a contract between themselves, whereupon the middleman filed suit in arbitration against the British company, alleging that the British company had committed economic delicts and should pay compensation. It was agreed that Ukrainian law was the applicable law since all negotiations and the conclusion of the contract between the Ukrainian company and the British company occurred on the territory of Ukraine. The middleman did not bring suit against the Ukrainian company, although there was little doubt that the Ukrainian company had breached its contract with the middleman to supply the specialized product to the foreign market solely through the middleman.

The middleman brought suit on the basis of the Civil Code of Ukraine (Article 1166), which provided that "Property harm caused by the unlawful decisions, actions, or failure to act to personal nonproperty rights of a natural or juridical person, and also harm caused to the property of a natural or juridical person, shall be compensated in full by the person who caused it".

It was common ground between the parties to the arbitration that no physical damage had been caused to any property of the middleman and that a delict, if committed, occurred on the territory of Ukraine.

Claimant Arguments. The claimant argued that the respondent British company had committed what under English law were classified as "economic torts" (unfair competition, interference in contractual relations, conspiracy to interfere in contractual relations) and that Article 1166 of the Civil Code of Ukraine should be understood to extend to such situations.

The respondent British company argued that Article 1166 of the Civil Code of Ukraine was virtually identical to the equivalent provision of the 1963 Civil Code of the Ukrainian SSR and did not encompass "economic delicts" as understood by English law. No Ukrainian doctrinal writings could be found which supported the application of Article 1166 to cases of economic harm analogous to the circumstances here, nor any relevant Ukrainian judicial or arbitral practice. "Economic torts" in the meaning of Anglo-American legal systems did not exist in Ukraine. The activity engaged in by the Ukrainian and British companies was entirely legal under Ukrainian law, merely an attempt by the Ukrainian company in a competitive situation to get the best possible price for its products. While there might be liability of the Ukrainian company to the middleman for breach of their contract, this did not affect the British company, which had no relation to that contract and was ignorant of its precise terms, although it was aware that such a contract did exist.

The claimant argued that Ukrainian law cannot be treated in isolation from other civil law systems to which it is related. The position of the respondent emphasized "form and structure" only, whereas when comparing different legal systems it is essential to look beyond formal differences and to concentrate upon the actual functions of the different institutions, concepts, principles, and techniques being compared. The claimant in effect argued that the arbitrators should apply the doctrine of "functional equivalence" as elaborated by K. Zweigert and H. Kötz in the English-language version of their treatise.[8]

In denying that Ukrainian law recognizes "individual torts" and the torts of inducement and conspiracy in civil law, counsel for the British company was comparing only the organization and form of civil law delictual regimes. All civil law systems structure their delictual regimes under a general principle of responsibility or obligation to compensate harm caused. In contrast, the Anglo-American legal tradition organizes its tort regime along the lines of individual torts with specific regimes. From this observation the middleman believes that precisely because there is no "individualization" of torts in civil law, there is no limitation at all on the types of harmful conduct that may give rise to an obligation not to compensate unless this is limited by legislation, and in Ukraine there is no such specific legislation.

Quoting Zweigert and Kötz again, counsel for the middleman noted:

> If we leave the history and attend to the particularities of the law of tort, we quickly see that underneath the doctrinal variations, the groups and types of case which appear problematical owing to the exigencies of actual life, are much the same in all legal orders under consideration even if they are dealt with in different portions of the legal system and even, occasionally, with different results ... To give an example, every legal system is familiar with cases where one person induces another to break his contract with a third party. Here the Common Law has the special tort of inducing breach of contract. For the German lawyer, such a case falls under the general clause of Art 826 BGB, but when he goes to the commentaries on this section, he immediately looks under the key word "Inducement of breach of Contract" (Verleitung zum Vertragsbruch) to find a careful collection of all the judicial decision and asks whether the case before him satisfies the conditions laid down in those decisions. The French lawyers and judges operate in exactly the same way (p. 39).

[8] K. Zweigert and H. Kötz, *An Introduction to Comparative Law*, transl. T. Weir (3d rev. ed.; 1998). The claimant quoted the following passage: "The beginner often jumps to the conclusion that a foreign system has 'nothing to report' on a particular problem. The principle of functionality applies here. Even experienced comparatists sometimes look for the rule they want only in the particular place in the foreign system where their experience of their own system leads them to expect it; they are unconsciously looking at the problem with the eyes of their own system" (p. 34).

Counsel for the British company replied that absolutely no Ukrainian commentaries and judicial practice had been identified that would be analogous to the German or French resources mentioned by Zweigert and Kötz. There is no positive support whatsoever in Ukrainian doctrine for such an application of Article 1166 of the Civil Code of Ukraine, but neither, it must be observed, is there any mention whatsoever of the point. In other words, Ukrainian silence is being construed to reject the possible application of Article 1166 to "economic torts" as understood in English law.

It was further objected by Counsel for the respondent that foreign legal practice, in this instance German and French practice with regard to an inducement to breach a contract as evidenced in commentaries and judicial practice, is not a source of Ukrainian law. There is no Ukrainian legislation that would authorize a Ukrainian court or arbitrator to turn to foreign legal systems for evidence of how to construe Ukrainian legislation. Claimant's response was that Ukraine was unquestionably within the civil law tradition, even if the law of Ukraine was part of a "socialist" or "post-socialist" sub-group of the civil law family.

Counsel for the claimant disagreed that recourse to German and French commentaries for assistance in understanding the Civil Code of Ukraine meant that foreign law was being used as a "source of Ukrainian law". This is merely the "practical use" of comparative law for the purpose of interpreting national rules of law. It has been observed that courts in Anglo-American and civil-law jurisdictions "make use of comparative law and make open use of it to an unprecedented extent", quoting the First President of the Cour de cassation in this connection:

> Citizens and judges of States which share more or less similar cultures and enjoy an identical level of economic development are less and less prone to accept that situations which raise the same issues of fact will yield different results because of the difference in the rules of law to be applied. This is true in the field of bioethics, in that of economic law and liability. In all these cases, there is a trend, one might even say a strong demand, that compatible solutions are reached regardless of the differences in the underlying applicable rules of law.[9]

[9] Guy Canivet, quoted in Mads Andenas and Duncan Fairgrieve, "Finding A Common Language for Open Legal Systems", in G. Canivet, M. Andenas, and D. Fairgrieve (eds.), *Comparative Law Before the Courts* (2004), p. xxxi. Also see Cees van Dam, *European Tort Law* (2006), pp. 169-171, and generally, B. Markesinis and J. Fedtke, *Judicial Recourse to Foreign Law: A New Source of Inspiration?* (2006).

CONCLUSION

Whether one considers the above example to be a justified use or an abuse of comparative law may depend upon a variety of factors. So far as the present writer can determine, Ukrainian civil law has resisted extending the application of Article 1166 of the Civil Code (and its predecessor) to economic torts such as inducement or conspiracy to breach a contract, including for reasons inherent in a planned economy. The silence of Ukrainian legislation and doctrine here is to be construed as rejection of this type of economic delict, not indifference, not ignorance. If this perception is correct, whether it is in the interests of Ukraine to continue to reject economic delicts while continuing to aspire to achieve a market economy is another matter.

On the other hand, it is apparent that in this particular case Counsel for the claimant was suggesting that Ukraine already is required to understand Article 1166 in this light precisely because (a) Ukraine is part of the European civil law family and (b) other members of the European civil law family recognize economic torts, including conspiracy or inducement to breach a contract. In effect, the affiliation to the civil law family of legal systems should predetermine the Ukrainian position on this matter.

To paraphrase the well-known expression of the late Professor Otto Kahn-Freund at Oxford University, is that a "use or misuse" of comparative law?

The Periodization of Comparative Law: In Search of an Acceptable Model

O. V. KRESIN*

The periodization of the evolution of comparative law in the broad sense assumes a certain view of the nature and basic benchmarks in its development. The few Ukrainian studies devoted expressly to the history of comparative law,[1] and also their primarily descriptive character, the

* кандидат юридических наук, Docent, Senior Scholarly Associate, Section of International and Comparative Law, Volodymyr M. Koretskyi Institute of State and Law, National Academy of Sciences of Ukraine; Learned Secretary, Ukrainian Association of Comparative Law; Associate Member, International Academy of Comparative Law

[1] In Ukraine and other post-Soviet countries scholars use the expression *порівняльне правознавство* (in Ukrainian) or *сравнительное правоведение* (in Russian) that might translate more precisely as *comparative jurisprudence* or even *comparative legal science.* This term encompasses the methodology or way of studying legal phenomena as well as an autonomous field of study or scholarly discipline built on the systematic use of the comparative method. Some European and American scholars have preferred the term *comparative jurisprudence* – among them Sir Frederick Pollock, William Ewald, and others. In this article the term *comparative law* is used, being the more traditional English usage. The term *comparative legislation* is used herein only when describing works where it was used or in official names where it was originally used.
O. M. Lysenko, Порівняльне правознавство як наука та його мшсце в системі юридичних наук [Comparative Law as a Science and its Place in the System of Legal Sciences] (Kiev, 2001) (abstract of kand. iurid. nauk diss.); O. D. Tykhomyrov, «Виникнення порівняльно-правових досліджень в Україні» [Origin of Comparative Law Research in Ukraine], in Часопис Київського університету права [Journal of Kiev University of Law], no. 4 (2005); I. Babych, «Виникнення та розвиток порівняльного правознавства як навчальної дисциплін» [Origin and Development of Comparative Law as an Instructional Discipline], Підприємництво, господарство і право [Entrepreneurship, State and Law], no. 4 (2007), pp. 141-144; and also works by the present writer: O. V. Kresin, «Розвиток порівняльних історико-правових досліджень» [Development of Comparative Historical Legal Research],

lack of resort to primary sources so typical of the respective sections in many general works and textbooks, testifies to the weak conceptualization of this subject-matter in Ukrainian legal comparison, the failure to form a retrospective view thereof, and accordingly the contemporary position and further prospects.

Despite the substantial number of publications, there are no serious conceptual works on this problem either in European or American scholarship. In our view, new fundamental studies of the principal stages of the evolution of comparative law should, *inter alia*, assist in helping to overcome the methodological crisis in comparative law and clarify its nature. The present article is a retrospective survey and comparative analysis of works devoted to the development of legal comparativistics.

The development of comparative law became the subject of scholarly research in the nineteenth century. This was connected with an awareness by European scholars of comparative law as a science and/or as a sphere of research and attempts to isolate it, and even to juxtapose the modern state thereof with the pre-scientific stage of development.

The first Ukrainian scholar who investigated the history of the origins of comparative law was Nikolai Karlovich Rennenkampf (1832-1899) in an article (1869) on the contemporary polishing of comparative law.[2] Formally,

---

in Iu. S. Shemshuchenko (ed.), Порівняльне правознавство у системі юридичних наук [Comparative Law in the System of Legal Sciences: Problems of Methodology] (2006), pp. 37-83; id, «Передмова» [Preface], in O. V. Kresin (ed.), Порывняльне правознавство: Антологія української компаравістики XX-XX століть [Comparative Law: Anthology of Ukrainian Comparativistics XIX-XX Centuries] (2008); id, «Соціологічний напрям у порівняльному правознавстві у другій половині XIX – на початку XX ст.» [Sociological Orientation and Comparative Law in the Second Half of the XIX and Early XX Centuries], in Порівняльно-правові дослідження [Comparative Law Research], no. 1-2 (2007), pp. 44-50; id. «Розвиток порівняльного правознавства в Україні в межах школи соціологічного позитивізму» [Development of Comparative Law in Ukraine in the Era of the School of Sociological Positivism], Право України [Law of Ukraine], no. 5 (2006), pp. 162-166; id, «Розвиток порівняльному правознавства в Україні в межах історичноі школи права» [Development of Comparative Law in Ukraine in the Era of the Historical School of Law], Бюлетень Міністерства юстиції України [Bulletin of the Ministry of Justice of Ukraine], no. 4 (2006), pp. 90-96; id, «Цивілізаціоністський напрям у порівняльному правознавстві» [Civilist Orientation of Comparative Law], Держава и право [State and Law], no. 31 (2006), pp. 476-482; id, «Розвиток методології порівняльного правознавства: історичний аспект» [Development of Methodology of Comparative Law: Historical Aspect], Право України [Law of Ukraine], no. 2 (2006), pp. 128-130; id, «Функціональний підхід у порівняльному правознавстві» [Functional Approach to Comparative Law], Держава и право [State and Law], no. 30 (2005), pp. 536-541; id, «Методологія та інституціоналізація порівняльних історико-правових досліджень у радянський період» [Methodology and Institutionalization and Comparative Historical Legal Research in the Soviet Period], Держава и право [State and Law], no. 29 (2005), pp. 691-698; id, «Перспективи розвитку порівняльного правознавства в Україні» [Perspective for the Development of Comparative Law in Ukraine], Правова держава [Rule of Law State], no. 14 (2003), and others.

[2] See N. K. Rennenkampf, «О современной обработке сравнительного правоведения»

the article is a review of the first issue of the French journal *Revue de droit international et de législation comparée*. Rennenkampf did not agree with the notion set out in an article by Gustave Rolin-Jaequemyns (1835-1902) that comparative law methodology used in the works of thinkers of the seventeenth to the early nineteenth centuries remained relevant for modern comparative studies. Rennenkampf said it had outlived itself and lost its scholarly authoritativeness. In Rennenkampf's view, although scholars of the past had compared the law of various times and peoples, there was no science of comparative law, no respective methodological base had been created, and comparative studies themselves were unsystematic.

Rennenkampf believed that comparative law had become scientific in the 1820s and that this was linked with the origins of and disputes between the historical and philosophical schools of legal thought. Thus, for the first time the development of comparative law was divided into two periods – prescientific and scientific, and the principal schools of comparative law were identified.

The first study known to us devoted to the history of comparative law proper was by the English legal scholar, Sir Frederick Pollock (1845-1937). It took the form of a report[3] delivered to the First International Congress of Comparative Law at Paris in 1900, later published as an article.[4] In Pollock's view, the scientific foundations of the comparative method had been set out in ancient Greece by Aristotle (384-322 B.C.). But after him this method had not developed further until the seventeenth century. Pollock linked its renaissance with the works of William Fulbeck (1560-1603?), Gottfried Wilhelm von Leibnitz (1646-1716), Charles Louis de Secondat Montesquieu (1689-1755), and others. Nonetheless, in his view, comparative law in his day had still not come into being by reason of methodological weaknesses and the few comparative studies being linked with the dominance of natural-law orientations in legal thought.

The formation of comparative jurisprudence, Pollock believed, was linked with the crisis of the revolutionary movement in Europe and the development of the historical school of law (national-historical orientation). Pollock regarded the comparative historical method elaborated by Sir Henry Maine (1822-1888) as a qualitatively new modern stage in the

---

[On the Contemporary Polishing of Comparative Law], in Kresin, note 1 above (Anthology), pp. 90-96.

3 The text was summarized in F. V. Taranovskii, «Сравнительное правоведение в конце XIX века» [Comparative Law at the End of the Nineteenth Century], in Kresin, note 1 above (Anthology), pp. 179-182.

4 See F. Pollock, "The History of Comparative Jurisprudence", *Journal of the Society of Comparative Legislation*, V (N.S., 1903), pp. 74-76.

development of comparative law, the basis of which was the notion that legal development in the world had passed through stages.

Fedor Vasilevich Taranovskii (1875-1936) briefly considered the evolution of comparative law in his textbook on the encyclopedia of law in 1917. He noted that the "comparative method" of the investigation of law was known since Antiquity. Unlike other scholars, Taranovskii suggested that the development of comparative legal studies had not ceased either during the Middle Ages or the early Renaissance notwithstanding the dominance of the natural-law school. He even distinguished within the framework of the last an "empirical orientation" in the context of which comparative legal studies has developed more intensively.[5]

Among the more recent schools of legal thought within whose framework the methodological foundations of comparative law were being formed, Taranovskii analyzed the historical school and the school of those who followed Georg Wilhelm Friedrich Hegel (1770-1831). Nonetheless, Taranovskyi was of the view that the scientific foundation of comparative research in law was to be found only within the sociological-positivist school.[6]

In 1922 an article by the English scholar, Harold Cooke Gutteridge (1876-1953) appeared. It is the first study known to us devoted to the development of comparative law in individual countries – France and England.[7] By its nature the article was a survey and devoted principally to the modern state of teaching comparative law in the universities and the creation of respective specialized chairs.

One of the best-known and detailed studies of the development of comparative law is an article by Walther Hug (b. 1898) published in 1932.[8] He surveyed several comparative legal studies commencing with Antiquity and even described individual periods of the development of legal thought and the influence of dominant paradigms of legal thought on the development of comparative studies. Hug noted that in the Ancient World comparative legal studies were rather the exception, whereas in the Middle Ages, unlike his modern day, comparisons were made between supranational (canon and Roman law) and particular (customary law and others) legal systems and an "internal comparative law" developed.

[5] F. V. Taranovskii, «Сравнительно-исторический метод и сравнительное правоведение» [Comparative-Historical Method and Comparative Law], in Kresin note 1 above (Anthology), pp. 201-205.

[6] Ibid., pp. 205-207.

[7] H. C. Gutteridge, "The Study of Comparative Law in France and England", *Journal of Comparative Legislation*, IV (3d ser., 1922), pp. 84-88.

[8] W. Hug, "The History of Comparative Law", *Harvard Law Review*, XLV (1931-32), pp. 1027-1070.

Hug considered the comparative law studies of Hugo Grotius (1583-1645), Montesquieu, and other scholars to be another exception to the dominance of natural law ideas in the early Renaissance.

Hug believed that John Selden (1584-1654) was the founder of the comparative history of law, for he accentuated the need for comparative studies and consciously engaged in comparison when investigating the law of various countries at various periods and the influence of legal systems upon one another. But Hug considered that Grotius, Samuel Pufendorf (1632-1694), and Giovanni Battista Vico (1668-1744) used foreign legal materials only as an illustration for their ideas. The "foremost precursor" of modern comparative law, in Hug's view, was Montesquieu, who applied the comparative method for the purpose of studying the possibilities and means of improving legislation and developing legal science. At the same time, Hug observed, the shortcomings of Montesquieu's research approach were: lack of criteria for the selection and uncritical use of sources; overrating some (climate, geographic location) and underrating other (traditions, national culture) factors of legal development, and not taking into account the stability of the historical development of law. However, Hug emphasized, in any event comparative law studies in the seventeenth and eighteenth centuries remained exceptional, and the attention of jurists was absorbed by the formation of national legal systems and the development of natural law ideas, which became the orientator for implementing law reforms.

In Hug's view, at the outset of the nineteenth century jurists turned to interpreting the newly-created codes, and interest in foreign law and comparative legal research was considered to be impractical. To be sure, the historical school of law which arose at the time facilitated the growth of the interest of jurists in comparing national law with Roman law.

But the science of comparative law proper, Hug said, was born in Germany under the influence of classical German philosophy. And the first comparatist should be considered to be Paul Johann Anselm von Feuerbach (1775-1833), who in 1810 emphasized the need for the development of comparative law in the likeness of comparative linguistics as an instrument of transformation of legal science from national to universal, and later elaborated this idea in others of his works. Comparative studies should supplement philosophical and theoretical legal research. Hug also noted the contribution to the origins of comparative law made by Edward Gans (1798-1839) and Anton Friedrich Justus Thibaut (1772-1840).

In parallel with the historical and philosophical school in the early nineteenth century Hug singled out the positivist comparative circle led by Carl Joseph Anton Mittermaier (1787-1867) and Karl Salomo Zachariae von

Lingenthal (1769-1843). Moreover, he stressed that the efforts of both groups of German jurists created no serious interest in society in comparative law.

Also not entirely successful were the efforts of Jean Louis Eugene Lerminier (1803-1857), Jean Jacques Gaspard Foelix (1791-1853), and other scholars in France; nonetheless, they founded positivist comparative law in France, the first specialized chair of comparative law and a journal. Despite the general indifference towards comparative law in the Anglo-American world in the early nineteenth century, there too, as Hug noted, individual scholars stated the need for its development and the introduction of a respective discipline in the universities.

However, Hug noted, a movement unfolded during the first half of the nineteenth century for reforming national law, and with it came interest in foreign experience and comparative studies, rather primitive, seeking ready solutions for their problems. By the mid-nineteenth century this interest had significantly weakened, especially under the influence of positivism.

On the whole Hug divided the development of comparative law into two periods: (1) embryonic – to the mid-nineteenth century; and (2) contemporary – from the mid-nineteenth century, when it "emerged as a distinct branch of legal science".

The English comparatist, H. C. Gutteridge, devoted significant attention to the evolution of comparative law in his introductory monograph.[9] In his view comparative law emerged in the mid-nineteenth century. Before then the historical school of law and the attraction of jurists to the codification of law did not encourage recourse to foreign experience and comparative studies. The emergence of comparative law Gutteridge linked with the early comparative law journals and chairs. With their decline, in his view, a period of stagnation transpired which lasted until the ideas of evolution penetrated legal science.

Modern comparative law, in Gutteridge's view, began with evolutionism and the sociological school linked with it – the appearance of Sir Henry Maine's work *Ancient Law* and the creation in 1869 of the Society of Comparative Legislation in France. From this time onwards, Gutteridge noted, comparative law "... no longer consists in the inspired but isolated efforts of a few men of genius, but takes its place as a recognised instrument for the development of law, ... as a branch of legal study". The publication of specialized scholarly journals was an external expression of the recognition of comparative law, in the author's view.

[9] H. C. Gutteridge, *Comparative Law: An Introduction to the Comparative Method of Legal Study and Research* (rev. ed.; 1949).

In the early twentieth century, Gutteridge noted, interest in comparative law grew substantially in connection with an awareness of the importance of not allowing legal isolationism and a change of attitude towards foreign experience as having an instrumentalist value.

The evolution of comparative law was the subject of an article by the American legal scholar, Roscoe Pound (1870-1964), on comparative law in space and time.[10] The author noted that comparative law began to develop in the last third of the nineteenth century and that the dominant orientation at that time was historical comparison (evolutionary; other scholars define this as sociological positivism), which emanated from Hegelian philosophy and was influenced by evolutionary theories in biology and the social sciences. This was replaced in the early twentieth century by an analytical orientation which, in Pound's view, developed under the influence of the natural law school in the form of comparative legislation through the aspiration of scholars by means of comparing legal norms to determine which of them was the most rational.

A distinctive feature of comparative law in the nineteenth century, in Pound's view, was the search through comparison for a single correct embodiment of a certain metaphysical idea, a conception of the development of law along one line. But in the twentieth century comparatists gradually began to understand that the ideal element is contained in the law itself, and not without, that it is a value in and of itself and cannot be brought under one universal model.

Among the most detailed surveys of the history of comparative law is to be found in the first volume of a treatise on comparative law by the Romanian scholar, Léontin-Jean Constantinesco.[11] In his view the school of natural law dominant in European legal thought until the end of the eighteenth century precluded the existence of comparative law, save for the existence of eternal and immutable principles of "historical reality and specific legal orders being subject to some material differences and specific features".[12] The prerequisites for comparative law to arise the author saw in the gradual formation, on one hand, of national legal systems and, on the other, a certain understanding of law. At the outset of the nineteenth century, the "comparative method transcends the framework of incidental efforts of individual people". The author then divided the development of

[10] R. Pound, "Comparative Law in Space and Time", *American Journal of Comparative Law*, IV (1955), pp. 70-80.

[11] L.-J. Constantinesco, *Rechtsvergleichung* (1971-83). 3 vols.

[12] Quotations are drawn from the Russian-language version in L.-J. Constantinesco, «Развитие сравнительного правоведения» [Development of Comparative Law], in V. A. Tumanov (ed.), Очерки сравнительного права [Essays on Comparative Law] (1981), p. 108.

comparative law into three periods: 1800-1850; 1850-1900; and 1900-1950. The criteria for this periodization are "on one hand, the means and forms with whose assistance comparative law was affirmed, and on the other, the understanding itself of its essence, conceptions which expressed this understanding".

In the first period comparative law had not yet separated itself from the study of foreign law, and the essence and subject-matter thereof had not been precisely defined. At this time, together with the codification of law, the forming of a number of national legal systems had been completed, and the attention of scholars in their quests for the best legal models moved from internal to external comparison. In jurisprudence the place of the logical-speculative discourse of natural law was taken by historical legal studies of positive law. The first specialized chairs and journals were created.

Constantinesco names the historical school of law, in particular, and notes that its contribution to the development of comparative law may be considered to be both a turning point and a barrier. The turning point was linking legal development and its specific distinctive features with the historical realities of specific countries. However, he observed, the historical school was interested solely in the law of the German-speaking countries and Roman law and ignored other law. It proclaimed that law is linked with the development of a specific people, and therefore its use by another people may have only negative consequences. Comparison accordingly has no practical interest and the interaction of legal systems is not the subject-matter of research.

The Kantian and Hegelian schools are singled out by Constantinesco as developing in parallel with the historical school. The Kantian Feuerbach, in criticizing the natural law and historical schools, noted that in general law is developing in the direction of unity, but there are serious differences in the law of various peoples. Therefore, when considering the law of individual peoples one should investigate both individual and common features and take their evolution into account: "Philosophy, history, and comparison should be recognized as equal components on the basis of which legal science is developing". Feuerbach proclaimed the possibility of the creation on a comparative basis of the universal history of law based on the principle of evolution.

Hegel noted that legal concepts might be elaborated only on the basis of a comparison of the law of all peoples. His follower, Edward Gans (1798-1839), believed it possible on the basis of diachronic comparison to determine the stages of the development of law on a universal scale – as the "stages of the development of reason advancing the universal course of history". In general, Constantinesco observed, this school was directed towards using foreign law to improve national law; it "opened the door to positivism, but also to comparative law".

The first to transform comparative legal research into an "instrument to resolve practical tasks" was, in the view of Constantinesco, Mittermaier, who primarily investigated the modern law of several European States in order to determine the norms and institutes of foreign law whose borrowing might help to improve national law.

During the second period (1850-1900), comparative law became, Constantinesco believed, a separate legal discipline, although not completely disengaged from the method of comparative law and the study of foreign law. It developed primarily in the form of positivist comparative legislation. A number of works appeared which were devoted to the General Part of comparative law, especially its subject-matter, objects, theoretical problems of the interaction of legal systems, and their classification. A number of specialist societies and journals were founded. The results of comparative studies began to be used by national parliaments.

Constantinesco distinguished at this time among comparative-historical, comparative-ethnographic, and philosophical orientations of comparative law. He asserted that comparatists believed their task to be identifying the laws of universal legal development, the coming together of legal science in general and of comparative law in particular to the natural sciences.

The third period of development of comparative law encompassed, in Constantinesco's view, the years 1900 to 1950 and commenced with the International Congress of Comparative Law in Paris. A practical applied orientation of comparative law came to replace the dominant historical approach, and comparative research became systematic. He also pointed to the enlivened interest in comparative law after the Second World War. This was expressed in the creation of new associations of comparatists, an increase of the place of comparative legal disciplines in legal education, the holding of regular international congresses of comparatists, the publication (incomplete) of the *International Encyclopedia of Comparative Law*, and others. The periodization of comparative law proposed by Constantinesco was accepted in many later studies, including in part by Ukrainian scholars.[13]

One of the early works in the former Soviet Union devoted to the history of the development of comparative law was an article published in 1974 by

[13] See, for example, O. L. Lvova and L. O. Makarenko, «Формування та розвиток ідей порівняльного правознавства» [Formation and Development of Ideas of Comparative Law], in O. V. Zaichuk and N. M. Onishchenko (eds.), Порівняльне правознавство (теоретико-правове дослідження [Comparative Law (Theoretical Legal Studies)] (2005), p. 45ff.

Tille and Faiziev.[14] Scientific comparative law, the authors suggested, arose in the nineteenth century under the influence of economic needs, especially the development of international trade. They singled out three periods in its development: (1) up to 1917; (2) from 1917 to the end of the 1940s; and (3) the modern stage. The first period "is characterized by significant interest in a new phenomenon in legal science, modest successes, and limited tasks". Comparatists at that time shared the idea of a world law, which retained vitality into the second period.

During the second period, the attention of scholars concentrated upon seeking the community of various legal systems; attempts were made to practically embody the unification of ideas. The comparison of Anglo-American and Romano-Germanic law became the fashion. However, the ignoring of non-western legal systems by western comparative law became typical, especially of Soviet and Islamic law, as being non-comparable. In general during the second period interest grew in this discipline and comparatists were more active.

The third period is characterized by a departure from the idea of creating a world law. As Tille and Faiziev noted, interest lessened in the theory of comparative law, and its practical application became the principal object of attention. The world socialist system was being formed at the time, and Soviet law, the law of socialist and post-colonial countries, became the subject-matter of studies in "bourgeois comparativistics". The other subject-matter of research was the unification of the institutes and branches of law of the member countries of various economic unions. A powerful institutionalization of comparative law also was characteristic of this period.

In his critical reflections on comparative law the Puerto Rican scholar, Jaro Mayda, distinguished among four stages in the development of modern legal comparison.[15] The first encompassed the second half of the nineteenth century to the early twentieth century, being basically characterized by the notion of a "common legislative law", a substantiation and servicing of unification projects. The second stage lasted from the 1920-1940s, an era during which the idea that comparative law is not an individual science

[14] A. A. Tille and M. M. Faiziev, «Основные этапы в развитии сравнительного правоведения» [Basic Stages in the Development of Comparative Law], in A. I. Ishanov (ed.), Проблемы сравнительного исследования законодательства союзных республик [Problems of Comparative Research of Legislation of the Union Republics] (Tashkent, 1974), p. 25.

[15] Jaro Mayda, "Some Critical Reflections on Contemporary Comparative Law", in K. Zweigert and H. Puttfarken (eds.), *Rechtsvergleichung* (1978), p. 367; we summarize this work on the basis of M. N. Marchenko, Курс сравнительного правоведения [Cours of Comparative Law] (2002), pp. 107-108.

or branch of knowledge, but merely one of the special methods of research in law. The third stage, from the 1940-1950s, was characterized by an understanding of comparative law as being an instrument for resolving practical tasks, and also by its extensive introduction into legal education, especially in Europe and America. The fourth stage commenced in the 1960s and was linked with the elaboration of the doctrine of families of legal systems. Mayda's position is shared by the Russian legal scholar, M. N. Marchenko, at Moscow University.

Significant attention was devoted to the evolution of comparative law in a work by the Ukrainian scholar, V. N. Denisov, in 1985.[16] Although Denisov considered the development of the use of the comparative method in jurisprudence, commencing from Antiquity, he believed that comparative law originated at the turn of the nineteenth and twentieth centuries. The prerequisites for comparative law to arise the Ukrainian scholar considered to be the confirmation of capitalist relations and the arising of national legal systems, development of conflicts law, unification of private law, reception of law, and colonial policies of the large States.

The proper date of the origin of legal comparativistics, in Denisov's view, may be considered to be the year 1900, when the International Congress of Comparative Law was held in Paris, "at which an attempt was first made to formulate the concept of comparative law". The views most widely shared at the time were that comparative law was the comparative history of law and an augmentation to analytical jurisprudence. The majority of scholars believed it to be a separate branch of legal science. Thereafter, Denisov observed, the functional approach to comparative law became rather influential, which regarded comparative law above all as a means, an instrument, of creating a single world law.

After the end of the First World War and 1917 October Revolution in Russia, it became obvious in Denisov's view that universalist schemes had become bankrupt and came down to private international law, whereas comparative law gradually ceased to be considered to be a science and instead was treated as a "conception of the comparative method" whose purpose is to classify objects of foreign law. Denisov noted, *inter alia,* the classification of legal systems into such groups as legal families – "world models of law" elaborated by René David (1906-1991). This was an effort to overcome the positivist limitations of a functional approach to comparative law and move on to pluralist criteria for comparison which would make it possible to take into account the impact of religion, ideology, and culture

[16] V. N. Denisov, «К критике буржуазных концепций сравнительного правоведения» [On a Critique of Bourgeois Conceptions of Comparative Law], in Kresin, note 1 above (2008), pp. 237, 253-256.

on law. These methodological changes made it possible to incorporate in the subject-matter of comparative law research non-western law, especially socialist and religious legal systems. Nonetheless, in Denisov's view, these changes were to a certain extent of a mechanical nature because they combined elements of different approaches without having been purposely rethought, and that on the whole predetermined the eclecticism of modern western comparativistics.

The American scholar, Rudolf B. Schlesinger (1909-1996), noted in 1995[17] that comparative law arose as a routine activity of jurists at the end of the eleventh and early twelfth centuries together with the formation of the school of glossators. This period lasted until the era of codification in the second half of the eighteenth century and was characterized by the use of Roman law and doctrine and the formation of the European *jus commune* in the domain of private law. To be sure, Schlesinger pointed out, these legal systems were not regarded as foreign, but as elements of law in force. The "process of comparison was to a greater degree integrative rather than contrastive".

The next period was characterized by the development of national codified law written in the national languages. Accordingly, legal scholars, teachers, and practitioners had no opportunity to adequately become familiar with the enormous mass of foreign law and in foreign languages at that. Therefore, "in these new circumstances comparative law became a specialized sphere of legal research" and contrastive comparison came to dominate.

The third period in the development of comparative law commenced in the second half of the twentieth century. Under the impact of globalization, the integrative method once again came to dominate, and "legal science began a search for a common core of legal systems".

Ewald suggested that comparative law had ceased to become the subject of research by "isolated individuals" and become an "organized academic discipline" in the nineteenth century.[18] He identified two periods in that century in the development of comparative law. He considered the year 1814 to be the date of the appearance of the last when Thibaut's work was published containing an appeal to imitate the Code Napoleon in Germany.

The first period lasted until the death of Gans in 1839. In characterizing this period, Ewald noted that comparative law was the offspring of Hegelian and Kantian philosophy. It was elaborated chiefly by German

[17] R. B. Schlesinger, "The Past and Future of Comparative Law", *American Journal of Comparative Law*, XLIII (1995), pp. 477-479.

[18] W. Ewald, "Comparative Jurisprudence (I): What Was It Like to Try a Rat?", *University of Pennsylvania Law Review*, CXLIII (1995), pp. 2116-2119.

scholars who taught at Heidelberg University, and comparison was undertaken primarily between German and French law. A distinctive feature of this group of scholars was that they turned to the comparison not only of written law, but also of ideas and theories. Comparative law in this period became a "systematic scholarly activity". But, as Ewald noted, this school was "in the shadow" of the historical school of law which actually condemned the appearance and results of the interaction of legal systems and "considered comparative research to be illegitimate".

During the 1840s to 1860s, in Ewald's view, a relative stagnation occurred caused by the death of a number of comparative legal scholars and a general indifference of jurists towards comparative research. But the main reason was the spread of legal positivism, which was not well disposed towards comparative law, regarding law as the will of the sovereign not limited by tradition, rational grounds, and foreign influences.

The second period of development of comparative law commenced in the 1870s and lasted until about 1900. The "new birth" was due, in Ewald's opinion, to practical requirements, especially the renewal of German private law which eventually lead to the adoption of the German civil code. The interest of German and French scholars in comparative legal research was linked with this. Comparative law was transformed in this period into a "professional academic discipline" expressed in the creation of specialized associations, chairs, and journals. Comparative law in the spirit of legal positivism was understood to be comparative legislative and considered to be an element of legislative technique, and the subject-matter of research was primarily norms of legislation. The periodization proposed by Ewald was interrupted by this.

In an article on comparative law[19] the American comparatist, Hyland, noted that despite a long history of comparative research, modern comparative law arose in 1869 (the creation of the Society of Comparative Legislation in France, and the Chair of Historical and Comparative Jurisprudence held by Sir Henry Maine at Oxford University). Hyland considered that the development of comparative law represented a replacement of certain paradigms and accordingly determined its periodization.

The first period (from 1869 to the First World War) he calls the "universalist", during which the idea of evolution dominated together with such elements as faith in a worldwide targeted development of law and the staged nature of such development, as well as the aspiration to create

[19] R. Hyland, "Comparative Law", in D. Patterson (ed.), *A Companion to Philosophy of Law and Legal Theory* (1999), pp. 185-197.

an ideal law which might be adopted and applied in all countries. The International Congress of Comparative Law in 1900 was the culmination of this period, the universalist paradigm being dominant there. The shortcomings of this orientation and period in comparative law, for which it was subjected to criticism, were: the derivation of universalist theories not from a comparison of modern legal systems of the world, but from Roman law and from Christian and natural law doctrines; the failure to recognize the place and significance of distinctions in the process of comparison, and of reducing the reasons for the existence of differences to historical accident.

The second, functional, period commenced after the First World War. It was linked with the process of unification in private law. Functionalism was directed towards a comparison of how different legal systems resolve certain legal problems, ignoring national institutional, doctrinal, and technical-legal specific features. The fundamental features of similarity between legal systems were established on this basis. However, functionalism did not take into account the historical, cultural, religious, and linguistic contexts of legal norms and decisions; the presumption proclaimed of the identity of legal decisions determined the result of comparison even before it was undertaken.

Hyland indirectly singled out a third period without indicating precisely when it began. He believed the theory of differences to be dominant in this period, according to which each legal system has inherent visions of equity, conception of law and its place in the life of man; it is impossible to determine the level of the development of law at which the distinctions disappear; the distinctions are of the same value as the features of similarity, and in comparative legal research they should be taken into account and not deprecated.

The Uzbek legal scholar, Saidov, in his treatise on comparative law[20] noted that it emerged in the early nineteenth century in Germany and was represented by the historical, Neo-Kantian, and Hegelian schools and, over time, by an ethnological orientation. During the second half of the nineteenth century, France became the developmental center of comparative law, where practical applied research was predominant, or "comparative legislation", but by the end of the century theoretical works had emerged.

During the first half of the twentieth century, European comparativistics sought a "common legislative law". The new doctrine of "comparative law" had in mind an expansion of the group of comparable sources of law,

[20] A. Kh. Saidov, *Comparative Law*, transl. W. E. Butler (2003).

theoretical views, and even took into account the historical evolution of legal systems. Commencing from the 1920s, the comparatists of continental Europe who previously had compared their own legal systems also turned to investigate the Common Law countries.

In the second half of the twentieth century there occurred the formation of groups of socialist legal systems and a significant number of new post-colonial States, which led to a revision of the traditional conceptions of comparative law. Interest grew in the theoretical problems of comparative law, and comparative research in public law became widespread. In parallel with the positivist orientation a legal-sociological orientation emerged representing functionalism and the so-called "critical theory of comparativism". Saidov asserted that during the 1980-90s there was a crisis in comparative law occasioned by generational differences of scholars.

The Italian scholar Sacco noted in his article[21] on a century of comparative law that he regarded as rather late the date for the origin of comparative law proposed by some scholars – 1900. Nonetheless, in his view, this date marked a stage. Prior to 1900 comparatists sought to find the sole most correct legislative resolution of legal problems. As Sacco observed, "scholars subjected solutions to verification, but they could not compare them" since they regarded their own in any event as the best. Implicitly, these propositions were aimed at the unification of law. Legal scholars were also interested in and occupied themselves with foreign law and comparative law in parallel with their other research projects and preferences. Surveys of national and foreign legislation were the principle products of comparatists which contained the parallel exposition thereof. In Sacco's words, "the unitary and universalist mentality" met the embryonic stage of the science of comparative law.

The gradual formation of a pluralist mentality and substantiation of legal diversity has been characteristic of comparative law since 1900. These may be considered to have formed after the two world wars, when legal nationalism began to be discussed and the legitimacy and value of Anglo-American and socialist law were recognized. During the second half of the twentieth century, systemology permeated comparative law, which also reflected the recognition by comparatists of "law as such, as it is, and not as it was formalized", and an understanding of the various sources of law and the multifactoralness of its functioning emerged. In the course of the twentieth century comparative law became a science concerning the essence of legal differences and finally separated itself from legal

21 R. Sacco, "One Hundred Years of Comparative Law", *Tulane Law Review*, LXXV (2000-01), p. 1165.

"polyglotism", offering an understanding of foreign law instead of simply an acquaintance with it. Comparatists became aware that the quality of science does not depend upon its "practical advantages".

The dissertation of a Ukrainian comparatist, Lysenko, suggests that six stages be identified in the development of legal comparavitistics.[22] The first stage encompasses the period up to the nineteenth century and is characterized by individual attempts to compare normative acts. At the second stage, the comparative method is used in the history of law; at the third, "as an instrument of law-creation, in particular codification"; at the fourth, to investigate legal systems "for the purpose of deepening the study of the phenomenon of law itself and trends of its development". During the fifth stage a theory of comparative law was formed, and at the sixth, comparative law gradually matured into an autonomous science: the group of topics being investigated has enlarged, the subject-matter of comparative law was formed and its conceptual apparatus, and its place in the system of legal sciences is being studied.

The Ukrainian comparatist Tykhomyrov suggested an unusual and original approach in his monograph on legal comparativistics.[23] Having regard to the "historical and geographical pluralism in understanding comparative law", he noted that it "does not exist outside national sciences". Therefore, the development of comparative law should be regarded "in the context of the origin and development of its national schools". However, Tykhomyrov speaks about the leadership of certain countries in certain periods (obviously, in the international science of comparative law), and, in considering the development of comparativistics in Japan, points to the methodological approaches characteristic of European and American sciences. He thus actually acknowledges that schools and orientations in comparative law of various countries were not deeply national.

The Ukrainian scholar Skakun in 2006 identified three stages in the development of comparative law: (1) the formation thereof as a legal science – accumulation of knowledge about the comparative legal method and legal systems of the world; (2) origin as an autonomous branch of legal knowledge with its own subject-matter, method, and conceptual apparatus; (3) formation into an integral system – theory of legal systems.[24]

22 Lysenko, note 1 above.

23 O. D. Tykhomyrov, Юридическая компаративистика: философские, теоретические и методологические проблемы [Legal Comparativistics: Philosophical, Theoretical, and Methodological Problems] (Kiev, 2005), pp. 47, 78.

24 O. F. Skakun, «Место общего сравнительного правоведения в системе юридических наук и его официальный статус» [Place of General Comparative Law in the System of Legal Sciences and Official Status Thereof], in Iu. S. Shemshuchenko and O. V. Kresin (eds.), Порівняльне правознавство: сучасний стан і перспективи розвитку: Збірник наукових

Bekhruz, from Ukraine, in his textbook on comparative law[25] elaborated and improved the periodization proposed by Saidov. He noted that comparative law has passed through four stages of evolution. The first was the stage of forming the idea of comparative law between 1800 and 1900. To be sure, in his view it became "recognized as a scientific orientation" after the International Congress on Comparative Law of 1900, so that the nineteenth century is the pre-history of comparative law. The development of national legal systems and international economic links were a prerequisite for its formation. Throughout the first period, comparative law did not separate itself from the study of foreign law, and the first specialized journals and chairs appeared.

The second stage in Berkhuz's periodization in the formation of comparative law as a recognized scientific orientation commenced with the Congress of 1900 and lasted until 1945. He noted that at the 1900 Congress conceptions were sounded out: goals, tasks, subject-matter, methods, and spheres of practical applications. Characteristic features of the second period were affirmation of the idea of creating a "world law" as the tasks of comparative studies and the emergence of specialized international associations of scholars.

The third stage he linked with the intensification of the development of comparative law after the Second World War, which lasted until the 1980s. During these years, Bekhruz observed, the number and quality of comparative legal studies grew, and some were directed towards elaborating theoretical problems; the focus of comparative studies was the interaction of legal systems; the geography of research expanded; and in addition to private law, greater attention began to be devoted to public and procedural law; the number of specialized comparative congresses and conferences increased tremendously.

The fourth, and present, stage in the development of comparative law, in Bekhruz's view, is linked with major geopolitical changes – globalization, the dissolution of the former Soviet Union, a change in the character of the development of the legal systems of post-Soviet countries, the principles of international order connected with this change, and the intensification of European integration. At this stage legal comparativistics is finding greater affirmation as an autonomous sphere of scientific knowledge, and comparative legal studies in post-Soviet space are proceeding in reality.

статей [Comparative Law: Contemporary State and Prospects for Development: Collection of Scholarly Articles] (2006), p. 7.

25 Kh. Bekhruz, Сравнительное правоведение [Comparative Law] (Odessa, 2008), pp. 84-91.

* * *

And so the evolution of comparative law began to be studied at 140 years ago and was transformed into a specialized subject-matter of research more than a century ago. Despite the rather broad spectrum of views on the subject, in our view one may identify rather typical positions of comparatists relating to the time of the origin and the principal factors and periods in the development of comparative law. To be sure, having regard to the basic materials involved by investigators, one may speak only about the view in western, that is, European and American, legal comparativistics.

Irrespective of whether scholars devoted attention to the development of comparative law research from Antiquity to the Enlightenment or not, virtually all of them agreed to some extent that in the nineteenth century cardinal qualitative changes occurred from which modern comparative law is calculated. The period prior to the nineteenth century is described by scholars as having these distinctive features: (1) lack of system, fragmentary research, all of which were the works of a few individual scholars; (2) the lack of a definite and consistently applied research methodology; (3) the dominance of a natural-law orientation in legal thought and the logical-speculative study of law; (4) the absence of form on the part of the objects of comparison – national legal systems; instead comparison was undertaken between supranational and particular legal blocks which were simultaneously applied to the fragmented law of a certain region – so-called "internal comparative law".[26]

A significant number of scholars see the emergence of comparative law in the development of legal thought, namely, the appearance of the historical and historical-philosophical (Hegelian and Neo-Kantian) schools in Germany in the 1810-20s and the polemic between them.[27] The methodological approaches of these schools, in the view of the majority of scholars, comprised the conceptual content of a certain period in the development of comparative law (up to the 1860s). However, some scholars consider the role of the historical school of law in the formation

[26] T. P. van Reenen, "The Comparison of Law in Medieval Legal Thought", *Journal of South African Law*, no. 4 (1995), pp. 665-667; J. M. Kelly, *A Short History of Western Legal Theory* (2003), pp. 258, 264ff.; R. Brooks, "The Emergence of the Hellenic Deliberative Ideal: The Classical Humanist Conception of Comparative Law", *Hastings International and Comparative Law Review*, XXX (2006-07), pp. 43-44; M. Richter, "Montesquieu's Theory and Practice of the Comparative Method", *History of the Human Sciences*, XV (2002), pp. 21-26.

[27] See H. Kötz, "Comparative Law in Germany Today", *Revue international de droit comparé*, no. 4 (1999), p. 754.

of comparative law to be contradictory, both positive and negative (L.-J. Constantinesco)[28] or frankly negative (H. C. Gutteridge, W. Ewald).[29]

Another manifestation of the origin of comparative law in this period was, in the view of scholars, positivist comparative studies of the first half of the nineteenth century (Mittermaier, Zachariae, Jean Louis Eugène Lerminier (1803-1857), and Jean Jacques Gaspard Foelix (1791-1853), and scholars within this group). Some scholars point to the early manifestations of the institutionalization of comparative law at this time – the emergence of the first specialized chair and journals. However, the beginning of the nineteenth century as the date of the appearance of legal comparativistics, also is based on other, non-scientific factors, such as the crisis of the revolutionary movement in Europe and the completion as a result of the codification of law of the formation of a number of national legal systems.[30]

Among the distinctive features typical of this period of comparative law the scholars note: (1) the redirection of the attention of scholars from internal to external comparison with a view to seeking successful legal solutions for various problems; (2) the inseparability of legal comparativistics from the study of foreign law and the ambiguity of the essence and subject-matter thereof; (3) the application of comparison primarily to the legal systems of continental Europe; (4) the leadership of German scholars in comparative studies. Proceeding from this, in our view, the essence of the period that extended from the early nineteenth century to the 1860s is more precisely identified by Schlesinger: comparative law became a specialized sphere of legal research. However, from the standpoint of the origin of a separate legal discipline, this period should, following Hug, be characterized as "embryonic".

The next period in the development of comparative law, in the opinion of some scholars, is linked with the sociological-positivist (or evolutionary) orientation in the 1860s, the founding the Society of Comparative Legislation in France and the Chair of Historical and Comparative Jurisprudence at Oxford University in 1869, together with specialized journals.[31] Some

[28] Also see M. Franklin, "Legal Method in the Philosophies of Hegel and Savigny", *Tulane Law Review*, XLIV (1969-70), p. 767; Compare I. Babich, «Виникнення та розвиток порівняльного правознавства як навчальної дисципліни» [Origin and Development of Comparative Law as an Instructional Discipline], Підирисмництво, господарство і право [Entrepreneurship, Economy, and Law], no. 4 (2007), p. 141.

[29] Also see K. Zweigert and H. Kötz, Введение в сравнительное правоведение в сфере частного права [Introduction to Comparative Law with Respect to Private Law] (2000), I, pp. 79, 84.

[30] See I. Iu. Bogdanovskaia, [Comparative Law: Beginning of a Century], [Yearbook of Comparative Law 2001 (2002), p. 39; L. S. C., "Civil and Criminal Laws of Modern States", *American Jurist & Law Magazine*, XXI (1839), pp. 56-57, 69.

[31] P. de Cruz, *Comparative Law in a Changing World* (3d ed., 2005); M. H. Hoeflich,

scholars point to the movement for the revival of German private law which led to the adoption of the German civil code (Ewald) and the emergence of an ethnological orientation (Saidov).

The characteristic distinctive features of the period which lasted from the 1860s to about 1910 (or the early twentieth century) noted by comparatists are: (1) the notion of the unidimensional, staged, and developmental nature of worldwide legal development and an understanding of comparative law as the comparative (general, universal) history of law; (2) the aspiration to seek for each specific situation a single correct legal solution, the best legal norm among different national legal systems which may be adopted and applied in any country, the notion of a "common legislative law", the substantiation and servicing of unification projects; (3) comparative law existed primarily in the form of comparative legislation in which the subject-matter of research was principally legislative norms; (4) theoretical thought commenced, although this had not separated itself from the comparative method. A significant number of comparatists who were the authors of the works analyzed here see comparative law being transformed into an individual branch of legal science, or domain of research, or scientific discipline. Some scholars believed that this happened in 1869 (for example, Hug and Hyland)[32], and others considered this to be merely an embryonic period (for example, Sacco).[33]

A new period in the development of comparative law, as some scholars note, commenced at the turn of the nineteenth and twentieth centuries; the benchmark was the International Congress of Comparative Law at Paris in 1900.[34] Some comparatists consider the year 1900 to be the date of the origin of legal comparativistics. Others believe that this period commenced between 1910 and 1920.

The various approaches to comparatists to periodization were affected by sundry criteria. The Paris Congress undoubtedly was an outstanding event which certified recognition of the existence of comparative law

---

"Comparative Law in Antebellum America", *Washington University Global Studies Law Review*, IV (2005), pp. 536-545.

[32] Also see A. Tille and M. Faiziev, «Из истории сравнительного правоведения» [From the History of Comparative Law], Общественные науки в Узбекистане [Social Sciences in Uzbekistan], no. 5 (1970), p. 39; R. A. Saidov, Становление, развитие и применение сравнительно-исторического метода в юридической науке [Origin, Development, and Application of the Comparative Historical Method in Legal Science] (Tashkent, 1990), p. 17 (abstract diss. kand. iurid. nauk); L. N. Brown, "A Century of Comparative Law in England: 1869-1969", *American Journal of Comparative Law*, XIX (1971), pp. 232-236.

[33] Also see E. Orücü, "Critical Comparative Law: Considering Paradoxes for Legal Systems in Transition", *Electronic Journal of Comparative Law*, IV (2000), p. 2.

[34] Also see A. Riles, "Introduction: The Projects of Comparison", in A. Riles (ed.), *Rethinking the Masters of Comparative Law* (2001), p. 4.

and a certain "corporation" of comparatists. It also became an occasion for scholars to systematically set out their views on the nature, subject-matter, and object of this scientific discipline. But those who pursued the history of comparative law do not point to any other material changes: internal – theoretical-methodological;[35] in the character and orientations of comparative law research; in the external conditions for the development of legal comparativistics – the legal, political, or other contexts thereof. The 1900 Paris Congress, just as the annual congresses overshadowed by it and undeservedly forgotten of the International Association for the Progress of Social Sciences (from 1862) and the Universal Congress of Lawyers and Jurists at St. Louis, Missouri (1904),[36] did not signify the beginning of a new era in the development of comparative law, although it materially affected the intensification thereof. In our view, the years 1910-1920 should be considered to be the beginning of the next stage.

The new period is linked, on one hand, with the dominance of legal positive in comparative law and a practical applied orientation, and on the other, with the functional approach. One important event which signified its emergence was the end of the First World War. As Denisov noted, there was skepticism relating to the possibility of creating a world law, and unification projects thereafter encompassed only private law.

The distinctive features of this period, which roughly lasted until 1945, became in the opinion of comparatists: (1) the idea that comparative law is not a science or a branch of knowledge, but merely a method; (2) a new doctrine of comparative law instead of comparative legislation, which meant an expansion of the subject-matter of research in which various sources of law, doctrines, and historical evolution were involved; (3) active investigation of the Common Law by continental European jurists;[37] (4) a change of attitude towards comparative law from an instrumentalist (especially as a means of unifying law) to an integral (means of not allowing legal isolationism, and so on) approach.

The next period in the development of comparative law began after the Second World War. By this time, on one hand, the subject-matter of research had greatly expanded – a number of post-colonial States had formed, the legal systems of countries which were on a socialist path of development

[35] E. Jenks, "On the Study of Comparative Jurisprudence", *Journal of Society of Comparative Legislation*, II (1900), p. 448.

[36] On these see, for example, D. S. Clark, "Nothing New in 2000? Comparative Law in 1900 and Today", *Tulane Law Review*, LXXV (2000-01), pp. 874, 888-889; Clark, "Establishing Comparative Law in the United States: The First Fifty Years", *Washington University Global Studies Law Review*, IV (2005), pp. 583-585.

[37] See J. C. Gardner, "The Study of Comparative Law in Great Britain", *Journal of Comparative Legislation and International Law*, XIV (3d ser., 1932), pp. 201-203.

had been materially transformed, and the religious fundamentalization has commenced of many legal systems which showed the failure of the tasks which comparative law confronted did not meet the standard of legal comparativistics. On the other hand, this was a period of the dominance and crisis of the functionalist approach, and also of the "critical theory of comparativism".[38]

This period, which in the view of comparatists extended until the 1980-90s, had these distinctive features: (1) study commenced of socialist, post-colonial, and religious law; (2) systemology came to comparative law with the elaboration of the doctrine of legal families, and with this, recognition of the equal value of "nonwestern" law; (3) the development of the "theory of distinctions": the formation of a pluralist mentality of comparatists, substantiation of legal diversity, and an understanding of the various sources and multi-factored nature of the development of law; (4) the extension of comparative studies to public and procedural law and to the interaction of legal systems; (5) the institutionalization of comparative law and its introduction into legal education significantly intensified.[39]

The most recent, contemporary stage of comparative law, in the view of scholars, especially of Saidov and Bekhruz, began in the 1980-90s. This period is based on the discussion relating to the essence and tasks of legal comparativistics under conditions of the development and awareness of the processes of globalization, the dissolution of the former Soviet Union, and cardinal changes in post-Soviet legal systems, intensification of European integration which led to the formation of a new supranational legal system of the European Union, the emergence of a number of new national legal systems as a result of the dissolution of federative States, and so on. As

[38] See A. Kh. Saidov, «О современном состоянии буржуазного сравнительного правоведения» [On the Contemporary State of Bourgeois Comparative Law], in Критика буржуазных политических и правовых концепций [Critique of Bourgeois Political and Legal Conceptions] (1984), p. 48; V. A. Tumanov, «О развитии сравнительного правоведения» [On the Development of Comparative Law], Советское государство и право [Soviet State and Law], no. 11 (1982), p. 41; Saidov, Теоритеческие проблемы советского сравнительного правоведения [Theoretical Problems of Soviet Comparative Law] (1984), pp. 1-3, 20 (diss. kand. iurid. nauk); M. Reimann, "The Progress and Failure of Comparative Law in the Second Half of the Twentieth Century', *American Journal of Comparative Law*, L (2002), pp. 672-673; Tumanov, «Вступительная статья» [Introductory Article], in V. A. Tumanov (ed.), Очерки сравнительного права [Essays on Comparative Law] (1981), pp. 5-7; M. Ancel, «Методологические проблемы сравнительного права» [Methodological Problems of Comparative Law], in Tumanov, ibid., pp. 39-41.

[39] Also see V. V. Palmer, "From Lerotholi to Lando: Some Examples of Comparative Law Methodology", *Global Jurist Frontiers*, II (2004), pp. 25-29; G. A. Bermann, "The Discipline of Comparative Law in the United States", *Revue international de droit comparé*, no. 4 (1999), pp. 1048-1052.

Saidov noted, the distinctive features of the modern period are crisis and a rupture in the succession of generations of scholars.[40]

The differences among scholars with respect to the periodization of the development of comparative law are, in our view, affected by these factors: (1) various views on the nature of comparative law, both as a science or as a method. For example, those who believe it to be a science are inclined the place greater emphasis on its institutionalization as an element of intellectual legitimation; (2) the countries of origin of the scholars and their command of languages. Comparatists rely on rather diverse materials known to them which influence their approach to periodization. The contribution of their country by a particular author is exaggerated, and the knowledge of foreign traditions of comparativistics is inadequate. Therefore, for example, the assertions of scholars as to by whom and when the term "comparative law" was first used differ dramatically. Moreover, materials from outside Western Europe and the United States are not taken into account. Familiarization with the works of eastern European scholars, for example, who are proponents of the historical school of law (the so-called school of Slavonic law) might remove any doubts relating to the weight of the contribution which this orientation made to the development of comparative law. And the distinctive features of the work of respective Soviet and now modern Ukrainian, Russian, and Uzbek scholars is separate from the world (in reality – western) consideration of a national or eastern European tradition of comparativistics.[41] There are, of course, other distinctions affecting the various legal understandings and other distinctive features of comparatists.

In our view, the five-pronged periodization of comparative law proposed herein is not the result of a simple collation of various views, but structured on the comparison thereof and a critical rethinking; and it takes into account, and to a certain extent is capable of reconciling, the basic positions of scholars.

[40] Also see Palmer, "Insularity and Leadership in American Comparative Law: The Past One Hundred Years", *Tulane Law Review*, LXXV (2000-01), pp. 1093-1094.

[41] See, for example, O. D. Tykhomyrov, «Виникнення порівняльно-правових досліджень в Україні» [Origin of Comparative Law Research in Ukraine], Часопис Київського університету права [Journal of Kiev University of Law], no. 4 (2005), p. 33.

Typologies of Modern Legal Systems of the World

L. A. LUTS*

Material changes in the infrastructure of the world order inhere in the modern stage of development of mankind, which means the study of social reality needs to take into account these realities. The requirements of social practice have intensified the need for comparative law studies, the renewal of the methodology of comparative law, and the creation of new conceptual approaches.

In defining the methodology of comparative law as a system of methods and means of comparative legal research (as well as doctrines on these), and the method of investigating them, several components are to be seen in the structure thereof: (1) a comparative typological approach; (2) a theory of the method of comparative law; (3) methods and means of comparative legal research; (4) the method of comparative law analysis.

The comparative typological approach is consistent with the laws of the poly-variationality of law and is based on the principle "from comparison to typological coincidence"; it depicts the diverse systems of comparative legal knowledge, and in jurisprudence – the aggregate of comparative legal knowledge. This approach enables the poly-variationality to be established of states in law: links, similarities and differences, typological changes, interactions, and others.

Underlying the comparative law approach is the principle of the unity of the comparative and typological methods of research, the combination of which creates a methodology of research that is new in principle, specific means of portraying the poly-variationality of the existence of law. A leading role in so doing is accorded to the typological method. A legal typology with whose assistance single-type legal systems are identified

* Доктор юридических наук, professor. Head, Chair of Theory and Philosophy of Law, Ivan Franko Lviv National University.

with a generalized legal model enables specific indicia to be abstracted and the common indicia to be singled out (essential for the creation of the ideal type of legal system).

Taking into account the fact that the "legal map of the world" is not uniform, but consists of individual national and inter-State legal systems between which complex integrative, multi-functional processes occur, scholars endeavor to classify them on the basis of various criteria. The importance of these classifications is predetermined as cognitive reasons and practical necessity or significance (harmonization of legislation, reception of law, and others). The problem of the classification of legal systems is one of the important problems of both the theory of law and of comparative law. Various criteria or factors are used for classification: ethnic, historical, racial, geographical, legal, and so on, which today in sum amount to several dozen. At one time, such criteria in comparative law doctrinal writings included: the distinctive features of the historical formation of legal systems (Ernest Désiré Glasson, 1839-1907); general structure and distinctive indicia (Adhémar Esmein, 1848-1913); the extent of similarity with other law or origin therefrom (Pierre Arminjon, 1869-19?; Boris Emmanuilovich Nolde, 1876-1948; Martin Wolff, 1872-1953); large cultural spheres (Adolf Friedrich Schnitzer); relationship with Roman law, the jus gentium, and canon law (Enrique Martinez Paz, 1882-1952); racial element (Georges Sauser-Hall, 1884-1966); the role of various sources of law (Henri Lévy-Ullman, 1870-1947); municipal indicia (René Rodière); ideology and legal technique (René David, 1906-1991); "legal style" (Konrad Zweigert, 1911-1996), and others.[1]

The American legal scholar Wigmore combined all modern and past legal systems into sixteen principal ones.[2] Although his work contains much legal historical informational materials, it does not demarcate the synchronic and diachronic aspects of classifying legal systems.[3]

Among the groups of classifications those most widely propagated are those by the French comparatist, David, and the Germans, Zweigert and Kötz. David singled out legal families such as the Anglo-Saxon, Romano-Germanic, socialist, religious, and traditional.[4] Zweigert and Kötz

1 R. Rodière, *Introduction au droit comparé* (1979); A. Esmein, "Le droit comparé et l'enseignement du droit", *Congrès international du droit comparé* (1905), I, p. 45; P. Arminjon, B. Nolde, M. Wolff, *Traité de droit comparé* (1950), I, p. 42; *Glowne kultury prawne wspolczesnego swiata* (1995), pp. 28-30; R. David, *Traité elementaire de droit civil comparé* (1950), I, p. 556; K. Zweigert, *Rechtsvergleichung* (1978); E. Glasson, *Le marriage civil et le divorce dans les principaux pays de l'Europe* (1879).

2 J. Wigmore, *A Panorama of the World's Legal Systems* (1928), I, p. 87.

3 A. Saidov, *Comparative Law,* transl. W. E. Butler (2003).

4 David, note 1 above, I; His work has been through several Russian language editions.

proposed a classification of legal families that contains eight varieties and is based on the concept of "legal style". Among the determinative factors, they considered there to be: (1) historical origin and development of a legal system; (2) dominant legal doctrine; (3) distinctive legal institutes; (4) sources of law and methods of interpreting them; (5) ideological factors.[5]

Ebert, a Swiss comparatist, used the Zweigert/Kötz classification as one of the possible working schemes for distinguishing and ordering legal systems. He observed that the ethno-historical theory identifies for each group of legal systems the dominance of a particular legal idea or legal order: in the Romanist, the French Code civil; in the Germanic, the German 1897 Civil code; in the Anglo-American, the Common Law, and in the Far Eastern, the Confucian theory of law.[6]

A global typology of law was rather extensively illuminated in Soviet legal doctrine,[7] within which an intra-typological classification was undertaken.[8] This classification (on the basis of formal indicia) assumed a division into a social and bourgeois (capitalist) type[9] and answered the question only of whose will of which social group the law reflects. This classification did not answer why, within the bourgeois type, legal systems of Common and continental law may exist, or democratic and totalitarian;[10]

[5] K. Zweigert and H. Kötz, *Introduction to Comparative Law*, transl. T. Weir (3d ed., 1998).

[6] K.-H. Ebert, *Rechtsvergleichung: Einführung in die Grundlagen* (1978), pp. 39, 44.

[7] Общая теория государства и права [General Theory of State and Law] (Leningrad, 1974), II; V. K. Babaev (ed.), Общая теория права: курс лекций [General Theory of Law: Cours of Lectures] (Nizhnii-Novgorod, 1993), pp. 38-39; Марксистско-ленинская общая теория государства и права: исторические типы государства и права [Marxist-Leninist General Theory of State and Law: Historical Types of State and Law] (1971), II; S. S. Alekseev, Общая теория права [General Theory of Law] (1981), I, pp. 107-122; V. E. Krasnianskii, «Классификация правовых систем» [Classification of Legal Systems], Правоведение [Jurisprudence], no. 5 (1969), pp. 41-46; A. A. Tille, Социалистическое сравнительное правоведение[Socialist Comparative Law] (1975), p. 178; O. A. Zhidkov, «История и опыт развития правовых систем» [History and Experience of Development of Legal Systems], in Мирное сосуществование и социально-политическое развитие [Peaceful Coexistence and Socio-Political Development] (1977), pp. 101-107.

[8] I. Szabo, Социалистическое право [Socialist Law] (1964), pp. 125-155; id, "The Socialist Conception of Law", *International Encyclopedia of Comparative Law* (1972), II, pp. 75-82; V. Knapp, «Крупные системы права в современном мире» [Large Systems of Law in the Modern World], in Сравнительное правоведение [Comparative Law] (1978), pp. 211-235; G. Eörsi, *Comparative Civil (Private) Law* (1979), pp. 31-225.

[9] A. Kh. Saidov, Введение в сравнительное правоведение [Introduction to Comparative Law] (1988), p. 49; A. Lopatka, «Польське право: від соціалістичного до капіталістичного (1989-2000)» [Polish Law: From Socialist to Capitalist (1989-2000)], in Європа, Японія, Україна: шляхи демократизації державно-правових систем [Europe, Japan, Ukraine: Paths of Democratization of State-Law Systems] (2000), pp. 35-38; V. Knapp, "Velke pravni systemy" [Great Legal Systems], *Pravnik*, no. 9 (1971), pp. 696-718; L. J. Constantinesco, *Traité du droit comparé* (1974), II, p. 18; G. Haney, *Sozialistisches recht und personlichkeit* (1967).

[10] V. I. Goiman-Chervoniuk, Очерк теории государства и права [Survey of Theory of State and Law] (1996), I, p. 196.

what the American, French, Islamic, and Japanese legal systems may share in common (within the bourgeois type of law) in accordance with a formation typology.[11]

At the same time, as Krasheninnikova observed, "it is impossible to elicit from the means of production (or socio-economic formation) the distinctive features of legal systems of different social systems and supranational legal communities".[12]

In western legal writings ideological criteria were also used, *inter alia*, to distinguish western and socialist law.

MODERN APPROACHES TO CLASSIFICATION

In contemporary legal doctrine the classification of legal systems of the world is made on the basis of various criteria: types of sources of law and model of legislative procedure;[13] elements of general and legal culture;[14] legal traditions;[15] commonality of principles of legal regulation of social relations, unity of terminology, legal categories and concepts;[16] together with complex or aggregate criteria, among which there are: (a) historical genesis, system of sources of law and structure of legal system;[17] (b) distinctive features of law creation orientated towards a particular element of the legal system and legal ideology;[18] (c) methodology of law, infrastructure of law, and structure of procedural law;[19] (d) legal ideology and legal technique;[20] (e) legal style;[21] (f) historical experience and development of law, method

11 A. P. Semitko, Развитие правовой культуры как правовой прогресс [Development of Legal Culture as Legal Progress] (Ekaterinburg, 1996), pp. 7-8.

12 N. A. Krasheninnikova, «Цивилизационные подходы к изучению истории государства и права» [Civilized Approaches to the Study of the History of State and Law], in Методологические проблемы правоведения [Methodological Problems of Jurisprudence] (1994), pp. 7-8.

13 H. Rot (ed.), *Prawo socialistyczne: wspolczesne problem teoretyczne* (Wroclaw, 1989).

14 V. N. Siniukov, Российская правовая система: введение в общую теорию [Russian Legal System: Introduction to General Theory] (Saratov, 1994), pp. 171-177.

15 J. H. Merryman and R. Pérez-Perdomo, *The Civil Law Tradition: An Introduction to the Legal Systems of Western Europe and Latin America* (3d ed., 2007); H. P. Glenn, *Legal Traditions of the World: Sustainable Diversity in Law* (3d ed., 2007).

16 Теория государствав и права [Theory of State and Law] (1997), pp. 509-510.

17 Saidov, note 3 above.

18 S. S. Alekseev, Право: азбука, теория, философия: опыт комплексного исследования [Law: Alphabet, Theory, Philosophy: Attempt at Integrated Study] (1999), p. 48; id, Теория права [Theory of Law] (2d ed., Kharkov, 1994), pp. 195-196.

19 C. Osakwe, Сравнительное правоведение в схемах: Общая и особенная части [Comparative Law in Diagrams: General and Special Parts] (2000).

20 J.-L. Bergel, Общая теория права [General Theory of Law] (2000).

21 O. F. Skakun, Теория государства и права [Theory of State and Law] (Kharkov, 2000), p. 553.

of legal thought, legal institutes, types of sources of law, and structural and axiological pre-determined link between them.[22] Views on the issues of classification have been expressed in Ukrainian doctrinal writings.[23]

The list of sundry classifications might be continued by using various approaches to select criteria and differentiation of the principal types of legal systems.[24] But as Rodière noted, there are almost as many classifications of legal systems as there are comparatists.[25]

Consequently, the choice of criteria is important for the classification of legal systems both theoretically and practically, but even more important is the definition of "classification". In accordance with the notions elaborated in doctrinal writings, "classification" (LATIN: *classic* is class or category; *facere*, to make) is regarded as a "system of dividing subject-matter, phenomena, or concepts into classes, groups, and so on according to common indicia or properties".[26]

From the standpoint of logic, this is a variety of a logical operation of dividing concepts and is regarded as a systematic division of subject-matter by classes on the basis of any general indicator, as a result of which each class occupies with respect to other classes a precisely determined place. Scientific classification is the division of subject-matter by classes on the basis of the most material indicia,[27] and is best when the subject-matter are similar to one another by the largest number of indicia.[28]

Classification is treated in philosophy as a special instance of the application of a logical operation of the extent of the concept and

[22] *Główne kultury prawne współczesnego swiata* (Warsaw, 1995), p. 30.

[23] Skakun, note 21 above, pp. 562-567; P. M. Rabinovich, Основи закальноï теорiï права i держави [Fundamental Principles of General Theory of Law and State] (Kiev, 1995); E. Kharitonov and O. Kharitonova, «Європейські правові системи: проблеми класифікації» [European Legal Systems: Problems of Classification], Вiсник Академiї правових наук України [Herald of Academy of Legal Sciences of Ukraine], no. 2(29) (2002), pp. 3-14.

[24] J. H. Merryman and D. S. Clark, *Comparative Law: Western European and Latin American Legal Systems: Cases and Materials* (1978), p. 9; Ugo Mattei, et al., *Schlesinger's Comparative Law: Cases, Text, Materials* (7th ed., 2009); M. N. Marchenko, Сравнительное правоведение [Comparative Law] (2001), pp. 243-262; Iu. A. Tikhomirov, Курс сравнительного правоведения [Cours of Comparative Law] (1996), pp. 112-140; A. Kh. Saidov, Сравнительное правоведение и юридическая география мира [Comparative Law and Legal Geography of the World] (1993); Babaev, Теория государства и права [Theory of State and Law] (1999), pp. 548-553; M. Ancel, «Методологические проблемы сравнительного права» [Methodological Problems of Comparative Law] in V. A. Tumanov (ed.), Очерки сравнительного права [Essays on Comparative Law] (1981), pp. 47-48.

[25] Rodière, note 1 above, p. 27.

[26] I. S. Shatilo, Общество как развивающаяся система [Society as a Developing System] (1998), p. 258.

[27] Логика [Logic] (Minsk, 1974), pp. 79-83; Навчальний посiбник з логiки [Elementary Manual on Logic] (Lviv, 1996), pp. 60-61.

[28] G. I. Chelpanov, Учебник логики [Textbook on Logic] (1946), p. 117.

"systematic division and placing in order of concepts and subject-matter" and occurs when there are all possible important indicia underlying it.[29] Similar notions of classification exist in foreign doctrinal writings. To be sure, significant attention is devoted not only to the general indicia of objects, but also to their distinctive features.

In classifying such legal objects as national legal systems, scholars have given attention to everything that is in some measure interconnected. However, some of them more similar indicia than others and are distinctive because of dominant distinctive features. Similar indicia are predetermined by the typological proximity of societies, general conditions of the historical development of society and religion, or other analogous circumstances.[30] The presence of common indicia is the basis for their classification and division by certain criteria into groups. However, the complexity and multifacetedness of problems which arise in connection with the classification of legal systems does not give precise, unequivocal results. Issues not only relating to the criteria for classification, but the use of simple, unequivocal, or complex criteria are controversial.

In western comparative studies especially intensive discussions are being held with regard to the factors which directly affect the forming of common indicia of legal systems and, consequently, the choice of criteria for their classification.[31] Economic, political, ideological, religious, historical, geographical, demographic,[32] and military-political[33] are among these factors. Marchenko sets out a number of requirements with respect to factors influencing the formation of common indicia of legal systems and criteria for their classification, among them: (1) permanence, fundamental nature (and not incidental) factors; (2) precise definiteness of indicia – criteria; (3) objectiveness; (4) dominance of one indicator within complex criteria; (5) recording of both objective and subjective factors which directly affect the process of forming common indicia of legal systems.[34]

Various terms are used to designate groups of legal systems with similar legal indicia and combined in the process of classification: "families of legal system" (David), "legal circles" (Ebert and Rheinstein); "form of legal systems" (Szabo), "structural community" (Alekseev), "legal style" (Kötz/

[29] E. F. Gubskii, G. V. Korableva, and V. A. Lutchenko (eds.), Философский энциклопедический словарь [Philosophical Encyclopedic Dictionary] (2000), pp. 212, 220, 221.

[30] M. Borgan, *Comparative Law* (1994).

[31] Marchenko, note 24 above, p. 253.

[32] Borgan, note 30 above, p. 71.

[33] P. de Cruz, *A Modern Approach to Comparative Law* (1993), p. 28.

[34] Marchenko, note 24 above, p. 254.

Zweigert). Terms such as "legal order", "legal culture",[35] and the like also are used. The term "legal family"[36] is encountered most frequently. David, however, noted that the concept of a "legal family" is not a biological reality; it is used merely for didactic purposes to identify the similarities and differences in a system of law in force.[37]

Some authors believe that a legal family is a category which serves to determine the relative unity of legal systems that have similar legal indicia and also reflects those peculiarities of legal systems which predetermined the similarity of their specific historical development.[38]

Without casting aside that which is positive on the level of classification of legal systems and their combination into "legal families" by legal doctrine (forms, circles, and so on), it must be said that there are controversial moments. First, the aforesaid classification groups of legal systems do not give a full impression of the "legal map of the world" as a whole; second, so far precise criteria of classification have not been defined; third, the category of "legal family" does not reflect objective legal indicia of groups of legal systems which are not within it. It seems that the resolution of these and other cognitive tasks would further the use of the concept of a legal system of a society which would meet modern realities and also a typologization of modern legal systems of the world.

Such a concept of legal system might be formulated by applying systems analysis and identifying the principal indicia, among which there may be the following: (1) existence of such elements as subjects of law and their structural sequence; (2) ensuring of permanent links between subjects of law thanks to their activity and legal means; (3) manifestation of links between subjects of law principally through legal relations; (4) orientation towards achieving legal order, which is an essential condition for the existence of a social system as a whole.

In considering a legal system of society as an integral phenomenon one must take into account its internal structure. The structural organization of a legal system of society includes those parts thereof which are advisable and necessary, and also enable the stability and alterability of the legal system to be expressed. These are the institutional part (aggregate of subjects which have the properties of elements of the legal system); functional part (aggregate of links between subjects of law which would

[35] T. Stawecki and P. Winczorek, *Wstep do prawaoznawstwa* (1999), pp. 20-21.

[36] R. David and C. Jauffret-Spinosi, Основные правовые системы современности] Principal Legal Systems of Modern Times] (1996), p. 20.

[37] Siniukov, note 14 above, p. 166; Saidov, note 3 above; Osakwe, note 19 above, pp. 22-47.

[38] V. K.Babaev, V. M. Baranov, and V. A. Tolstik, Теория права и государства в схемах и определениях [Theory of Law and State in Diagrams and Definitions] (1999), p. 198.

be objectified as legal relations through their activity); normative part – the aggregate of legal means which are mediators in the arising and existence of stable links between subjects of law.

On the basis of the foregoing one should understand as the legal system of a society – the structurally stable interaction of subjects of law in place with the assistance of legal means and ensuring the attainment of legal order – to be an essential condition of the functioning of a social system. This concept has regard to the recent achievements of the social sciences and is predetermined by modern realities, especially the modern infrastructure of the world. It facilitates the resolution of a number of scientific and practical tasks and enables the principal modern legal system of the world to be typologized. The objectivity of typologization also further the concept of "type of legal system of society".

TYPOLOGIES OF LEGAL SYSTEMS

The concept "type of legal system" (which differs from the concept "type of law" traditionally used in Soviet legal doctrine) enables the stable, most material legal indicia to be identified that are inherent in a particular legal system, the societal-developmental links to be elicited, and the indicia of individual legal systems to be singled out so as to be identified with a certain type.

This is a concept fundamental to typology. A typology is determined variously by: (1) the method of scientific cognition with whose assistance the aggregate of objects is divided into certain groups; (2) the type of scientific systematization and classification of articles or phenomena by the community of material indicia; (3) the grouping of phenomena with the assistance of a generalized model, type, or result of typological description and contrast.[39]

Both the process of dividing the cognitive aggregate of objects into groups and the result of such division determine a typology. Some authors use the term "typologization" to designate the process of dividing and "typology" to designate the results of this division. In the view of Kagan, typologization is the direct continuation of classification, according to which a group of heterogeneous objects is divided until a level of qualitative homogeneity is achieved at which modified categories (aggregate of single-type objects) are formed. A theoretical model (archetype) is created in the

[39] Типология и классификация в социологических исследованиях [Typology and Classification in Sociological Research] (1982), p. 8; I. T. Frolov (ed.), Философский словарь [Philosophical Dictionary] (1991), p. 193; A. M. Prokhorov (ed.), Большая советская энциклопедия [Great Soviet Encyclopedia] (1976), XXV, p. 265.

process of typologization, a sample of which gives us an image, and this model is "realized in the diversity of modified variations".[40]

Modern sociological literature defines typological analysis as the highest level of generalization in comparison with grouping and classification, distinguishing in so doing empirical and theoretical typologization. Theoretical typologization consists of generalizing the indicia of social phenomena on the basis of an ideal theoretical model and theoretically-substantiated criteria. The method of theoretical typologization leads to an explanation of what is formulated in the hypotheses of the respective theory.[41]

The literature variously approaches demarcating the concepts of classification and typology. A division on the basis of indicia which are used to construct classes is called a typology or a typological grouping, but if respective forms are established in so doing, the theoretical links between various aspects of the system being studied are called a classification.[42] Sometimes the term "classification" is used for a typological grouping.[43] In other instances the term "classification" is used together with the term "typology",[44] although in sociology the term "typology" is used in connection with the substantive character of the respective division of an aggregate into groups, and the term "classification" is never used for this purpose because of the absence of respective properties.[45]

In legal doctrine the concepts of typology and classification often are used as synonyms.[46] Sometimes a typology is defined as a type of classification.[47] However, although these are generic means of cognition, they are relatively autonomous. Rozhkova believes that a typology is distinguished from classification by two material indicia: (1) the subject-

[40] M. S. Kagan, «Системное рассмотрение основных способов группировки» [Systemic Consideration of Basic Means of Grouping], Философские и социологические исследования [Philosophical and Sociological Studies] (1977), p. 24.

[41] Iadov, V. A., Стратегия социологического исследования [Strategy of Sociological Research] (1999), pp. 320-334.

[42] B. G. Mirkin, Анализ качественных признаков (Математические модели и методы) [Analysis of Qualitative Indicia (Mathematical Models and Methods)] (1976).

[43] P. P. Maslov, Статистика в социологии [Statistics and Sociology] (1971).

[44] T. I. Zaslavskaia and I. B. Muchnik, «Об одном методе классификации и объектов в социологии» [On One Method of Classification and Objects in Sociology], Социологические исследования [Sociological Research], no. 1 (1974), pp. 150-159.

[45] Note 39 above (1982), p. 11.

[46] Tille, note 7 above, p. 152; id, «Сравнительный метод в правовых исследованиях» [Comparative Method in Legal Research], Методологические проблемы советской юридической науки [Methodological Problems of Soviet Legal Science] (1980), p. 255; A. I. Denisov (ed.), Теория государства и права [Theory of State and Law] (1980), p. 76.

[47] V. M. Syrykh, Метод правовой науки: основные элементы и структура [Method of Legal Science: Basic Elements and Structure] (1980), p. 162.

matter of a typological classification is objects of a determined sphere of activity as integral systems; (2) classification types are the highest classification categories.[48]

The existence of the second of the said indicia is denied by Silchenko, who believes that the highest categories of classification are called classes, and in typology, are called types. However, the main thing is not the level of these categories, but the means of obtaining them and their special-purpose designation. In addition, classification is not in a position to give integral knowledge about an object and identify system-forming links. The purpose and essence of a typology lies in working out notions about the organic unity of the system of material indicia (properties) as elements of a single type.[49]

The method of modeling is closest to the process of typologization, with its gnosiological status. The similarity between them is that a model and a type reproduce the object of study. However, they are not identical and often do not coincide in the object of study. The purpose of modeling and of a typology also is different. The special-purpose designation of the last lies in the study of various aspects of the object by means of singling out individual indicia and properties from the entire system of links (in that understanding one may speak about an ideal type as a model of true reality). The investigator abstracts from a number of real properties, thanks to definitions of indicia and properties necessary to form an ideal type. Thus, if the schematism and abstracting of a typological method constitute one of the essential prerequisites for its application, the essence thereof does so in the method of modeling.

On the basis of the foregoing, it should be noted that an incorrect substitution occurs in doctrinal writings with the concepts of "typology", "typologization", and "classification". It is suggested that typologization and classification are autonomous methods of scientific cognition, but if we define classification as the division of a concept into types, groups, or other classification multiples on the basis of a determined indicator or property,

[48] L. P. Rozhkova, Принципы и методы типологии государства и права [Principles and Methods of Typology of State and Law] (Saratov, 1984); id, Принципы и методы типологии государства и права [Principles and Methods of Typology of State and Law] (Saratov, 1980), p. 7 (abstract diss. kand. iurid. nauk).

[49] S. V. Polenina and N. V. Silchenko, Научные основы типологии нормативно-правовых актов в СССР [Scientific Foundations of Typology of Normative Legal Acts in the USSR] (1987), pp. 15-19; N. V. Silchenko, «Роль и место понятия «типология» в понятийном аппарате общей теории государства и права» [Role and Place of Concept of "Typology" in Conceptual Apparatus of General Theory of State and Law], in Право и правотворчество: вопросы теории [Law and Law-Creation: Questions of Theory] (1982).

then typologization is the process of grouping certain systemic phenomena of true reality on the basis of a theoretical model (or type).

The aggregate of generalized knowledge concerning typologization and the creation of respective types and bringing them into a determined system should be considered to be a typology. Consequently, the concept of the type is the basic concept of a typology.

A type (from the Greek – typos) is a representation, sample, form, or model. A new interpretative dictionary of the Ukrainian language treats the meaning of "type" as a "sample, model, form to which a determined group of articles, concepts, or phenomena correspond".[50] Other similar views relative to the concept of "type" exist.[51] Legal doctrinal writings understand the concept of "type" to mean the most stable combining of properties and indicia of objects and phenomena of State law reality with a view to creating an example or model thereof.[52]

Constructing an ideal type based on an impression of the close link and interaction of indicia and properties not only provides an understanding of a type in the systemic unity thereof. That is, these indicia are not a simple aggregate, but an organic whole, a system, where each indicator is a distinctive element of the system of indicia, and their stable links form the structure of an ideal type.

The concept of "homogeneity" as conditioning particular phenomena by the same causes is important in the process of forming a type, as is emphasized in sociological works.

In addition, the existence of certain prerequisites is important for determining a type. All indicia must have a final number of significances. Objects (or phenomena) which have the same selection (or aggregate of selections) of indicia essential for each type belong to a single type. The base selection of indicia must not only be sufficient, but also necessary, that is, must not include "superfluous indicia" which do not bear information about the nature of the type of classified objects.[53] The ideal type is one of the types of models of thought. It is based on the separating out of certain indicia and properties of reality essential for forming a type. It differs from other models by a special form of abstraction – the abstraction of idealization, whose essence consists of separating out basic elements and

[50] V. V. Iaremenko and L. M. Spipushko (eds.), Новий тлумачний словник української мови [New Interpretative Dictionary of the Ukrainian Language] (Kiev, 1998), IV, p. 524.

[51] See Prokhorov, note 39 above, XXV, p. 561; note 39 above (1982),; Gubskii, et al., note 39 above, p. 455.

[52] Polenina and Silchenko, note 49 above, p. 9.

[53] G. S. Arefeva, «Социальная активность» [Social Activeness], in Проблема субъекта и объекта в социальной практике и познании [Problem of Subject and Object in Social Practice and Cognition] (1974), p. 110.

relations typical of a certain phenomenon or process and abstracting from the nonessential, incidental, and secondary.[54]

Thus, a type is a model (or example) of determined phenomena (or processes) which contain the essential selection of material indicia for the grouping thereof.

LEGAL SYSTEM AND THE SOCIAL SYSTEM

On the basis of the above it should be noted that the basic parameters of indicia of a type of legal system are determined by the place and role of the legal system in the social system, and also by its special-purpose orientation. A legal system is a subsystem of a social system, and it may function only therein in accordance with the purposes and tasks which it is called upon to resolve. The general development of a legal system is part of the development of society, as an organic system (or origin thereof as an integral whole) which occurs within the limits of determined general laws of societal development.

The development of society from simple forms (the stability and procedure of which is ensured by customs, traditions, and the like) to complex ones (with a specific regulatory system in the form of law) leads to the development of systemic qualities, and later, to the acquisition by the legal system of wholeness, the accumulation of legal properties, the formation of subsystems (systems of law, systems of external forms or sources of law, systems of subjects of law, systems of legal activity, and so on) and a weakening of the role of other social regulators and enhancing the role of legal ones.

The legal system is determined by numerous requirements and interests of participants in social relations, the need to coordinate and regulate them. The social function of the legal system determines the purpose the purpose, structure, and procedure for the functioning thereof.

The history of the development of human civilization testifies to its unequal social development. National social systems today have different levels of development influencing their perfection and the effectiveness of their legal systems. An analysis of the genesis of national legal systems shows the various levels of their normativeness at various periods of development; however, their genesis is a complex and lengthy process which depends upon various factors: economic, political, spiritual, and so on. The genesis of a legal system happens simultaneously with the

[54] A. F. Iatskevich, Диалектика объективного и субъективного в проявлении законов общества [Dialectics of Objective and Subjective in Manifesting Laws of Society] (Minsk, 1982), p. 152.

genesis of other subsystems of society, although in various periods of the development of society a reduction of the role of the legal system may occur. In such periods the social value (or significance) of law is reduced as an effective means for the management of society, legal means are replaced by other means of regulation: customs, morality, religion, and others.

In a society where an optimal correlation exists between subsystems of the social system and none of them swallows up the other, some functions are not substituted by others, the need arises for a high level of normativeness in the legal system. This level is ensured by the effective mechanism of legal impact which depends upon the requirements of society and individual subjects thereof and is a part of the mechanism of social impact. It is formed under the influence of a world-outlook recognition by society of law as a social value. The mechanism of social impact may have a number of levels – lower, medium, and high – each of which depends upon the weight of legal regulators within the system of social regulation.

The concept of the mechanism of legal impact enables the legal system to be analyzed within s systemically-dynamic state, specific functions to be illuminated which particular legal phenomena fulfill in the legal system, and their links and interaction to be shown.

As already noted, the mechanism of legal impact is part of the system of social management, which consists of managing and managed subsystems, the principal element of which is people, and the management comes down to the influence of some of them on the consciousness and behavior of others. Within the system of management of a society the mechanism of legal impact is one of the important normatively-organized factors which ensure the effectiveness of the practical activity of people.

The mechanism of legal impact is a system of general and special legal means with whose assistance legal requirements are introduced in social behavior of subjects and the normative-legal behavior of an organization (regulation) of social relations is effectuated. The concept of a "means" is general-scientific and interdisciplinary. In philosophy it is understood to be methods or instruments of action. Legal means are those legal phenomena which represent the social value of law and ensure the achievement of legally and socially significant results.

Legal means within the mechanism of legal impact may be divided into general and special.

With the assistance of general means (legal consciousness, legal culture, legal principles, legal order) moral-psychological, ideological, and informational impact is effectuated. The principal function of special means (norms of law, normative-legal prescription, sources of law, law-executing, law-realization, interpretative-legal acts) is effectuated by putting in order (regulation) of social relations. And this is the principal function thereof.

Their respective correlation in the mechanism of legal impact determines the level of normativity, is an indicator of the level of legal culture of society and the individual, their legal possibilities and level of legal development, testifies to the demand for legal forms in bringing order to social links, the competitiveness of legal values with non-legal ones (moral, religious, and so on), and enables legal conflicts to be prevented or resolved.

At the same time, legal impact has certain limits since legal means are created in the legal system that are necessary in order to ensure legal order in society. These means ensure the functioning of the legal system and other subsystems of society.

All this testifies to the importance of the use of knowledge concerning the mechanism of legal impact, in particular, the legal means, with a view to the typologization of modern legal systems of the world.

IDEAL MODELS OF LEGAL SYSTEMS

In effectuating the typologization of modern legal systems, it is essential to create "ideal types", models, on the basis of which the grouping of legal systems will be carried out. These models should have characteristic features needed to care an "ideal type", and also indicia by which the identification of real legal systems of the respective type is effectuated.

In order to elicit such types the essential indicia are: (1) the distinctive features of the institutional, functional, and normative parts (they determine the "selection" of the most material legal indicia of a specific type); (2) the presence of a respective mechanism of legal impact, in particular, the respective level of its normativity. Additional conditions also are important, such as: (1) the character of a legal norm and respective means and forms of its objectification, which determine the level of normativity of the mechanism of legal impact, in particular, the mechanism of legal regulation; (2) the existence of a respective mechanism for ensuring the realization of legal norms by means of the effectuation of respective legal activity (especially judicial). These parameters of the type of a legal system are determined by the place and role of the legal system within the social system of its structural organization and targeted orientation.

In effectuating the typologization of modern legal systems of the world on the basis of such a theoretical model as "type of legal system" one may separate out several types: (1) Romano-Germanic (continental); (2) Anglo-American (Common Law); (3) mixed with subtypes: dualist (Latin American and Scandinavian), religious community (Muslim, Hindu), traditional-philosophical (Japanese, Chinese), custom-community (African); (4) inter-State legal with subtypes: European (for example, the legal systems of the Council of Europe, European Union), American, Asian, African, and so on.

An analysis, for example, of the Romano-Germanic type of legal system testifies to the optimal combining of general and special legal means in the mechanism of legal impact, and also an adequate selection of the last, which enables one to speak about a high level of normativity of the system.

However, the absence of diversity in the system of sources of law and the optimality of their combining leads to the excessive formality of the legal system, the absence of flexibility in legal regulation. This, in turn, may influence the effectiveness of legal regulation and the level of normativity of the respective type of legal system.

In the Anglo-American type the combining of general and special means is characterized as follows: a significant part of the general means are within the mechanism of legal impact on an equal basis with the special, and the optimality of their correlation is disturbed to the benefit of the former. At the same level the normativity is reduced at the expense of the less general and abstract character of the legal norm, and also the possibility of its objectification not only in normative legal acts, but also in judicial precedents. Therefore, the level of normativity of this type of legal system is – medium or average.

In the religious subtype of the mixed type the low level of normativity is explained by the fact that general legal means (and often non-legal) have priority over special ones. The undifferentiated character of the norm also plays its role in the reduction of the level (the lack of a precise demarcation of the normative and individual prescription; legal, moral, religious, customary, and traditional rules), and hence the specific means of their objectification (traditions, customs, religious sources, and so on).

As regards the Scandinavian subtype of the mixed type, it is characterized by a high level of normativity in the Scandinavian subtype both from the optimal combining of general and special legal means and the coordination of various means and forms of the objectification of norms of law, and also the adequacy of their application in the respective spheres of regulation. Legal unification has importance in ensuring the high level of normativity in the group of Scandinavian legal systems.

The course of the development of mankind, the need for resolving general humanitarian (worldwide) problems, and also globalization and integration, have facilitated the formation of a qualitatively-new infrastructure of world order, the emergence of inter-State (international) associations of a universal and regional nature, effectuating the structuring of the respective space. All this has promoted the emergence at the modern stage of development of a new type of legal system – inter-State legal. The emergence thereof is objectively determined by a number of such laws of societal development as: expansion of the group of participants of international relations, complication and increase of the number of international relations; recognition of many humanitarian problems to be worldwide and global; the need to change legal means in accordance with the purposes of international legal regulation, and the growing role of law in the regulation of international relations.

The level of normativity of the inter-State legal system at this stage is medium because of the lack of an adequate selection of special legal means. This is explained by the insignificant period of the functioning of these systems and the absence so far of precise parameters thereof. Although the trends of their development testify to the increase of their number: the growth of powers relative to the structuring of social space; the creation of a significant number of legal standards in various social spheres; and the growth of the pace of legal unification.

In applying the method of comparative-legal analysis to legal systems of the Romano-Germanic type one may single out general identifying features: (1) the presence of a subject of law creation with extensive powers; (2) the presence of constitutional justice agencies; (3) a precise delimitation of law-creation, law-application, law-interpretative activity; (4) a high level of normativity of the system; (5) the abstract nature of a norm of law and extensive use of norms of material law; (6) the precise branch structure of the system of law and division of the system of law into public and private law; (7) the hierarchy of normative legal acts: constitution, laws, subordinate acts; (8) branch codification.

At the same time, legal systems of the Romano-Germanic type are materially changing, to which the following trend testifies: the growth of the importance of international treaties; the increased significance of judicial precedents; the unification of legal regulation by international legal standards; the coming together of the Romano-Germanic and Anglo-American types of legal systems; the increased significance of general-civilized principles of law.

UKRAINE AND COMPARATIVE LEGAL MODELS

In applying the comparative law method to an analysis of the legal system of Ukraine it should be noted that the aforesaid indicia enable it to be identified with the Romano-Germanic type (existence of a legislative organ – Supreme Rada of Ukraine and other law-creation agencies with extensive law-creation powers; Constitutional Court of Ukraine; precise separation of law-creation, law-application, and law-interpretation activities; precise branch structuring of norms of law within the system; division into public and private law, and so on).

Such identification is affirmed also by the genesis of national law (sources of Magdeburg Law, Constitution of Pilip Orlik of 1710, constitutions, codes, and laws adopted at various periods of the history of Ukraine, doctrine; adoption of the 1996 Constitution on the European democratic model; formation of agencies of constitutional justice, adoption of new Civil Code of Ukraine in connection with the expansion of the limits of private-law regulation of social relations).

The identification of the legal system of Ukraine with the Romano-Germanic type is acquiring significance from the standpoint of the need to determine the place of Ukraine among modern legal systems of the world. Although the view is held in Ukrainian doctrinal writings identifying the legal system of Ukraine with continental law, other views all the same are expressed. Some scholars adhere to the position of Russian scholars concerning the trends of a Slavic legal family being formed (V. N. Siniukov) or a Eurasian family (Iu. N. Oborotov). It seems inadvisable for the classification and identification of legal systems to investigate the culturological, world-outlook, or other (non-legal) criteria. The substitution of concepts and criteria in comparative legal studies, just as in any other scientific research, is fraught with mistakes and subjective conclusions far removed from objective reality.

Therefore, it seems that for the legal community of modern times an important task is the creation of an effective methodology for comparative law research.

Although the processes of forming the legal system of Ukraine have been accompanied by certain difficulties: the reduction of the quality of law-creation and law-application activity, legal idealism and nihilism, lack of a normative-legal base for the activity of certain agencies of State power, multiplicity of laws (more than 3,500) and other deformations, positive trends are in evidence. In particular, an institutional, functional, and normative part of the legal system is being formed and is being brought into conformity with international legal standards; the system of sources of law of Ukraine being shaped is becoming more diverse. In legal doctrine the possibility is being discussed of using judicial precedent as a source of law.

Legal Systems of the Modern World: Problems of Identification

V. V. OKSAMYTNYI*

EXTENT AND FRAMEWORK OF LEGAL SYSTEM: PARADIGMS OF NEW REALITY

Modern legal realities are extremely complex to reflect with the assistance of old, stable, but rather narrow constructions. The new millennium is characterized by the complexity of problems confronting it passed on by the preceding century and the aspirational beginning of the present century. The processes of identification of modern States in the world community actualize recourse to laws of societal development and manifestations of their politico-legal development and trends in the functioning of law under conditions of globalism and integration. Then an awareness comes of the societal law of introducing into jurisprudence complex categories, scholarly operations flexible and adequate to the challenges of the day and leading to the achievement of higher levels of generalization.

The legal system is becoming one of these, capable of making it possible to analyze all legal reality as a whole, and not individual components thereof. There is no need for a change of concepts, especially a substitute for the conception of law by the conception of a legal system since this should become and is becoming an integral part of the doctrine on law as being more significant and multi-aspectual. However, an understanding of so obvious a fact for the modern specialist comes not at once, but gradually,

* доктор юридических наук, professor. Meritorious Jurist of the Russian Federation; Director, Scientific Center of Comparative Law, A. S. Griboedov Institute of International Law and Economics; author of numerous monographs on international and comparative law.

stumbling against numerous conceptual and categorical impediments and ideological taboos which operated in the legal understanding of eras past.

An analysis of the complex, specialized, and mixed studies to some extent affecting the systemic problem in law affirms that the juridical category "legal system" is used intensively and multifariously, representing an equivocal and multi-functional phenomenon belonging just as other sub-systems of the universal social system as a whole to complexly organized communities. At the same time, the very concept of legal system in legal science is defined variously by different specialists.[1] This is to be explained not only by the various individual approaches of authors to this issue, but also their affiliation to different branches of jurisprudence. The unifying principle of these approaches until the end of the twentieth century was their use almost solely to describe legal phenomena, means, and processes existing within a specific State or typical of a certain group of countries.[2]

A legal system is primarily or most often considered in the context of the link with the State as the principal bearer of public power. And comparative law, being an integral part of the general theory of legal science applied to State law phenomena of the modern world, separates out as a result of juxtaposition, types of legal systems of States on various grounds or their legal families. The classifications in the works of comparatists are rather diverse, but they most often consider the similarities or differences in the creation and actions of various components of legal systems called States, turning to the legal understanding dominant in a country, the ways of forming sources of law, the normative legislation of the State, mechanisms for the operation of legal prescriptions, or to the results of such action.

Even René David, the most noted comparatist of the second half of the twentieth century, noted the multiplicity of legal systems both within an individual State and between States: "Every State has its own law in the

[1] In connection with the sundry approaches to an understanding of legal system it is even suggested to create a special international conference, a result of which might be a respective convention on the legal system based on "international standards". See S. O. Serebrova, «О необходимости законодательного закрепления дефиниции «правовая система» [On the Need for Legislative Consolidation of a Definition of "Legal System"], in V. M. Baranov, P. S. Patsurkivskii, and G. O. Matiushkin (eds.), Законодательная дефиниция: логико-гносеологические, морально-психологические и практические проблемы [Legislative Definition: Logical-Gnosiological, Moral-Psychological, and Practical Problems] (Nizhnii Novgorod, 2007), p. 397.

[2] See V. V. Oksamytnyi, «Правовая система как объект сравнительно-правового исследования» [Legal System as Object of Comparative Law Research], in Россия в период реформ: задачи, пути, решения [Russia in the Period of Reforms: Tasks, Paths, Solutions (2006), pp. 112-119; id, Правовые системы современных государственно-организованнчх обществ: особенности в многообразии [Legal Systems of Modern State-Organized Societies: Distinctive Features in Diversity], in Россия: перспективы развития [Russia: Prospects for Development] (2007), pp. 173-182.

modern world, and it happens that several competing legal systems operate within a single State".[3] Non-State communities and the international community have, in his view, legal systems.[4]

Nonetheless, other aspects directly arising from the essence of a legal system as the objectively formed and historically conditioned aggregate of inter-connected legal phenomena and institutions not only of a specific State, but also other formations existing in the modern world, remain in the shadows or are insufficiently investigated. Therefore it is vital in principle to say the following: legal systems are singled out not only at the level of the State. An understanding of a legal system is broader and more in accord with the laws of societal development when specialists do not confine themselves to the framework of the State or to a society "unified into a State".

It is proposed to regard as State legal systems both municipal and international (inter-State) legal systems.[5] However, the incompleteness of such a classification should be noted.

State-organizational formations of very different types are elements of the public structure of societies or communities throughout practically the last five and a half millennia of their development. To be sure, most often we link the history of statehood directly with States which are counted for the last three or so millennia. Among them were oriental despotisms, empires of antiquity and the Middle Ages, bourgeois republics, and socialist and supranational States.

One should not overlook the significant number of formations similar to States and other State-organized societies in world history. They might precede the early States recognized by history, such as, for example, the Upper and Lower Nile later united into the Ancient Egyptian State. Or be city-States autonomous in administration later assembled into a unified Greece only under Alexander of Macedonia. Dozens of duchies, princedoms, and "free" cities are a typical example of such formations in the Middle Ages which became part for hundreds of years of the Holy Roman Empire of the German nation (962 to 1806). No less than half of modern

[3] R. David, Основные правовые системы современности [Principal Legal Systems of Modern Times] (1988), p. 37.

[4] Ibid., pp. 37-38.

[5] See V. V. Gavrilov, «Понятие национальных и международных правовых систем» [Concept of National and International Legal Systems], Журнал русского права [Journal of Russian Law], no. 11 (2004), pp. 76-87; I. G. Dudko, «К вопросу о «правовой системе» субъектов Российской Федерации» [On the Question of the 'Legal System' of Subjects of the Russian Federation], Государство и право [State and Law], no. 9 (2003), pp. 96-99; S. O. Serebrova, Общетеоретические основы формирования европейской правовой системы [General Theoretical Foundations of Forming a European Legal System] (Nizhnii Novgorod, 2005) (abstract diss. kand. iurid. nauk).

States were colonies, protectorates, or dominions under the administration of European countries but had a certain amount of self-government. And the last and the present centuries give us numerous examples of State formations not recognized by the international community but nonetheless having own legislative and other law-creation agencies. The beginning of the new century cannot be imagined without the active integration of States, without inter-State unions which have become dominant in the modern world order.

What unites them in the context of the present study? All these State-organizational societies (or communities) have a normative-organized system formed in the process of their functioning and based on own law and the law-realizing activities of special institutions.

If one attempts to summarize the varieties of modern State-organized formations existing in the theory of the State, in our view in practice there are:

- *States* representing special organizations of sovereign public power capable of effectuating through law the supreme direction of the population of the country throughout its entire territory;
- *municipal formations* enjoying a certain autonomy as part of a complex unitary, regionalist, or federated State;
- *dependent territories*, pre-State formations under the authority of so-called governing States but having own power structures which organize the direct administration of the population by means of normative prescriptions;
- *State-similar formations*, which are so-called unrecognized States (or quasi-States);
- *inter-State associations* as formations based on an international treaty of States which voluntarily cede a number of sovereign powers to the created supranational agencies.

In considering the multi-aspectual essence of the legal system, which is inseparable from the distinctive features of countries and societies possessing this, we set out our own treatment of the legal system as an historically conditioned and objectively formed aggregate of legal phenomena, institutions, and processes consolidated and supported by normatively stable relations in a State-organized society (or community).

One should take into account the fact that within the world community unique legal systems of individual States and other State, State-similar, or inter-State formations continue to be formed. They have their own law in which characteristics of principle are manifest, the state of its development at a particular historical stage is reflected, legal ideals and philosophical-legal structures consolidated by the beliefs of a people and its traditions, and the distinctive features of legal consciousness and legal culture peculiar to a society are fixed. Therefore, different legal systems with their base principles, legal conceptions and categories, legal constructions, system of sources of law, internal structure thereof, distinctive features of the law-creation process and the exercise of a right are inherent to various State-organized societies.

The proposed scheme of the components of a legal system, having regard to the comparative law studies undertaken in legal science, draws attention to the consistency of the emergence of its structural parts and inter-linkages between them, regarding them as universal categories:

- *law-understanding* in the aggregate of dominant legal institutions of a society and the level and distinctive features of legal thought of a people and the ruling elite;
- law-creation as a cognitive and procedurally-fixed means of the formalization (preparation, formalization, adoption, and introduction into operation) of normative rules of behavior as generally-binding;
- *legal block*, including legislation in force in a State-organized society as a system of officially established and inter-connected normative legal acts of general significance;
- *legal institutions*, created in a State-organized society for the functioning of its legal system;
- *mechanism for the effectuation of law*, in which the processes for the realization thereof have been concentrated;
- *results of operation of law*, consisting of the establishment in a State-organized society of a legal order determined by the regime of legality and legal culture of its subjects.

It is essential to point to the orientation of a legal system, a certain hierarchy of its functions. This is crowned by the fact that they may be combined into a primary orientation – the aspiration when achieving a common purpose to preserve the unity and integrity of the system itself. The watchword is integration, whose essence both in the unification of all legal systems of a State-organized society into a single whole and in the amalgamation of all structural elements thereof on the basis of general principles of law (supremacy of law, legality, equity, humanism, equality, and others). It should organize and stimulate their solidarity with legal requirements adopted and upheld in the respective formation.

The integrative function is directed towards the unification of social communities (groups, strata, peoples, ethnic groups, all of society).[6] Other

[6] See N. M. Kolosova, Интегративная функция правовой системы [Integrative Function of Legal System] (1990) (abstract diss. kand. iurid. nauk).

functions are closely connected with this leading function of the legal system. This view corresponds to modern socio-economic and political realities since there is a possibility to resolve a priority task – the achievement of political and legal consensus as an adequate understanding of the content and values of the legal prescriptions by all members of society.[7]

Accordingly, we propose the following classification of the basic orientations of the legal system:

- *functions of highest level,* deemed to ensure the existence of the system itself as an integral phenomenon and therefore representing an integrative orientation to which the basic, and especially more special, clarifying elements of the legal system should conform;
- *functions of basic level,* which determine the processes to be effectuated by the legal system as a whole. To these should be relegated: (a) *axiological function,* which is manifest in the establishment of the purpose of the legal system, among which the main ones are legal order, equity, lawful behavior, that is, that which leads to the forming, preservation, and stabilization of the existing social community; (b) *informational function,* connecting components of the system between themselves, facilitating the creation of their symmetrical order, bringing order to the conscious activity of subjects, and thereby orientating the legal system to achieve the necessary result; (c) *regulatory function,* reflected in the forming of a normative foundation establishing the positive rules of behavior, respective models of activity, and the incorporation thereof in the legal culture of the person and human communities; (d) *protective function,* the assignment of which is to defend generally-significant socially important political, economic, cultural, ethno-national, and other values and, accordingly squeeze out phenomena deemed to be socially dangerous, harmful, and wrongful;
- *functions of ensuring the level* presented by the orientations which are directly linked with the constituent elements of the structure of the legal system and are specifically determined: orientation of legal understanding in a State-organized society depending

[7] This is the prevailing, but not the sole, view. Reutov believes that at the level of an all-social, global approach (the most general function of a legal system may be called the submission of the organizing principle into social relations". See V. P. Reutov, Структурирование правовой системы как выражение ее функциональных возможностей [Structuring a Legal System as an Expression of Its Functional Possibilities] (Nizhnii Novgorod, 2004), p. 25 (abstract diss. doctor iurid. nauk). However, he contradicts himself further on when he clarifies that this function rather belongs to society as a whole as a system and determines its structure, including the existence of a sub-system of normative regulations and the varieties thereof: moral, legal, religious, and others.

upon the historical, religious, ideological and other factors of legal development; by means of forming sources of law meeting the specific nature of individual types thereof, peculiarities of the development of various societies and civilizations, forms of Statehood; consolidation of basic institutes and branches of legislation in which are traditionally included the entire system of laws and subordinate normative acts based on them regulating relations which have significance on the scale of a State-organized society as a whole; status and activity of legal institutions, that is, organizations having powers with regard to the adoption of legal acts or application of law; the practice of the exercise of a right connected with the realization of legal acts, interpretation thereof, overcoming gaps in law and resolution of legal conflicts; consolidation of the results of the exercise of a right that is determined by the qualitative legal status of a person and levels of his legal consciousness and legal behavior.

LEGAL SYSTEMS OF MODERN STATES

There are more than 200 States in the world, the "oldest" of which is more than one thousand years (Japan with a monarchical form of rule which has existed 2,680 years), and the youngest, about four years (Montenegro). The possession by each of the States of own law leads to the formalization of an own national legal system reflecting its socio-economic, political, and cultural distinctiveness. The qualitative characteristics of the last are the conditions of association in legal families or groups of legal systems. Both the distinctive features peculiar to various State forms and characteristic for a country with a determined type of law are noticeable in the content of national legal systems.

A national legal system has its own specific feature, structure, and purposes, is formed, develops and functions in a determined segment of time, in a specific geographical region with certain ethnographic peculiarities of the population, and is created in societies with different traditions, professions of faith, and means of forming a system of sources of law.[8]

[8] Iu. A. Tikhomirov, Курс сравнительного правоведения [Cours of Comparative Law] (1996), R. David and C. Jauffret-Spinosi, Основные правовые системы современности [Principal Legal Systems of Modern Times] (2001), H. Koch, U. Magnus, and P. Winkler von Mohrenfels, Международное частное право и сравнительное правоведение [Private International Law and Comparative Law] (2001); M. N. Marchenko, Курс сравнительного правоведения [Cours of Comparative Law] (2002); A. Kh. Saidov, *Comparative Law*, transl. W. E. Butler (2003); A. E. Chernokov, Введение в сравнительное правоведение [Introduction

A differentiated approach to the legal systems of various States formed in legal doctrine throughout the twentieth and twenty-first centuries by taking into account that the so-called legal map may not be one-dimensional; it reflects numerous multi-functional processes. And therefore the classification of legal systems of States becomes one of the major problems for both the theory of law and for comparative law.

More productive are the gradations based on combining legal systems of States into certain classification groups – legal families. They are separated on the basis of taking into account many factors, among which the following deserve attention:

- community of historical fate (for example, the family of Scandinavian law, family of Latin American law);
- voluntary re-creation in a country of the basic schemes for the structuring and functioning of other legal systems (adjacent States autonomously choose structures acceptable for them of systems of legislation, law-application, and so on);
- former colonial dependence, as a result of which the metropolitan countries impose their legal ideology and legal institutions (for example, the former colonies of France received the basic institutes of legislative law, and the former components of the British Empire – the ideas of judicial law);
- ideological dependence connected with the establishment in a country of regimes of a certain orientation (for example, the creation of socialist law and its expansion in postwar Eastern Europe);
- religious identity determining the adherence of a region or individual countries to certain dogmas and canons (an example might be the dissemination of Islam and Muslim law).

Legal families may be stable (and exist for centuries in such capacity) or provisional, dependent, in particular, on the form of a determined State-political regime in certain countries. In any event, the existence of legal families is the basis for their classification. There may be regarded as criteria for their identification:

- community of legal ideology, in accordance with which general principles of law are structure in the family of the associated States;
- proximity of legal methodology as the aggregate of means and methods of embodying law in life, including, for example, similar sources of law, the structure thereof, legal technique, legal language and terminology, and so on;
- similarity of systems of legal education and training of jurists;

to Comparative Law] (Spb., 2007).

- identical structure of legal professions and spheres of activity of legal practitioners;
- common legal traditions and legal culture, and so on.

In Soviet jurisprudence there dominated for long years the so-called intra-type classification, which meant the division of legal systems and families into socialist, bourgeois, and those "vacillating" between the antipodes of the types of law.[9] It might only answer the question: the will of what social group is reflected by law but not explain why within, for example, the framework of the bourgeois type the existence is possible of groups of legal systems of Common and continental law, what determines the differences between North American and Latin American law, between Germanic and Romano legal families, between Hindu and Japanese law. And that is why the comparativist conception of René David, who introduced socialist law among the recognized legal families, was needed somewhat later.

The influence of the "triad" approach which dominated the 1970-80s to the present is not so obvious since in modern post-Soviet comparative law, which has avoided the generally obligatory ideological postulates of the recent past, a number of works have emerged based on the legacy of sources of the Russian/Ukrainian and foreign comparativistic heritage. An analysis thereof makes it possible to come to a view on the diverse grounds for distinguishing national legal systems. In our view, the most acceptable are the quantitative and qualitative-element criteria.

Under the first approach we refer to the number of legal systems in specific States, their mutual links and mutual relations. Thus, quantitative characteristics determine the proposed division of national legal systems into:

- *uni-level legal systems of unitary States*, understanding by these the aggregate of law, legal culture, and legal practice of a centralized State taken individually. In such a State-organized society the entire territory is divided into administrative units (regions, counties, woewody, departments) whose State-law status is determined entirely and regulated by the legal system of the particular State (the legal systems of the countries of the Baltic, Poland, or Belarus are such, for example);
- *two-level legal systems of complex unitary States*, which arise and are formalized in countries allowing the creation and functioning of

[9] Марксистско-ленинская общая теория государства и права: Исторические типы государства и права [Marxist-Leninist General Theory of State and Law: Historical Types of State and Law] (1971), Chapter 1; A. A. Tille, Социалистичкское сравнительное правоведение [Socialist Comparative Law] (1975), p. 178.

individual self-governing territorial or nationality-territorial units enjoying a certain autonomy within the framework of a centralized State. They take into account especially the legal distinctive features of one or several autonomous formations (Denmark with the autonomous Faroe Islands and Greenland; Ukraine with the Autonomous Republic of Crimea) in the absence of a similar autonomy for all remaining parts of the state;

- *two-level legal systems of regionalist States (semi-federations),* which are regarded as transitional, subsequently being transformed into federated States. As examples there may be mentioned: United Kingdom, who has granted great legal autonomy to Wales, Scotland, and Northern Ireland; South African Republic, defined by its constitution as a unitary State with elements of federalism in which the nine provinces comprising it have been endowed with autonomous powers, including legislative; Spain, which is called a State of autonomous communities where the status of being autonomous is acquired not only by historical regions inhabited by national minorities (Basques, Catalonia, Galicia), but also each municipality and province;
- *two-level legal systems of federated States* having a federal legal system which determines "kompetenz-kompetenz" – by the law of the federation through constitutional innovations to establish and regulate its powers and the supremacy of federal law, and also regional legal systems. The last may be such subjects of the federation as states (Mexico), territories (Federal Democratic Republic of Ethiopia), provinces (Argentina), lände (Germany), or cantons (Switzerland);
- *tri-level legal systems of federated States,* the sole unique example being the Russian Federation, where besides the federal and regional (as of 1 February 2011, 83 subjects of the Federation) legal systems there function dual systems of a number of territories (Altai, Krasnoiarsk) and regions (Tiumen, Archangel) in which there are autonomous national areas (Khanty-Mansiisk, Iamalo-Nenets, and others);
- *parallel (dualist) legal systems of States* represented by a significant number of countries located in various parts of the globe. In these States by virtue of historical, ideological, regional, and other factors there exist, besides the officially formed and functioning legal systems, and exert a significant impact on national law systems built on religious views, customs, traditions, and the way of life of the people. Such systems (Near East, Tropical Africa, Pacific Ocean

basin, and a number of other regions) supplement national law, regulating primarily the private-law status of the native population;
- *competing legal systems of States* in which historically formed customary or religious binding rules of behavior are in contradiction with the requirements of the State legal system. An example is the secular States of the so-called East, where religious dogmas operating for hundreds of years often obstruct the effectuation of official consolidated legal prescriptions (India, Turkey).

When choosing a particular classification, the widely-shared qualitative characteristics of legal systems of States are taken into account in the event of their being combined into legal families. Such qualities singled out are rather numerous, but any approaches to the choice of criteria for singling out systematizing indicia are subjective. Without claiming the "ultimate truth", we acknowledge for comparatists the right to choose particular criteria when singling out the types of legal systems. However, as specialists in legal systems themselves recognize, in real life there is no perfected legal or other classification or any other classification, which inevitably makes any of the legal families relative. And therefore one must concur with Marchenko, who advanced a number of requirements relating to the indicators of impact on the forming of common indicia for legal families, and also criteria for their classification.[10]

They should, in particular, meet the following conditions: (a) have as their foundation permanent, fundamental, and not provisional and incidental, factors; (b) whenever possible, there should be more definite indicia-criteria; (c) have a stable objective character; (d) in instances when not one, but several, indicia-criteria underlie the classification of legal systems, one should be fundamental, dominating; (e) when investigating common features of legal systems-criteria, their classification should take into account not only objective, but also subjective, factors exerting a direct impact on the process of their formation.

According to the trends forming in the theory of law and comparative law, the consideration of the basic legal systems of States is increasingly necessary through the prism of stable groups thereof on the basis of the civilizational approach to State-law typologies. The civilization theory enables uniqueness to be shown, the non-repeatability of a certain society, thanks to the consolidation therein of a definite culture because civilization is a determined type of human community and each, according to Toynbee, "is a culture which has achieved the limits of self-identification".[11]

10 M. N. Marchenko, Сравнительное правоведение [Comparative Law] (2001), p. 254.
11 A. J. Toynbee, Постижение истории. Избранное [A Study of History] (2001), p. 14.

The scale of criteria for the classification of civilizations is for Toynbee flexible; however, two criteria remain stable: the existence of a "universal" church and the form of its organization, and the "degree of remoteness from that place where a particular society initially arose".[12] He believed that a particular type of States corresponds to a particular type of civilization.

The followers of this approach among jurists assume the existence of types of legal systems corresponding to a particular modern civilization and make the State-legal identification thereof. More consistent, in our view, are Zweigert and Kötz, who introduced the concept of "legal style" as the distinguishing peculiarity of a certain legal family.[13] On this basis they single out western law (Romano-Germanic, Scandinavian legal family and the Common Law), and the remaining legal families (socialist law, countries of the Far East, Islamic law, Hindu law) are defined as "non-western law".

These legal families dominate in comparative jurisprudence at present, being the base for clarifying and making specific the classifications, in particular with regard to types of sources of law, models of legislative procedure, and other law-creation peculiarities, elements of general and legal culture, legal traditions, infrastructure of law, and the structure of procedural law.

Osakwe is pursuing this direction, considering as the principal types of law western law (Romano-Germanic, Anglo-American, and Scandinavian), quasi-western law (socialist and systems transitional to the Romano-Germanic), and nonwestern law (religious legal systems, southeastern and African customary law).[14] Within the religious group Osakwe singled out Muslim (Islamic) law, Jewish, canon (Catholic Church), and Hindu law. He notes other approaches, including when within this group Zweigert and Kötz separate Muslim (Islamic) and Hindu law; David – Muslim (Islamic), Jewish, and Hindu law; and Iu. A. Tikhomirov – Islamic (Muslim) and Hindu law. In our view it would be logical to relegate to the religious group Confucian (Far Eastern) law, excluding canon law from this ranking, as long since having "dissolved" into the secular law of Europe and Latin America. Also justified would be the inclusion within the sphere of customary law, the legal systems of the Pacific Ocean basin.

A number of modern specialists in their search for own classification interpretations have turned to a different conceptual category, singling

12 Ibid., pp. 82-85.

13 K. Zweigert and H. Kötz, Введение в сравнительное правоведение в сфере частного права [Introduction to Comparative Law in the Sphere of Private Law (2000), I, pp. 106-117.

14 C. Osakwe, Сравнительное правоведение в схемах: Общая и особенная части [Comparative Law in Diagrams: General and Special Parts] (2002), pp. 56-60.

out the "type of legal system". Luts contributes the "aggregate of the most material legal indicia inherent in a group of legal systems which are within the boundaries of a determined space and time".[15] The principal typologization criteria are the distinctive features of the institutional, functional, and normative parts determining the essential indicia of a specific type and level of normativity of the mechanism of legal impact. Additional criteria are the character of norms of law; conformity of means and forms of objectivization of norms of law; mechanism for ensuring the realization of norms of law.

On the basis of these characteristics the following types of modern legal systems are modeled: (a) Romano-Germanic (continental law); (2) Anglo-American (Common Law); (3) mixed (with sub-types – dualist, Scandinavian, Latin American; religious-community: Muslim, Hindu; traditional-philosophical: Japanese, Chinese; customary-community); (4) inter-State.[16]

In this classification, based also on a civilization approach, there may be traced: first, a clear "discrimination" against socialist law whose impact was adhered to by almost a quarter of the population of the world; second, Northern Europe and Latin America actually turn out to be in the sphere of influence of the Asian-African legal group; third, the typology of the legal systems of States includes the legal systems of inter-State unions. And, finally, the post-Soviet States, including those so different in degree and direction of legal development, such as Ukraine, Kirgizia, Armenia, or Turkmenia, without having regard to the processes continuing therein, are brought within the "scope" of the Romano-Germanic type of legal systems. It is appropriate in this connection to refer to the compatriots of the author of this classification, who with reason characterize their own country as a "European State, but one which constantly is in a state of worldview reflexes".[17] The processes of legal adaptation in the former Soviet republics are far from completed that would give grounds for a formal association thereof with an individual group of legal systems.

Can one find an alternative to the seeming contradictory example of grouping legal systems of States? Logically formalizing the trend in the theory of law and comparative law with respect to the classification of legal

[15] L. A. Luts, Типологізація сучасних правових систем світу [Typologization of Contemporary Legal Systems of the World] (Kiev, 2007), p. 12.

[16] Ibid.

[17] E. O. Kharitonov and O. I. Kharitonova, Деякі питання класифікації європейських систем приватного права [Some Questions of the Classification of European Systems of Private Law] (Kiev, 2007), pp. 24-25.

systems of States, we suggest to single out the following stable associations of legal families which have formed in the modern world:

- *western law* (European and Anglo-American groups of legal families), the criteria for which may be: continental legal tradition embodied in the ideas of natural law doctrines and an individualistic approach; concepts of equity, equality and freedom of expression of will; autonomy of the person in society; noninterference of the State in the affairs of the person;
- *eastern law* (religious and traditional legal families and systems), based on an interpersonal approach, priority concepts of debt and duty, dependence of the person in society, subordination of man to the State, on "sacral" doctrines requiring self-sacrifice of the individual to social and State interests;
- *ideological law* (socialist and post-socialist legal systems), which arose artificially by revolutionary means between the basic types of law in the world based on the primacy and principles of the communist idea to which the legal development of the country is subordinate.

Within the framework of these associations, groups are distinguished of legal families and individual sub-groups – original legal systems of States having for various reasons a mixed nature (for example, in the United Kingdom, the country of classical Common Law, an integral part thereof – Scotland – adheres to the principles and institutes of continental law. In the legal system of Israel one may find elements of Jewish, Muslim, English, and Roman law. And the legal system of socialist China takes into account the distinctive features of the Confucian thought of the population).

[1]. **Western law.** Within the framework of such a complex concept as western law, the continental (European) law is regarded as the aggregate of legal families and individual legal systems formed on the basis of and with the active use of the Roman legal heritage and associated community of principles of building law, the structures thereof, sources, and conceptual legal apparatus.

The term "continental law" is a qualified one; it points to the roots, origin, and initial "natural habitat" of formation and development. By virtue of the historical traditions of comparative law and the positions taken from the nineteenth century by French and German comparatists, it continues to be called a "Romano-Germanic" type of law, giving due to the joint efforts which were exerted by the universities of the Latin countries and States of Central Europe in the cause of developing a common European legal science. But in addition to the Romano (southern European) and Germanic (central European) legal families, the Scandinavian (northern European) legal family is part of continental law, as is the Latin American legal family beyond the limits of Europe. In English speaking countries this group is called the "civil law countries", pointing to the Roman past of European law. Now European law often is associated with the legal system of the European Union,[18] which is formally and actually incorrect since the European Union is an inter-State union combining a large part, but far from all, of Europe (27 States of 50) and cannot itself substitute for European institutes.

Thereafter European law stepped across the boundaries of the continent and thanks to many factors (including missionary support of the Catholic Church, military conquests, colonization, and the voluntary acceptance of ideas, constructions, and institutes) was transformed into the most widespread and influential group of legal families of those existing in the world.

Summarizing the characteristics of continental law, the principal features are:

- common historical foundations which it is accepted to regard as the European or western tradition of law[19] that was made up of the Roman legal legacy and the reception thereof (doctrinal and actual) in Europe, the canon law of Catholicism, the philosophy of natural law and historical jurisprudence, and the pluralism of jurisdictions and legal systems;
- similarity of basic legal concepts and the community of a European legal language as a whole. A single legal dogma, that is, conceptual-category apparatus, gradually formed under the influence of the mastery of the Roman legal legacy in medieval European universities, the work of doctrinal legal scholars and legal practice of countries which determined the legal policy of individual legal families (so-called identifier-States);
- general principles of vocational education for jurists and the methods of study, assuming two stages of training for the legal profession – general and specialized;
- recognition of law as statutory (written),being the result of law-creation in the name of the State, the legislator (in the broad meaning) being the actual creator of law;
- dualism of law manifest in the combining therein of public law protecting the general State interest and private law, ensuring

[18] B. N. Topornin, Европейское право [European Law] (2002); L. M. Entin (ed.), Европейское право [European Law] (2007); S. Iu. Kashkin (ed.), Право Европейского Союза [Law of the European Union] (2006).

[19] H. J. Berman, Западная традиция права: эпоха формирования [Western Tradition of Law: Era of Formation] (2000), pp. 20-27.

the interests of a civil society in the person of individuals and associations thereof;

- dominance of material law over procedural, playing an "ensuring" role in legal regulation;
- coinciding attitude towards the hierarchy of sources of law, where binding normative documents headed by a law and international treaties play the principal role;
- the growing binding role of principles and norms of contemporary international law in the municipal legal system, the commencement of which was laid by the 1949 Basic Law of the Federal Republic of Germany and the integrating (uniting) processes in Europe (Council of Europe, European Union);
- the special role of legal doctrine (jurisprudence), with the assistance of which the basic principles are being worked out of building a legal system, a law-creation process is being constructed, and the interpretation of law is being effectuated;
- attitude towards the judicial process as a non-obligatory source of law since, as Bergel stressed, judicial decisions "are not rules having binding legal force for anyone except the parties to the proceeding".[20] However, in continental legal systems "the uniformity of judicial practice is actually encouraged, which is basically formed in the process of activity of the highest judicial instances";[21]
- the existence of a system of judicial control over the constitutionality of legal norms manifest in the creation and functioning of a special constitutional court whose decisions are binding on subjects of law;
- similar trends in the processes of the codification of law requiring the presence of codes in the principal branches of law;
- a uniform scheme for structuring the system of law, where the base branch is constitutional law and the profile branches are civil, criminal, and administrative law, and the respective procedural branches.

The second group of legal families of western law – Anglo-American law – unites an adherence to the English doctrine of judicial precedent, which may be summarized by the following: "once formulated a judicial decision is binding both on the court which issued it and all inferior courts in analogous situations".

20 J.-L. Bergel, Общая теория права [General Theory of Law] (2000), p. 136.
21 Chernokov, note 8 above, pp. 43-44.

There may be relegated to case law countries at present: the European countries of the Common Law (England, Wales, Northern Ireland, Republic of Ireland, Malta, Cyprus, and the territory of Gibraltar); former dominions of the British Empire, so-called quasi-monarchies (Canada, Australia, New Zealand, and about fifteen other States) where many British constitutional traditions, judicial precedents, and legislative acts (commencing from the Magna Carta of 1215) are considered to be in force on their territories; the former colonies of the United Kingdom in which judicial precedent is recognized as a source of law and judges are granted significant powers, including of a law-creation nature; the United States of America, whose legal system is regarded as an autonomous branch having specific features when applying the principle of judicial precedent.

Being a consequence of the distinctive origin directly of the English Common Law, the Anglo-American group of legal families differs from the continental system as determined by the following characteristics:

- historical distinctiveness in the formation of law which emerged especially in the rejection of the reception of Roman Law despite England being part of the Roman Empire for four centuries;
- a uniform approach to legal understanding based in the principle of the "rule of law", according to which all are equal before the law since lex is not the sole (or primary) source of legal norms.[22] And the last are regarded not so much as general abstract rules as means of authorization of a right;
- own legal terminology, many positions of which differ materially from the European (continental) legal language;
- separation of law into statute (or legislative) and precedential (or judicial); the last is regarded as law consisting of norms and principles created and applied by judges in the process of adopting judicial decisions, and also as methods which judges use when creating a precedent and as a special legal judicial culture;
- distinctiveness of the system of sources of law, where judicial precedent occupies the leading position;
- recognition of the "persuasiveness" of foreign judicial precedents if such have been created in Common Law countries (especially in Australia, New Zealand, and Canada);
- priority of procedural law over material, reflected in the fact that these legal systems have a primarily procedural and pragmatic nature more than legislative-systematic;

[22] A. K. Romanov, Правовая система Англии [Legal System of England], intro. W. E. Butler (2004), pp. 79, 85-89.

- distinctive features of the system of legal education providing for the specialization of students from the first year of study and legal professions in the Anglo-American law countries.

In fixing the distinctive features of two groups of legal families of western law we direct attention to the modern processes of their approximation, underlying which is the similarity of the foundation of functioning groups. The common economic (market economy), socio-political (uni-type social and political system), ideological (liberal and neo-liberal ideas and conceptions), culturological (including law-cultural uni-typeness) foundations of the law are determined by western civilization. This not only formed fundamentally similar State and legal systems, but also exerted great influence on other civilizations existing in parallel and the types of law and State that arose within their framework.[23]

In the English-speaking countries the role of lex and general norms of codification have been enhanced, in continental Europe the trend towards forming more abstract norms has brought to life a counter trend that follows the logic of legal systems: intensification of the role of judicial agencies in the process of legal regulation and the development of their individual law-creative activity. The drafting in the course of European integration (especially by the European Court of Justice) of provisions and constructions which unite previously incompatible, qualitatively different provisions of continental and Common Law is a noteworthy fact. This is conditioned by the fact that under modern circumstances the common cultural foundation, processes of integration, and following of European principles of law acquire principled significance for legal systems relegated to the category of, or close to, western civilization.

[2]. **Eastern law.** The term "dualism" also is acceptable when describing the legal systems of eastern law; however, it is understood as duality in the normative-legal impact on social relations and behavior of people in these States. They also are called religious—traditional legal systems. To this category are relegated countries with a Muslim, Judaic, Hindu, and Confucian law, and countries of Tropical Africa, Southeast Asia, and the Pacific Basin, where tribal and community customs and traditions are strong.

In such States together with the law officially in force (often the external forms of western law received – conceptual apparatus, legal institutions and institutes, system of sources of law, allocation of legal functions according to the principle of separation of powers, external legislative attributes, and procedural rituals) extensively and frequently use in priority own socio-

[23] See Marchenko, translated elsewhere herein.

normative regulators incorporating religious, community-traditional, and customary rules of behavior determine the way of life of the majority of the population.

In addition to the legal family of Muslim law, the legal systems of the countries of the so-called East (understood as broader than its geographical significance) do not form unified groups which, however, does not prevent the presence of common features in dualist legal systems:

- the presence of so-called sacral (righteous) doctrines or beliefs indicating the traditional priority of duties of a believer and subject (or citizen) with the secondary significance of social prerogatives recognized for them;
- syncretism (from the Greek, *synkretismos* – combination) of law, religion, and morality in the normative system of society exerted a principled influence on the behavior of its members;
- an understanding of lex to a great degree as a prohibition and instrument of punishment, and to a lesser degree as a means of positive regulation of social relations;
- separation of the sphere of the rights of believers and of non-believers with the domination of the rights of the former. Thus, the "Islamic position with respect to human rights is linked with the conviction that by virtue of the division of subjects into non-Muslim and Muslim, securing the rights of the last is the task solely of the Islamic community";[24]
- separation of the rights of the native population of one profession of faith between castes of the dominant and subordinate on the principles of a hierarchical caste system. Thus in Hinduism and in Confucianism people are divided into castes from birth, each of which has its own system of rights and duties;
- subsidiary character of positive (established and ensured by State power) law which, in turn, is affected by those conceptions of State and law which formed in the said regions.

The conception of the theocratic State and society is widespread in Muslim countries.[25] In India and the countries of Southeast Asia the role of Brahmin views on State and society is considerable. The Tao-centrist idea of State-law structure dominates in China, Japan, and other countries of

[24] Kh. Bekhruz, Исламская традиция права [Islamic Tradition of Law] (Odessa, 2006), pp. 212-213.

[25] See L. W. C. Van den Berg (1845-1927), Основные начала мусульманского права согласно учению имамов Абу Ханифы и Шафии [Basic Principles of Muslim Law according the Doctrines of Imams Aboe Hanifa and Sjafe'i], transl. from the Dutch (2006), pp. 182-190.

the Far East. On this occasion one may cite the view of Harold J. Berman (1918-2007). Concerning the reception of western law in Japan and China at the end of the nineteenth and early twentieth centuries, the American legal historian asserted that this law regulated certain relations in official and higher circles, but practically had no impact on the traditional legal structure of peoples as a whole.[26] It should be noted that past and modern State-law modifications in these and other countries are far from leading to a rejection of millennial traditions. The structures and institutes of western law introduced in the East for the most part remain simply a façade behind which the regulation of social relations occurs according to traditional models.

If one endeavors to typologize the approaches of States, for example, to Muslim law, one may state that there exist three contemporary models of their reflection in national legal systems of the East:

- the model of secularization, characteristic for countries which by constitutional means have separated religion from State life (Turkey, CIS countries with a Muslim population). The proclaimed secular character of the State requires all citizen to comply with official rules of behavior; however, believers may follow norms of Islam and the Shariat in their personal life if their behavior in so doing is not contrary to secular laws;
- model of harmony, in accordance with which countries proclaim Islam to be the State religion and the Shariat is admitted to the legal system as one of the sources of law (Egypt, Syria, Tunisia);
- model of Koranization, under which the State proclaims norms of the Shariat to be official legislation and extends the operation thereof to everyone on the territory of the country (Saudi Arabia, Iran).

Such models arise especially in countries with traditional (or customary) legal systems.

[3]. **Ideological law**. Ideological law invaded during the twentieth century the space between the two historically-formed types of legal systems in the legal world, denying the succession and interconnection with preceding and other legal systems. Initially created by revolutionary means in one country within the framework of the Soviet legal system, it contrasted sharply with the western and eastern traditions of law.

Formed after the Second World War on the basis of communist ideology in various regions, the States came to be relegated to a special group – socialist legal family. Although their number today is limited

26 Berman, note 19 above, p. 58.

to only several countries (China, Korean People's Democratic Republic, Socialist Republic of Vietnam, Laotian People's Democratic Public, and Cuba), more than a quarter of the world population lives in this family, which preserves the actuality of analyzing the distinctive features of this phenomenon of legal history. Socialist legal systems are characterized by the following features:

- denial of the succession with law of the preceding eras, previous State-law regimes, national distinctiveness, and historically-formed traditions of peoples;
- proclamation of socialist law to be the highest historical type of law, juridically consolidating new State-law values;
- class nature of law based on the principle of the "dictatorship of the proletariat" and the "will of workers and peasants" embodied in lex;
- domination in the system of actual sources of law decisions of organs of the ruling Party of various levels not fixed as normative acts (congresses, plenums, ruling Party elite);
- predominance in the system of socialist law of public-law institutes and, accordingly, neglect of the private-law interests of citizens;
- simplification of procedural forms and limitation of the rights of the accused and persons on trial to defense, and others.

On the territory of the former Soviet Union States were created after its dissolution in which new own national priorities were affirmed. Their legal systems may be conditionally combined under the concept of "post-ideological law" and relegated to the "post-Soviet legal family" formed on the basis of a comparatively homogeneous legal space of the Commonwealth of Independent States. This group by virtue of its recent past and not entirely consistent break with it is in a transitional state between the principal associations of legal families with the gradually strengthening trend of approximation with continental law.

The legal system existing in the republics of the Soviet Union for more than seven decades of the last century reflected basic legal ideas, institutes, and processes of the so-called identifier-countries of the socialist legal family, that is, the USSR – States in the development of which the very essential indicia of States being combined on the basis of an ideological principle was embodied. A number of post-Soviet States, especially Ukraine, are more precisely associated with a certain group of legal systems, that is, with continental (European) law.[27] This process is proceeding otherwise in other former parts of the Soviet Union.

[27] L. A. Luts, Европейські міждержавні правові системи та проблеми інтеграції з ними

The contemporary state of Russia is become the subject-matter of integrated and special studies which combine into one statement of fact: the legal system today is so distinct from socialist law that one cannot speak about its return to the former family. But the problem of legal identification remains.

During the 1990s and early twenty-first century several variants of the choice confronting the legal system of Russia were intensively discussed – either accede to one of the existing families of western law (that is, return to historical roots), or transform yourself into a new generic (Eurasian) legal family together with certain other former republics of the Soviet Union, or proclaim a new so-called Slavic legal family.[28]

Comparatists now are inclined to the view that the process of approximation or integration of the Russian legal system with European law is noteworthy. Saidov asserts that the "kinship of Russian law with Romano-Germanic law gives rise to no doubt".[29] Chernokov, clearly ahead of reality, convincingly declares, for example, that "this, finally, is recognized by practice and science, that is, the return to the Romano-Germanic model has occurred".[30]

More cautious in his assessment of the real state of the Russian legal system is the American comparatist, Osakwe, who declared: "The measurable trend of development of contemporary Russian law gives every reason to suppose that it is moving in the direction of accession to the Germanic sub-group in the family of Romano-Germanic law",[31] having shown itself to be a "worthy candidate for membership in this family".[32]

правовоі системи Украіни (теоретичні проблеми) [European Inter-State Legal Systems and Problems of Integrating the Legal System of Ukraine with Them (Theoretical Problems)] (Kiev, 2003); L. O. Korchevna, Проблема різноджерельного права: Дослід порівняльного правознавства [Problem of Different Sources of Law: Study in Comparative Law] (Kiev, 2004); N. M. Onishchenko, Правова система проблеми теорії [Legal System: Problems of Theory] (Kiev, 2002); O. F. Skakun, Правова система України на правовій карті світу [Legal System of Ukraine on Legal Map of the World] (Kharkov, 2004).

28 See on this problem: V. N. Siniukov, Российская правовая система: Введение в общую теорию [Russian Legal System: Introduction to General Theory] (Saratov, 1994); Iu. A. Tikhomirov, Курс сравнительного правоведения [Cours of Comparative Law] (1996); M. N. Marchenko, «Является ли правовая система России составной частью Романо-германской семьи» [Is the Legal System of Russia Part of the Romano-Germanic Family?], Правовая политика и правовая жизнь [Legal Policy and Legal Life], no. 1 (2001); C. Osakwe, «Типология современного российского права на фоне правовой карты мира» [Typology of Contemporary Russian Law Against the Background of the Legal Map of the World], Государство и право [State and Law], no. 4 (2001).

29 Saidov, note 8 above, p. 337.

30 Chernokov, note 8 above, p. 109.

31 Osakwe, note 14 above, p. 28.

32 Ibid., p. 42.

However, we are impressed more by the processes occurring under which the following is indicated: "there is no need, it seems, to run ahead of events and artificially twist Russian ("national") law under the Romano-Germanic ("inter-nationality", European) or any other law".[33] Indeed, in any sphere of the life of society, including legal, artificially forcing processes and events already noted as in process is hardly justified.[34]

LEGAL SYSTEMS OF OTHER MODERN STATE-ORGANIZED SOCIETIES (OR COMMUNITIES)

Legal systems of municipal formations. Municipal formations or regions are a reality of the administrative-territorial structure of modern countries. There are more than 300 regional structures in the world with the rights of self-governing entities as part of unitary or federal States.

All these formations share in some degree the conducting of legal policy within their region autonomously which is agreed with the central authorities and have own legislative, executive, and judicial agencies adopting and/or realizing legal acts on the territory of the formation. They include certain constructive elements of a regional legal family, such as:

- the aggregate of legal values reflecting the cultural-historical, religious, national, domestic, and other distinctive features of this region;
- law-creation as a normatively-regulated process of creation, change or repeal of legal acts of this formation;
- effectuation of own legal regulation up to the adoption of laws of the State on matters relegated to the subject-matter of joint jurisdiction of the center and the regions (so-called forestalling law-creation);
- creation and functioning of a mechanism for overcoming contradictions between central and regional legislation;
- hierarchy of organized legal corpus of territorially-operating acts of regional significance;
- real process of law-application on the territory of the particular region.

[33] Marchenko, Правовые системы современного мира [Legal Systems of the Modern World] (2001), pp. 232-234.

[34] See, in this connection, Правовая система Российской Федерации в условиях глобализации [Legal System of the Russian Federation Under Conditions of Globalization (2004). 2 vols.; R. A. Romashov, «Законодательная дефинпция: в условиях интеграции правовых систем: проблемы унификации» [Legislative Definition under Conditions of Integration of Legal Systems: Problems of Unification], in Baranov, et al., note 1 above, pp. 112-117.

It is possible to fix directly in municipal formations, depending upon their contemporary varieties:

- *legal systems of self-governing territorial entities* within a centralized unitary State which is an autonomy regulated by the constitution of the country and general laws of the State. Examples are: Faroe Islands within Denmark, which are an enlarged internal autonomous formation; the archipelagoes of the Azores and Madeira as autonomous regions of Portugal having political and administrative status and own governmental organs; Gagausia (Gagauz Yeri) in Moldova, whose status is determined by a republic law as a "territorial autonomous formation with special status as a form of self-government of the Gaguzes"; the Autonomous Republic of Crimea within Ukraine, having its own parliament and government; however, the sphere of its powers is limited and is basically regulated by Kiev; and others;
- *legal systems of autonomous formations of regionalist States*, which are considered to be unitary States with elements of a federal, transitional, or semi-federated. Among them, in particular, the United Kingdom, a country which was formed 300 years ago in 1707, when England, Scotland, and Wales, and later Northern Ireland, combined. Significant changes are now being observed in the relations between the components of a once centralized State, which has delegated a series of powers, among them legislative and others of a law-creation character. These changes are called devolution,[35] which in essence is a process of the federalization of the country. Another example is the Chinese People's Republic. On one hand, it is composed of territorial entities administered entirely from Beijing – 23 provinces and four cities of central subordination. On the other, China extensively used the administrative form of autonomy: compactly living national minorities may create various types of autonomous formations, which has led to the forming of five autonomous districts, thirty autonomous regions, 124 autonomous uezds, and more than a thousand autonomous volosts.[36] In addition there are the special administrative areas of Hong Kong and Macao, which have a high degree of autonomy and the plenitude of legislative, executive, and judicial power;

[35] A. Brenton, «Британия и Россия – сходство в разнообразии» [Britain and Russia – Similarity in Diversity", Известия [News], 21 June 2007.

[36] «Китай. Китайская Народная Республика» [China. Chinese People's Republic], in A. Ia. Sukharev (ed.), Правовые системы стран мира: Энциклопедический справочник [Legal Systems of the World: Encyclopedic Manual] (2003), p. 374.

- *legal systems of subjects of federations as form of territorial structure,* represented by individual State formations which as a whole comprise a single union State. Among the characteristic features of legal systems of intra-federal regions we single out the endowing of subjects of federations with constitutive power, that is, they possess the right to own law-creation, the adoption of own constitution (or charter, statute) as the basic law of the region and, naturally, the right to have their own legislative, executive, and judicial agencies;[37]
- *inter-subject legal systems,* which have been actually formed in the modern Russian Federation. In addition to federal and regional legal systems dual systems in Russia function in the Krasnoiarsk Territory and a number of regions (Irkutsk, Tiumen, Archangel) in which there are national autonomous areas. The intertwining of legal powers and their co-subordination and interlinkage in such formations and between them creates many difficulties for the new Russian statehood, as a result of which there is a trend towards merger processes, among them relations in inter-regional legal systems. Examples are the emergence of Perm Territory on the base of the Perm Region and Komi-Permiats Autonomous National Area, Kamchatka Territory, which combined into a single whole the Kamchatka Region and Koriak Autonomous National Area, and the Transbaikal Territory, which combined the Chita Region and Agin-Buriat Autonomous National Area.

Legal systems of dependent territories (or territories with transitional legal regime). Since the United Nations was founded in 1945, more than sixty territorial formations whose peoples were previously under colonial rule have become sovereign States and received membership in the United Nations.[38] In addition, many other territories achieved self-determination thanks to

[37] See V. V. Oksamytnyi, «Правотворческие полномочия субъектов зарубежных федераций» [Law Creation Powers of Subjects of Foreign Federations], in Проблемы правотворческва субъектов Российской Федерации [Problems of Law-Creation of Subjects of the Russian Federation] (1998), pp. 144-152; I. R. Metshin, Правовая система республики в составе Российской Федерации (на примере Республики Татарстан) [Legal System of Republic Within the Russian Federation (Example of the Republic Tatarstan)] (1999), pp. 6-7, 12 (abstract diss. kand. iurid. nauk); M. A. Buganova, Правоохнанительная система субъекта Российской Федерации [Law-Protection System of Subject of Russian Federation] (2002), pp. 9-18 (abstract diss. kand. iurid. nauk); V. E. Chirkin, «О сущности субъекта федерации: традиции и реалии» [On the Essence of a Subject of a Federation: Traditions and Realities], Государство и право [State and Law], no. 7 (2003).

[38] Department of Public Information of the United Nations, Основные факты об Организации Объединенных Наций [Basic Facts on the United Nations] (2005), pp. 359-363.

political unification or integration with independent States. However, despite great progress achieved in the process of decolonization, there are in the world about twenty non-self-governing territories under the external management of the United Kingdom, the United States, France, and New Zealand.

There are, however, examples of dependent territorial structures having governmental management institutions, including legislative and judicial, adopting normative decision and realizing them throughout the entire space of the formation and with respect to the entire population. Among them is Puerto Rico, which received under the Constitution adopted 25 July 1952, from the metropolitan the status of a "State freely acceding to the United States". This territory has been given extensive self-government exercised by its own bicameral legislative assembly, government, headed by a governor, advisory council, and courts.[39] This points to the functioning in this territorial formation of an own legal system, which differs to a great extent from the legal systems of Common Law family countries. The norms of civil law in force in the "acceding State" were drawn up on the Spanish model, and the procedural and a large part of other legal norms correspond to Latin American models.

The Palestine National Authority, created on the basis of the 1993 Washington Declaration of Principles on Interim Self-Government Arrangements providing for the creation of interim Palestinian self-government, is another typical example of a territorial with a transitional regime. The creation of the post of president in this formation as the head of the self-governing territory, government, and Palestinian legislative council testify to the forming of own organs of power and administration and, as a consequence, legal system. Its foundations are based on Islamic conceptions and classical institutes of Muslim law.

Recent events (having in view the uprising of Muslim fundamentalists in summer 2007 and their seizure of power in Gaza), called a coup d'etat by the extraordinary meeting of ministers of foreign affairs of the members of the League of Arab States, may threaten the separation of the sector from the rest of the territory and defer for some time the possibility of creating a sovereign Palestinian State.[40] Moreover, the real possibility is predicted of the consolidation in this Near Eastern region of two self-governing territorial formations controlled by ideologically irreconcilable groups

[39] S. V. Lavrov (ed.), Страны мира: справочник 2006 [Countries of the World: Manual 2006] (2006), pp. 341-343.

[40] G. Kosach, «Палестинский разлом: бомба под государство, которого и так нет» [Palestinian Break: Bomb under a State Which Is Not Yet One], Профиль [Profile], 25 June 2007, pp. 26-30.

(Hamas, the Islamic Resistance Movement) and Fatah (Palestine National Liberation Movement) with their own State-law systems.

Legal systems of State-Similar Formations. At present the recognition by the world community of a particular territory as an independent State cannot be ignored – this is an indicator of principle that public power has been consolidated in a State. An example is membership in the United Nations – the most authoritative universal international organization of modern times in which there are 192 States.

Therefore, one cannot agree with Baburin who asserts that "Statehood and sovereignty of a State do not depend upon their recognition by other States".[41] The Russian politician, in essence, upholds the position previously maintained by the USSR of the declarative theory which was based on the absolute right of nations to self-determination and excluded any dependence of the status of a new State on the fact of being granted recognition. Today Russia and other former socialist countries directly in own practice have encountered sharp manifestations of separatism and attempts at self-proclamation by individual territories as States.

Nonetheless, there are a number of formations in the modern world with elements of Statehood which contest their affiliation to "mother countries" (that is, to those of which they are formally a part or were a part), claim the creation of own States, and considered themselves to be such. Among these are Abkhazia, Kosovo, Dniester Moldovan Republic, Karabakh, Northern Cyprus, Taiwan, and other so-called quasi-States. Such State-similar structures have virtually all the attributes of State power, including representative legislative and law-applying institutions. Often their legal systems are qualitatively different from the States within which they formally continue to be, and this chasm continues to become greater.

Thus, before the actual self-separation of the Dniester Moldovan Republic (DMR) from Moldova the legislation of the Moldavian SSR operates on the territory of the DMR. From 1990 their legislation began to develop independently and the differences between the "mother" and "departed" legal systems began to grow. Whereas the new law of Moldova was orientated towards the traditions of the Romano countries, the legislation of the DMR from the moment of the proclamation of statehood followed the Russian model on the whole.[42]

[41] S. N. Baburin, Мир империй: территория государства и мировой порядок [World of Empires: Territory of a State and World Order] (Spb., 2005), pp. 507-509.

[42] «Приднестровская Молдавская Республика» [Dniester Moldovan Republic], in Sukharev, note 36 above, pp. 631-634.

Thus, unrecognized States with own law-creation agencies and legislative may exist for decades. The present legal system of Taiwan – an island whose authorities officially call it the Republic China is for more than sixty years the "heir" of the legal system of continental China, having basic principles and institutes of continental (European) law with certain elements of Anglo-American law. Historically, the Confucian tradition of the Chinese has influenced to some degree the legal consciousness and legal culture of the population of the island.[43] At the time when the Chinese People's Republic, proceeding from the ideas of Mao Tse-tung and Deng Xiaoping are building a "socialist rule-of-law State" with Chinese characteristics, on Taiwan the 1947 Constitution of the Republic of China continues to operate and many codes drafted and introduced into operation in the 1920-30s.

Both the constitution and principal codes of Taiwan were subjected at the turn of the Millennium to certain democratic changes that followed changes in this formation after isolation in the international arena. The powers of the president are growing with the simultaneous enhancement of the role of the legislative chamber, which was given the function of control over the activities of the Government. In the view of a number of experts, the concept of "sovereign democracy" so popular today among Russian politologists was born on Taiwan, which having lost membership in the United Nations to the Chinese People's Republic, sought an own politico-legal identity distinct from that of Communist China.[44]

Legal systems of inter-State associations. The postwar era witnessed a significant growth in the number of international organizations, which reflects the objective progress of world civilization. At the contemporary stage about seven thousand international organizations exist, among which about 300 are intergovernmental organizations.

Inter-State associations are of special interest as permanent formations of States having own legal systems.[45] In such formations own inter-State legal systems function. Such a system should be regarded as an integral structure created on the basis of principles and norms established by the inter-State association and limiting (with their consent initially expressed

[43] «Тайвань» [Taiwan], in Sukharev, note 36 above, pp. 757-762.

[44] D.Orlov, «Политическая доктрина суверенной демократии» [Political Doctrine of Sovereign Democracy], Известия [News], 30 November 2006.

[45] See V. G. Vishniakov (ed.), Право и межгосударственные объедининия [Law and Inter-State Associations] (Spb., 2003); R. A. Kalamkarian and Iu. I. Migachev, Международное право [International Law] (2004), pp. 218-295; Iu. M. Kolosov and E. S. Krivchikova (eds.), Международное право [International Law] (2007), pp. 305-312.

in the constitutive treaty) the sovereignty of national law in determined spheres.

The principal indicia (their presence of absence determines the extent and limits of functioning) of inter-State legal systems are becoming:

- treaty-law character of the association establishing the principles of the legal order being formed between member States;
- permanent character of the functioning of inter-State formations and the normative-legal corpus created by them;
- equality of member States in relations between themselves and with the formation being created;
- uniform legal policy, proposed activities according to general legal principles, purposes, and tasks, forecasting of legal processes, creation of mechanism for legal regulation within the framework of inter-State associations;
- existence of common legal space as a result of the interaction of the inter-State legal system with national legal systems of member States;
- supranational (as a rule) nature of the competence of inter-State organs having powers to adopt imperative decisions for all member States of the association with the right to apply enforcement measures;
- expansion of the number of so-called self-executing decisions of law-creation organs of inter-State associations not needing additional transformation into municipal legislation.

The legal systems thereof correspond to autonomous types of State associations, among which there are:

- *inter-State legal system of commonwealth* – a union of sovereign States coordinating their activities in determined spheres. The basis for the association may be an historical community, cultural and linguistic homogeneity, religious ties, economic integration, legal compatibility (affiliation to a single group of legal systems or legal family). The legal system of a commonwealth. The legal system of a commonwealth is confined in its impact on member States by virtue of the absence of supranational powers in the union structures, which in essence are called upon to perform only coordinating functions, and also the possibility of the participants in such a formation not to fulfill decisions of permanent organs of the commonwealth (Commonwealth of Independent States – CIS). The ambiguity of the legal status of the CIS also does not facilitate making its more active within the framework of the own legal system. The principal way out from this situation may only be the transformation of the CIS into a more integrated inter-State structure similar to a community, or its division into a number of more solid associations of States;

- *inter-State legal system of Union State* – a local (bilateral) union of States on the basis of historical, political, economic, socio-cultural, and ethnographic proximity. Examples of such unions are the Union State of Serbia and Montenegro (2002-2006) and the Union State of Belarus and Russia, that is, one no longer existing and the other still unformed inter-State associations. In both instances insuperable obstacles on the path of creating a single State-law system were obvious and latent political and economic contradictions, a clear lack of desire to introduce supranational structures with imperative powers or to subordinate oneself to the supranational organs created.
- *inter-State legal system of community* – a centralized form of State association assuming the voluntary limitation by member States of their sovereign rights to the union structures. Communities have clearly expressly features of a State nature, materially distinguished them from international organizations of the traditional type both from the standpoint of their institutional structure and internal law regulating their mutual relations with member States and the outside world.

To a greater extent that other State associations the European Union has succeeded in embodying special features of communities, its legal system being a structure that has been formed and facilitates the further integration of the European States, including the working out of their uniform legal policy.

As a consequence, an inter-State association of the confederated-federated type has formed on the basis of a single European legal space. In modern western legal doctrine the European Union is regarded as a "supranational" organization, "closely integrated post-State formation, which exercised sovereign powers".[46] Moreover, a number of authors assert that by its status the European Union already is not an international organization, but a "confederation with elements of a federal structure" which soon will be transformed into a proper federation, or already is a new type of federation – a "federation of national States".[47]

[46] S. Iu. Kashkin and A. O. Chetverikov, «Комментарии к проекту Конституции Европейского Союза» [Commentary on the Draft Constitution of the European Union], Журнал зарубежного законодательства и сравнительного правоведения [Journal of Foreign Legislation and Comparative Law], no. 1 (2005), p. 11.

[47] Serebrova, note 5 above, pp. 19-20, 28-29; V. A. Tolstik, «Проблемы иерархического соотношения российской и европейской правозащитных систем» [Problems of Hierarchical Correlation of Russian and European Right-Protection Systems], in Российская

It is believed that this assumption has plainly outlived itself and was dictated by the euphoric anticipation of the adoption of the Constitution of Europe. However, in the present state of the legal system of the European Union the primacy of so-called European legislation is not in doubt over the national laws and subordinate acts of all 27 countries within that community. The legal means for ensuring the realization and confirmation of the priority of the law of the EU have been created.

Universal international legal system. Other approaches to singling out the legal systems of the modern world remain outside the scope of this study. In recent years especially, the recourse of international lawyers to conceptions of an "international inter-State legal system", an "international normative system", and a "global legal system" is noteworthy.[48] Such a worldwide normative construction must be a generalization of world legal experience embodied in the aggregate of general humanitarian (or civilization) principles and norms by which the international legal order is established and maintained.[49]

The end of the "cold war" era led to the forming of real prerequisites for intensification of the regulating role of international law in relations between States, and also between other members of the world community. The internationalization of traditionally municipal issues is being accompanied by theoretical generalizations of this process. These, in turn, require special studies by theoreticians of law and international lawyers.

Nonetheless, the discussions around a universal system of international legal regulation also favor a conclusion concerning the limited nature of the consideration of a legal system only within the framework of State limits. A legal system as a politico-legal phenomenon reflects the diversity of the modern world, requiring more sustained attention. In essence the aspiration to regard both municipal and international law not only as a stable aggregate of binding principles and rules of behavior, but also a dynamically developing construction accommodating the processes of globalization is in evidence.

и европейская правозащитные системы: соотношение и проблемы гармонизации: Сборник статей [Russian and European Right-Protection Systems: Correlation and Problems of Harmonization: Collected Articles] (Nizhnii Novgorod, 2004), p. 53.

48 See V. V. Gavrilov, «Развитие концепции правовой системы в отечественной доктрине права: общетеоретический и международно-правовой подходы» [Development of the Conception of Legal System in the Fatherland Doctrine of Law: General Theoretical and International Legal Approaches], Журнал российского права [Journal of Russian Law], no. 1 (2004), pp. 76-87.

49 Saidov, "Comparative Law and Law-making", *Journal of Comparative Law*, II (2007), pp. 75-76.

Comparative Law Hermeneutics: Cognitive Possibilities

M. A. DAMIRLI*

In this article, as is evident from the title, we reflect principally upon comparative law. However, the main idea transcends this limited comparative domain and is linked more with socio-humanitarian comparative studies as a whole.

The point of departure for my reflections in this study is the following circumstances. First, the conception of hermeneutic methodology has been elaborated to date chiefly with respect to the humanities (literature, linguistics, art history, pedagogy, psychology, history, and others). In these conceptions hermeunetics is considered to be a specific means of cognition of the humanities and is linked with elaborating various methods of interpreting historical, philological, religious, mythological, and legal texts (or rather – legal norms).

Second, the majority of representatives of existing conceptions of hermeneutics proceeded from the juxtaposition and differentiation in principle of the natural sciences and the humanities, the "sciences of nature" and "sciences of the spirit", without taking into account the specific nature of the social sciences. The positions of Max Weber (1864-1920) and Paul Ricoeur (1913-2005) are exceptions. Whereas Weber combined all disciplines not within the natural sciences into the category of historical and social sciences, Ricoeur defined the social sciences as the sciences concerning man and society and relegated to this group such diverse disciplines which "fall between linguistics and sociology", including the historical and legal sciences.

* доктор юридических наук, профессор. Chair of European Union Law and Comparative Law, Odessa National Legal Academy

In light of this attention should be drawn to the correlation of the social sciences and the humanities. The fact is that they both to a considerable extent overlap (the reason for using them together). Nonetheless, they are not the same. This problem is considered to be controversial in socio-philosophical literature. Some believe that not all the social sciences may be qualified as humanities; the humanities are, first of all, those sciences such as pedagogy, psychology, literary studies, linguistics, social anthropology, and others, whereas, for example, the socio-economic sciences are relegated to the social sciences, not being sciences of the humanities cycle proper. However, it is stressed that these sciences possess a humanities quality.[1]

Others are of the view, on the contrary, that the class of humanitarian sciences is broader than the class of social sciences. Any social science is relegated to this class, but not all the humanities are social sciences (for example, language, art history).[2] Without dwelling on details, we note here merely the essential point that is directly relevant to the matter under consideration – the recognition in both instances of the humanities quality of all social sciences.

The humanities quality of any social cognition, especially comparative law, is stipulated above all and in no small degree by the special configuration of relations within the system "subject-object" and the important role in that system of subject-man who is simultaneously an object. Here another point of contiguity is discovered – the link of the social (including legal) knowledge with texts, since the "text is that specific distinctive feature which separates man as an object of humanities cognition".[3] Hence the conclusion that social (including legal) cognition has humanities quality.

However, merely stating the humanities quality of the nature of social (legal) cognition, for all of its importance, is insufficient. More important is the identification of the specific nature of socio-humanities cognition, including with respect to the application of the tenets of hermeneutics therein.

On one hand, the humanities quality of social cognition enables the cognition of respective tenets of hermeneutic methodology elaborated purely in regard to the humanities to be applied in this sphere. But, at the same time, the distinctive nature of the subject-matter of social cognition proper to some extent limits the possibilities for the application of these

1 See A. M. Korshunov and V. V. Mantatov, Диалектика социального познания [Dialectics of Social Cognition] (1988), p. 165.

2 Ia. Iu. Prosperini, Проблемы человека и гуманитарные науки (философско-методологические аспекты) [Problem of Man and the Humanities (Philosophical-Methodological Aspects)] (2000), p. 15 (diss. kand. filos. nauk)

3 V. G. Kuznetsov, Герменевтика и гуманитарное познание [Hermeneutics and Humanities Cognition] (1991), p. 134.

tenets (whether we are studying reality in law and, say, poetry is not the same thing) and requires certain modifications, which is an important scientific-cognitive task. Comparative law cognition is no exception.

Modern hermeneutics, in elaborating a general theory of understanding, regards it as a means of the being of man (ontology of understanding) and as a method of humanities cognition (gnosiological understanding), to be sure without building a Chinese Wall between them. By analogy, one may single out two modes, in the socio-humanities sphere in general and in the comparative law sphere in particular: the mode of being and the mode of cognition. We consider them consecutively.

COMPARATIVE LAW UNDERSTANDING

In considering this mode it is appropriate to follow Ricoeur in putting the question: "what is a substance whose being lies in understanding"?[4] In other words, understanding is the main hermeneutic problem which "becomes by a means of being, that being which exists in understanding".[5] Indeed, is the domain "controlled" by legal comparativistics a being which exists in understanding?

The ontological status of understanding as an appendage of this domain lies above all in the fact that it acts as a means of the being of law in the world. Legal orders are actually formed from acts of understanding and interpretation in the process of practical legal life. Under modern conditions law-creation always or nearly always passes through a comparative stage which confronts understanding with an important task. Law as a regulator of social relations in various spheres of the life of man requires consent not only with individual legal systems, but also between them.

The being of law on a world scale is distinctive for its mixed character and diversity and is constructed from various systemic legal formations (international, supranational, and national legal systems) and the intertwining thereof. None of these legal systems can exist in isolation. Constant interaction and mutual influence occurs. The dynamic of law, just as the dynamic of any phenomenon of culture, "cannot be represented as either an isolated immanent process or as a quality of a passive sphere of external influences. Both these trends are realized in mutual tension, from which they cannot be abstracted without distorting their very essence".[6]

[4] P. Ricoeur, Конфликт интерпретаций. Очерки о герменевтике [Conflict of Interpretations. Essays on Hermeneutics] (1995), p. 8.

[5] Ricoeur, note 4 above, p. 10.

[6] Iu. M. Lotman, Культура и взрыв. Внутри мыслящих миров [Culture and Explosion. Within Thinking Worlds] (1992), p. 116.

A genuine dialogue is happening between existing legal systems; in other words, the being of law has a dialogical nature. The dialogical being of law includes synchronic and diachronic aspects. The synchronic aspect of the dialogical being of law accentuates attention to the interlinkage and mutual influence of the various co-existing legal systems. The diachronic aspect – the dialogue of the past, present, and future of legal systems. An especially vital moment of this interaction is the dialogue of innovation and tradition, the injection of innovation into a regenerating legal order. One of the main tasks is to identify the mechanism for dialogue in the legal sphere.[7]

A comparativistic interpretation, just as any interpretation, has the aim of overcoming distance.[8] In our case – between a legal system to which a text belongs and the interpreter himself and the context thereof, and ultimately – between legal systems. In the "encounters" of various legal systems and cultural-legal traditions as a whole, an understanding of the other, a search for sameness and self comprehension, an awareness of one's own legal system through correlation with "the other's" legal system, the achievement of consent and mutual understanding are essential conditions of modern legal life.

In conditions of globalization the processes of interaction and mutual influence of legal systems are large-scale, dialogue is conformed as a norm of modern legal development, integration processes are deepening and expanding, facilitating the establishment of profound and comprehensive interlinkages and mutual dependencies. Transnational links and contacts are expanding, new integrative regional combinations are being created, the coming together and mutual-facilitation of national legal systems is occurring, and so on. Consequently, the role and significance of understanding is enhanced.

Under modern conditions, understanding acts as a determinative characteristic of the existence, functioning, and development of law (or legal systems) itself, means of the being thereof.

[7] The theoretical foundations of the mechanism of such dialogue with respect to culture have been presented by the noted culturologist, Lotman. The basic propositions of his conception, especially with regard to the process of perception from the standpoint of the "receiving" side, may be taken into account also with respect to law. Lotman, note 6 above, pp. 268-276.

[8] Ricoeur, note 4 above, p. 25.

COMPARATIVE LAW UNDERSTANDING: MODE OF COGNITION

Here we refer to comparative law understanding as a methodological operation. The weak elaboration of this mode makes the structuring of special methods of understanding a vitally urgent task.

Certain theoretical-methodologically significant propositions are set out below by way of a special resolution of this task; these relate to heuristic possibilities and distinctive features of comparative law understanding as a means of cognition.

First, the application of the tenets of hermeneutics in legal comparativistics logically derives from the nature of the being of law itself since, as noted above, the existence of legal systems is a means of being. Legal comparativistics thus acts as a hermeneutic discipline.

Second, Unlike purely humanities cognition, which gravitates towards a preference for methods of understanding, there is a special mutually-reinforcing dialectal correlation between explanation and understanding in comparative law cognition since the explanation fulfills the function of summing up the special under the general, and understanding – a grasp of the sense of the individual, the unique. Eliciting the general and the special is an important subject-matter task of comparative law.[9]

Third, The hermeneutic circle whose material construction is the correlation between the part and the whole is an important hermeneutic instrument. Here the movement of understanding constantly passed from the whole to the part and from the part to the whole (H.-G. Gadamer); knowledge of the whole assumes knowledge not only of the parts thereof, but all possible links between them (P. Ricoeur). The process of comprehension the whole proceeds with the assistance of the constant clarifying construing of the whole. There are two types of relations of "part-whole": the first type – the relation of the part to the entire whole; the second type – the relation of the whole as parts to the entire aggregate of external and internal conditions of life as a whole.[10]

From the standpoint of the hermeneutic circle it is impossible to understand the law of any people without having determined the place thereof in the system of social regulation, and the lace of social regulation – in the context of social values, standards, rules, beliefs, and institutions whose aggregate creates the specific face of culture and form the socio-

[9] On the correlation of explanation and understanding in the social sciences the reader is referred to Ricoeur, Герменевтика и метод социальных наук [Hermeneutics and Method of Social Sciences]. www.philosophy.ru

[10] Kuznetsov, note 3 above, p. 62.

cultural context of the law of a given people. Further, if one dwells on the positions of hermeneutics, we should, on one hand, determine the place of the legal system being studies within the system of kindred legal systems – respective legal family, and on the other, consider its interlinkages with international law, and also with integrative, supranational law, if the State whose legal system is studies has integration links with other States.

In the context of hermeneutics, as noted, knowledge of the whole assumes knowledge not only of the parts thereof, but also of all possible links between them. With regard to comparative law, this, *inter alia,* means that the study of foreign law is merely "preliminary knowledge" and assists comparative law cognition (the deeper our knowledge of individual parts, the greater our possibilities to create an integral picture of the sphere of reality being studied), But there is no comparative law proper yet. For example, the constitutional law of foreign countries is merely summary knowledge received with the assistance of the individual study of the constitutional law of each country; here the part is studies without its linkages with the whole.

Fourth, A distinctive feature of comparative law understanding is also its dialogue-relatedness. Although, as Bakhtin noted, understanding is always in some measure dialogue-related,[11] the dialogue-relatedness of understanding here logically derives from the dialogical nature of the being of law being studies. This circumstance, consequently, requires the application of the dialogical methodology.

Fifth, one of the research tasks of comparative legal science is an understanding of the "other" (other legal system). In this event a model of understanding "getting accustomed" (or "resettlement") must be applied. Another's culture should be analyzed from the standpoint of this other's culture, speaking in hermeneutic terminology, from the standpoint of the author and his context.

In a comparative law understanding, a material role belongs to the socio-cultural context. This is conditioned by the existence of differences between the legal systems to be compared which belong to different cultures, peoples, civilizations, and traditions within whose framework law is perceived differently. In so doing to understand legal cultures of various peoples while comparing them from the standpoint of one of them is not correct because it leads to one-sided conclusions: "If we seek to approach research of law in the life of particular nationalities, ethnic

[11] M. M. Bakhtin, Эстетика словесного творчества [The Aesthetics of Oral Creativity] (1979), p. 292.

groups, and communities from the position of own understanding of law and legal norms, we may not find it there".[12]

Here there is not and cannot be a place for Eurocentrism or any other manifestation of "centrism" excluding the possibility of identifying the special, the unique. Dialogical methodology "requires the 'placement' of the author of the text and interpreter in identical conditions relative to time, language, culture, and so on".[13] The realization of this requirement assumes, especially, knowledge by the comparatist-researcher of the language to be studied of the "other" legal system. It also is essential to achieve the distinctive features of world-understanding, cultural-legal traditions, legal style, and so on in the legal systems to be compared.

The search for sameness and self-understanding and an awareness of one's own legal system through correlation with the "other's" legal system and overcoming thereby the "alienness of the others's" is another task of dialogical comparative-law cognition. The model of "getting accustomed" is inadequate for this. As Lotman properly observed, the "external" culture in order to intrude into our world must cease to be "external" for it.[14] This means with regard to our domain that understanding of "the other's" legal system should happen from the position of the interpreter and the context thereof. An interpreter of the other's legal culture should analyze from the standpoint of his own legal culture, should approach the other's legal system from the specific nature and problems of his own legal system. On this plane to understand the other's legal culture means to know how to find answers to questions which arise in our legal culture.

The foregoing enables one to conclude that the dialogical movement of comparative legal understanding includes various models of understand and should pass through the following stages: from the outset – understanding a legal system from the standpoint of the particular culture; next – understanding a legal system from the standpoint of its context; finally – understanding a legal system from the position of an interpreter and the context thereof, and thereby an awareness of one's own legal system through the correlation with the "other's" legal system.

Sixth, unlike humanities cognition proper, where the question of truth is moved to the back, in social (including comparative legal) cognition this question is of material importance. Whereas in humanities cognition the problems of objectivity (or adequacy) and truth are separated, do not

12 A. I. Ovchinnikov, Правовое мышление в герменевтической парадигме [Legal Thinking in the Hermeneutic Paradigm] (Rostov-on-Don, 2002), p. 43.

13 Kuznetsov, note 3 above, p. 143.

14 Lotman, note 6 above, p. 116.

coincide,[15] in the social sciences in general and legal comparativistics in particular the problem of the adequacy of interpretation, the elaboration of criteria for evaluation of the results thereof, is an important problem.

Finally, at present primary attention is being devoted in comparative law to a description of individual legal families, the contrasting and juxtaposition of legal systems, and problems of their interaction remain beyond the purview. In this writer's view, legal comparativistics must transcend the framework of a traditional typological approach to the study of legal systems in space. Research on the interaction of legal systems should become a major orientation of comparative law theory.

[15] Kuznetsov, note 3 above, p. 132.

Functionalism and the Development of Comparative Law Cognition

A. V. TKACHENKO*

The correlation of comparative legal and philosophical-methodological cognition have determinative significance for understanding the nature and gnosiological possibilities of legal comparison. Under modern conditions the correct description of such a correlation is possible only thanks to the formalization and critical comprehension of the referential construction of methodological thought embodied in the functionalism of comparative law. This article is devoted to substantiating this thesis.

THE METHODOLOGICAL APORIA OF THE FUNCTIONALISM OF COMPARATIVE LAW

Any reflection of functionalist methodology in comparative law sooner or later encounters a logical contradiction. On one hand, functionality is postulated to be the "basic methodological principle of comparative law",[1] the center of all methodological discussions;[2] and, on the other, there is no place in functionalism for the "methodological" contemplation of the functional method.[3] Moreover, the functionalists themselves consciously

* Docent, Chair of Theory and History of State and Law, Kiev International University

[1] K. Zweigert and H. Kötz, Введение в сравнительное правоведение в сфере частного права [Introduction to Comparative Law in the Sphere of Private Law] (2000), I, p. 50.

[2] Michaels points out that the functional method is the "focal point of almost all discussions about the field of comparative law as a whole -- centres versus peripheries of scholarly projects and interests, mainstream versus avant-garde, convergence versus pluralism, instrumentalism versus hermeneutics, technocracy versus culture, and so on". R. Michaels, "The Functional Method of Comparative Law" in M. Reimann and R. Zimmerman (eds.), *The Oxford Handbook of Comparative Law* (2006), p. 340.

[3] Illustrations of this are frequent in comparative law literature and basically consist of

affirm the secondary importance of methodology[4] and even if "such a thing as a sui generis functional method" of comparative law does not exist,[5] its existence would lead to a "clear paradox".[6]

The exceptional significance of the said aporia (simultaneous affirmation and denial of the functionalism of methodology) lies in the fact that the relationship of functionalism to methodological work influences and even determines the methodological situation in comparative law as a whole. In particular, the mixing of epistemological and social purposes caused by a search for the legitimacy of comparative law studies in the practical consequences of their application is now proclaimed to be the main reason for the stunning theoretical weakness, emptiness, and lack of content of comparative law.[7]

Proceeding from this, the widespread references to the marginal role of theory and methodology as a major feature of comparative law discourse are natural.[8] In our view the clearest and completely depressing state of

---

an emphasis on the practical and pragmatic nature of the argumentation of such noted functionalists as E. Rabel, D. Esser, and K. Zweigert, as a consequence of which their attitude towards functionalism was exclusively instrumental and not expressed in a detailed elaboration and substantiation of the method or an adequate understanding of function as the center of comparative legal studies. See Michaels, note 3 above, p. 362. In view of this, the general characterization of functionalism was made by Gerber with respect to Rabel: "Ironically, there is little method in his method". D. J. Gerber, "Sculpting the Agenda of Comparative Law: Ernst Rabel and the Façade of Language", in A. Riles (ed.), *Rethinking the Masters of Comparative Law* (2001), p. 198.

4 J. H. Merryman, "Comparative Law and Scientific Explanation", in id, *The Loneliness of the Comparative Lawyer* (2001), p. 501.

5 A. E. Plastas, "The Functional and the Dysfunctional in the Comparative Method of Law: Some Critical Remarks", *Electronic Journal of Comparative Law*, XII, no. 3 (2008), p. 2. See www.ejcl.org/123

6 Plastas, note 5 above. In our view, being guided by the argumentation in the "canonical" work of comparative legal functionalism by Zweigert and Kötz, the last is defined as a *principle* and not as an autonomous *method*.

7 R. Sacco, "Legal Formants: A Dynamic Approach to Comparative Law", *American Journal of Comparative Law*, XXXIX (1991), p. 2; G. Samuel, "Comparative Law and Jurisprudence", *International and Comparative Law Quarterly*, XLVII (1998), pp. 822-823.

8 M. A. Damirli, «Теоретико-методологические проблемы сравнетельного правоведения: попытка актуализации и некоторые размышления» [Theoretical-Methodological Problems of Comparative Law: Attempt at Actualization and Some Reflections], Журнал зарубежного законодательства и сравнительного правоведения [Journal of Foreign Legislation and Comparative Law], no. 3 (2006), p. 47; A. Kh. Saidov, «Современное сравнительное правоведение: методология и новые парадигмы» [Contemporary Comparative Law: Methodology and New Paradigms], Порівняльно-правові дослідження [Comparative Law Studies], no. 1-2 (2007), p. 16; Saidov, Сравнительное правоведение и юридическая география мира [Comparative Law and the Legal Geography of the World] (1993), p. 49; G. Frankenberg, "Critical Comparison: Re-thinking Comparative Law", *Harvard International Law Journal*, XXVI (1985), p. 416; U. Mattei and M. Reimann, "Introduction: Symposium 'New Directions in Comparative Law'", *American Journal of Comparative Law*, XLVI (1998), p. 597.

comparative law is captured in the metaphors "reverse alchemy" of Rosen[9] and the "boggy locale"[10] and "neglected garden" of Brand.[11]

In our view these utterances, whose general sense may be formulated as an assertion that functionalism does not inject methodological thought into the sphere of comparative law cognition, but obstructs this, being correct in content but simultaneously is methodologically deficient or even non-methodological entirely. The simple denial of functionalism stands as remotely from methodology as does its canonization. It is essential to answer: (a) why does functionalism not promote the constituting of the methodology of comparative law cognition? (b) what should this methodology be? (c) and by what means may it be constructed? However, the answers to these questions assume not a denial of functionalism, but the comprehension thereof, reflection.

Therefore, the observation by Michaels deserves attention, that "other disciplines have discarded functionalism only after utilizing its insights. Functionalist comparative law has not yet made sufficient use of the benefits of functionalism".[12] In our view, methodological thought is a fruit of functionalism. And since, according to Örücü, comparative law "can only be approached as an enigma",[13] the link between functionalism and methodology also is a mystery – although since the functionalism of comparative law is not methodological, the path towards forming a methodology of comparative legal research lies only through the contemplative overcoming of functionalism and reflections on the foundations of functionalist thought.

[9] "Comparatists in a sort of reverse alchemy … have managed to turn gold into lead, the subject being far more interesting than some of the things done with it". L. Rosen, "Beyond Compare", in P. Legrand and R. Munday (eds.), *Comparative Legal Studies: Traditions and Transitions* (2003), p. 495.

[10] The locale of comparative law is boggy since "comparatists try to reach firm ground without the guidance of serious thoughts on methodology". O. Brand, "Conceptual Comparisons: Towards a Coherent Methodology of Comparative Legal Studies", *Brooklyn Journal of International Law*, XXXII (2006-07), pp. 407-408.

[11] The contemporary picture of "comparative-legal methodology as a garden filled with withering or infertile flowers". Brand, note 10 above, p. 435.

[12] Michaels, note 2 above, p. 381.

[13] E. Örücü, *The Enigma of Comparative Law: Variations on a Theme for the Twenty-First Century* (2004), p. 1.

Gnosiological-Epistemological Bases of Functionalist Reference. It is a matter of principle for the correct understanding of functionalist thought that the denial by it of the need for an autonomous, problemizing reflection of the methodology of comparative law cognition does not mean a denial of this methodology itself. The fact is that functionalists do not make the existence and adequacy of methodological provision for their studies dependent upon their own methodological efforts. That is, in fact the postulation of the methodology of comparative law studies exists, but such postulation is external to comparative law and is effectuated outside (or instead of) autonomous methodological work of comparatists.

The source of the said understanding of methodology by functionalists coincides with the source of the functionalism of comparative law as such. This source is the formalization by Rabel of "functional comparability" effectuated by him when resolving the problem of the conflict of qualifications.[14] This solution laid down a gnosiological-epistemological model defining and identifying any attempt to implement the functionalist program in comparative law.

The essence of functional gnosiology is the problem of constructing a theory of cognition, that is, delimiting thought and methodology; this is resolved by means of the external perception of methodology, that is, the use of methods belonging to other, with respect to comparative law, disciplinary spheres.[15] This solution derives from a key idea of functionalism: the complete independence of functional concepts from national legal concepts.[16]

This resolution by functionalism of the gnosiological issue pre-determines its resolution of the fundamental epistemological dichotomy of the source of cognition, which Samuel described as a schism between *research* and *authority*.[17] The epistemological content of Rabel's solution

[14] M. Graziadei, "The Functionalist Heritage", in Legrand and Munday, note 9 above, pp. 103-104; Michaels, note 2 above, p. 378, n. 200.

[15] G. Samuel, "Taking Method Seriously", *The Journal of Comparative Law*, II, no. 2 (2007), p. 211.

[16] One of the best known and influential formalizations of this idea is Zweigert's assertion that the "comparatist when considering problems should abstract himself from his own doctrinal and legal views and cultural milieu and use only neutral concepts". Zweigert and Kötz, note 1 above, p. 23.

[17] As Samuel pointed out, the epistemological orientation towards authority, being absolutely inevitable for national jurists, is hermeneutic text determined by its object, but basically a motivating question – determination of the significance of this text. Research is a natural-science orientation; its motivating objective is explanation of the phenomenon

of the problem of qualification lies in the substitution of the orientation towards authority (which is a synonym of natural comparability)[18] with an orientation towards research which at the time motivated the social sciences and which should have corresponded to the concept of functional comparability.[19]

Rabel's solution of the gnosiological problem of structuring a theory of cognition and the epistemological problem of the source of condition stipulated the absence in the functionalism of comparative law of a philosophical-methodological interpretation of those cognitive means which he exploited. That is, in comparative law a gnosiological-epistemological model of functionalism exists not in the form of an exposition thereof, but only by reference,[20] by an implicit indication thereof.

It is understandable that the gnosiological-epistemological model of comparative legal functionalism also determines its understanding of methodological thought. In other words, functionalists in fact postulate a methodology of own studies, but such postulation is not constitutive, but by reference.

Functional Reference as Sociology. Sociology is postulated to be the methodological reference for comparative legal functionalism and comparative law as a whole.[21] It is explicitly indicated in functionalist

---

received as a result of a precise investigation of all accessible physical data. See Samuel, note 15 above, p. 116.

[18] Natural comparability acts as a foundation of cognition affirming the absence of material distinctions between the perception of national law and legal comparison based on an assumption of the conformity to an identical symbolic form, identical legal idea. Finding universal legal ideas thus becomes possible without the need to exit beyond the limits of the field of ideas of the national legal system of the investigator. It is considered sufficient merely to adequately perceive the correlation between form and idea in the national legal system.

[19] Functional comparability is a structure of an analysis in which "the technical-juridical constructions, are to be discarded". R. Hyland, "Comparative Law", in D. Patterson (ed.), *A Companion to Philosophy of Law and Legal Theory* (1999), p. 187 (quoting E. Rabel). It is assumed that "… comparison was only useful if it was 'grounded' in the realities of those way legal systems actually solved problems". Gerber, note 3 above, p. 201.

[20] By reference is understood the "separating out and specification into strict ideas by means of the correlation thereof with a reference without taking into account the role of contexts in forming the meanings of scientific terms". T. A. Novolodskaia and V. N. Sadovnikov, Философские проблемы социально-гуманитарного знания [Philosophical Problems of Socio-Humanitarian Knowledge] (Spb., 2008), p. 42.

[21] It is indicated in the literature that the participants of the First International Congress of Comparative Law in 1900 "arrived under the influence of A. Comte and the progress of biology, especially the theory of evolution". W. J. Kamba, "Comparative Law: A Theoretical Framework", *International and Comparative Law Quarterly*, XXIII (1974), p. 488. It is evident that they shared also Comte's classification of sciences, according to which 'law is regarded as part of sociology'". N. N. Tarasov, Методологические проблемы современного правоведения [Methodological Problems of Modern Jurisprudence] (Ekaterinburg, 2002), p. 148 (diss. doktor iurid. nauk). The following words of one of the Congress participants,

literature that the aspiration to comprehend the social functions of law as such inevitably leads to the comparative law of the sociology of law.[22]

Thus, affirmation of the methodological identity of comparative law and sociology is the content of referential thought of the functionalists. Comparative law is proclaimed to be a science having a clearly expressed sociological nature in which "all the principal methods of cognition of law must be regarded not so much from the standpoint of formal logic as by proceeding from their sociological aspect"[23] since "all methods used in the process of the cognition of legal phenomena also have a place in the other sociological sciences".[24] In so doing functionalism naturalizes the assertion of the identity of the methods of comparative law and sociology, pointing only to the general recognition of such identity.[25] Proceeding from this, the idea of methodological reference turns out to be one of the basic elements of the *a priori* horizon of functionalism, transcending the limits of the subject-matter of comparative legal reflection.

The basic heuristic potential of the relationship of reference to problems of methodology is the assumption that sociology elaborates concepts applicable in comparative law. It is the "sociological origin" of these concepts that is the circumstance which relieves comparatists from the need for their individual theoretical study in order to impart to them scientific substantiation[26] since the results of these methods in other disciplines may persuade jurists of their reliability and fruitfulness.[27]

Interpretation *tertium comparationis* as a sociological reality reflecting an understanding of the meta-juridical character of the criterion of comparability as the sociological character thereof is the instrument for the effectuation by functionalism of a methodological reference.[28] It should

F. V. Taranovskii, are testimony to this: "comparative law is a part of sociology as the unified, synthetic science concerning society". F. V. Taranovskii, «Сравнительно-исторческий метод и сравнительное правоведение» [Comparative-Historical Method and Comparative Law], in O. V. Kresin (ed.). Порівняльне правознавство: Антологія українскої компаративістики XIX-XX століть [Comparative Law: Anthology of Ukrainian Comparativistics XIX-XX Centuries] (2008), p. 208.

22 Max Rheinstein, «Предмет и задачи сравнительного правоведения» [Subject-Matter and Methods of Comparison in Law], in V. A. Tumanov (comp. & transl.), Очерки сравнительного права (Сборник) [Essays on Comparative Law (Collection)] (1981), p. 92.

23 S. Popescu, «Цели и методы сравнения в праве» [Purposes and Methods of Comparison in Law], in Tumanov, note 22 above, p. 204.

24 O. L. Bigich, «Місце порівняльного методу в правовій методології» [Place of the Comparative Method in Legal Methodology], Правова держава [Rule of Law State], vyp. 13 (2002), p. 450.

25 Zweigert and Kötz, note 1 above, p. 21.

26 R. Cotterell, "Comparatists and Sociology", in Legrand and Munday, note 9 above, p. 133.

27 R. Lukich, Методология права [Methodology of Law] (1981).

28 Zh. Stalev, «Сравнительный метод в социалистической правовой науке»

be stressed in principle that the functional reference acquires the form of epistemological optimism – assumptions that comparative law "may escape the need for working out an adequate methodology".[29]

Epistemological optimism determines not only the form, but also the content of the functional reference – the last assumes a theoretical (or substantive) perception of sociological methodological provision for comparative law studies.[30] In so doing, since the functionalism of comparative law "... focuses ... on a particular problem ... [and] is not the province of theorizing, pattern identification or generalizations",[31] it is possible to suppose that this does not in general form an autonomous sphere of theoretical knowledge. In turn, this precludes even the need to substantiate sociology as a theory of a higher level with respect to functionalist comparative law – the link between them turns out, respectively, to be the correlation of theory and practice.

Thus, in comparative legal functionalism the content of referential thought proves to be exceedingly broad – from sociology there is injected not only methodological instrumentation, but also sociological conceptions about the status and the gnosiological characteristics of the subject-matter of knowledge. Comparative legal functionalism turns out to be merely the practical sphere of the application of sociological theory and methodology.

Functionalist Reference as Methodological Positivism. From the philosophical-methodological standpoint, the said theoretical-methodological understanding of a functional reference required adjustments of principle. The functionalist understanding of comparative law as a "manifestation of sociological laws in the sphere of law"[32] is incomplete since sociological laws proper do not exist. Sociological methodology itself lacks autonomy, which is conditioned by the "nonrepeatable localization" of sociology in

---

[Comparative Method in Socialist Legal Science], in V. A. Tumanov (ed.), Сравнительное правоведение: Сборник статей [Comparative Law: Collection of Articles] (1978), p. 28.

29 M. Van Hoecke, "Deep Level Comparative Law", in id, *Epistemology and Methodology of Comparative Law* (2004), p. 173.

30 One of the imperatives of methodology is the assertion that "on the substantive plane theory cannot be the methodological means of scientific research since it is concerned with the subject-matter of research and not to the research procedures relating to this subject-matter". N. N. Tarasov, «Метод и методологический подход в правоведении: попытка проблемного анализа» [Method and Methodological Approach to Jurisprudence: Attempt at a Problem Analysis], Правоведение [Jurisprudence], no. 1 (2001). The sole exception to this rule is the possibility to assert that "each theory of a more general (or abstract) level fulfills the methodological role with respect to a more specific theory, and also to practice". O. G. Danilian (ed.), Философия права [Philosophy of Law: Textbook] (2007), p. 30.

31 Gerber, note 3 above, p. 204.

32 F. V. Taranovskii, «Сравнительное правоведение в конце XIX века» [Comparative Law at the End of the XIX Century], in Kresin, note 21 above, p. 192.

the common space of science, with its pretensions to status of a "social physics" capable in a single disciplinary space of combining natural scientific and humanities cognition by means of the transformation of the second according to the canons of the first.[33]

Thus, since the point of departure for the functionalist program is an implicit affirmative answer to the question of whether the methods used in sciences concerning nature can possibly be applied to explain legal relations, the true sense of the reference style of methodological thought of functionalists assumes a reference not to sociology itself, but through it to natural science methodology as such.[34] Functionalist comparative law proves to be an expression of a draft methodological positivism[35] – an attempt at a natural scientific interpretation of comparative law cognition.

Since natural scientific cognition has to do with laws, that is, affirms a necessary, causal, and universal link,[36] the carrying over by functionalism of similar aspirations in the sphere of comparative law is natural.[37] Based on this, functionalism is understood as an instrument of the scientification of comparative law – the creation of a universal legal science with a unified conceptual apparatus and material, structured according to a

[33] Max Weber said concerning this that sociological theories consist not so much of assertions similar to law as they use the last. Therefore, sociology is more the consumer than the producer of laws. Heinrich Rickert (1863-1936) also did not relegate sociology to socio-humanitarian cognition precisely because it uses the same methods of generalization as the natural science. Therefore Rickert criticized the division of sciences by subject-matter and, referring to sociology, showed that this science concerning society uses those methods which make it more similar to the natural sciences than with the sciences concerning culture. See V. G. Fedotova, et al., Социальные знания и социальные изменения [Social Knowledge and Social Changes] (2001), p. 67.

[34] We completely share the view that the "purpose of functionalism is to ensure the carrying over of the methods of the natural sciences to the social sciences". G. L. Saidler, Юридические доктрины империализма [Legal Doctrines of Imperialism] (1959), p. 129. Consequently, the principal methodological aspiration of functionalism is achieving that state of affairs under which legal analysis would not concede to the precision of natural scientific knowledge. See E. V. Kolomenskaia, «Функциональный подход к исследованию договора»[Functional Approach to Investigation of the Contract], Журнал российского права [Journal of Russian Law], no. 5 (2005), p. 116.

[35] The author uses the concept of "methodological positivism" in G. H. von Wright's interpretation, who pointed to it as a "philosophy defending methodological monism, the mathematical ideal of the scientific and deductive =Nomic conception of scientific explanation". See Georg Henrik von Wright (1916-2003), Логико-философские исследования [Logical-Philosophical Studies] (1986), p. 42.

[36] V. A. Lektorskii, Эпистемология классическая и неклассическая [Classical and Non-Classical Epistemology] (2006), p. 210.

[37] Rheinstein especially, in defining comparative law as an observation and precise science, asserted that it needs laws such as Newton's law of gravity or Gresham's law in economics, laws as they are understood by the natural sciences. M. Rheinstein, "Teaching Tools in Comparative Law", *American Journal of Comparative Law*, I (1952), p. 98.

common scheme which would be supranational in character.[38] Since the substantiation of the last thesis is the assertion that "German physics, Belgian chemistry, or American medicine no longer exist",[39] in our view Legrand is right when he asserts that for functionalism "law emphatically should be more 'like', say, mathematics than, say, art history".[40]

Proceeding from this, the functionalism of comparative law proves to be the basis for the idea of ontological naturalism – the assertion that social phenomena are a continuation of natural ones and fall under the same mechanisms,[41] and that law is a "kind of object totally external to and independent [of judges], and studied, in fact, like other natural objects".[42] Ontological naturalism "must be embodied in methodological naturalism",[43] which also is expressed as the "idea of a unified science encompassing all spheres of existing, universal mathematics".[44]

An understanding of the referential style of functionalist argumentation as attempts to realize the project of methodological positivism in the sphere of comparative legal cognition enables the community of the functionalism of comparative law and that intellectual tradition which may be called a naturalist paradigm to be asserted and which from the philosophical-methodological point of view acts as a classical scientific rationality.[45] Thus, comparative legal functionalism, being subordinate to the spirit of Cartesianism, acts as an instrument of the mathematization of

[38] Zweigert and Kötz, note 1 above, p. 73.

[39] Zweigert and Kötz, note 1 above, p. 27.

[40] P. Legrand, "Comparative Legal Studies and the Matter of Authenticity", *The Journal of Comparative Law*, I, no. 2 (2006), p. 401.

[41] See Samuel, note 15 above, p. 113; Fedotova, note 33 above, pp. 60-61.

[42] M. Zirk-Sadowski, "Legal Epistemology and Transformation of Legal Cultures", in Van Hoecke, note 29 above, p. 22.

[43] Lukich, note 27 above, p. 94.

[44] Tarasov, note 21 above, p. 86. In this respect in order to understand the functionalism of comparative law the suggestion of Edmund Husserl is important "geometry necessarily possesses ... the respective horizon of the geometric future; it acts as such for each geometer endowed with a consciousness (stable, implicit knowledge) of how to behave and cognitive progress in this horizon". E . Husserl, Начало геометрии. Введение Жака Деррида [Origin of Geometry. Introduction of Jacques Derrida] (1996), p. 213. On this proposition rests the assertion of Husserl fundamental for both the system of eidetic phenomenology and for comparative legal cognition, that the natural sciences, being most fully embodied in geometry as an *a priori* horizon in which the progress of any specific science is inscribed from the outset. See Z. A. Sokuler, «Э. Гуссерль о геометрической традиции: к смене парадигм в теории познания» [Edmund Husserl on the Geometric Tradition: To a Change of Paradigm in the Theory of Cognition] in Философия науки [Philosophy of Science (1999), vyp. 5.

[45] This enables an important comment of a methodological nature to be made. The fact is that the "functionalist turn" from essentialism to functionalism, to which Michaels, for example, refers as a source of functionalist thought did not in fact have a paradigmatic nature, but was effectuated within a naturalist paradigm. See Michaels, note 2 above, p. 344.

legal language and legal thought; the contextual language of national legal orders is replaced by mathematical (semantically invariable) language of functional concepts.[46]

A determining distinctive feature of comparative legal functionalism manifest in the modern methodological situation is that thanks to its exclusively referential style of methodological and theoretical argumentation, a fundamentalism is a basic feature. By the fundamentalism of functionalism we understand its ability to illuminate not only classical thought, but also the metaphysical purpose on which this thought is based.

The content of this metaphysical is a determination of the existing as the subject-matter of a concept and truth as the reliability of the concept.[47] And the essence of the mathematical is the essence thereof, that is, the "means of thought which contains within itself a reference to something already known (*tertium comparationis*). As Heidegger noted, "Tά μαθηματα means that when considering the absolute and treating with things, man knows in advance".[48]

This essence of the mathematical determined for all subsequent history of European thought was formulated by Socrates as a "pyramidal" construction of thought. The content of this construction is the requirement "to give a definition to concepts and then determine whether such a concept exists which would be common to them and which concept might be highest so that they are distinguished as lower concepts with respect to it".[49]

The pyramidal (mathematical) model of thought is identical to the construction of a functionalist comparative statement which means that the look similar, that they share a certain common property, that they are

[46] Legrand points to this, characterizing the method of Descartes as a "general mathematization of reality", and observes that "functionalism is actualized in the sphere of comparative legal studies as a version of Cartesianism". P. Legrand, "Paradoxically, Derrida: For a Comparative Legal Studies", *Cardozo Law Review*, XXVII (2005), p. 647. Grosfeld also emphasized that underlying mathematical thought lies the postulate that "mathematical and geometrical concepts as the appropriate instruments to understand and order the world as a cosmos and, therefore, as constituting the core of legal concepts". B. Grosfeld, "Comparatists and Language", in Legrand and Munday, note 9 above, p. 170.

[47] M. Heidegger (1889-1976), «Время картины мира» [Time of Picture of the World], in id, Время и бытие [Being and Time: Articles and Addresses] (1993), p. 48.

[48] Heidegger, note 47 above, p. 43.

[49] V. Shtegmaier, «Жак Деррида: деконструкция европейского мышления. Баланс» [Jacques Derrida: Deconstruction of European Thought. Balance] in V. Shtegmaier, et al. Герменевтика и деконструкция [Hermeneutics and Deconstruction] (Spb., 1999), p. 72. After Socrates, the most significant retranslation of the principle of "tertium comparationis" is by Aristotle (Topics 1, 8, 103 b15) and Thomas Aquinas (Summae Theologiae, 1, Question 3, Section 5, Conclusion). Thanks to them, this logical construction of thought became so embedded that it came to be regarded as reason itself.

a "triadic relation between two objects and a certain quality, the *tertium comparationis*.[50] Therefore, functionalist comparative law within the limits of this pyramidal construction of thought plays an exceedingly important role. In the Plato dialogues with his interlocutors Socrates sought to obtain only acknowledgement of the same reality for all universal knowledge, "functionality pursues uniform elements of thought",[51] using the concept *tertium comparationis* to "ascribe to comparative law studies a logical structure",[52] representing an "nontimely and static point of view".[53]

ERROR OF FUNCTIONALIST REFERENCE

The basic problem and possibility of comparative legal cognition is an awareness that the referential style of methodological and theoretical thought of functionalism cannot fill comparative law with methodological content, making problematic its existence as an autonomous discourse.

Philosophical Problematic Nature of Functionalist Reference. The first reason for this is the transformational processes in philosophical-methodological thought of the twentieth century, which led to the destruction of the classical gnosiology and classical (mathematical-pyramidal) thought as a whole. This destruction was a consequence of transcending the limits of classical thought effectuated by Kurt Gödel's second incompleteness theorem, quantum mechanics, and Heidegger's nonclassical conception of truth as unconcealed.[54]

[50] N. Jansen, "Comparative Law and Comparative Knowledge", in Reimann and Zimmerman, note 2 above, p. 310. Having arisen as a Rabel variation of resolving the problem of qualification, functionalism confronted the task of building a logical pyramid in which the legal solutions for two or more legal orders would correspond to a common denominator (*tertium comparationis*), which unambiguously stipulated to apply the already-known (mathematical) in advance. This stipulation extended to sketches, a draft, of that which should be compared in law in advance of the unknown cognition: a pyramidal construction of thought built according to the model of *tertium comparationis*. Any comparative law study must fine its place within this general scheme introduced as a known fact. Law falls within the field of vision as such only in the horizon of this general scheme. This draft of comparison receives its provision at the expense of the fact that a comparative law study is linked in advance to it at each of its investigative steps.

[51] Plastas, note 5 above, p. 12.

[52] Legrand, note 46 above, p. 649.

[53] Samuel, note 15 above, p. 115.

[54] The new rationality which arose from these three sources led to the transformation of the conceptions concerning the nature of facts. The substance of this transformation lies in the recognition of ontological intervals, and not conceptuality, knowledge, the impossibility of the existence of privileged systems of reporting (absolute truth), the conditional nature of facts as a system of thought, and in consequence, affirmation of the paradigmatic dependence of knowledge. For comparative legal cognition this transformation means confirmation of the conditionality of any description of reality by a conceptual structure of a legal system,

Proceeding from this, the assertion in the contemporary methodological situation by functionalism of the borrowing of a theory and methodology for comparative legal studies from the sociology of law not only fails to substantiate the scientific status thereof and explanatory claims, but, on the contrary, is the most obvious source for criticism of it. The fact is that if an inter-disciplinary theoretical-methodological reference would be possible in general, today it would to correct to speak about the carrying over not of the methodological instrumentation of functionalism from sociology to comparative law, but the criticisms destroying it. The reason is that within the confines of the referent itself (sociology), an erosion of the pivotal idea from which the functionalist world outlook arose and on which it is based is occurring under the influence of the general-scientific process of overcoming classical thought – from the contrast of structure and function. The last, as Shtompkin noted, comprised for more than a hundred years the heart of sociological language, being the "principal sin of sociology".[55]

The mechanism for overcoming functionalism in sociology was launched by two assumptions "of a new paradigm of functional analysis in sociology" posited by Merton: (1) a transition from a monist to a dualist understanding of the nature of function and respective demarcation of clear and latent functions. For comparative law this signifies the impossibility of effectuating one of the major intentions of comparative legal functionalism – the use of law for social engineering;[56] (2) the assertion that resolution of

---

and also the impossibility of a comparatist transcending the limits of legal discourse and, consequently, of a juridically neutral approach to reality insisted upon by functionalism. In view of this, the pivotal idea for functionalism that focusing on practical functions enables the objectivity of facts to be asserted proves to be erroneous, that is, their independence from the methodology of comparative legal research, and that such objectivity makes possible a perception of the phenomenon of law uniform and universal for all legal systems.

55 P. Shtompka, Социология социальных изменений [Sociology of Social Changes] (1996), p. 19. Shtompka noted: "recently sociology cast doubt on the reliability of systemic-organism models of society and the dichotomy of statics and dynamics … Two circumstances are increasingly important: first, the aspiration to concentrate attention on the penetrating properties of social reality, that is, on the perception of society in movement (procedural image), and, second, the aspiration not to regard society as an object, that is, dematerialization of social reality (image of field)". Ibid.., p. 26.

56 The reason for the impossibility of social engineering is that neither the legislator nor the judge by definition can now the latent functions. Rozin pointed out that the cause of the gnosiological bankruptcy of the ideology of social engineering is its ignorance of the distinctions of social reality from phenomena of first nature and effective social action – from engineering activity. The essence of such distinctions lies in the fact that all elements of social action cannot be assigned once and forever; on the contrary, they change as they unfold, are rethought, in the broad sense are reconstituted; social action is directed not only to the achievement of the purposes put, but also to the creation of conditions which enable these purposes to be realized; discourse is the essence of a social action, and not only the substantiation thereof, that is, a substantive discussion of the nature and sense of all its basic elements. See V. M. Rozin, Типы и дискурсы научного мышления [Types and Discourses

the question concerning the level of integration of society and functionality of an institution (in comparative legal functionalism three "functionalist presumptions" correspond to it: the answer of law to the problems of society; the universality of problems, and the identity of the legal solution for identical problems) cannot be assumed *a priori*, but must be established within the limits of a specific empirical study.[57]

Since, as Nagel said, functionalism in sociology proved to be incapable of performing its principal postulate concerning the possibility of value-neutral social science,[58] it has been deprived of its basis. Michaels noted that in sociology there has been a "cultural turn" – "… functionalism made way for cultural and hermeneutic methods …".[59]

Thus, the successive unfolding of the logic of referential thought requires from functionalists either to extend into the sphere of comparative law not only the theory and methodology of functionalism, but also the criticism thereof, or to assert the existence of a unique link between functionalism and comparative law, which makes irrelevant for the last any criticism of functionalism in sociology. It seems to us the acceptance of the first scenario is equivalent to a denial of functionalism, and the second relates to the sphere of teleology, and not methodology, since not reflection, but faith, is required.

Lack of Substance of Functionalist Reference. Reflection of the functionalist reference demon-strates its lack of substance, even from the standpoint of functionalism itself. The fact is that the basic purpose and evidence of the existence of such a reference should be the empirical character of comparative legal research.[60] However, the principal characteristic of functionalism in comparative law is the failure of the empiricism of research to conform to the very requirement postulated by it. Hyland, in describing the state of affairs, expressly indicated that the functionalists avoid an empirical investigation by means of a central premise of functionalist

of Scientific Thought] (2000), p. 136.

57 This means that "functionalist presumptions" must be the subject-matter of reflections and not an *a priori* horizon of comparative legal studies, as happens in functionalism.

58 E. Nagel, "A Formalization of Functionalism", in id, *Logic Without Metaphysics* (1956), p. 247.

59 Michaels, note 2 above, p. 354.

60 As Örücü pointed out, "… a comparative lawyer is expected to describe, juxtapose, identify similarities and differences and then venture into the field of explanation". Örücü, note 13 above, p. 54. Peteri also stresses that "comparison in the social sciences cannot replace experimental cognition". Z. Peteri, «Задачи и методы сравнительного правоведения» [Tasks and Methods of Comparative Law], in Tumanov, note 28 above, p. 80.

studies, asserting that there is an identical solution for practical problems across different legal cultures.[61]

Since functionalists confine themselves to postulating Nomic links between legal phenomena (in the nature of presumptions of the identity of problems, or presumptions of the identity of practical solutions) while refraining from empirical verification,[62] we are concerned with an absorbing phenomenon – on one hand, functionalist comparative law aspired to be sociological, and, on the other, it does not in fact bind itself with a sociological empirical methodology. As a result, it is impossible to determine the reference declared by functionalists is expressing.

It must be emphasized in principle that this dissonance between functionalist declarations and the actual methodological situation testifies not to a rejection of the gnosiological ideal, which may and should be overcome, but to the incorrectness of idealization itself taking the form of the common logical-methodological inadequacy of the functionalism of comparative law.

This logical-methodological inadequacy of functionalism is manifest when analyzing the correlation of the Nomic and empirical in scientific cognition. One may single out positive (problem of induction)[63] and negative (problem of falsification) aspects of their correlation.

Functionalism sees the positive aspect of the correlation as the possibility of verifying the Nomic, that is, affirms the possibility of an empirical substantiation of the laws of comparative legal cognition.[64] The literature on the philosophy of science has long since acknowledged the erroneousness of such a position and, consequently, the impossibility of substantiating and verification of laws of cognition by empirical observations, in particular because the objects which relate to these laws have a logical, and not an empirical, nature.[65] Moving from the sphere of the

[61] Hyland, note 19 above, pp. 188-189.

[62] Brand qualified this strategy of behavior: "they generally fail to discuss how one establishes 'likeness' and 'sameness' as a starting point for comparison". Brand, note 10 above, pp. 417-418.

[63] As Carnap pointed out, the problem of induction arose from the need to answer the question: "on what do we rely when we move from direct observation of facts to a law expressing certain regularities of nature"? Rudolf Carnap (1891-1970), Философские основания физики: Введение в философию науки [Philosophical Foundations of Physics. Introduction to the Philosophy of Science] (2d ed.; 2003), p. 59.

[64] We refer to Zweigert's assertion concerning the empirical origin of the presumption of identity, which he illustrates by examples of an analysis of the binding character of offer in German and Anglo-American law, and registration systems of rights to property under German, French, English, and United States law. See Zweigert and Kötz, note 1 above, pp. 58-59.

[65] See Carnap, note 64 above, p. 307. Lektorskii, note 36 above, p. 136; G. Samuel, "Epistemology and Methodology of Comparative Law: Contribution from the Sciences and

empirical to the sphere of the Nomic is possible only in the negative aspect. Carnap noted this: "although a means does not exist with the assistance of which it would be possible to verify a law, means do exist with whose assistance we can refute it. To do so one must find one instance which is contrary to it".[66]

In comparative legal functionalism, however, the empirical inadequacy acquires a special content – we refer not to the presence of specific empirical instances which would refute it, but to the impossibility of indicating any empirical instances which it confirmed.[67] This means that the empirical inadequacy of functionalism excludes the possibility of the falsification thereof. It is ironic that from the standpoint of methodology this casts doubt on the scientific status of the functionalism of comparative law.

Methodological Impossibility of Functionalist Reference. The functionalist reference also proves to be methodologically incorrect insofar as it is not coordinated with the concept of methodological transmission. The last also investigates the question of interdisciplinary methodological influence and the influence of metascientific spheres on disciplinary ones.

Unlike the functionalist reference, which allows the formation of a methodology of comparative legal studies by means of a simple indication of its affiliation to an external methodological tradition (sociology as a stage of the development of the naturalist paradigm), methodological transmission assumes the possibility of the *adaptive* and *transforming* carrying over only of schemes of methodological thought formalized in respective methodological approaches. This means that a correct understanding of methodological transmission in general excludes the possibility of interdisciplinary movement of the methodological instrumentation.[68]

Since methodological approaches involve particular schemes of scientific thought, the influence of methodologies of other disciplines or

---

Social Sciences", in Van Hoecke , note 29 above, p. 45.

[66] Carnap, note 63 above, p. 61. Also see Samuel: "actual facts may be relevant in the falsification of a theory". Samuel, note 65 above, p. 45.

[67] A demonstration of the empirical inadequacy of functionalism is Legrand's analysis of the presumption of the identity of problems using the example of the problem of pre-contractual information in England and France. In formulating the conditions (Legrand points to twelve conditions, separately stipulating their nonexhaustive character) which a comparatist must take into account in order to properly establish the identity of the problem of pre-contractual information in these two countries, the author concludes that "even in advance of empirical study, I argue that the sameness that is postulated is simply unrealistic". Legrand, "The Same and the Different", in Legrand and Munday, note 9 above, p. 275.

[68] Such movement obstructs the major purpose of considering science in an inseparable link with its subject-matter and method, as a consequence of which method belongs only to a particular science and works only within the limits of its subject-matter, and this means also is not carried over to the subject-matter of another science. See Tarasov, note 30 above.

metascientific spheres on the methodology of jurisprudence is exercised intermediately. The conversion of such schemes of thought into the research instrumentation of jurisprudence (including – comparative law) acts as a result of internal processes emanating in legal science itself and is based on referential thinking of the research experiment.

Thus, a referential construction of functionalism excludes the formation of an adequate methodological provision for comparative law studies. The forming and reflection of such methodological provision may be effectuated solely within the limits of comparative law itself, requiring a constitutive and not a referential purpose for methodological thought.

Functionalism – Disciplinary Paradigm of Biology. Finally, functionalism cannot be transmitted into comparative law since it is not a scheme of methodological thought capable of trans-disciplinary movement. The fact is that in the modern philosophy of science the circumstance is recognized that functionalism may be adequate only if it can be regarded as a legitimate means of research. It is vital in principle that such legitimation be accomplished by means of reducing function to an adaptation to concepts of natural selection and, consequently, confining its applicability to biology.[69]

Such reduction is an attempt to demonstrate the "metaphysical purity" of functions. Sober noted that "if function is understood to mean adaptation, then it is clear enough what the concept means. If a scientist or philosopher uses the concept of function in some other way, we should demand that the concept be clarified".[70]

Reduction and, in essence, the elimination of function to adaptation as the sole possible means of retaining its scientific status and substance has defining significance. It turns out that functionalism may have methodological-theoretical significance only on condition of the recognition of its disciplinary status exclusively within the limits of biology.[71]

[69] McLaughlin pointed out that "... the philosophical literature on natural functions emerged after the definitive work of C. G. Hempel and E. Nagel in the early 1960s has concentrated almost exclusively on biological examples to the neglect of social science, and the followers of Hempel also show a strong tendency to favor an analysis of functional explanation in terms of natural selection that can apply only to biology". P. McLaughlin, *What Functions Explain: Functional Explanation and Self-Reproducing Systems* (2007), p. 80. Similarly, in the modern philosophy of science Alexander Rosenberg, on one hand, stressed the erroneousness of delegitimating functional explanations in biology and, on the other, discarding any explanatory value of functional explanations in the social sciences. See A. Rosenberg, *Philosophy of Social Science* (1988), p. 133.

[70] E. Sober, *The Philosophy of Biology* (1993), p. 86.

[71] Such judgments are called in the literature "an argument for the absence of a mechanism". P. Pettit, "Functional Explanations and Virtual Selections", *British Journal for the Philosophy of Science*, XLVII (1996), p. 291. Jon Elster says that "natural selection offers itself as a feedback

CONCLUSION

The foregoing enables one to state that the referential construction of functionalist argumentation is completely unable to occupy the sphere of comparative legal discourse adequate to its nature with theoretical and methodological content. Michaels statement in this connection is illustrative: "This functional method is a chimera, in both theory and practice of comparative law".[72] If one concurs with the aforesaid metaphor of the overgrown garden as an image of modern comparative law, the principal task of comparatists becomes activity which would cultivate it. The need to cultivate the garden answers the appeal of Samuel to seriously address issues of methodology. However, his understanding of a serious attitude towards methodology as "sold grounds in the history and constructions of law as a discipline, and also in epistemology and methodology of sciences and the social sciences" in our view is a half-measure and does not fully respond to the appeal confronting comparative law in the modern intellectual era.[73]

For us, a serious attitude towards methodology is a change of conceptions concerning the correlation of philosophical-methodological and comparative legal cognition. Such a change is formalized by us as a transition from the fundamental nature of comparative legal cognition to its foundation-formation. The content of this approach lies in an awareness of the impossibility of substantiating comparative legal knowledge by a reference to some external *a priori* basis which can never be reflected. Instead, the constant regeneration of grounds for comparative legal cognition by this cognition itself is essential, that is, the incorporation of this into the subject-matter of scientific reflection. Thus, foundation-formation assumes an understanding of the grounds of cognition as signs, the meaning of which exists only in discourse, are not stationary but dynamic, affirmed by semantic improvement and advance in shades of meaning.

A change in the referential style of thought to constitutive is the methodological correlative of this gnosiological schism of fundamentality and foundation-formation. The substantive component of constitutiveness encompasses: first, "metadigmal" interpretation of the methodological reflection of comparative law, according to which it must encompass

---

mechanism that can explain why the effects of tokens of a particular type can be causally relevant for the existence of other tokens of the same type at a later time. Because there is no comparable mechanism generally available in the social sciences, functional explanations must remain mysterious and therefore ought not to be advanced ...The metaphysical price is said to be too high". McLaughlin, ibid., p. 93.

[72] Michaels, note 2 above, p. 340.

[73] Samuel, note 15 above, p. 237.

all levels of methodology, including philosophical; second, disciplinary limitation of such methodological reflection.

Thus, the modern criterion for the existence of autonomous discourse becomes the possibility to effectuate therein, by its means and in its interests, a special philosophical-methodological comprehension of the foundations of cognition. In our view, such a forming of the philosophical-methodological content of comparative law is possible, in particular, by means of the reflection of the circular construction of comparison proposed by Legrand.[74]

[74] P. Legrand, "Comparing in Circles", in P. Nicholson and S. Biddulph (eds.), *Examining Practice, Interrogating Theory: Comparative Legal Studies in Asia* (2008), pp. 6-8.

Comparative Law and the Integrating Role of International Law

IU. A. TIKHOMIROV*

Under conditions of globalization the role of legal integration is growing. Comparative law is successfully fulfilling this role. However, not all legal means are treated and used systemically. To some degree the international legal block is "disappearing" in the general mechanism of comparative law. Recognition of the enormous role of international law is so far not accompanied by the full incorporation of its instruments in the comparative legal context, which as before emanates from recognition of the parallel development of national legal systems and methods of their study. The root cause is concealed in the traditional treatment of comparative law.

René David (1906-1991), who substantiated the subject-matter and basic concepts thereof, may be regarded as the founder of the theory of comparative law.[1] The typology of legal systems as legal families is based on historical-cultural and political-ideological criteria and with the recognition of the socialist legal family in earlier editions. Ancel,[2] Zweigert and Kötz,[3] and others continued studies in this direction. The American

* доктор юридических наук, профессор, Заслуженный деятель науки РФ; Associate, International Academy of Comparative Law; First Deputy Director, Institute of Legislation and Comparative Law attached to the Government of the Russian Federation.

1 R. David and C. Jauffret-Spinosi, Основные правовые системы современности [Basic Legal Systems of Modern Times] (1996).

2 See M. Ancel, «Методологические проблемы сравнительного правоведения» [Methodological Problems of Comparative Law] in V. A. Tumanov (ed.), Очерки сравнительного права [Essays on Comparative Law] (1981).

3 See K. Zweigert and H. Kötz, Введение в сравнительное правоведение в сфере частного права [Introduction to Comparative Law in the Sphere of Private Law] (2000). 2 vols.

professor, Osakwe, separates out the General Part and the Special Part in comparative law.[4]

The International Academy of Comparative Law has long held a stable position. The congresses held once every four years reflect the interests of comparatists of the world towards traditional and new legal topics. On the agenda of the XVII Congress (July 2006) were such topics as constitutional guarantees of justice, precedent and law, referendum, responsibility of judges, limits of the law of ownership, legal status of migrants, legal machinery for eliminating corruption in public service, the formation of a European constitutional law, and others.

In Russian doctrinal writings of the 1960-80s works appeared on socialist comparative law (Tille, Tumanov, and others).

It is noteworthy that in years past and now textbooks on the theory of State and law allocated chapters to the basic legal systems of modern times. Their content is elicited through the concept of a "legal family", which encompasses the aggregate of national legal systems with similar sources of law, concepts, branches, and moral-religious roots.[5] In another definition a legal system represents an integral complex conditioned by objective laws of societal development having mutually-dependent and agreed special and general legal means of legal impact on social relations.[6] But in all instances the treatment of the problems of the theory of law is in parallel with the characteristics of foreign legal systems.

During the past decade and a half special works on comparative law have appeared distinguished primarily by one criterion – that comparative law is a scientific method or a scientific discipline. They consider issues of the history, methodology, and functions of comparative law and the criteria for and types of legal systems. The level of comparison is either a national legal system as a whole, or a branch thereof.[7] An analysis of the correlation of national and international law is being introduced not without our influence. The "choice" of legal systems is approximately the same, although in certain works there is an interest in the socialist family and post-Soviet legal systems. A "satiation" with the philosophical and culturological aspects is noticeable.[8]

[4] C. Osakwe, Сравнительное правоведение в схемах: общая и особенная части [Comparative Law in Diagrams: General and Special Parts] (2002).

[5] See Теория государства и права [Theory of State and Law] (2006), pp. 587-614.

[6] See O. F. Skakun, Теория государства и права: Энциклопедический курс [Theory of State and Law. Encyclopedic Cours] (Kharkov, 2005), pp. 326-384.

[7] See A. Kh. Saidov, *Comparative Law*, transl. W. E. Butler (2003); M. N. Marchenko, Сравнительное правоведение: Общая часть [Comparative Law: General Part] (2006).

[8] A. D. Tikhomirov, Юридическая компаративистика. Философские, теоретические и методологические проблемы [Legal Comparativistics. Philosophical, Theoretical, and

During the past decade there has been a transition from raising general questions to a comparative analysis more subject-oriented – branches of law, by country, the institutional principle.[9] New journals have emerged – the Журнал зарубежного законодательства и сравнительного правоведения [Journal of Foreign Legislation and Comparative Law], the Ежегодник сравнительного правоведения [Yearbook of Comparative Law], and, in Ukrainian, Порівняльно-правові дослідження [Comparative Law Research] (Kiev), among others.

The development of research in the field of comparative law is welcome. But the concept of "legal system" is treated too narrowly. The instrumental-methods aspect does not suffice when means of analysis, comparison, evaluation are elaborated, and conclusions of the study and practical proposals are presented. The accent is placed primarily on contrasting laws, leaving other phenomena of legal life in the shadows. Jurisprudence is not a synonym of law in the strictly normative sense; it embraces all sources of law, State and other institutions, legal institutions, law-application, legal education, and science.

Proceeding from this, the present writer proposed a broader spectrum for the elements of the legal system being investigated and introduced the norms of international organizations and inter-State associations as a type of common denominator, as a criterion, as an accelerator of the coming together of national legal systems.[10]

In another work a scheme was used for structuring a book of the Kluwer Publishing House, when legal and institutional elements were considered and the means of comparison, coming together, harmonization, and unification of norms of various legal systems. An analysis of the development of public and private law and branches of Russian law encompassed by them is given in contrast with the respective branches of foreign law.[11] A stricter subject-matter-instrumental comparison was achieved by this.

Methodological Problems] (Kiev, 2005).

9 See I. Ia. Kiselev, Сравнительное трудовое право [Comparative Labor Law] (2005); Основные институты гражданского права зарубежных стран: Сравнительно-правовое исследование [Basic Institutes of Civil Law of Foreign Countries: Comparative Law Study] (1999); A. A. Malinovskii, Сравнительное правоведение в сфере уголовного права [Comparative Law in the Sphere of Criminal Law] (2002); Административное право зарубежных стран [Administrative Law of Foreign Countries] (2003); Институты конституционного права зарубежных стран [Institutes of Constitutional Law of Foreign Countries] (2004); Saidov, Национальные парламенты мира [National Parliaments of the World] (2005).

10 Iu. A. Tikhomirov, Курс сравнительного правоведения [Cours of Comparative Law] (1996).

11 Iu. A. Tikhomirov and E. V. Talapina, Введение в российское право [Introduction to

Continuing to develop this conception, this writer suggests that it is advisable to alter the appearance of certain concepts within comparative law. While retaining as the base object the concept of "legal system", it is possible, first, to refrain from identifying it with the concept of "legal family", which has more stable historical-culturological roots. Second, the group of objects of study should be expanded by relegating four types of macro-legal systems to them – the national legal family, the legal family, the legal system of inter-State associations, and systems of international law. A change in the vectors of attraction is occurring – together with "paired" comparisons the role of "multi-limbed comparisons" is growing. In this way one may speak about the modern legal map of the world, where the boundaries and intersecting of systems are evident.

These are macro-levels of comparative legal analysis. The second block thereof comprises: (a) legal norms; (b) laws and other legal acts; (c) legal institutes; (d) sub-branches of legislation; (e) branches of legislation; (f) legal masses; (g) systems of legislation; (h) subject-matter and methods of legal regulation; (i) legal concepts and terms; (j) legal technique. The third block is situational-targeted, when new legal solutions are sought for transnational projects, and so on. In the fourth block or group of comparison one may single out: (a) legal conceptions; (b) legal consciousness; (c) legal culture; (d) lawful and unlawful behavior. The fifth block encompasses: (a) legal education; (b) legal profession. The sixth block includes State and social institutions mediated by law.

The autonomous and "intersecting" existence of the said objects of analysis is a mysterious tangle which should inspire scholars and practitioners to disentangle it. Comparison may be voluntary at the discretion of any country, arise from its contractual obligations with another country, or from obligations of membership in an international structure.

What are the typical legal differences of national legislation? An analysis within the framework of comparative law to a great extent predetermines its functions – informational, analytical, critical. They provide a special-purpose orientation and program of study, contrasting, evaluating, and preparing conclusions and proposals. We refer to the complex cognitive-analytical process. Legal distinctions are not identical in their nature or from the standpoint of possibilities to overcome them. One may speak of temporary and long-term distinctions and about distinctions ineradicable even in the remote future.

Legal distinctions may be:

Russian Law] (2003).

(a) material – for example, certain dogmas of Islamic law, in particular, the principle of the Constitution of Iran: "Recognition of the Last Judgment";
(b) theoretical – for example, the predominance of procedural institutions and norms in administrative law of the United States and Germany, and the concept of public services in the public law of France;
(c) systems and branches of law different in structure – for example, in Israel there is no Constitution and codes, eleven Basic Laws operate, and in Germany there is no labor code among the sources of labor law;
(d) dissimilar forms of codification – for example, in France codes include non-legislative norms, and in Ukraine civil and economic codes co-exist;
(e) specific concepts and terms;
(f) the specific nature of concrete legal institutions and norms and legal solutions – for example, in the ecological law of Germany the accent is placed on stimulation, and in the Criminal Code of Sweden electronic control is provided for over persons sentenced to not more than two months of imprisonment;
(g) the distinctive features of legal technique and structuring of laws;
(h) various paces of innovation – for example, in Ukraine a Code of Administrative Procedure has been adopted; in Kazakhstan a Law on Administrative Procedures is in force; in Belarus administrative justice is being developed. Russia is merely planning the innovation;
(i) contrastive State institutions.

With regard to identifying and evaluating legal differences and overcoming them, in addition to the cognitive aspects there is the activeness aspect. Depending upon the purposes which confront States, the rates and level of their political, economic, and social development, and the character of international relations, legal links are formed with other States. National branches of legislative are modified accordingly. Military-political cooperation (pacts, alliances, and so on) "gravitate" towards a change of certain norms and institutions of constitutional and administrative law. The accelerated and large-scale economic integration encourages the legislation on companies, transport, customs, technical rules and regulations, and so on to become identical more rapidly. Other branches develop as before with minor changes or await "their time".

Membership in international and inter-State structures and their norms exerts a strong influence.

I

The integrating role of international law with respect to national legal systems is reflected in ensuring their "inclusion" in the resolution of such problems of the world community as ensuring security, ecological equilibrium, economic growth, and others. This is achieved through the introduction of general normative orientators and rules of legal regulation and by means of coordinating the activities of State and non-State structures. The hierarchal nature of principles and norms of international law should be taken into account in full, reflected both as the correlation thereof between themselves and the unequal radius and extent of influence on national law.[12] Treaty obligations signify equal requirements for the parties to adjust their own legislation. Model laws form examples of national laws. Functional standards sharply prescribe compliance with specific prescriptions and normative standards. The role of recommendatory resolutions is appreciable.

The general trend is remarkable that certain major principles of development of both States and the world community recognized in national and international law are coming together. The principle of sovereignty of people and the State, the principle of territorial integrity, the principle of equality and self-determination of peoples. The principle of ensuring human rights and basic freedoms, the principle of sustainable development and well-being, and the principle of democratism have been consolidated in the constitutions and laws of virtually all States of Europe, Latin America, Africa, and Asia, on one hand, and in international documents such as the United Nations Charter, treaties on the creation of the European Union, Commonwealth of Independent States, Eurasian Economic Community, international covenants on human rights, and others, on the other hand.

The question is how to combine legal and other means of the guarantees thereof and to ensure both the practical actions of States and international structures. Regrettably one observes with regard to the last approval or tacit consent to violations of internal principles by external actions.

The mechanism of comparative legal analysis and overcoming differences in national legislation is therefore important. We proceed from the fact that the first part thereof contains programmatically-ensuring means – agreeing of scientific legal conceptions; programs for the harmonization of national legislation; treaties on legal cooperation; agreements on legal

[12] See Курс международного права в семи томах [Cours of International Law in Seven Volumes] (1989), pp. 182-219.

assistance; consulting; exchange of informational surveys; procedures for agreeing national programs of draft law activity.

The second part encompasses the complex of such legal means as joint and coordinated legal actions and measures; fulfillment of common obligations of States in accordance with international acts and treaties; drawing up a general dictionary of terms and concepts (glossary); a common or extended legal regime (investing, taxation, and others); recognized equal extent of rights of subjects (investors, entrepreneurs, and others); model laws; unified acts; uniform norms (or servicing), and so on; uniform standards; equalization of levels of legal security (pensions and others); recognition of legal documents (diplomas on education, and others); introduction of simplified procedure (acquisition of citizenship, and so on); equal legal defense of subjects; permitted legal privileges and incentives; extension of sanctions. A special role belongs to international legal means in this mechanism.

An international legal block is essential in the mechanism of comparative law for several reasons. The expanding integration of States in the economic, scientific-technical, informational, trade, ecological, and social spheres imposes new and higher requirements for the coordination thereof and uniform activities. There are few "paired" arrangements, strict "carrying over" of legal experience, or verbatim copying of another's norms. Various forms of carrying over law – subordination, assimilation, adoption of a foreign model – depends both upon political and other purposes and upon the specific nature of the culture and traditions of a country.[13]

The noted German jurist, Kniper, justly criticizes the practice of "throwing" norms and institutes through the efforts of consultants and foundations without having regard to the extensive legal context and specific features of countries.[14] Some former socialist countries were convinced of this. The generally-recognized objectivity of international legal solutions found in public procedures enables such contradictions to be avoided.

But it is appropriate to note that international lawyers consider the topic of the correlation of international and national law to be "theirs", losing from sight all aspects of internal law. Lawyers specializing in branches of law do not consider links with international norms anything

[13] Norbert Rouland, Историческое введение в право [Historical Introduction to Law] (2005), pp. 360-406.

[14] R. Kniper, «Возможности и границы сотрудничества в области права с точки зрения зарубежного консультанта» [Possibilities and Limits of Cooperation in Domain of Law from Standpoint of Foreign Consultant], Журнал зарубежного законодательства и сравнительного правоведения [Journal of Foreign Legislation and Comparative Law], no. 4 (2007).

more than fragments of their branches. Often instead of comparative analysis information is merely given on foreign law,[15] and the criteria for the influence of international legal norms are not set out precisely.[16]

A turning point in the complex analysis must be "made" within the framework of the theory of State and law and all branches of law simultaneously. One of the early attempts in this direction is a book on the results of the II International Practical School of Legal Scholars held on 24-26 May 2007.[17]

II

What is the strain of the influence of international law on national legal systems? In concise form one may speak about the conceptual impact of humanist and peaceloving principles and norms of international law furthering the formation of the peace-minded worldview of people and the actions of States in this direction.

The role of international legal principles recognized by States as binding in their coordinated and joint activities is rather significant. They have been consolidated in the United Nations Charter, declarations, and elsewhere.

We especially single out the adoption and application as normative orientators model legal acts of the Bustamante Code type, uniform laws and unified rules,[18] codes of entrepreneurship and business ethics, and model laws of the Inter-Parliamentary Assembly of the Commonwealth of Independent States and Eurasian Economic Community.

We note the direct or indirect use of norms of international legal acts in order to create similar or homogeneous norms and institutes of national legislation. This simulating impact is especially noticeable in the process of the realization of the 1985 European Charter of Local Government and the 1950 European Convention for the Protection of Human Rights and Fundamental Freedoms.

Means of encouraging gaps in national legislation to be filled are useful. Uniform functional regulations of the ecological standards type, technical regulations for the operation of aircraft and motor vehicles, standards for

15 See, for example, V. N. Shapoval, Сравнительное конституционное право [Comparative Constitutional Law] (Kiev, 2007).

16 See, for example, E. A. Vystorobets, Экологическое право. Мотивации в международном сотрудничестве [Ecological Law. Motivations in International Cooperation] (2006).

17 See Влияние международного права на национальное законодательство [Influence of International Law on National Legislation] (2007).

18 T. P. Lazareva, Международное торговое право. Расчеты по контрактам [International Trade Law: Settlements of Accounts Under Contracts] (2003).

petrol and diesel fuel, the strict rules of the World Health Organization, International Labor Organization (ILO), and other international organizations are extensively utilized. They have no legal alternatives; otherwise, sanctions would be applied.

We note the application of ILO, UNESCO, and other recommendations containing a normative orientation for law-creation and law-application in national States in the domains of education, culture, labor, and others. The gradual formation is occurring of international branch law introducing in concentrated form standard concepts, principles, institutes, and procedures contained in branches of national law. These include international economic law, international banking law, international criminal law, and others.

The formation of similar law-application practice, especially in courts, is of importance.

It is not difficult to note that many international means concern all or almost all countries. Others in greater measure concern legal systems encompassing respective inter-State associations (European Union, Eurasian Economic Community, Organization of African Unity, World Trade Organization, and others). For the last greater structuring of own legal acts and stronger influence on national legal systems of member-States is characteristic.

We turn to the domain of legal provision for technical regulation in the Commonwealth of Independent States (CIS). It is developing at various rates in various countries. Laws on technical regulation have been adopted in Moldova, Kazakhstan, Kirgizia, and Russia; in Azerbaidzhan – a Law on Safety Technical Safety; in Ukraine – a Law on Standards, Technical Reglaments, and Procedure for Evaluating Conformity". A Statute on Technical Regulation is being drafted in Tadzhikistan. The objects of technical regulation in these countries do not always correspond to the European Convention. With a view to eliminating technical barriers when engaging in trade and ensuring free circulation of products on the market the CIS on 21 November 2007 at an enlarged session of the Committee of the Soviet of the Federation of the Federal Assembly of the Russian Federation approved a draft Conception of Technical Regulation in Countries of the Commonwealth. The terms, principles of harmonizing national legislation, coordination, and stages of work are the elements of this Conception.

III

The fulfillment of international obligations by States is a major imperative for their activities. Whereas in the past a State acted while being guided only by the principle of good faith and freely resolved the issue of the applicability of international treaties in domestic law, now domestic law extensively regulates the means of implementation.[19] Scholars single out three groups of States – those realizing international obligations by means of material incorporation, those adhering to the principle of formal (or procedural) incorporation, and those automatically integrating international treaties into national legal systems. A comparative analysis of municipal procedures to express consent to the bindingness of international treaties, the agencies called upon to express such consent, and the procedure for the realization of international obligations in the national legal system has been very fruitful.[20]

Worthy of note is that the principle of sovereignty and sovereign equality of States, the basic principles of legal systems, and the possibilities of States taking proper legislative and administrative measures are noted in many international legal documents specially. This is explained by the primary status of national-State institutes – as a consequence of constitutional law of States to transfer to inter-State structures part of their powers in accordance with international treaties if this is not contrary to the foundations of the constitutional law of the country. This is a vital condition.

Without touching upon the vast complex of issues of implementation, we mention comparativistic aspects. We observe here: the free determination of the time of ratification or approval of international treaties, which sometimes creates undesirable time breaks in the actions of States and the making of changes in their legal systems. We note the free choice by States of the forms of legal acts which they adopt and change. The determination of the types of State agencies which are assigned to fulfill international obligations occurs variously. And one is struck by the varying real extent of norms subject to implementation when some countries either slowly or incompletely realize them, or they remain without legal consequences entirely. One cannot agree with the practice of applying so-called double standards to assessing the degree and nature of the fulfillment by individual States of their international obligations – the "forgiveness" of some and severe criticism and even sanctions against others. Where is the equality?

The problem of law-application is no less important on the international than on the national-State level. Recognition of this requires overcoming the "normative fetishism" and orientation in the activity of all international. State, and non-State structures towards undeviating fulfillment of

[19] I. I. Lukashuk, «Внутреннее право государства и соблюдение международного договора» [Domestic Law of a State and Compliance with an International Treaty], Юрист-международник [International Lawyer], no. 3 (2004).

[20] B. I. Osminin, Принятие и реализация государствами международных договорных обязательств [Adoption and Realization by States of International Treaty Obligations] (2006).

normative arrangements and own acts. Thus, delay in the ratification of treaties and agreements concluded, in bringing national legislation into conformity with the norms thereof, weak fulfillment of decisions of the Council of Heads of States of the CIS and Inter-Parliamentary Assembly of the CIS on the creation of a free trade zone, on the procedure for customs formalization, and customs control of goods moving between States-Parties to the Agreement on the Creation of a Free Zone tells negatively on the level of development of the economies of the Commonwealth countries. In general the 200 model laws of the CIS are being realized weakly since the executive organs of States are not fully orientated in this direction.

International structures undertake monitoring over the fulfillment of national procedures and actions. An example is the comparative analysis of legislation in the struggle against corruption. Attaching importance to overcoming this phenomenon on a world scale, the United Nations adopted on 31 October 2003 the Convention against Corruption. We also note the Council of Europe on Criminal Law Convention on Corruption of 27 January 1999. The Group of States against Corruption (GRECO) operates, of which Russia, Ukraine, and other countries are members. Ratification of these conventions required serious changes in various branches of legislation, searches for solutions to questions concerning a public official, responsibility of juridical persons, a national anti-corruption agency, and others. The replies of countries to questionnaires of GRECO, monitoring of changes, reports of States, study of evaluation missions of GRECO, changes in travel to States, reports concerning the conformity of changes to international standards, publicity of information, recommendations, and again monitoring. Such is the cycle.

IV

Special attention should be drawn to the new trend in the development of international law: its national-legal institutionalization. Whereas in past centuries primarily the external interests of States in the form of political, military, and trade treaties were reflected within the framework of international law, during the past half-century the law-forming role of national systems in international law is noticeably growing. A significant part of its principles and institutions have been "brought in" from national legal systems and reflect the best and stable experience of a number of or many States with regard to local self-government, elections, courts, entrepreneurial structures, and so on. The generalization and concentration of national-legal regulators lead next to their "return" in the form of international principles and norms to the "bosom" of national legal systems. This cycle is becoming typical and reflects the closer link of domestic and international law. The primacy of the principle of the sovereignty of nations, peoples, and States is reflected therein and simultaneously the recognition permitted by constitutions of the priority of international norms in the respective spheres. But there are extreme forms of the exaggeration of national-legal interests.

In the United States drafts in recent years of "Global Governance and Global Administrative Law in the International Legal Order" have been undertaken which contain a number of radical provisions. Globalization and the emergence of global governance are transforming the structure of international law. Differences between municipal and international law are becoming less substantiated, and soft forms of creating norms are becoming more widespread; the sovereign equality of States is gradually being undermined, and the grounds for the legitimacy of international law is to a greater degree becoming doubtful.

Global administrative law means that the greater part of global management may be understood as regulation and administration. Global administrative space is being generated in which the strict dichotomy (or separation) between municipal and international law is to a great extent being disturbed and administrative functions are being effectuated often in a complex interaction between officials and institutions.

It is being asserted that international law is becoming obsolete thanks to the spontaneous system of legal force of resolutions and decisions of the United Nations General Assembly and Security Council recognized and not recognized by the States thereof. A global administrative order within the framework of global administrative space means a broader, more mobile, legal formation responsive to modern requirements, harmoniously intertwined in law, politics, the economy, culture, and other spheres of social relations which are not based on sovereign equality of States, as is international law, but are distinctive for transparency, multi-functionality, and adaptiveness not only to public law, but also to private law institutes. New forms of global administrative law will be the results of the consolidation of international, municipal, and administrative law, a means for the emergence of new "conglomerate norms". These "conglomerate norms" may emerge from the implementation of norms not only of international law in municipal law, but, on the contrary, in the implementation of norms of global administrative management in the system of international law.[21]

[21] *European Journal of International Law*, XVII (2006); *Law and Contemporary Problems*, LXVIII (2005).

As is evident, on the scientific and political levels the accent is on the "dissolution" of the State as a system, on the transfer of its functions to commercial structures and to supranational institutions. Specialized norms of "agencies" have priority. A theoretical foundation is thereby laid under any arbitrary actions in the international arena in the interests of a super-State and transnational corporations.

However, the question is whether national and international interests are correctly understood and realized. Legal provision for their harmonious combination is an urgent task,[22] although deviations from the legal model are all too obvious.

The practical "way out" of this and similar theories is the stability of sovereign States. The sharp actions of the United States and its allies against Yugoslavia and Iraq, the effort to break up Serbia and to institutionalize Kosovo break down world order and violate principles of international and constitutional law under the flag or priority of fictitious national interest, or the defense of human rights and prevention of a nuclear threat.

CONCLUSIONS

First, there is a trend towards the growing influence of international law on national law and the mechanism of comparative law. Second, the application of international-legal criteria for comparison and evaluation of national systems, branches, and institutes of law and individual laws and subordinate acts is called upon to harmonize the legal regulators of national and global processes. Third, the issue of a correct understanding and application of international legal principles and the character and limits of the influence of national interests is acquiring special urgency. Substantial scholarly studies are needed in this domain which would enable the dynamics of public and private law regulators of social processes to be forecast.

[22] Правовое обеспечение национальных интересов [Legal Provision for National Interests] (2005).

Comparative Legal Research in an Era of Globalization

KH. N. BEKHRUZ*

GLOBALIZATION: GENERAL CHARACTERISTICS

The contemporary stage of the development of civilization is conditioned by the inter-linkage and interdependence of all spheres of the life of society. This process also intensifies the interdependence of peoples, States, public institutions and movements, and separate individuals residing and existing within the framework of various civilizations.

A multitude of factors are facilitating the processes of inter-linkage and inter-penetration, especially the new conditions of the existence of mankind creating the real prerequisites for the joint activity of peoples acting outside the framework of national States, socio-cultural spaces, and religious convictions. The aforesaid processes also reflect the essence of globalization, which is the most widespread concept in the modern lexicon of not only politicians and economists, but also ecologists, jurists, and others.

The theoretical comprehension of the phenomena and globalization trends requires a new approach enabling the potential to be mobilized of various civilizations in resolving the problems confronting mankind.

A significant number of scholarly works analyzing the problems which mankind faces at the modern stage of development are furthering a proper understanding of globalization and the societal laws and trends of development in national and international legal consciousness. This also has great practical significance connected with the future of not only individual States, but mankind as a whole.

*доктор юридических наук, professor, Chair of Law of the European Union and Comparative Law, Odessa National Legal Academy.

Various views exist as to when the process of globalization commenced: from times ancient, in the era of the Hansa Union, or only after the Second World War, or under conditions of a comprehensive liberalization of world trade. In the interpretation of Manfred Steger, the first (pre-historical) period of globalization encompassed the fifth to third millennia B.C.; the second – fifteen centuries A.D. (early globalization); the third from 1500 to 1700 (pre-modern globalization); the fourth, 1700 to 1970 (modern globalization). And the fifth (contemporary), dates from the 1970s to today. Another view holds that the process of globalization and, accordingly, the concept of globalization itself were first formulated in an article by an American: T. Levitt, "The Globalization of Markets", *Harvard Business Review*, LXI, no. 3 (1983), pp. 92-102. By virtue of the interdependence of States one may say that the roots of globalization processes extend deep into history, but all the same, globalization is a phenomenon of the twentieth century which became an object of comprehensive scientific studies in recent decades.[1]

In the view of some authors, the term "globalization" received extensive currency during the 1980s thanks to the work of Immanuel Wallerstein (b. 1930). In his three-volume work *The Modern World-System* (1974-89), written from Neo-Marxian positions, he considers globalization to be a new stage in the development of capitalism, as a new strategy for the subordination of some countries to others. This posing of the issue, not openly contested by anyone, naturally could not be supported by all social scientists by reason of their being involved in various socio-political forces of the modern world.[2]

Common in the various conceptions of globalization is that they explain it as a modern form of the internationalization of economic life. Fisher considers the globalization of world economic relations to be: first, the scope of the world economy and world economic relations as a single whole; second, the interlinkage and interdependence of all spheres, components, and forms of world economic relations; third, of principled importance at the contemporary stage is the interaction of world economic relations with other components, spheres, and forms of international relations (political, social, legal, moral, cultural, aesthetic, religious, and others).[3]

[1] R. F. Khabirov, «Глобализации, государственный суверенитет, права человека» [Globalization, State Sovereignty, Human Rights], Юридический мир [Legal World], no. 10 (2007), p. 45.

[2] V. P. Kultygin, «Незападные концепции глобализации» [Non-Western Conceptions of Globalization], in Личность. Культура. Общество [Individual. Culture. Society] (2002), nos. 1-2, p. 80.

[3] G. Fisher, Глобализация мирохозяйственных связей: сущность, формы, перспективы [Globalization of World Economic Ties: Essence, Forms, Perspectives] (1999), p. 10.

Globalization is indeed a stage of internationalization, but a qualitatively new stage thereof. This is a process of forming a global human community connected with the movement of human activity beyond national frameworks and its transformation into transnational forms, cardinally changing not only the conditions of the existence of individuals, social groups and communities, peoples and States, but also individual, national, and supranational legal consciousness. This leads to the creation of a global community within whose framework the existing nation-State formations act as more or less autonomous structural entities.[4]

Globalization has cardinally affected the communications characteristics of modern society, which strengthens contacts between countries and regions. As a result the harmonious coexistence of peoples is ensured since stability and predictability of the world order depends directly upon the stable development of every society individually.

The political dimension of globalization processes, encompassed by the concept of geopolitics, has direct relevance for various models and forms of world order. This is reflected in the concepts of "international division of labor", "international organizations", "world economy", "international relations", "international law", and others. In the strategic sphere geopolitics has displayed itself in the conception of living space, augmented by homogeneous ideological and power components extending to the territory of "others".[5]

The economic dimension of globalization processes is expressed in the concept of geoeconomics. There is an awareness of a new division of the world, and not only by political (administrative-geographical) boundaries within whose limits a homogeneous ideological, politically, and power milieu is arranged – the world has become transboundary. The extending of economies beyond national limits laid the basis for the forming of geoeconomics and geofinances, and economic boundaries have emerged. Other mobile boundaries (civilization, culturological, demographic, innovation, and others) have appeared with them. All this creates a complex system of relations, and not only international. A new field has been formed for legal regulation. In this situation the State as the central personage of geopolitics is qualitatively changing. Under the impact of globalization the evolution of State forms is occurring. Now one may

4 A. V. Torkunov (ed.), Современные международные отношения и мировая политика [Contemporary International Relations and World Politics] (2005), pp. 92-93.

5 E. G. Kochetov, «Ослепление геополитикой. Глобализирующийся мир и Евразийский континент у опасной развилки» [Blindness of Geopolitics. Globalizing World and the Eurasian Continent at a Dangerous Fork], Безопасность Евразии [Security of Eurasia], no. 4 (2001).

speak about different types of States: (1) the classical form of State within which sovereignty extends strictly within national-territorial boundaries; (2) a State within the framework of mobile economic boundaries ("country-systems" overturned "from without" or "from within"); (3) non-adjacent States ("nucleus plus diaspora"); (4) State within a State.[6]

Globalization as a complex process encompassing economic, political, social, cultural, legal, and other spheres of human life is perceived contradictorily. The contradictoriness is manifest in the elaboration and description of common models of globalization, which impede understanding the operation of fundamental laws of societal development in the evolution of the world community as a system of the highest complexity. This has led to the forming of an anti-globalist orientation.

Anti-globalism, which at the turn of the twenty-first century became a noteworthy social current that has gone far beyond the framework of national boundaries is at attempt at an intellectual and organizational rejection of global conceptions and theories directed towards tying the world to its model of a single-polar world.

In the view of anti-globalists, it is globalization that generates the multiplicity of problems furthering the enrichment of the wealthy and impoverishment of the poor countries. The possibilities of national States to resolve own problems are simultaneously narrowed. This is a threat to national culture and traditions.

The concentration observable in the world economy of economic power and might is construed as a direct threat to democratic institutions and the possibilities for the broad masses to influence the course of events. Accordingly, a struggle is unleashed to uphold the democratic foundations of a society, strengthen national democratic institutions and their use to influence the centers to adopt world economic solutions.

One of the major theses of the anti-globalists is that the conception of globalization legitimates not only social inequality in the modern world, but also leads to a renunciation of the struggle to achieve social equality in the future. Consequently, the basic aim of the struggle against globalization is, in their view, a struggle for social justness.

An illustrative example of anti-globalist ideas is the statement of K. Bivak, who noted that under contemporary conditions not only the United States, but also Europe, should be considered to be imperialists since it uses the fruits of globalization to the prejudice of third world countries. Analyzing the social movements in the United States, she declares that

[6] Kochetov, «Основные характеристики глобализационного процесса и правовое измерение мира» [Basic Characteristics of Globalization Process and Legal Dimension of the World], Журнал российского права [Journal of Russian Law], no. 3 (2003), p. 89.

in the United States there is, together with the globalists, a strong anti-global movement of both the left and the right. She singles out four aspects of the analysis of globalization. The first aspect is economic (most often globalization is in the form of the Americanization of entrepreneurship). The second aspect is social (the cardinal change of accents in the hierarchy of values and character of social relations). The third aspect is political (the most important of the political moments are constitutional changes, and also the origin and expansion of the influence of transnational subjects of power and the narrowing of the sovereignty of national governments). The fourth aspect is cultural (linked basically with the intensive Americanization of the life of many countries of the world).[7]

In the view of Pantin, globalization should be regarded in the context of global history. This view helps to overcome the limitedness of "Eurocentrism" and "western-centrism", "eastern-centrism", and "Russian-centrism" in treating the past and the present. This limitedness is rather dangerous since it, for example, represents the modern "American-centrist" model of globalization with all of its disproportions. Only a global vision of historical development is capable of re-creating an adequate and integral picture of the past and the future, thereby cautioning us against nationalism, chauvinism, self-adoration, which already more than once have brought peoples and civilizations to disaster.[8]

Thus, modern globalization is among the stages of a lengthy and complex process of forming mankind into a global community. Globalization processes reflect the objective conditions of life of modern society and conditioned the development of new technologies. Globalization should be perceived not as a purpose in itself, but as a means for the development of modern society.

LEGAL DIMENSION OF GLOBALIZATION PROCESSES

The trends and processes uniting and binding various countries and peoples into a single world whole are called globalization. Globalization creates conditions for forming a single social, political, economic, and cultural space which affects for forming of a single legal space.

Globalization processes lead to the forming of a global social system in which global problems accumulate connected with forming institutional and normative mechanisms having a supranational character.

[7] Kultygin, note 2 above, pp. 87-88.

[8] V. I. Pantin, Циклы и волны глобальной истории. Глобализация в историческом измерении [Cycles and Waves of Global History. Globalization in Historical Dimension] (2004), pp. 19-20.

The functioning of the global social system is impossible without respective legal regulation, which is a means of averting conflicts of law, conflicts of interests, and so on.

A revision of the system of legal regulation lies in a search for modern forms and methods of legal regulation within the framework of a new world order. For example, in recent times a stormy process of forming gigantic networked reproduction systems has occurred, the development of a "new economy" on the basis of advanced information technologies (internet economy), movement of geologistic models to a priority level, and others. However, the legal provision for these processes and the formation of models for their legal regulation do not correspond to their contemporary state.

The internationalization of transboundary financial flows has threatened the existence of stale national financial systems on the basis of national legal regimes. However, problems exist connected with the functioning of transboundary legal systems.

The legal dimension of globalization processes affects, as already noted, the revision of the entire existing system of legal regulation of social relations. This is linked with the emergence and strengthening of the influence of modern subjects of the world economy, not of a national but rather of a supranational character.

A typical feature of the globalization processes is the transformation of the status of supranational organizations as subjects of international law which under modern conditions have more powers than the member States of these organizations.

This affects the uniform regulation of a determined sphere of the life of States. Supranationality, on one hand, has a functional character (is the functional framework for unification trends, an expression of the practical interdependence of States) and does not transcend the limits of their field of influence, and on the other has an autonomous being, independent, within certain limits, of the initial will of States.[9]

The contradictoriness of globalization processes is also manifest in the fact that decentralization trends exist in legal regulation which is expressed in a redistribution of the role and amount of central and local legislation.

It is noteworthy that although the principal subjects of domestic and international law are the State and its agencies, non-State and social institutions and large economic structures are ever more active. The weight of international and inter-State institutions is growing, which creates a

[9] V. M. Shumilov, «Концепция Глобальной правовой системы» [Conception of Global Legal System], Юрист-международник [International Lawyer], no. 3 (2003), p. 52.

greater coincidence with regard to subject-matter, levels, and forms of regulation. The approximation of the typology of acts and norms furthers the European Convention on Information on Foreign Law of 7 June 1968 and published texts and collections of national, foreign, and international legal acts and means of overcoming legal differences.[10]

Globalization processes affect the socialization of law manifest in the expansion of the social activity of the State.

The legal manifestation of globalization processes also lies in strengthening the role of procedural as well as material law, which leads to an expansion of the sphere of procedural regulation, increased number of procedural norms, complication of the procedure, improvement and procedural forms. Procedural regulation becomes more precise and detailed.

GLOBAL LEGAL SYSTEM

In connection with globalization a change is occurring in all the base fundamental principles of the socio-political life of mankind. The legal component also is subject to serious changes, as a result of which law is surviving the phase of active development. This is manifest in qualitative changes in the substance and content of many legal mechanisms.

Globalization processes are leading to the formation, as already noted, of a global social system whose functioning is impossible without forming a global legal system.

In a global legal system, according to Shumilov, one may single out several levels of relations requiring regulation:

- relations in the sphere of national jurisdiction of States; these relations are regulated by municipal law (especially municipal relations and relations of a private-law character with a foreign element);
- relations between States (more broadly – between "public persons"); they are regulated by international law;
- relations between private persons of different States on those matters which are not regulated either by domestic or by international law (or are regulated by generally permissible means in which the principle is applied: "all is permitted unless expressly prohibited"). In this instance private persons of different countries, being interested in ensuring order, create an own autonomous

[10] Iu. A. Tikhomirov, «Глобализация: взаимовлияние внутренниего и международного права» [Globalization: Inter-Influence of Internal and International Law], Журнал российского права [Journal of Russian Law], no. 11 (2002), p. 10.

system of regulation – something in the nature of international contract law (so-called transnational law);

- relations in the sphere of supranational jurisdiction affecting global problems and interests and regulated by norms which may be provisionally called supranational law.

The qualitative unity between the said four legal phenomena Shumilov calls a global legal system.[11]

The basic components in the structure of a global legal system are, on one hand, international law and, on the other, national law. The specific nature of their mutual relations is the main problem of the functioning of this legal system.

As a result of forming a global legal system fundamental changes occur which are connected with the constant expansion of the sphere of regulation of international law at the expense of issues which traditionally were within the jurisdiction of national law, as a consequence of which international law is penetrating into the fabric of national law. An intensification of the mutual influence between the two legal systems leads to their being intertwined, which one may described as a new quality. Moreover, transnational law and supranational law are incorporated in the process of growth.

The influence of norms of national legal systems influence the formation of international law, and accordingly international law selects the most progressive ideas embodied in the law of States which are subjects of international law. Thus, international law is a factor in the improvement of national legislation.

One objective law of societal development in law is the deepening of the interaction of international and municipal law, which reflects a more general law of societal development – the deepening of the interaction of national society with the world community. The deepening interaction of international and municipal law affects the so-called internationalization, or homogenization.

One of the manifestations of globalization processes in the legal sphere under conditions of the functioning of a global legal system is the substitution of the primacy of national law with the primacy of international law.

Whereas earlier many international legal documents containing international legal norms were initiated by States on the basis of norms of national law, in the new conditions national States more often are obliged to bring norms of national law into conformity with international law. For

[11] Shumilov, note 9 above, p. 47.

example, the mutual relations of the European Union and member States are structured on precisely this principle.

Within the framework of the global legal system the principle subjects in the private international law sphere are transnational corporations. They create own autonomous economic system whose legal superstructure is translational law as supranational law.

The supranational level differs from the international especially because relations are structure not on a bilateral basis between individual States, but on the principle of direct, interpersonal relations between individuals whose nation-State affiliation does not have material importance.

Supranational law, or a single legal space, is called upon to fulfill an integrative function on the level of mankind as a whole, having ensured other legislative guarantees to all people on Earth irrespective of their nationality affiliation and citizenship that exceed those which exist in national legislation.[12]

Moreover, transnational corporations form own transnational interests which may diverge from State interests of the investing country and country of registration of the enterprise and often are contrary to the requirements of the international economic order as a whole.

The general sense of the conception of a global legal system lies in the fact that the participants of international relations themselves work out the norms of behavior which, it seems, are beyond the framework of domestic and international law.

The origin and development of a global legal system evidently will follow approximately the same path as the legal order of the European Union. This legal order consists of several components: international law, the law of the European Union, and national law of member States. These three parts have formed a distinctive division of labor. The subjects of the law of the European Union are States and private individuals simultaneously.[13]

As Harold J. Berman (1918-2007) observed, the developing system of world law includes not only public international law, that is, law created by national States in the process of mutual relations, including law regulating the activities of the United Nations and its specialized inter-State organizations, but also the enormous system of norms of treaty and customary law which regulate relations between natural and juridical persons involved in voluntary activity outside national boundaries. World law is the new name of what which we sometimes have called the law of

[12] N. B. Zazaeva, «Право как составляющая цивилизации» [Law as a Component of Civilization], Общество и философия [Philosophy and Society], no. 2 (2007), p. 73.

[13] Shumilov, note 9 above, p. 52.

nations, the common law of mankind, encompassing common features of various legal systems, various peoples of the world.[14]

In describing the transformation occurring at present in the legal firmament, Alekseev also identified the process of the creation of a global legal system with the formation of a "law of civilized peoples". From this standpoint he singled out the primary cause of world order for all these processes: the global crisis in the development of human civilization, the development and confirmation of civilizations of a liberal type, and this means, of modern civil society whose center and sense is Man, his dignity, and high status in the social system, his inalienable rights.[15]

Thus, the global legal system is a complex structure in which both subjects of international law and subjects of national law interact. The group of issues subject to regulation within the global legal system is not confined only to economic matters; to them should be added especially administrative law, procedural, conflicts norms, and others. In this understanding many branches of international law will come into contact with transnational law.

GLOBAL PROCESSES AND COMPARATIVE LAW

The process of globalization affects fundamental changes and the transformation of the modern humanitarian sphere. For the first time the world has begun to be perceived in its inextricable unity, community, integrity, has opened a new panorama which it is impossible to describe from traditional (or technogenic) scholarly positions. This requires a new approach to its theoretical comprehension by the humanitarian sciences.

New scientific disciplines have emerged in the era of globalization, especially globalistics and its sub-branches (geoeconomics, geofinances, geoinformatics, geoculture, geologistics, and others). Globalistics as a science is directed towards working out new approaches enabling the globalization processes occurring to be studied in the modern world. Legal globalistics as a component of globalistics investigates the contemporary state of legal science, its prospects under conditions of universal globalization encompassing economic, political, social, and other spheres

[14] H. J. Berman, «Мировое право: экуменическая юриспруденция Святого Духа» [World Law: Ecumenical Jurisprudence of the Holy Spirit], Представительная власть – XXI век: законодательство, комментарии, проблемы [Representative Power – XXI Century: Legislation, Commentary, Problems], no. 1 (2005), p. 13.

[15] S. S. Alekseev, «Право на пороге третьего тычячелетия: Некоторые тенденции мпрового правового развития – надежда и драма современной эпохи» [Law on the Eve of the Third Millennium: Certain Trends of World Legal Development – Hope and Drama of the Modern Era] (2000), p. 226.

of the life of modern society affecting the formation of general legal spaces beyond national law.

The role of law in the era of globalization lies first in working out a general legal policy ensuring the uniform regulation of social relations not so much in the framework of national law as in the framework of supranational law. This relates directly to a legal science such as comparative law.

Edouard Lambert (1866-1947) at the beginning of the twentieth century noted that, for comparatists, comparative law plays the same role as Roman law once played.[16] According to Raymond Saleilles (1855-1912), the purpose of comparative law to serve the progress of national law, to become an instrument of national legal technique. Comparativistics now is not primarily the subject-matter only of academic legal research. Possibly this is why more often it is called the "school of the precise method". Saleilles suggested that the result of comparative legal research should become singling out the common law of civilized mankind (in place of natural law), which is coming, however, to play a subsidiary, subordinate role, facilitating the interpretation and development of national law. He insisted that the proposed innovations were harmonious with national law as a whole and did not disturb its structure.[17]

The primary functional purpose of comparative law lies in investigating the general laws of societal development of forming and functioning of legal systems in order to identify the general and the special in them with a view to the mobilization of their potential and possibilities in resolving problems confronting mankind in the era of globalization. Comparative studies have been called upon to suggest legal solutions supporting the virtues of globalization and reducing its negative manifestations. The value grows in this connection of studies of the distinctiveness of national legal cultures which retain stability and diversity and satisfy the requirements and serve the interests of local communities.

Some writers note that together with the consolidation of the interdependence of the world globalization stimulates trends towards separatism, religious and localist sectarianism, autonomization of local cultures, often accompanied by a concentration of poverty in certain regions. Globalization, as Igor I. Lukashuk (1926-2007) correctly indicated, challenges both liberal democracy and legal unification since it is accompanied by economic, social, cultural, and political crises.[18]

16 E. Lambert, *La function du droit civil comparé* (1903).

17 R. Saleilles, "Rapport sur l'utilité, le but et le programme du Congrès", *Procès-Verbaux* (1905).

18 I. I. Lukashuk, «Взаимодействие международного и внутригосударственного права в условиях глобализации» [Interaction of International and Municipal Law in Conditions

Our task, in the view of Imre Szabó (b. 1912), lies in elaborating a single legal science which may treat law in various aspects, both vertically and horizontally, in various degrees and at various levels.[19] This statement has not lost its relevance in modern conditions, in an era of globalization.

The interest of comparatists is growing in the investigation of legal cultures, not only of the western type (intercultural and intracultural comparison), but also of the non-western type since doubts arise as to the universality of the western idea of law.

The comparison of legal cultures assumes an accent on the socio-political prerequisites of forming legal systems and institutions, the economic and ideological "bonds" of law, that is, a contextual analysis of legal norms in force. Law always has been closely intertwined with business interests, economic forces, the social interaction of an era.

It is necessary to develop comparative law studies within the framework of branch legal sciences, including the public-law block (constitutional, administrative, and municipal law). The issue of branch comparative disciplines is controversial since many noted comparatists (for example, M. N. Marchenko) suggest that the essential organizational-personnel prerequisites for this are for the moment lacking.

Of great topicality at the contemporary stage of comparative legal research is the problem of elaborating objective criteria for assessing legal models of particular institutions ensuring the effectuation of the functional purpose of law in an era of globalization.

LEGAL ACCULTURATION AND SIGNIFICANCE THEREOF IN THE APPROXIMATION OF LEGAL SYSTEMS

As Jean Carbonnier has noted, the cultural-historical process is developing as the interaction of sundry local cultures (polylineal) and at the same time a cultural unity of people is being formed (monolineal). Today many specialists speak about the unity of world culture; however, the loss by national culture of certain features under the influence of acculturation does not signify in the foreseeable future differences between cultures in general and legal systems in particular being lost. It is understandable that the modern world cannot exist under conditions of legal culture being closed off. Processes of legal acculturation are proceeding, that is, the

---

of Globalization], Журнал российского права [Journal of Russian Law], no. 3 (2002), pp. 115-128.

[19] I. Szabó, «Теоретические проблемы сравнительного правоведения» [Theoretical Problems of Comparative Law], in V.A. Tumanov, Сравнительное правоведение: сборник статей [Comparative Law: Collection of Articles] (1978).

destruction, overcoming of this closedness, when one legal system may be supposedly grafted on to another.[20]

National legal systems do not exist in isolation. They interact and engage in endless cultural dialogue. The legal system of an individual State is subject to constant pressure on the part of fragments of other legal cultures, legal texts, procedures, and legal constructions. The "bombardment" of culture by the texts of another culture leads to a new interpretation both of these "imported" texts and the context itself of an "aborigine" culture. From such new interpretation there inevitably arise new thoughts to be realized in human activity.[21]

Moreover, the great legal systems which have come down to us, as a rule, commenced with borrowing (Athenian, Roman, Western law, and so on). This may happen through individual legal institutions, elements of legal technique, and law-application practice. There also is borrowing of legal principles, legal ideas. In other words, borrowing may be fragmentary, called legal acculturation, or global, called legal reception. If during legal acculturation the borrowing occurs of legal provisions, then in the event of legal reception the fundamentals of the legal system change in general.

Legal reception is regarded as a variety of legal acculturation, called total acculturation, or a "cultural mutation".[22]

Fragmentary legal acculturation is a widespread phenomenon occurring within the framework of a constant dialogue of legal systems and legal cultures. As regards total legal acculturation, that is, legal reception, this is an exceptional phenomenon. An example is the reception of Roman law, on the basis of which the Romano-Germanic legal family was formed.

In the view of Osakwe, comparative law encourages and approves borrowing the ideas of various legal systems, comprising the axiom of this discipline. But carrying over ideas from one legal system to another requires a careful analysis for compatibility. Legal borrowing is externally similar to the medical surgical operation to transplant individual parts of the human body. The comparatist is similar in his work to a surgeon in the sense that he takes part of another's legal system and "transplants" it into his own. In order to achieve a successful result the legal institution taken from system "A" and transplanted in system "B" must combine with system "B" and not be "rejected" by it. For example, before borrowing the institution of the jury from the Anglo-American Common Law system and introducing it into the continental European legal system of Russia,

20 J. Carbonnier, Юридическая социология [Legal Sociology] (1986), p. 199.

21 Iu. M. Lotman, Внутри мыслящих миров. Человек – текст – семиосфера – история [Within Thinking Worlds. Man – Text – Semiosphere – History] (1999), pp. 21-22.

22 Carbonnier, note 20 above, pp. 198-201.

it is essential to understand whether this institution is compatible with the complex mechanism of Russian criminal procedure law.[23]

Legal acculturation is effectuated by various means and paths: with the assistance of legislation and judicial practice, by means of the conclusion of treaties, and also by special paths. For example, legal acculturation effectuated by scholars and teachers occurs on the level of legal science and legal education. On this basis Oborotov singled out the following types of legal acculturation: legislative, judicial, treaty, and doctrinal.[24]

Thus, the modern world cannot exist under conditions of the closedness of legal cultures. The processes of legal acculturation are going on, as a result of which the problems of their further development are becoming more problematic and may not correspond to the requirements and interests of modern society. Comparative law furthers such a dialogue, the mobilization of potential which various legal systems (or families) possess and legal cultures for resolving all-planetary issues. Going beyond the framework of a national vision of law, the primacy of general humanitarian values in the development of civilization and its legal components are becoming the main requirement in the development of modern society. The modern world is characterized by a growing trend towards integration by means of the interaction of legal systems.

Legal borrowing is one of the most characteristic features of legal evolution since no single legal system has a monopoly on original legal discoveries. In any event effective borrowing may not be uncritical since copying may turn out not to reproduce what was achieved in the past, but lead to failure.

COMPARATIVE LAW AND THE APPROXIMATION OF LEGAL SYSTEMS

Comparative law and the approximation of legal systems are directly connected, which is conditioned by the internal logic of their development. In 1900 Lambert in his Report to the I International Congress of Comparative Law set out his vision of this problem. One of the distinctive features of his approach to a comparison of national legal systems and the creation of a real

[23] C. Osakwe, «Размышление о природе сравнительного правоведения: некоторые теоретические вопросы» [Reflection on the Nature of Comparative Law: Certain Theoretical Questions], Журнал зарубежного законодательства и сравнетельного правоведения [Journal of Foreign Legislation and Comparative Law], no. 3 (2006), pp. 61-62.

[24] Iu. N. Oborotov, Традиции и новации в правовом развитии [Traditions and Innovations in Legal Development] (Odessa, 2001).

base for unification lay not in taking from all legal systems which existed at the time, but only those which were at the same level of development.[25]

Comparative law encountered not only traditional problems which accompanied the development of science as a whole, but also problems caused by each subsequent stage of societal development. The basic problem, which comparatists now consider to be one of priority, is the approximation of legal systems, conditioning their legal integration and forming not only local, but also general legal spaces. The modern processes generated by the era of globalization post to jurisprudence as a whole and through comparative law in particular the task of using the potential of various legal families (or systems) in resolving tasks affecting all mankind.

Comparative law as an obvious scientific phenomenon of modern times on one hand, and the approximation of legal systems as an objective process of modern international practice, on the other, organically reinforce one another. As a result of comparative legal studies, the approximation of legal systems is becoming more pragmatic, transparent, and predictable since this process has scholarly substantiation within the framework of the theory of comparative law. In turn, the processes of approximation of legal systems create a favorable base for the approbation and further elaboration of various conceptions which have emerged within the framework of comparative law.

Thus, with the assistance of the methodology of comparative law the basis for the approximation of legal systems is being formed by identifying the common and the special in the objects being compared. In addition, as a result of comparative law studies the most optimal methods and forms of the approximation of legal systems are identified. In some instances the optimal form of such approximation is considered to be the unification of legal norms, for example, within the framework of integration processes in the European Union, and in another instance the more effective is the adoption of model legislative acts. This type of harmonization of legislation, for example, is used in the legal practice of the United States as a form of approximation.

Thanks to comparative law studies, the establishment of the possibility and limits of the approximation of legal systems is becoming real since the method of comparative legal analysis identifies the limits of such borrowing of legal provisions by one legal system from another. Legal borrowing gives the anticipated result if are based on the methodology of comparative law.

[25] Lambert, note 16 above.

Drafts within the framework of comparative law further the formation of a single category-conceptual apparatus which is an essential component of a formal-legal character augmenting the substantive aspect of the approximation of legal systems. This has special importance in working out model legislative acts and unified legal norms and is manifest in the drafting of European normative legal acts which are intended to be complied with in States belonging to the Romano-Germanic and Common Law systems.

The question constantly arises within the framework of theoretical works in the sphere of comparative legal studies about the forming of a general "universal" law adequately reflecting the requirements and meeting the principal challenges of modern society in the domain of legal regulation.

The approximation of legal systems cannot happen outside the influence of globalization processes which stimulate changes in the world economy, including the growing economic interdependence and technological possibilities. One factor in forming geoeconomic space is the "mutual penetration" of legal systems.[26] The globalization process developing in the political domain differs from globalization in the socio-economic sphere. States to a significant degree retain their autonomy. Therefore, with respect to States, and also legal systems, the more precise term is "internationalization", signifying especially the approximation of political and legal systems of States and the deepening of their interaction and cultural influence.[27]

TEACHING COMPARATIVE LAW IN THE CONTEMPORARY STAGE

Research into global laws of societal development and trends in the development of law in the modern era are the task of legal science and legal education together with the study of national law. The importance of the analysis of the experience of world development, including the study of processes occurring in modern society, are conditioned by the requirements of legal progress. Therefore, legal science should rest on theoretical elaboration, the object of which is legal systems.

Comparative law is not only an autonomous science, but an instructional discipline which is based on the science of comparative law. Comparative

[26] E. G. Kochetov, Геоэкономика [Geoeconomics] (1999), p. 3.

[27] I. I. Lukashuk, Глобализация, Государство, право. XXI век [Globalization, State, Law. XXI Century] (2000).

law as an instructional discipline represents knowledge about the state of the science of comparative law and its past, present, and future.

The study of comparative law is an important condition for the development of modern legal science and legal education. Comparative law should occupy an important place in the instructional syllabus of an institution of legal education since modern jurists work in national legal systems belonging to different legal families.

As Osakwe noted, comparative law destroys legal xenophobia among students, facilitates an understanding of foreign legal systems, furthers the study and use of own national law, raises the cultural level of those studying and, finally, strengthens the fundamental nature of legal education. Under conditions of the contemporary interaction of world legal cultures and mutual relations between different legal systems the graduate of an institution of higher legal education in any country cannot consider himself to be a literate jurist without a knowledge of comparative law. A study of own national law reaches its height and gives an optimal result only when the scientific method of comparative (or contrastive) analysis of law is applied.[28]

Comparative law facilitates the consideration of the legal system as a phenomenon directly dependent upon the distinctive features of various societies. This enables the link to be emphasized between legal phenomena reflected in a legal system with such components of public consciousness as religion, culture, morals, politics, ideology, and so on. This, in turn, enables not only the evolution of legal systems to be considered, but also the legal panorama of the modern world to be objectively determined.

The main task of comparative law is to identify the innovation processes in the content and teaching of comparative law and determine the most effective ways of the optimization thereof. In other words, the further strengthening of comparative law as an instructional discipline is possible on the basis of new works in the sphere of the methods of teaching it.

As Saidov noted, comparative law as an instructional discipline also concretizes the general theory of law, history of law, philosophy of law, and the general theoretical part of the branch legal sciences.[29]

The teaching of comparative law enables students to be armed with skills of conducting comparative legal studies, so essential for the development of legal science and legal practice. In addition, comparative law as an instructional discipline enables students not only to deal with national law,

[28] Osakwe, note 23 above, p. 59.

[29] A. Kh. Saidov, *Comparative Law*, transl. W. E. Butler (2003).

but also to enlarge their horizon through the study of foreign law by means of contrasting this on the basis of the methodology of comparative law.

The objective study of legal systems, their past, modern state, and also prospects for their development condition changes in the structure of comparative law as a science, which requires also a structural change in setting out the instructional cours.

It is essential to note that at present primary attention is devoted in instructional literature to Romano-Germanic and Common Law. As regards the other legal families, sufficient attention is not being devoted to them. Instructional and scholarly literature devoted to this problem establishes the succession of legal families: study of the cours commences with a consideration of the Romano-Germanic legal family, then the Common Law system, mixed legal systems (Scandinavian, Latin American), and then the religious-traditional legal systems are considered (Islamic legal system and Hindu legal system, systems of customary and Far Eastern law).

A study of the essence and content of legal systems with a link to political, religious, ideological, philosophical, and other factors of social life requires a revision of the sequence of the material identifying the formation, evolution, and functioning of various legal systems.

An objective study of the legal panorama of the world affects the need to study legal families with regard to their origin and development, thanks to which the succession of the basic elements of legal families is ensures and their functioning. The criterion of sequence in setting out the material illuminating legal families should become a civilization-chronological approach, according to which the illumination of legal families begins not with the Romano-Germanic and Common Law, but with the traditional and religious legal systems. This integral character of the materials enables not only the mechanism for the functioning of legal systems to be understood, but also predictions to be made with respect to the prospects for their development.

Thus, comparative law offers an integral impression about the legal panorama of the world, the mutual relations between legal families (or systems), legal cultures within the framework of the dialogue of legal systems conditioned by legal acculturation. Erudition is thereby enlarged, the level of legal consciousness and legal culture is enhanced. As a result, an attitude of respect is formed not only with regard to own law, but also to "alien" law. The knowledge and skill received within the framework of studying comparative law further the effective professional activity of jurists.

Unified Potential of Comparative Law as a Science and Instructional Discipline

A. IU. SALOMATIN*

The fact that comparative law as an individual orientation in legal science arose during the era of modernization, when the process of modernizing spread to various countries with astonishing speed, was to be expected. The internationalization of legal transformations and intensification of economic and cultural contacts in the nineteenth century inspired jurists to go outside the law of their own countries and to study foreign law. Soon interest was displayed in comparative analysis, affirmed by the appearance of the early studies, professional societies, and journals. As sociological-positivist orientations in comparativistics spread during the 1860s. the notion of a single means of world legal development and an understanding of comparative law as the universal history of law were confirmed. Scholars sought to seek each specific situation of a single correct solution, the very best norm among various national legal systems.[1]

The idealist position was in evidence at the First International Congress in Paris when, in 1900, the French comparatists expressed confidence in the coming unification of law of various countries. Modern specialists, living in the post-modernizing era of accelerating globalization, are more cautious in their forecasts about the creation of an all-planetary law. The uneven nature of the modification of national legislation is noted. "Military-political

* доктор юридических наук, доктор исторических наук, профессор. Head of Chair of Politology and Foundations of Law, Director of Center for Comparative Law and Political and Socio-Legal Monitoring, Penza State University

[1] O. V. Kresin, «Проблемы периодизации развития сравнительного правоведения» [Problem of Periodization of the Development of Comparative Law], in A. Iu. Salomatin (ed.), Сравнительное правоведение в российском высшем образовании [Comparative Law in Russian Higher Education] (Penza, 2010), pp. 105-106.

cooperation (covenants, alliances, and so on) 'nudge' the modification of certain norms and institutes of constitutional and administrative law. The accelerating and large-scale economic integration inspires legislation on companies, transport, customs, technical rules and regulations, and so on to be made the same more quickly. Other branches are developing in their former context with minor changes or await "their hour".[2]

Simultaneously, pessimistic sentiments resound with regard to comparative law itself. The noted American scholar, Reimann, pointed to significant successes of the discipline after 1945, when a large number of textbooks, casebooks, monographs, and articles appeared, especially on private law and, to a lesser degree, on criminal and constitutional law and judicial law in comparative perspective. Published works may be divided into: (1) works on foreign law primarily of a descriptive character with elements of comparison; (2) works on the world geography of legal families; (3) works on the purposes, methods, and shortcomings of the comparative legal method. Their geographical scope is broad: Europe, United States, Asia, former socialist countries, Latin America, and, to a minimal degree, Africa. Despite, however, the abundance of works and approaches, Reimann has reason for saying "the small amount of statistical data on the legal systems to be studied and compared is laughable". Moreover, the abundance of uncoordinated works without a solid theoretical foundation leads to dissonance about what it is necessary to compare.[3]

What is it in fact – modern comparative law? Does it possess the minimum theoretical assurance or is it in chaos? What are the possibilities for its integration into legal education?

COMPARATIVE LAW: MULTI-ASPECTUALNESS AND PLURALISM OF APPROACHES

On the whole we are witnesses to the preserved multi-aspectualness of comparative law. The time is gone when the majority of jurists perceived comparativistics only as a scientific method; proponents of this approach were many in the ranks of jurists, primarily those professing the views of the Common Law.[4] On the European continent and in the countries of the

[2] Iu. A. Tikhomirov, "Comparative Law and the Integrating Role of International Law", *The Journal of Comparative Law*, V, no. 1 (2010).

[3] M. Reimann, "The Progress and Failure of Comparative Law in the Second Half of the Twentieth Century", *American Journal of Comparative Law*, L (2002), p. 686.

[4] See, for example, C. Osakwe, «Размышления о природе сравнительного правоведения: некоторые теоретические вопросы» [Reflections on the Nature of Comparative Law: Some Theoretical Questions], Журнал зарубежного законодательства и сравнительного правоведения [Journal of Foreign Legislation and Comparative Law], no. 3 (2006), p. 56.

CIS adherents who understand comparative law to be a science dominate. "Now it is demonstrated and acknowledged – comparative law has earned its right to exist".[5] Another question on which individual authors make an important clarification: «comparative law understood in the meaning of a comparative legal scientific method may be used by various legal sciences, and comparative law as a scientific discipline claims to scientific autonomy formalized as a subject-matter, object, functions, and methods".[6]

Several approaches to the teaching of comparative law have come into being. The simplest is the *selective institutional-problem method*, when a limited number of countries and limited number of topics are taken for comparative analysis. A lecturer at Nizhnii Novgorod State University, V. Luzin, familiarized students with "various legal systems of the world (system of continental law, systems of Common and customary law). The subjects for discussion in class were: sources in different legal systems, judicial control, models of separation of powers, right to inviolability of private life (regulation of searches and arrests, right to abortion, right to die, right of sexual minorities, and so on). The list of countries whose legislation and judicial practice was used included the United States, United Kingdom, France, Germany, and Russia".[7]

The *systemic-legal approach realized with respect to the principal legal families*, as is done in the textbooks of Professor Marchenko, has an assured methodology and high theoretical level. The notion is successfully implemented in them of the objectively penetrating processes of legal globalization and convergence of legal systems. On one hand, not without grounds does Marchenko point to the trend of the Europeanization of the English Common Law. On the other hand, a certain Americanization of European continental law is noted – especially as regards finance leasing, contracts for the lease of enterprises, franchising, ensuring the secrecy of bank accounts, protection of the rights of ownership and consumer rights. However, the author is undoubtedly right that the degree of rapprochement

[5] M. A. Damirli, «Теоретико-методические проблемы сравнительного правоведения: попытка актуализации и некоторые размышления» [Theoretical-Methodological Problems of Comparative Law: Effort to Actualize and Some Reflections], Журнал зарубежного законодательства и сравнительного правоведения [Journal of Foreign Legislation and Comparative Law], no. 3 (2006), p. 53.

[6] O. F. Skakun, Общее сравнительное правоведение: Основные типы (семьи) правовых систем мира [General Comparative Law: Basic Types (Families) of Legal Systems of the World] (Kiev, 2008), p. 17.

[7] V. Luzin, «Реформа юридического образования в России. Личный опыт» [Reform of Legal Education in Russia: Personal Experience], in Юридическое образование в посткоммунистических государствах: профессиональная подготовка в условиях переходного периода [Legal Education in Post-Communist States: Professional Training under Conditions of a Transition Period] (Ioshkar-Ola, 2001), p. 15.

should not be exaggerated, since if the United States and Europe have not only close economic, but also political interests, the "Americanization to a significant degree would touch not only European private, but also constitutional, administrative, criminal, and other respective branches of law".[8]

Another monumental work of more than a thousand pages[9] adds an analysis of the leading families and systems of law (Romano-Germanic, Anglo-Saxon, Muslim, Judaic, socialist, and post-socialist countries) with extracts from the world of leading jurists, which makes it especially valuable when conducting seminars.

The textbooks by Saidov have a broader range of legal geography. Saidov subjects to comparative consideration, besides the traditional three to five families and systems, also the Scandinavian, Latin American, Japanese, Hindu, and Far Eastern law and the customary law of Africa.[10] He emphasizes that he "endeavored, on one hand, to combine a country approach with the comparative-generalized and, on the other hand, to add a problem approach to the analysis of issues of legal comparativistics with a portrait of the views of leading representatives thereof".[11] Saidov gives considerable attention to the history of comparative law in the format of national schools and historical periods, and also to branch comparative law with regard to private law and constitutional law.

The textbook by the Ukrainian comparatist, Bekhruz, is distinctive for the originality in the sequence of the exposition of the material.[12] As the author himself notes, his book is structured on the chronological-civilization principle and "reflects the logic of the development of legal systems not only in static, but in dynamic measures". This also provides a sharper image of such elements of legal systems as legal traditions and legal mentality. A "study of the essence and content of legal systems in their linkage with political, religious, ideological, philosophical, and other factors of social life requires a revision of the sequential exposition of the material ...".[13] In other words, the author sets out the legal families and legal systems comprising them in chronological sequence, beginning with

[8] M. N. Marchenko, Правовые системы современного мира [Legal Systems of the Contemporary World] (2008), pp. 268-269, 271-272, 274.

[9] Marchenko, Курс сравнительного правоведения [Cours of Comparative Law] (2002).

[10] A. Kh. Saidov, Сравнительное правоведение: Краткий учебный курс [Comparative Law: Concise Instructional Cours] (2006).

[11] Saidov, Сравнительное правоведение. Основные правовые системы современности [Comparative Law: Principal Legal Systems of Modern Times] (2007), p. 19.

[12] Kh. Bekhruz, Сравнительное правоведение [Comparative Law] (Odessa, 2008).

[13] Bekhtuz, note 12 above, pp. 8, 49.

African customary law and ending with the western families of legislative and precedential law, as well as the post-Soviet legal systems.

The Russian comparatist, Lafitskii, just as his Ukrainian colleague, draws attention to the ethno-cultural and religious factors. In this two-volume study the author investigates the images of law in various systems. He studies not only the legislative aspects, but also "Holy scripture and monuments of literary and folk creation" because "they determine the spiritual essence, distinctive features, and, ultimately, the fate of the principal legal systems of the modern world".[14] The work includes systems relating to the Christian tradition of law: Slavonic, Romano-Germanic, Anglo-Saxon, Scandinavian, and Latin American.

Tikhomirov's classic work[15] is of interest to the teacher of comparative law because it contains a mass of ideas which may be used in the instructional process. The approach of the author may be described as a *systemic-branch* one, since together with the consideration of legal families, an analysis is given of the development of certain branches of law (constitutional, civil, administrative, financial, criminal) in individual States (including Russia). Tikhomirov is among the first to make a number of important comments: for example, the inadmissibility of a mechanistic and literal copying of western constitutional legal ideas, the inadvisability of substituting the analytical nature of passive information provision, retaining the differentiation of legal blocks when intensifying the inter-penetration of legal systems.[16] The legislative acts of various countries published in the book provide material for comparative analysis with a student audience.

The legal science of comparative law has developed in a positive direction through the *law-system approach*. Skakun, proceeding from the fact that "law-creation, law-application, law enforcement, and judicial agencies are a direct component of the legal system of society",[17] in her textbook on the structure of legal families and national legal systems comprising them considers not only systems of law, but also judicial systems and political systems. This expanded approach to comparative law should be acknowledged to be correct.

One must concur with Tikhomirov that the "accent on contrasting primarily laws leaves in the dark other phenomena of legal life. Jurisprudence is not a synonym of law, and it encompasses all sources

[14] V. I. Lafitskii, Сравнительное правоведение в образах права [Comparative Law in the Images of Law] (2010-2011), I, pp. 10-11.

[15] Iu. A. Tikhomirov, Курс сравнительного правоведения [Cours of Comparative Law] (1996).

[16] Tikhomirov, note 15 above, p. 28.

[17] Skakun, note 6 above, p. 52.

of law, State and other institutions, legal institutions, the application of law, legal education and science".[18] It is another matter that the search for additional material for comparative contrast presents certain difficulties for the lecturer in the subject. This especially concerns such a complex and difficult phenomenon as the legal culture of a particular country,[19] or such an under-generalized phenomenon as legal education. The time has come when we should in approximate form determine the differences in the perception of law in several leading countries of the world, having recourse, for example, to sociological studies. Eliciting the experience of teaching law in various countries would be useful, with an explanation of the specific features of education in each instance.

One should not forget the comparative branch disciplines, in particular, comparative civil law, where the problems are more linked with practical requirements.[20] Professor Osakwe, from the United States, who has repeatedly come to Russia and lectured in leading Moscow institutions of higher education, created a good educational undertaking.[21] Textbooks published on different branches of foreign law – criminal, administrative, commercial, labor,[22] and others – also are in essence comparative legal publications which even in the absence of formal comparative legal analysis presume such an analysis since the reader, being familiar with foreign legal realities, contrasts them with phenomena of Russian legal life.

Very original in content is an instructional manual by Marchenko and Deriabina on the law of the European Union.[23] It analyses typical features and structural peculiarities of the law of the European Union, the combination of elements of Romano-Germanic and English law, primary

[18] Tikhomirov, «Сравнительное правоведение: развитие концепций и общественной практики» [Comparative Law: Development of Conceptions and Social Practice], Журнал российского права [Journal of Russian Law], no. 6 (2006), p. 6.

[19] An example of a masterful study of the legal culture of various categories of French judges is J. Bell, *French Legal Cultures* (2001).

[20] A. Kh.Saidov, «Сравнительное гражданское право как наука и учебная дисциплина» [Comparative Civil Law as Science and Instructional Discipline], Журнал зарубежного законодательства и сравнительного правоведения [Journal of Foreign Legislation and Comparative Law], no. 1 (2007), p. 54.

[21] C. Osakwe, Сравнительное правоведение: Схематический комментарий [Comparative Law: Schematic Commentary] (2008).

[22] See, for example, G. A. Esakov, N. E. Krylova, and A. V. Serebrennikova, Уголовное право зарубежных стран [Criminal Law of Foreign Countries] (2009); A. N. Kozyrin and M. A. Shtatina (eds.), Административное право зарубежных стран [Administrative Law of Foreign Countries] (2003); I. Ia. Kiselev, Трудовое право России и зарубежных стран [Labor Law of Russia and Foreign Countries] (2005); A. Iu. Bushev, O. A. Makarova, and V. F. Popondupulo, Коммерческое право зарубежных стран [Commercial Law of Foreign Countries] (2003).

[23] Marchenko and E. M. Deriabina, Право Европейского Союза. Вопросы истории и теории [Law of European Union. Questions of History and Theory] (2010).

and secondary legal sources. The question is raised of the form of State structure of the European Union (federation, confederation, or international organization). An account is given of its institutions and judicial system. The authors consider the principal ways and forms of bringing European legal systems and families together, whether they be linked with the activities of the European Court of Justice or national courts, expansion of the practice of judicial supervision or the growing universalization of general principles of law. The issue of the interaction of the legal system of the European Union with the legal systems of member States is explored, as is the correlation of international, municipal, and European law.

Another innovation which might be applied to the teaching of comparative law is the expansion of the last to include "comparative State formation" – the subject-matter of which would encompass the "general and specific laws of societal development regulating the arising, development, and functioning of State-legal systems, legal forms and orientations of the activity of States, in their comparative cognition".[24] A step in this direction would be teaching a course on comparative State-formation, developed in substance and method by the St. Petersburg lecturers Golubeva and Chernokov.[25] In the future one may truly think about the merger of two courses – the more traditional (comparative law) and the less customary (comparative State science) into one, but this is a matter for the far future.

REALIZATION OF LAW-SYSTEM APPROACH TO TEACHING COMPARATIVE LAW

At Penza State University comparative law is taught in an enlarged format, that is, by means of the comparative analysis of legal systems (and not systems of law) of the leading States of the world, relying basically on an instructional-methods complex elaborated by the present writer and A. V. Malko.[26] We have brought in elements of other approaches of Russian and Ukrainian colleagues in recent years in the instructional plan (see Table 1).

Traditionally, about 10% of the instructional time is reserved for topics of a general theoretical nature (subject-matter and tasks, history

[24] N. N. Onishchenko, «К вопросу о понятии «сравнительного правогосударствоведения» (некоторые подходы к анализу и изучению» [On the Question of the Concept of 'Comparative State Formation' (Certain Approaches to Analysis and Study)], in A. Iu. Salomatin (ed.), Сравнительное правоведение в российском высшем образовании [Comparative Law in Russian Higher Education (Penza, 2009).

[25] L. A. Golubeva and A. E. Chernokov, Сравнительное государствоведение [Comparative State Science] (Spb., 2009).

[26] A. V. Malko and A. Iu. Salomatin, Сравнительное правоведение: Учебно-методический комплекс [Comparative Law: Instructional-Methods Complex] (2008).

TABLE 1

Approaches to Teaching Comparative Law

Topic	Title	Content of Lesson
1	Subject-Matter and tasks of comparative law	Comparative law. Scientific method or integrated scientific discipline? Content of comparative law. Inter disciplinary links
2	History of comparative law	Predecessors of science of comparative law in pre-industrial societies. Forming of national schools is XIX-XX centuries. International Academy of Comparative Law
3	Basic priorities of comparative law research	Legal systems – basic units of analysis in comparative law. Combining legal systems into legal families. Main and supplemental elements of legal systems in process of analysis. Diachronic and synchronic comparison
4	Legal system of England	English system of law – vanguard of Anglo-American legal family. Sources and evolution of Common Law and law of equity. Modern state and sources of English system of law. Slightly centralized judicial system. Judges. Role of jurors. Dualism of legal profession. Semi-centralized police system
5	Legal system of United States	Causes of Americanization of English Common Law across ocean. Pluralist system of law and judicial system. Constitutional federalism. US Supreme Court – Coordinator and initiator of legal policy, first institution of Constitutional justice. Recruitment of judges at federal and state levels. Status of legal profession. Special role of jurors. Decentralized police system
6	Legal system of British Common-wealth countries (examples of Canada and Australia	General and particular in colonization policy in Canada and Australia. Status of dominion. Canadian federation and difficulties of legal unification. Centralized judicial federalism. Dependence of Australia on British legal tradition. Unity of Common Law and preferential Codification at level of states. Strengthening of federal bonds. Partial dualism of legal profession

7	Romano-Germanic legal family	French coutume-Roman law and gradual unification under absolutism. Trend towards judicial-legal centralization by means of feudal regionalization and specialization. Basic turn in court organization and law in French Revolution and reforms of Napoleon I. Expansion of codes. Court organization with two lines of justice and specialized courts. Legal education and legal profession. National school of magistrates. Centralized police system. State fractionalization and legal particularism in Holy Roman Empire of German nation. Unification of Germany (1871) and judicial-legal optimization. Synthesis of codes and federal laws in modern system of German law. System of narrowly specialized branches of justice. High requirement for legal education. Semi-centralized police system. Distinctive features of legal systems of Spain and Italy
8	Legal systems of Scandinavian Countries	Influence of outlying position of Scandinavia and its socio-geographic conditions on law. Early trend towards legal systematization. French and German influence. Aspiration Towards legal integration in region. Partial filling of gaps in law with aid of precedents. Precedential decisions as instrument of unification. Simple and rational access to justice. Informal constitutional control
	Colloquium: "Convergence of western legal systems: dream or reality?"	Europeanization of English Common Law. Individual manifestations of Americanization of European continental law. Influence of economic and political factors, legal consciousness, historical and national traditions. Phenomenon of coming together of national systems of law within European Union framework
9	Countries of Muslim law	Religious schools in Islam and their influence on law. Classification of countries of Islam from standpoint of peculiarities of use by them of norms of Muslim law. Legal systems of Turkey, Egypt, Saudi Arabia
10	Hindu law	Hinduism as religious system and system of law. Influence of Muslim law and English law in India. System of law of modern India and its judicial system

11	Far Eastern legal family	Influence of Confucianism and legizm on law of China. Role of idea of socialism "with Chinese specifics" in legal system of CPR. Degree of influence of certain principles of Romano-Germanic law in modernization after 1911 revolution. Legal renewal after 1979. Centralized judicial system. Administrative commissions and conciliation commissions. Acknowledgement of guilt. Influence of Chinese ideology on medieval Japan. Law of Shogunate. Meiji revolution (1868) and basic orientations of Modernization. Influence of American law after World War II. Codes and special laws. Supreme Court as highest judicial institution, organ of constitutional justice, and director of justice in country. Significance of conciliation procedures and moral-ethical norms of hiri.
12	Legal systems of Latin America and Africa	Circumstances of legal reception in independent States of Latin America. European borrowings in private law and borrowings from United States in constitutional law. Amparo procedure. Shortage of judges and overburdening of courts. Great role of traditional (community) law in African countries. Significance of law of former Metropolitans and European and Muslim law. Combining Of State, community, and family courts
13[1]	Significance of comparative law for modern Russia	Specific features of legal development of Russia. Legal and judicial reforms in new millennium. Controversial aspects (Civil Code of Russia). Place of Russian legal system on legal map of world (is the Russian system of law part of the Romano-Germanic legal family?)
	Scientific student Conference	Theme of conference varies from year to year

[1] Topic 13 it is proposed to carry over to a separate module in a special course: "Problems of Theory of State and Law" given on the eve of the State examination.

of the discipline, basic priorities of comparative-legal research, including familiarization with recommended literature). Consideration of the specific legal systems begins with England as the founder of the Anglo-American legal family. We proceed from the fact for us as bearers of legal culture the Romano-Germanic law is genetically closer and it is more complicated to comprehend precedential Common Law and precisely for that reason should so commence the instructional process. At lectures and seminars connected with English law we aspired to transmit ideas concerning:

- the specific nature of the forming of State and law on the British Isles expressed in early centralization and constitutionalization of the State and dualism of the system of law;
- aristocratic evolution of British society which affected the insufficient centralization of the judicial system and the dragging out of legal reform.

The development of the jury, the motherland of which in the Anglo-American world is considered to be Great Britain, is analyzed.[27]

A logical approach to an analysis of the legal system of the United States gives the lecturer the possibility to compare the legal development of the former metropolitan and the North American colonies. Here the students are encouraged to find answers to questions:

- why in the colonial period did various versions of Americanized Common Law come to be used; why was a simpler and more convenient judicial system formed there;
- why after the War for Independence did legal differences deepen between the United States and the United Kingdom; what role was played here the by resettlement nature of society and the federal structure of the State;
- how does hyper-respect for the Constitution influence the institution of constitutional control and what political factors facilitated the strengthened position of the United States Supreme Court?

In general, consideration of the activity of the highest court of the country is considered to be extremely topical. An analysis of past and modern noteworthy decisions of the United States Supreme Court enables students to attach themselves to the not entirely comprehensible law of precedent developing in the context of the changing constitutional-political situation. An external outline of events and exposition of decisions is given in works by Zhidkov, Salomatin, and Chernilovskii. We have translated

[27] A. K. Romanov, Правовая система Англии [Legal System of England], Preface by W. E. Butler (2000), pp. 301-302.

into Russian several decisions which will make it possible for students personally to study primary sources.

Aspects connected with the legal development of the British dominions are interesting in that they demonstrate the degree of variation of the Common Law and the structures of the State-law system in Canada and Australia in comparison with the United Kingdom and the United States. On one hand, Canada and Australia remained for a long time in the orbit of British influence (in the more remote but economically and politically weaker Australia, this influence was stronger). On the other hand, Canada and Australia, unlike their metropolitan, are federated States which endeavored to borrow much from the United States in the political and constitutional domains.

The study of the Romano-Germanic legal family is noteworthy for students because one is addressing the dominance of legislation that is more familiar to them. France as the largest country of the European continent and as the motherland of classical feudalism, an estate-representative monarchy, and absolutism is worthy of special attention. Its coutume-Roman law and judicial system should be regarded until the end of the eighteenth century in the light of gradual unification and cautious centralization, leaving a niche for regional judicial parliaments. At the same time, after the events of 1789-1794 and 1799-1814, one must note the change of tempo and priorities in development. The Great French Revolution, the rule of the Directorate, and Napoleon I gave birth to an extremist revolutionary model of transformations of State and law, including a hierarchical centralized dualist judicial power strictly orientated towards legislation, the dominance of codes, and in the twentieth century, the expansion thereof.

In Germany, fractionalization of the State affected legal development for a long time. The optimization of the legal system commenced later there, at the end of the nineteenth century. Typical for it was a mild synthesis of codes and federal laws and a system of narrowly-specialized branches of justice. However, legal education is distinctive for the severity and high barriers to "exit". In this respect the professional training of graduates of law faculties to be judicial personnel in the National School of Magistrates in France impresses Russian students more than the exhausting system of compulsory apprenticeship and two State examinations in Germany.

The Scandinavian legal family is interesting for its reasonable and simple court proceedings and optimal combination of legislation and judicial precedent. Regrettably, the extent of literature in the Russian and English languages is insufficient to know the system in depth, for neither lecturers nor students have a knowledge of the Scandinavian languages. This topic serves as a logical transition to the colloquium on the subject of "Convergence of Western Legal Systems: Dreams or Reality?". It happens at the half-way point in the semester and psychologically enables the weaker students to be mobilized by involving them in the general discussion. In seeking examples of convergence – more or less successful – the students undertake an intensive search on the Internet and in journals and monographs; they recall materials from their courses on public and private international law.

The topics "countries of Muslim law" and "Hindu law" are optimally studied not in and of themselves, but as a comparison of two different systems of religious law (external comparison). We would recommend here to rely on the classical works by Russian comparatists.[28] When considering the Far Eastern legal family, one passes on to a comparative analysis of the legal systems of China and Japan (internal comparison). In this last instance one must be aware that despite a certain similarity in the close historical fates of these two countries and the strong Chinese influence on Japan in the early stage of development, they followed different paths. The legal development of China, so enormous in scale and resting on the Confucian tradition, legism, and the ideas of socialist with a Chinese orientation, is more autonomous from the West. The legal system of Japan, which experienced rapid modernization at the end of the nineteenth and pressure from the United States after 1945, bears strong borrowings from the Romano-Germanic and Anglo-American legal families. In any event, the legal cultures of these peoples have a strong traditional origin manifest, for example, in the preference for nonjudicial procedures to settle disputes and the influence of moral and ethical norms.

An analysis of the legal systems of the countries of Latin America and Africa as the concluding topic not only assumes their comparison with one another by virtue of their being fundamentally opposite. Usually we exhaust this topic with reports by students, and the entire course finishes with a student scientific conference which has a country or a problem-institutional theme. In the 2009-2010 academic year we turned for the first time to constitutional justice: the students prepared reports on the United States Supreme Court under the chairmanship of Chief Justice Roberts, the Conseil d'état of France, the Supreme Constitutional Court of the

[28] See N. A. Krasheninnikova, Правовая культура современной Индии [Legal Culture of Modern India. Innovative and Traditional Features] (2009); L. R. Sukiainen, Мусульманское право: вопросы теории и практики [Muslim Law: Questions of Theory and Practice] (1986); id, Шариат и мусульманско-правовая культура [Shariat and Muslim Legal Culture] (1997).

Federal Republic of Germany, and the Constitutional Court of the Russian Federation. The best reports were published.[29]

COMPARATIVE LAW AS CORE OF LEGAL EDUCATION

Comparative law can and should play a pivotal role in a legal education so exceedingly uncoordinated and differentiated by individual disciplines. Objectively the developing process is overcome by the abundance of legal material and the germination of new legal institutions and branches of law generated by the dynamism and complexities of modern life. But this does not mean that lecturers in law should not adapt to these processes. At present in the instructional process "attention is principally devoted to the mastery by a student of knowledge and skills within a single discipline, often without indications how they may be used thereafter when studying other disciplines or in practical activity".[30]

The segmentation of disciplines (that is, not linked with one another) is a serious problem for modern legal education. In the view of Romashov, this should be overcome by an inter-disciplinary synthesis, when instructional courses with a complex subject-matter of cognition are taught by representatives of various scientific orientations. As an example, "such a course may be called legal conflictology, within the framework of which the theory and sociology of law may be successfully combined with legal psychology and branch disciplines".[31]

In our view comparative law is one of the key disciplines in the modern instructional plan. The task of comparative law is not only to expand the intellectual horizons of future students, but to instruct them in matters of foreign legislation, judicial proceedings, and legal mentality, including for practical purposes, having regard to the processes of globalization and intensification of legal relations with a foreign element.

We do not agree with Tolstykh that "at present in Russian comparative law a threatening disproportion is observed" connected with excessive study of foreign constitutional law and insufficient study of foreign civil and

29 Salomatin, note 24 above, pp. 305-345.

30 V. P. Prokopev and S. A. Rogozhin, «Новое качество университетского образования» [New Quality of University Education], in Качество высшего профессионального образования в начале XIX века [Quality of Higher Vocational Education at Outset of XXI Century] (Tiumen, 2002), p. 3.

31 R. A. Romashov, «К вопросу формирования системы юридического образования в современной России» [On the Question of Forming the System of Legal Education in Modern Russia], Юридическое образование в России: в поисках современной модели [Legal Education in Russia: Seeking a Modern Model] (Saratov-Ekaterinburg, 2005), pp. 33, 35.

Diagram 1

Sequence of Studying Comparative Disciplines by Law Students

Bachelor's Degree

1 Year

Introduction to Comparative Law {special course devoted to principal legal systems within Discipline "Theory of State and Law"

Saturation of "History of State and Law of Foreign Countries" and "History of Russian State and Law" with comparative legal analysis. (concluding inter-subject discussion of problems of the model of modernization)

↓

2 Year

Saturation of "Constitutional Law of Foreign Countries" and "Constitutional Law of Russia" with comparative legal analysis (joint inter-subject measures to be conducted by teachers)

↓

3 Year

Accumulation of material on internationalization of law in course of studying Private International Law and Public International Law for subsequent comparative subjects

↓

4 Year

"Legal Systems of Modern Times" or "Foundations of Comparative Law" Basic comparative course considering legal systems grouped into legal families on integrated basis

Instructional module "Significance of Comparative Law for Modern Russia" within framework of instructional course "Problems of Theory of State and Law", which is studied on even of taking State examination

Incorporation of questions on comparative law in syllabus for State examination on theory of State and law

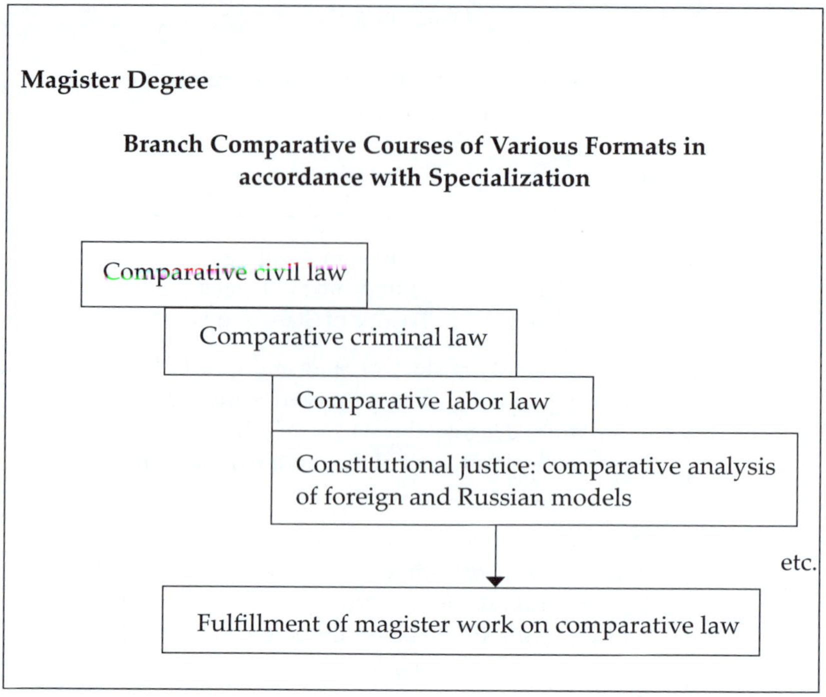

administrative law.[32] In our view, one should reduce the study of individual branches and institutions within the framework of comparativistics, but increase it in all directions. We suggest the scheme described in Diagram 1 for comparativistic courses.

The optimization of the instructional process we see as follows.

In the first year within the base disciplilne "Theory of State and Law" it would be desirable to single out a brief special subject "Introduction to Comparative Law" in which the initial notions are given of the three leading legal families (Anglo-American, Romano-Germanic, and Muslim) and legal cultures. For this Marchenko's study is excellent.[33]

During this same period of study with a view to closer coordination with the synchronically-taught disciplines "History of State and Law of Foreign Countries" and "History of Russian State and Law" one might consider in a comparative key the main problem of our civilization during

[32] V. L. Tolstykh, «Отечественное сравнительное правоведение: проблемы развития» [Fatherland Comparative Law: Problems of Development], Юридическое образование и наука [Legal Education and Science], no. 2 (2004), p. 8.

[33] Marchenko, note 9 above.

the past two centuries – the topic of modernization, relying, for example, of Salomatin and A. S. Tumanova, Политическая модернизация [Political Modernization].

An analogous approach in the second year may be used for the disciplines "Constitutional Law of Foreign Countries" and "Constitutional Law of Russia". Here the comparative analysis is of paths of development (for example, the United States, Russia, European countries) enriches the students' understanding of specific models of constitutionalism, avoiding abstract dogmas and stamps of differentiation.

In the third year in the process of studying "Public International Law" and "Private International Law" there is an abundance of material on the internationalization of law. The view is expressed in foreign literature that there is a sharp reduction in the significance of conflicts norms, but we do not share this view.

The fourth year is the principal link in comparativistics training. The sundry information accumulated by students of a comparative-law character relating to several legal disciplines must be systematized with the assistance of a concentrated semester subject (not less than four hours per week) called "Legal Systems of Modern Times" (or "Fundamental Principles of Comparative Law"). It is advisable to conduct a colloquium and scientific student conferences. In essence on the basis of this key comparativistic subject we have the possibility to encourage students to write diploma works on comparative law and to continue research at the level of magister or kandidat degrees.

The magister creates conditions to study branch comparative law subjects, depending upon the magister specialization. However, together with the basic branch disciplines ("Comparative Civil Law", "Comparative Criminal Law", and so on), provision should be made in the syllabus for subjects of another, problem-institutional format. At Penza State University the specialization 12.00.02 ("Constitutional and Municipal Law") is offered at magister level, with a special subject offered: "Constitutional Justice: Comparative Analysis of Foreign and Russian Models". This special subject, since it is linked with human rights and affects the activities of the most "activist-minded" courts, will also be of interest to other legal specializations, for example, 12.00.01 ("Theory and History of Law and State; History of Doctrines on Law and State").

The time has long since come to join comparative law to one of the specialities from the Supreme Attestation Commission nomenclature and, even more logically, the core base speciality in jurisprudence – 12.00.01.

Finally, the writing of magister theses on comparative-legal problems becomes the ultimate measure of comparativistic training.

In foreign countries the teaching of comparative law is rather extensive, but to various extends and on the basis of different traditions. In recent time it has come to be understood that such teaching may at least occur at four levels: (1) introduction to comparative law; (2) application of the comparative method in all branches of law; (3) use of the comparative approach to sources of law; and (4) the study of a particular special subject from the domain of international or foreign law.[34]

We suggest the various approaches be synthesized. We proceed not only from the informational-cognition actuality of comparative law, but also from its nurturing significance. One must agree with the Italian jurist that a "jurist, future lecturer, practitioner, or State employee must study a discipline which helps him better understand his own legal system and instills in him the nonacceptance of any dogmatism. A legal system in this event will not seem to be something indestructible and unshakeable (here I have in view legal education in the universities of continental Europe); one may not like it, but evaluate it, relating to it as a living organism with weaknesses, merits, and shortcomings. A student should understand that any rule, any institution, or mechanism was created by virtue of certain reasons of a different order. Therefore the natural aspiration arises in him to understand the entire socio-cultural reality conditioning the respective legal system".[35]

However, it also is true that the complexity of modern law and legal systems, and dynamism and periods of unpredictability force us to combine research efforts. We repeat the appeal which we made in 2008: we need new forms of instructional work (for example, collective lectures and discussion with the participation of not less than two lecturers); we urgently need collections of documents for seminars. One or the other might produce international cooperation, the first step towards which might be an international seminar at a particular institution of higher education. One wants to believe that Russian and Ukrainian comparatists will not be required to wait for long.

[34] See E. Krings, "Congrès de l'Academie International de droit comparé. Brisbane – Juillet 2002", *Revue de droit comparé*, no. 4 (2002), p. 414.

[35] A. de Vita, «Место изучения сравнительного права зарубежного стран в подготовке юристов» [Place of Study of Comparative Law of Foreign Countries in Training of Jurists], Юридическое образование: новые подходы в России и Западной Европе [Legal Education: New Approaches in Russia and Western Europe] (2001), p. 84.

Legal System: State, Society, Region, World?

O. F. SKAKUN*

The universal category "legal system" on which the scientific analysis of all legal reality rests often is used autonomously, without adding words which would explain what legal system one is referring to, that of a society or of a State. A number of modern scholars write about the legal system of a State, and others about the legal system of a society. During the Soviet period the category "legal system of developed socialism" was popular,[1] that is, a legal system was regarded in an ideological-historical foreshortening which had regard to a determined stage of the development of a socialist State or society. The term "statehood" in its correlation with the category of "legal system" is being actively used more recently.[2]

The need to consider this issue is that usually a legal system is linked with a State as the principal bearer of public power – even when "legal system of a society" is written. We use the word-combination legal system of Russia, England, United States, France, and so on, which means "national legal system" or "legal system of a State".

The question arises whether there may be several legal systems in a single State, that is, does it have municipal legal systems? May, for example, one speak about the legal systems of municipal formations which have relative autonomy in regional unitary States (political regions of

* доктор юридических наук, Professor. Associate Member, Academy of Legal Sciences of Ukraine, Meritorious Jurist of Ukraine. Emeritus Professor of Kharkov National University of Internal Affairs; author of more than 400 works.

1 N. I. Matuzov, «Правовая система развитого социализма» [Legal System of Developed Socialism], Советское государство и право [Soviet State and Law], no. 1 (1983).

2 V. A. Zatonskii, «Государство и личность в системе государственности (К вопросу о содержании базовых категорий теории государства и права)» [State and Individual in the System of Statehood (On the Question of the Content of Base Categories of the Theory of State and Law)], Государство и право [State and Law], no. 10 (2007), pp. 5-12.

Italy – Trentino-South Tyrol, Aosta Valley, Friuli Venezia, Giulia, Sardinia, Sicily; or the "autonomous communities" of Spain: the Basque country, Catalonia, Galicia, Andalusia, Valencia, and so on)?

Is it correct to speak in retrospect about the origin of a Muslim legal system, or more correct to refer to the legal system of Iraq, Iran, and other Muslim countries? Suppose that the systems of Hindu and Muslim law operate in Pakistan within the boundaries of certain groups or communities of the population which zealously preserve their traditions, especially religious law traditions. The succession of religious law traditions by each new generation of these groups or communities imparts distinctiveness to the legal system of Pakistan. Does this mean that the systems of Hindu and Muslim law function as legal systems within the legal system of Pakistan?

The question is whether it is theoretically proper and logical to analyze a legal system in connection with a society or a State, statehood or a social group, which is distinctive for religious and other weighty peculiarities (customary norms, as, for example, African communities) influencing positive and the entire mechanism of legal regulation of a society within State boundaries?

No less topical is the functioning of inter-State regional-continental legal systems (in Europe: the European Union and Council of Europe). Their existence emphasizes that "legal system" is a generalized theoretical model (or construction) of legal content which functions legitimately and may be multi-tiered.

The topicality of this issue is intensified by the need under conditions of globalization to clarify, concretize, which families (or types) of legal families exist on the planet.[3]

In a single article it is impossible to address all issues. Only the principal ones can become the subject-matter of consideration.

CONCEPT AND STRUCTURE OF LEGAL SYSTEM

First, To seek an answer to the issues raised it is appropriate to begin with the concept and structure of a legal system since these indicators determine the extent to which many legal phenomena are encompassed by a legal system. In doctrinal writings a legal system is a complex integrated category which incorporates all well-structured, organized legal reality and consists of the aggregate of components: norm-creation, administration of justice, legal practice; legal acts (normative, application, interpretative); legal

[3] To designate the full aggregate of legal systems the concepts are used in the theory of law: "legal map of the world" (V. A. Tumanov); "legal geography of the world" (V. Knapp, A. Saidov); "community of legal systems" (Zh. Stalev); "legal circle" (K. Zweigert and H. Kötz).

norms and legal relations; subjects of law and their subjective rights and duties; legal institutions – courts, procuracy agencies, advokatura, notariat, and others; and also legal responsibility, legal consciousness, legal culture, legality, and legal order.[4] A legal system is interpreted as a complex, collective, and multi-tiered concept which reflects the entire aggregate of legal phenomena of society,[5] or "legal phenomena, each of which within the framework of a single structure fulfills its specific service role".[6]

The socialization of legal knowledge provides for the consideration of the legal problem (and legal system is one of the central categories thereof) in the context of society as a whole, and not only its State organization mediating relations with regard to the forming and realization of State power.

The various approaches of modern scholars to defining the concepts and structures of "legal system" are determined by the types of understanding of law (positivist, sociological, natural law, psychological, integrated, and others). Moving away from the positivist interpretation of law inherent to the Soviet era, the majority of modern Ukrainian and Russian jurists link legal system with society, social relations, and place stress on the social conditionality of the components of a legal system. Thus, the Ukrainian scholars Kelman and Murashin believe that "legal system" is a complex of legal phenomena conditions by the objective laws of societal development.[7] Luts calls a legal system the "subsystem of society", a "subsystem of a social system", and regards European legal systems as "inter-State".[8] The Russian legal scholar, Babaev, classifies a legal system as the "aggregate of mutually-dependent, coordinated, and interacting legal means which regulate social relations ...".[9] His compatriot Perevalov, in referring to the conditionality of the complex of legal phenomena by objective laws

[4] Matuzov, Правовая система и личность [Legal System and the Individual] (Saratov, 1997), pp. 13-19; id, Актуальные проблемы теории права [Actual Problems of the Theory of Law] (Saratov, 2003), pp. 93-116.

[5] Matuzov, note 1 above, pp. 18-19.

[6] M. I. Baitin, «Право – связующее звено между политической властью, государством и правовой системой общества» [Law – Connecting Link Between Political Power, State, and Legal System of Society], Вопросы теории государства и права: Личность, право, правовая система [Questions of the Theory of State and Law: Person, Law, Legal System] (Saratov, 1988), p. 38.

[7] M. S. Kelman and A. G. Murashin, Общая теория государства и права [General Theory of State and Law] (Kiev, 2006), p. 277.

[8] L. A. Luts, Европейские межгосударственные правовые системы: общетеоретическая характеристика [European Inter-State Legal Systems: General Theoretical Characteristics] (Lviv, 2004), pp. 49, 109, 200ff (abstract diss. doctor iurid. nauk).

[9] V. K. Babaev, «Правовая система общества» [Legal System of Society], in V. K. Babaev (ed.), Общая теория государства и права [General Theory of Law: Cours of Lectures] (Nizhnii Novgorod, 1993), p. 85.

of societal development, strengthens his definition by stressing that legal phenomena which create a legal system are cognized and constantly reproduced by "people and their organizations (the State)".[10]

The majority of modern legal theoreticians write about the legal systems of States. According to the Russian scholar Siniukov, a national legal system is a historically-specific aggregate of law (or legislation), legal practice, and the dominant legal ideology of an individual country (or State).[11] The Ukrainian legal scholar Rabinovich noted that a legal system is a system of all legal phenomena which exist in a particular State or in a group of States of the same type.[12] These scholars do not confine the functioning of all legal phenomena inherent in a certain society merely to the normative (or specifically juridical) influence on social relations (or State legal regulation), but stress the primary influence of social relations in the sphere, boundaries, of level of State regulation and note the role of legal consciousness, legal nurturing, and other legal phenomena operating in one socio-cultural space. It is understandable that no single State, being a special social formation and a special institution of public power on the scale of a whole society, a super-institutional organization,[13] can effectively function outside a determined system of social relations. Society acts not only as a material, but also as a spiritual basis for the being of the contemporary state. The legal grounds for its activity a State derives in society.

The category "legal system" itself was introduced into legal science in order to designate law as a systemic social phenomenon with a view to the study of its structural elements in interconnection and interaction, and their internal integrity and relative autonomy of functioning. The structure of a legal system[14] serves as the internal organization of law or its

[10] V. D. Perevalov, «Правовая система общества» [Legal System of Society], in V. M. Korelskii and V. D. Perevalov (eds.), Теория государства и права [Theory of State and Law] (1997), p. 463.

[11] V. N. Siniukov, Российская правовая система: Введение в общую теорию [Russian Legal System: Introduction to General Theory] (Saratov, 1994), p. 163.

[12] P. M. Rabinovich, Основы общей теории государства и права [Fundamental Principles of General Theory of State and Law] (Kiev, 1994), p. 147.

[13] I. A. Gomerov, Государство и государственная власть: предпосылки, особенности, структура [The State and State Power: Prerequisites, Peculiarities, Structure] (2002), pp. 474-477.

[14] From the standpoint of a component (or elements) approach, the structure of a legal system may be represented by subsystems: (1) institutional subsystem – subjects of law: individual (legal individual) and collective (legal institutions); (2) normative subsystem – legal norms and principles; (3) functional-social subsystem – legal relations, legal activity, realization of law; (4) ideological subsystem – legal consciousness, legal nurturing, legal culture; (5) communicative subsystem – natural links between the said subsystems and other (economic, political, and so on) systems of society at the national and international levels.

individual parts and simultaneously reflects the stability and development of law, thereby giving the possibility to receive the static and dynamic characteristics of a legal system. The static nature of a legal system is expressed in the stable unity and linkage of elements which are an indicator of relations being in order. And the dynamism lies in the interaction, the substitution of means of linkage of components (and elements which comprise components) between themselves and the external milieu, which may lead to the transition of a legal system to another qualitative state.

NUCLEUS OF LEGAL SYSTEM

Second, the discussions among scholars as to what (or who) is the nucleus of a legal system – law or a subject of law, the bearer of rights and duties, has not resulted in a victory for any of the sides. Some of the Ukrainian and Russian scholars (T. Radko, V. Perevalov, M. Rassolov), being adherents of the humanization of the legal system, believe that the subject of law which acts on the basis of the legal imperatives of society is a central figure of the legal system. Other scholars (O. Zaichuk, N. Matuzov, and N. Onishchenko) call law and legislation the central link of a legal system. Matuzov, for example, writes that with the assistance of legal means a State exercises the necessary influence on social relations (consolidation, regulation, protection, defence).[15]

Indeed, law, which is a result of the interaction of agencies of the State and society in the creation of legitimate prescriptions, acts in the social system as a variety of social communication, and in the legal system as the normative foundation, its static and dynamic carcass. The norms of law are within the legal system as a link thereof with which the remaining portion of the elements thereof are connected in some way. An understanding of law acts as the conceptual foundation of the legal system. The repeated mediating exchange of legal activity, lawful behavior, legal relations are combining elements. Legal practice with its resultative elements (legality and legal order) is an obligatory condition and indicator of the effective functioning of a legal system.

In giving a proper role to the all-encompassing significance of law which penetrates each of the components of a legal system, one must take into account that the forming and functioning of a legal system is directed towards the satisfaction of the needs and interests of man as a person in a legal system. Law arose and exists in society because it is objectively called

[15] Matuzov, note 4 above (1997), p. 26.

upon to be a socially regulatory force, an element of the subjective sphere of the life of society. And society is the aggregate of persons as subjects of law who are endowed with legal personality, have simultaneously similar and dissimilar requirements and interest which may be realized only with the assistance of social communion.

In the legal system a person acquires the character of a person of law through internalization (legal nurturing) and legal socialization. Two counter processes occur: external (movement from society to man) and internal (movement to society proceeds from man).[16] Legal internalization is expressed in the social requirement to regulate, coordinate the activity of people and is effectuated through the system of legal norms, which orientate them towards specific models of behavior and limit activity – undesirable or prohibited. Legal socialization consists of attracting persons towards a system of legal values of society and in reverse their socio-legal activity directed towards adjusting social values.[17] In becoming internalized and socialized, a person acts as a source and a bearer of law, a creator of all legal phenomena, the values nucleus of the legal system.

It is assumed that a person has a legal essence which a natural person inherits as a participant (or party) of social relations, has a high level of legal consciousness expressed in legal self-nurturing and an active relationship with legal norms and values. Therefore rights and freedoms, both natural and inalienable, harmoniously are called upon to be combined with duties, and dignity and honour are to be respected. A person may not be a person of law who neglects the equality of duties and responsibility in relations, the freedom of another person, and disturbs the harmony of interest between a person and society, ignores legal order, that is, does not adhere to the principle of the rule of law. The 1996 Constitution of Ukraine affirms the significance of the subjects of law with their constitutional rights and duties as system-forming material factors of the legal system. The recognition of a person of law (or subject of law) as the central figure of the legal system does not diminish the role of law as a normative foundation of the entire legal system, the central link of the legal system, which connects all the elements thereof.

The present writer is guided by an integrated understanding of law which is based on a synthesis of the natural-law, sociological (including historical), and positivist theories of law, but not by means of their

16 See G. I. Ikonnikova and V. P. Liashenko, Философия права [Philosophy of Law] (2007), p. 115.

17 V. Iu. Shvachka, Правовая социализация лица в современных условиях [Legal Socialization of the Person in Contemporary Conditions] (Kiev, 2008), pp. 4-5 (abstract diss. kand. iurid. nauk).

mechanical summing up; rather by means of their establishment as a unifying base who is a person of law, an individual, his spiritual essence (internal genesis of law), social milieu, and State power (or agencies thereof) born of the milieu (external genesis of law). In perceiving law as a systemic phenomenon, it must be taken into account that society, the State, and the person represent an integral *socium* or distinctive statehood, although various functions are performed here. This statehood becomes the grounds for the development of the legal system thanks to a person of law as a subject of law who acts as the basic natural values sentry of the legal system and the purpose and means thereof.

TYPES OF STATE SYSTEMS

Third, If the view of those scholars who link the concept of "legal system" not so much with society as with the State is supported, it is essential historically to imagine a State-organized formation in which (on the basis of own social relations regulated by law) multi-tiered legal systems were formed during five and a half millennia. These are: (1) States as sovereign formations, the public power in which extended to its population (the majority of modern countries of the world); (2) municipal formations which have relative autonomy as parts of a unified State (subjects of the Federation, autonomous formations in regional unitary and federated States). They, as a rule, have a different legal status and are not constitutionally endowed with the right of withdrawal (secession) from their States; (3) dependent (colonial) State-organized formations which are under the power of a metropolitan but have power structures which administer the population with the assistance of imported law and also customary law (for example, countries of Asia, Africa, and Latin America to the mid-twentieth century); (4) State-similar formations which have been officially recognized as autonomous States but not by all countries of the world (Kosovo, which separated from Serbia, has a new status on the basis of the Declaration of Independence adopted by the Parliament of Kosovo on 17 February 2008) or are virtually unrecognized (Dniestr Moldavian Republic), and others.

To these may be added States which at one time had various degrees of national independence (or sovereignty) or international recognition (the RSFSR and the USSR were not recognized by the international community during the first ten to fifteen years of their existence) or were under the administration of other States.

Each of the said States or State-similar formations has a quality such as "statehood". This quality serves as the grounds for forming and transformation of the legal system. In the functional sense "statehood" assumes the existence of a mechanism for legal regulation and a mechanism for legal influence on social relations. The mechanism for legal regulation consists of a complex of special legal means (norms of law, acts for the realization of norms of law; legal relations; acts of interpretation of norms of law; and others). A mechanism of legal influence, besides the said special legal means, includes general derivative legal means which arise as a consequence of legal regulation (legal consciousness, legal culture, legality, legal order, and others). This mechanism of legal influence assists in determining the peculiarities of legal systems and in establishing families (or types) of legal systems of the world.

BASIS OF STATEHOOD

Fourth, for a proper impression of a legal system which is formed on the basis of statehood it is necessary to explain the understanding of the terms "basis" and "statehood". In Russian philosophical literature the basis is a phenomenon which acts as the necessary condition (prerequisite) and serves as the explanation of the phenomenon.[18]

The understanding of statehood as a complex, integrated organism which self-develops arose lone ago in Russian doctrine but has not been extensively elaborated. At the turn of the twenty-first century this became a "promising orientation of research".[19] The promising nature of this orientation is increased if the modern methodology of jurisprudence is taken into account where natural law theory as at the frontier and law is granted primary in the correlation of law and State. Therefore, the genesis of statehood (proto-States),[20] which is linked with the isolation of agencies of inter-kinship power in ancient times and often classified as legal-statehood. Even those scholars who believe that socio-genesis, law-genesis, and poly-genesis were born virtually simultaneously, they understand the State to be the "legal form of a common (public) power".[21]

In the meaning of "legal statehood" we consider next the term "statehood", thereby strengthening the role of law in the formation of the political, economic, and other systems which characterize the *socium*.

The view is widely shared that the State and statehood have the same root but are not identical concepts. There are various views with regard

[18] Философский словарь [Philosophical Dictionary] (1972), pp. 298-299.

[19] L. A. Morozova, Проблемы современной российской государственности [Problems of Contemporary Russian Statehood] (1998), p. 14.

[20] V. A. Grechenko, «К вопросу о сущности понятия «государственности» [On the Question of the Essence of the Concept of Statehood], Вестник Национального университета внутренних дел [Herald of the National University of Internal Affairs], no. 20 (2002), p. 245.

[21] V. S. Nersesiants, Философия права [Philosophy of Law] (2008), p. 56.

to the concept of statehood. One is that "statehood" is a broader concept that "State" and represents a system of social relations mediated by the State "which contains various phenomena"[22] connected with law and State. In this sense statehood is a system of inter-connected socio-legal, State-political, economic, moral, ethnocultural, and other components with whose assistance the authorities effectuate a regulatory-organizing, stabilizing, integrating, and activizing influence on social relations, and the subjects of a civil society (citizens) influence the State and State power through restraint, direction, norm-creative and organizational activity, and also through the levers of limitation.[23]

According to this view, the structure of statehood includes components which fulfill, at a minimum, these functions: (1) maintenance of equilibrium, defence, balance, and effectiveness of statehood; (2) constant restraint and braking of the development of statehood. Whereas in the first instance the stability is strengthened of both the legal and political systems, in the second their development is held back. The development of statehood in a certain social milieu is effectuated in this dialectical linkage of opposite functions. The legal and political systems are decisive in forming the foundations of any statehood. It follows that statehood arises as a broader concept than the political and legal system and is grounds for their development.

Must the State obligatorily be formed so that statehood is the basis of the legal system of a particular self-governing society? May one consider statehood to be a specific form of politico-legal organization of society which precedes the formation of the State itself (that is, proto-State) and on the basis of which a relatively solitary legal system is formed? May a politico-legal self-governing *socium* which is within a State as part thereof (for example, the Province of Quebec in Canada), be considered to be have statehood (quasi-State)?

In our view statehood cannot be connected solely with the State which was formed. One should take into account the state of statehood in State-similar formations (quasi-States) which: (1) are self-governing (regional) entities and on the path towards creating a State; (2) form their own self-governing structures within a formed State; (3) have not been recognized by international society, although *de facto* they are politically and legally self-sufficient.

The State is the nucleus of the political system of society, its major component. As a social phenomenon which administers, the State may not optimize this role without interacting with society. On the sociological

[22] J. Carbonnier, Юридическая социология [Legal Sociology] (1986), pp. 197, 276-277.

[23] Zatonskii, note 2 above, pp. 6-7.

plane the State is a "specific type of political society"[24] which arose as a result of permanent habitation on a certain territory by a relatively solitary community of people and is administered by an institutionalized authority which has a monopoly right to organized forms of coercion.

An understanding of statehood cannot be reduced solely to the politico-legal organization of society in a formed State; it must be considered more broadly, understanding by statehood the system of social relations mediating State-similar formations which exist or existed within complex States (federated, regional, imperial, unions). It must be recognized that the basis for such relations to arise is the stable, self-sufficient, self-governing *socium* which "virtually at all times is a mixture of the collective and the individual".[25]

Consequently, the legal system is formed on the basis of statehood not only in a sovereign State. Statehood is formed in an unstable State formation during the origin thereof. Statehood manifests itself in a State-similar formation (quasi-State) which is within a certain formed State. The sphere of operation of public power which its administrative apparatus exercises is limited in such a State-similar formation and, as a rule, there is no autonomous representation of its interests without. It is subject (according to the legislatively consolidated principle of the centralization of administration) to the central agencies of power, and also to administrative-supervisory structures and military forces of the metropolitan State on its territory. It does not have all the indicia which are inherent to a State, and the qualitative and quantitative augmentation of the indicia is materially less than a sovereign State has (for example, the absence of autonomous and permanent purposes, tasks, and functions).[26] In essence the term "statehood" may designate a qualitatively lower form of political organization of society that the State. However, the legal system which develops on the basis of such statehood is closely linked and interacts with the legal system of the complex State, of which the State-similar formation is a part.

For example, for centuries Ukrainian territories were part of various States (Poland, Russian Empire, Austrian Empire, and others). Ukraine did

[24] See Jean-Louis Bergel, Общая теория права [General Theory of Law] (2000), p. 240.

[25] E. Burlai, «К проблеме правогенеза: исторические и логические аспекты» [On the Problem of Law-Genesis: Historical and Logical Aspects], in Антропология права: философский и юридический измерения (состояние, проблемы, перспективы) [Anthropology of Law: Philosophical and Legal Dimensions (State, Problems Prospects)] (Lviv, 2006), p. 67 (Materials of First All-Ukrainian Round Table (Lviv, 16-17 September 2005).

[26] O. F. Skakun, Теория государства и права. Энциклопедический курс [Theory of State and Law. Encyclopedic Cours] (Kharkov, 2006), pp. 43-44.

not have an own stable State. However, one cannot deny the origins of the legal system in the early State formation on the territory of modern Ukraine – Kievan Rus (there State construction basically was completed under Yaroslav the Wise in the eleventh century).[27] The subsequent development of Ukrainian statehood is evidenced by the formation of the Galicia-Volhynia Principality (twelfth-thirteenth centuries), the Zaporozhian Sech (sixteenth-seventeenth centuries), and the Hetmanship (seventeenth and eighteenth centuries). The Hetmanship, in the words of the second President of independent Ukraine, Leonid Kuchma, "was incomparably more autonomous than the Ukrainian Soviet Socialist Republic over two centuries".[28] A distinctive statehood was formed on the territory of Ukraine in the twentieth century: the Ukrainian People's Republic (1917-1920), the Western Ukrainian People's Republic (1918-1919), and the Ukrainian Soviet Socialist Republic (1917-1991). Modern Ukrainian scholars note that "although Ukraine was considered to be a union republic within the USSR, an independent State, in fact this was a national-State autonomy".[29]

The form of statehood of the Soviet Union was determined by the dominance of the State over the *socium*, and the legal system of Soviet Ukraine in this sense became a copy of the legal system of the Soviet Union. Both in the USSR and in the Ukrainian SSR political and ideological factors were the basic ones in the development of Soviet law, which was reflected in the exclusive role of the Communist Party in the political system of society and the domination of Marxist-Leninist ideology.

Statehood concentrates the complex of various power, political, legal, and other phenomena and processes (relations, mutual actions) which include positive and negative elements. The nature of the interconnections and interactions to a great extent determines the effectiveness of the functioning of the legal system. Statehood as a political and social reality cannot avoid the prop of a legal system capable of maintaining legal order in society, overcoming negative phenomena with the assistance of legal means. One may judge the essence of statehood by the nature of law formed in a society.

LEGAL MAP OF THE WORLD

Fifth, if one reviews the legal map of the world in its historical dynamism, one may see that from the mid-1950s more than ninety new States arose on

[27] M. Kotliar and S. Kulchitskii, Справочник из истории Украины [Manual on the History of Ukraine] (Kiev, 1996), p. 26.

[28] L. Kuchma, Украина – не Россия [Ukraine – Not Russia] (2003), p. 143.

[29] Grechenko, note 20 above, p. 247.

the ruins of the former colonial empires in Asia, Africa, Latin America, and Oceania: some by means of armed struggle (Algeria, Angola, Mozambique, and others), some by peaceful means (Malagasay Republic, Tanzania). A number of States originated in the twentieth century by means of the "dissolution" or division of union States (Soviet Union, Yugoslavia, Czechoslovakia), or division – the direct withdrawal or secession of a large region from the former States with a view to creating an autonomous State (for example, with the secession of Eritrea from Ethiopia, Bangladesh from Pakistan), or unification (Federal Republic of Germany and the German Democratic Republic). On the basis of new State formations the transformation of former legal systems occurred.

Now Puerto Rico, the British Bermuda Islands, and Palestine are forming their own legal systems thanks to the fact that they have an own parliament, government, and judicial system. Palestinian autonomy was created in 1994. It exists (in the view of the Palestine Liberation Organization) as a transitional formation en route to the realization of a proposed "State of Palestine".[30]

About thirty territories exist in the twenty-first century (American Samoa, New Caledonia, Gibraltar, Falkland Islands, Guam, and others) which are under the external administration of the United Kingdom, France, New Zealand, and certain other countries. They do not have their own State-organized structure and, as classified by the United Nations, are nonself-governing territories since they have an own constitution; however, they are actually dependent with regard to many questions (defence, foreign policy, and so on) on the metropolitan – United Kingdom. New Caledonia (which since 1949 has the status of an "overseas department" of France and in 1998 changed its status on the basis of a treaty with France – received self-government and elects its own government. The French Government, however, appoints the High Commissioner as its representative. The administrative autonomous regions of Portugal (Azore Islands and Madeira in the Atlantic Ocean) are in the course of forming their own relatively autonomous legal system.

Among the determinative indicia which characterize the legal systems of modern municipal formations (quasi-States) one may name the following: existence of a right to own law-creation, adoption of an own constitution or charter as the basic law of the region, and naturally the guaranteed functioning of own legislative, executive, and judicial agencies.

[30] Formally, the State of Palestine was proclaimed on 15 November 1988 in Algiers at a session of the Palestinian National Council, the highest consultative organ of the Palestine Liberation Organization.

CLASSIFICATION OF LEGAL SYSTEMS BY STATE STRUCTURE

If legal systems of States of the world are classified according to the form of their State structure, the following one-tier, two-tier, and three-tier may be singled out among them.

One-tier: these are legal systems of unitary States which have an administrative-territorial division and do not contain other legal systems (Republic Belarus, Estonia, Poland).

Two-tier: these are: (1) legal systems of federal States which combine subjects of a federation (states in the United States; *länder* in the Federal Republic of Germany; and others), each of which have their own legal system since they were endowed with the right to form their own legislative, executive, and judicial agencies and to effectuate own law-creation, adopt a constitution, charter, or statute as the basis law of the said region; (2) legal systems of regional (or complex unitary) States (Italy, Spain, Sri Lanka, and others), within which autonomous formations of a political character function (regional structures). These are internal regional legal systems which are within a complex general national legal system. To this group of regional legal systems it is appropriate to relegate the administrative-political area of Hong Kong, which since 1997 is part of unitary China with the rights of an autonomous formation. It is endowed with the plenitude of legislative, executive, and judicial power and the right to effectuate an autonomous immigration and tax policy. Nominally, Hong Kong belongs to the Chinese People's Republic, but there a legal system continues to function with existed during the period of the Kuomintang.

It is necessary also to recall Scotland, Wales, and Northern Ireland within the unitary United Kingdom, who received real autonomy during the resolution of intra-regional problems and have own legal systems. Or the Faroe Islands within the unitary Kingdom of Denmark, which on the basis of the Act on Self-Government of 31 March 1948 received virtually complete autonomy on all questions except for defence and foreign policy. They conduct an autonomous policy within the European Union. Their legal system is developing according to the modern political structure of the Faroes consolidated in the Treaty on sharing responsibility of 12 May 2005 and in an inter-State agreement of 2006.

Among the Commonwealth of Independent States (CIS) countries which have a complex unitary structure one may cite the example of the Republic Moldova, part of which is Gagauzia, which formally has a base for the development of an own legal system. According to the Law of the Republic Moldova "On the Special Legal Status of Gagauzia (Gagauz Yeri)", adopted in 1994 (Article 1) on the basis of the Constitution of Moldova

(Article 111), Gagauzia is a "territorial autonomous unit with the special status as a form of self-government of the Gagausians".[31] Also reflected in the Basic Law (1998) is the legal status of Gagauzia, its legislative agencies (People's Assembly); executive agencies (Bashkan of Gagauzia and the executive committee (Bakannik committees); and judicial agencies – the Tribunal and courts.

The regulatory system of agencies of power in municipal formations determines the level of statehood on the basis of which the legal system develops.

Three-tier: the legal systems of federated States comprised of subjects of the federation which, in turn, are divided into regional structures such as autonomous national areas (for example, in the Russian Federation there are the following types of subjects of the Federation: Krasnoiarsk Territory; Tiumen Region; autonomous national areas thereof – Khanty-Mansiisk-Iurga, Iamalo-Nenets, and others.

Regional self-government of the second and third tiers of legal systems is a variety of statehood, but the level of their political development is various. The legal system of a country and the legal systems of its internal formations are in close interconnection and interaction since the last, having own statehood, base it on the statehood of the country. Thus, the system of agencies of State power of a subject of the Russian Federation form: legislative (or representative) and the highest executive agency, other agencies which are founded according to the constitution or charter thereof. They are subjects of legal norm-creation and form the normative basis of the legal system of the subject of the Federation.

For example, in the norm-creation, law-application, and other legal forms of activity of the authorities of Moscow Region (as a subject of the Federation), according to the Charter of 11 December 1996 the following take part: Moscow Regional Duma – the legislative (or representative) agency of State power of Moscow Region; the governor – the highest official of Moscow Region; the government – the highest executive agency of State power of Moscow Region; the central and territorial executive agencies of State power of Moscow Region; and the Charter Court of Moscow Region.

Even though the level of socio-economic development of subjects of the Federation depends significantly on the territory, geographical position, size of population, and historically formed structure of the economy, they all have legal equality, which is consolidated by the 1993 Russian Constitution (Article 73) in the principle of "residual competence", when subjects of the

[31] The structure of the administration of the autonomous unit consists of the Executive Committee of Gagauzia headed by the Bashkan and the People's Assembly comprising 35 deputies.

Federation possess the full plenitude of power outside the jurisdiction of the Russian Federation and powers of the Russian Federation with regard to the subject-matter of joint jurisdiction of the Russian Federation and subjects of the Russian Federation. The list of subject-matter of jurisdiction of subjects of the Russian Federation is consolidated in their constitutions or charters, The fundamental principles of legal regulation with regard to questions relegated to the subject-matter of jurisdiction of the Russian Federation, subject-matter of joint jurisdiction, and "residual competence" have been established on the constitutional level (Article 76, 1993 Russian Constitution).[32] Here there is the co-subordination of statehood, and consequently the legal system of each unit of the hierarchical structure of the Federation (the Federation, subject of the federation, and political unit) have distinctions which depend on the level of legal regulation exercised by their State agencies and agencies of local self-government and on the legal status of these agencies.

There are more than 300 regional structures in the world which are entities with self-governing rights (quasi-State) within unitary or federal States.[33] That is why the proposition "statehood – is a State in its relation to the *socium*" is not universal and must be expanded: "statehood – is a State or State-similar formation in their relations to the respective *sociums*".[34]

The existence of own legislative, executive, and judicial agencies which adopt, interpret, and apply legal acts on the territory of a municipal (or regional) formation make it possible to formulate certain constructive elements of their legal systems: the complex of legal values which reflect socio-cultural, moral-religious, national mentality, domestic, and other peculiarities; the constitutionality of phenomena of a legal character (adoption of own constitutions); regional law-creation and subordinate act law-creation which is exercised in strict conformity with State legislation and concerns the needs and interests of inhabitants of a certain region; the system of normative-legal acts of regional significance which are in hierarchical co-subordination; the application of these acts in regional territorial boundaries – the issuance of individual acts of one-

[32] See M. Iu. Karpechkina, «Проблемы законодательного регулирования предметов ведения Российской Федерации и ее субъектов» [Problems of Legislative Regulation of Subject-Matter of Jurisdiction of the Russian Federation and Subjects Thereof], Современное право [Contemporary Law], no. 3 (2007), pp. 25-30; for the text of the Constitution, see W. E. Butler (ed. & transl.), *Russian Public Law* (2d ed.; 2009), pp. 1-40.

[33] I. N. Mukienko, «Типология современных правовых систем: критерии и сравнительная характеристика» [Typology of Contemporary Legal Systems: Criteria and Comparative Characterization], История государства и права [History of State and Law], no. 3 (2007), p. 37.

[34] Iu. N. Oborotov, Современное государство: основы теории [Contemporary State: Foundations of Theory] (Odessa, 1998), p. 94.

off significance which contain prescriptions to a specific person or specific group of persons, and so on.

Municipal (or regional) legal systems also have indicia: they take into account geographical and natural position of the territory; have regard to national and domestic peculiarities of the region; are characterized by relative autonomy and dynamism of development; have common legislative competence with the center; have a sphere of legislative activity free from interference; expand and deepen legal regulation in the sphere of their own exclusive competence; exercise own legal regulation up to the adoption of laws of the State on matters relegated to the subject-matter of joint jurisdiction of the center and regions (so-called forestalling norm-creation); create and ensure the mechanism for overcoming disagreements between central and regional legislation, and so on.

CRIMEAN LEGAL SYSTEM

May the Autonomous Republic of Crimea, which is part of Ukraine, be relegated to State-similar formations which have their own legal system? This question may be answered in the negative. The Autonomous Republic of Crimea is an administrative-territorial unit, an administrative region, just as other regions of Ukraine and the cities of Kiev and Sevastopol. An executive agency (Council of Ministers) and a representative agency (Supreme Soviet) function in the Autonomous Republic of Crimea. To the powers of the Supreme Soviet of the Autonomous Republic of Crimea are relegated (according to Article 10(1), Law of Ukraine "On the Supreme Soviet of the Autonomous Republic of Crimea" of 10 February 1998;[35] Article 4(1), Constitution of the Autonomous Republic of Crimea of 23 December 1998;[36] and especially, Article 135 of the 1996 Constitution of Ukraine) the adoption of the Constitution of the Autonomous Republic of Crimea and making of changes therein with obligatory confirmation thereof by the Supreme Rada of Ukraine.[37] The Supreme Soviet of the Autonomous Republic of Crimea does not have autonomy in the sphere of legislation, however. Just as the soviets of regions, the Supreme Soviet of the Autonomous Republic of Crimea is now endowed with legislative functions.

[35] Офіційний вісник України [Official Herald of Ukraine] (1998), no. 8.

[36] Офіційний вісник України [Official Herald of Ukraine] (1999), no. 1.

[37] The Constitution of the Autonomous Republic of Crimea was adopted at the Second Session of the Supreme Soviet of the Autonomous Republic of Crimea on 21 October 1998, confirmed by Law of Ukraine "On Confirmation of the Constitution of the Autonomous Republic of Crimea" on 23 December 1998, and entered into force from the day of its publication – 12 January 1999.

With regard to law-creation terminology, the Constitution of the Autonomous Republic of Crimea is the sole law which is adopted by its parliament. However, neither the Constitution of Ukraine nor the Constitution of the Autonomous Republic of Crimea say that the Constitution of Crimea is a law. The Constitution of the Autonomous Republic of Crimea (Article 1) and the Law of Ukraine "On the Supreme Soviet of the Autonomous Republic of Crimea" precisely indicate that the Supreme Soviet of the Autonomous Republic of Crimea is the "representative agency of the Autonomous Republic of Crimea" and shall "exercise representative, norm-creative [not legislative – *O. S.*], control functions, and powers within the limits of its competence". In essence the Supreme Soviet of the Autonomous Republic of Crimea is not a parliament which represents the interests of citizens, but rather a regional soviet which represents the interests of territorial communities.[38]

With regard to questions which have a normative-legal character, the Supreme Soviet of the Autonomous Republic of Crimea issues decrees, and with regard to organizational-administrative questions – decisions. The decrees and decisions of the Supreme Soviet of the Autonomous Republic of Crimea, just as the Constitution thereof, are adopted at sessions thereof by open or secret ballot by a majority of votes of deputies of the total number in the Supreme Soviet. A unified departure is observed with respect to the entry into force of normative legal acts and the Constitution of the Autonomous Republic of Crimea: normative legal acts are signed by the Head of the Supreme Soviet of the Autonomous Republic of Crimea within fourteen days after their adoption and enter into force in the procedure established by the Constitution of the Autonomous Republic of Crimea and normative legal acts of the Supreme Soviet of the Autonomous Republic of Crimea. But the Constitution of Crimea, and changes and additions thereto made by the Supreme Soviet of the Autonomous Republic Crimea, before their entry into force are subject to publication after confirmation by the Supreme Rada of Ukraine – the sole agency of legislative power in Ukraine (Article 27, Constitution of Crimea). In addition, according to the Constitution of Ukraine and the Constitution of Crimea, normative legal acts of the Supreme Soviet of the Autonomous Republic of Crimea and the Council of Ministers of the Autonomous Republic of Crimea with regard

[38] This is affirmed by decision of the Constitutional Court of Ukraine relating to an official interpretation of Articles 3 and 5 of the Law of Ukraine "On the Status of Deputies of Local Soviets" (the case concerned the status of deputies of soviets). It is indicated therein that the Basic Law of Ukraine contains no provisions relative to prohibiting a deputy of a rural, settlement, district, or regional soviet to combine his mandate with other types of activity. This decision in essence extended to deputies of the Supreme Soviet of the Autonomous Republic of Crimea.

to issues of jurisdiction of Crimea must be consistent with the Constitution and laws of Ukraine.

The Constitution of the Autonomous Republic of Crimea, as a codified act whose content addresses competence and status, regulates the organization of State power and determines the status and competence of these agencies within the territorial framework of the autonomous formation.[39] According to the Constitution and other normative acts, the Autonomous Republic of Crimea is, as an administrative-territorial entity, a self-governing organization of the population – the local agencies of authority are elected by the population and have the right autonomously to decide the majority of issues of local life; however, the internal self-government thereof usually is limited by the sphere of administrative activity.

Thus, the Autonomous Republic of Crimea should not be regarded as a legislative unit analogous to the autonomous formations of Spain, Italy, Sri Lanka, and others. As the Constitutional Court of Ukraine pointed out, referring to the Constitution of Ukraine (Article 133), the Autonomous Republic of Crimea is an administrative unit within the administrative-territorial structure of Ukraine.[40]

RELIGIOUS AND STATE LEGAL SYSTEMS

It was noted above that the basis for the diversity of legal systems within a State is statehood having different degrees of development. But if one contemplates the coexistence of "parallel" legal systems of the religious type – contemporary official and inherited community-religious systems – the question arises as to whether religious law (and not statehood) is the basis for their development. To the category of historically-formed system of religious law one may relegated Muslim law in the countries of the Arab East, Hindu law in India, and Jewish law in Israel, where religious-legal teachings have been combined with the continuous preservation of a community structure and the development within the community of rules of behaviour set out in religious sources.

[39] The legal status of the Constitution of the Autonomous Republic of Crimea and its place among legislative acts of Ukraine should be officially determined in the Law "On Normative-Legal Acts of Ukraine", proceeding from the principle of "legal dominance". The draft is being discussed in the Supreme Rada of Ukraine.

[40] The decision of the Constitutional Court of Ukraine with regard to a constitutional submission by fifty people's deputies of Ukraine concerning the conformity to the Constitution of Ukraine (constitutionality) of the provisions of the Constitution of the Autonomous Republic of Crimea and Law of Ukraine "On Confirmation of the Constitution of the Autonomous Republic of Crimea", 16 January 2003.

May one consider that now in Iraq, Jordan, Kuwait, Morocco, Saudi Arabia and other countries, where Islam is the State religion, two types of legal systems coexist: one – contemporary and conditioned by statehood (so-called legal system of Muslim countries); the second – Islamic-religious, which arose within the Islamic community on the base of religious sources (Muslim law)? To answer this question affirmatively is possible only for certain countries of the Arabian Peninsula and the Persian Gulf. One should take into account that after the issuance of the Law of the Osman Empire on the Majalla (1869-1877)[41] and legislative acts on personal status, there was a gradual rejection of the fiqh as the principal legal form;[42] the leading source (or form) of Muslim law became the normative legal act. The legal systems of the most developed Arab countries with certain deviations began to be structured on two basic models: the Romano-Germanic (French) – Egypt, Syria, Lebanon and countries of the Maghreb, and the Anglo-American – Iraq and Sudan.

If the most recent secularization processes (or reduction) of Muslim law are taken into account which are occurring in connection with the adaptation thereof to the requirements of the modern world market and mutually-advantageous international cooperation, it turns out that the "spirit" and stable religious components of Muslim law are not identically part of all modern legal systems of the Muslim countries. By degree of retention of Muslim (or Islamic) law and use in national law of the norms of the fiqh, modern legal systems of Muslim countries may be roughly divided as follows:

[1]. legal systems which retained Islamic law as the core, the central link, an element of public order (Saudi Arabia, Iran, Pakistan, and others). The constitutions and laws of these States contain provisions concerning loyalty to the principles of Islam. The motherland of Islam, Saudi Arabia, is a model of functioning Muslim law. Here the shariat has higher legal significance than a law and even the "base system", the Basic Law (Constitution) adopted in 1992. It is indicated in the "base system" that this is an Arabian, Islamic, sovereign kingdom; the purpose of secondary and higher education is to introduce the Islamic faith into the consciousness of

41 The basis of the Madjali Code is works by representative of the Hanifa School of Muslim law, Ibn Nu'man ibn Thabit and Abu Said al-Hademi, whose interpretation was official in the Osman Empire from the sixteenth century. The Madjali Code operated in a number of Arab countries until the mid-nineteenth century and in Lebanon, Jordan, and Kuwait individual articles are applied even now.

42 Fiqh is a theory of Muslim law which is part of the shariat; principles of faith comprise another part of the shariat – moral behavioural provisions and prescriptions of the sect (regulation of prayer, fast, religious holidays, and other duties of a believer).

new generations. According to the 1979 Constitution of Iran all laws and decrees must be based on Islamic norms (Article 4); governmental edicts which are contrary to the principles of Islam may not be applied (Article 170). The islamicization of Pakistan in the last decades of the twentieth century was on a large scale, confirmed by these facts: a rejection of general elections if they do not meet the principles of Islam; creation of the Council of Islamic Ideology (1999) with a view to bringing legislation of Pakistan into conformity with the shariat; entry into operation of a law on the islamicization of the socio-political life of Pakistan;

[2]. legal systems in which Islamic law is not the central element but plays an important role in social life (Yemen Arab Republic, Qatar, Kuwait, Libya, Sudan, United Arab Emirates, Brunei, Bahrain). They are subjected to the influence of continental and Anglo-American legal systems; however, they have not lost loyalty to the Koran and other sources of Islamic law and, moreover, aspire to enhance the influence of the last. A distinctive renaissance is observed of Islamic legal culture and a return to traditional Islamic values. In the Constitution (Article 3) of unified Yemen (Yemen Arab Republic) the shariat is proclaimed to be the source of all legislation. Since 1975 Yemen has embarked upon the codification of norms of Islamic law, having created a special commission for this purpose. In Libya (official name: Great Socialist People's Libyan Arab Jamahiriya)[43] at the beginning of 1977 the Koran was proclaimed to be the "law of society", which replaces the Constitution. The 1985 Constitution of Sudan, together with custom, regards Islamic law as the principal source of legislation. The legislation of the United Arab Emirates regulates the legal status of imams and hatibs of mosques. Although Islamic courts have been eliminated or are in the process of liquidation, the adoption of judicial decisions is most often effectuated under the influence of a Muslim legal consciousness and not norms of law. For example, in the criminal codes of Kuwait (as amended in 1964) and Bahrain (1976) the influence of Muslim law is traced in punishment for use of alcoholic beverages and gambling. In Brunei a law on the limitation of the consumption of alcoholic beverages has been adopted.

[3]. legal systems where the influence of Islamic law is confined to the level of general principles, so-called "advanced" legal systems (Algeria, Egypt, Jordan, Iraq, Morocco, Syria). Preference is given to normative legal acts of the State which regulate broad spheres of legal relations. They are drawn

[43] Jamahiriya is a State of the masses, which means the participation of the entire population of the country in the administration of the State.

up not without borrowings from norms of Romano-Germanic and Anglo-American law. The declaration of Islam to be the State religion emphasizes that the State respects the Islamic religion which is professed by the majority of the population and in general form declares its favor towards certain Islamic traditions as the cultural heritage of the people.

The 1971 Constitution of Egypt (Article 1) provides that the "Egyptian people are part of the single Arab nation", which consolidates the idea of Pan-Arabism. In these countries, as a rule, it is established constitutionally that the head of State may only be a Moslem (Algeria); Islamic is a source of legislation (Algeria, Egypt). In the domain of family law laws have been adopted which are based on Islamic law (Egypt, Lebanon, Syria, and so on). One may state that the sphere of operation of Islamic law is limited, as a rule, by the "law of personal status". Islamic courts consider cases (on the basis of norms of Islamic procedural law) only to resolve disagreements connected with "personal status" relations, marriage, family, trusteeship, guardianship, and so on. The civil codes of Egypt (1948), Algeria (1975), Iraq (1951) recommend that judges fill gaps in the law by using the principles of Islamic law.

[4]. legal systems which preserved the least influence of Islamic law (Turkey, Tunisia, Morocco). Turkey, which now seeks to join the European Union, adopted European models of personal status in 1926, family law, and law of inheritance, thereby breaking off from traditional Islamic norms. In Turkey polygamy is condemned, as are the unilateral dissolution of marriage by the husband and the unequal division of property between sons and daughters of the deceased. The 1982 Constitution of Turkey declared the republic to be democratic, secular, and a social rule-of-law State, although it is a country of Islamic faith. There are no Islamic courts. The shariat, whose decisions and legal provisions are the foundation for Sunni Moslems, have retained influence only in civil society which used traditional Islamic methods for resolving disputes. The western European way of life has embedded itself more deeply in Turkey than in other Muslim countries.

In Tunisia Islamic law is officially recognized as a subsidiary source of law; however, the instances of rejection of the right of a Muslim women to inherit, if she has married a non-Muslim, are not unique. Polygamy has been prohibited in marriage and family relations by legislation, and various rights of women and men have been established. Islamic courts have been abolished, the independence of judicial power proclaimed, and the provision constitutionally consolidated that a court decree is rendered in the name of the people and fulfilled in the person of the President of the Republic. The Family Code of Morocco when regulating family law relations departed from Islamic law: the age of men who enter into marriage is raised (from 15 to 18 years); a girl may autonomously choose a husband without the trusteeship of a father or brother; children born out of wedlock may be officially registered, and the mother has the right to give them her own surname.

The said division of legal systems into groups – depending upon the degree of retention of Islamic law therein – is a rough one. The boundaries between these groups are flexible. In the majority of Muslim States an inclination is observed to subordinate market relations to general legislation which, as a rule, is not orientated towards Muslim criteria. In countries of the Muslim world statehood as the basis of the development of legal systems has not lost decisive significance for their formation and functioning. This has merely acquired a religious "spirit" as a consequence of the greater or lesser influence of Muslim law in the past and in the present.

The legal systems of the post-Soviet States with a Muslim population differ from the said legal systems of the Muslim countries: there Islamic law does not exert an impact of principle on socio-political and State-legal life, although individual spheres thereof are regulated – in various countries differently (Azerbaijan, Kazakhstan, Uzbekistan, Turkmenistan, Tadzhikistan, and others). It is not appropriate to speak about the existence of parallel legal systems even in some of them.

It is wholly inappropriate to accept the views of some "patriots" from non-Muslim States that Islam and its legal system are being "carried over" to European and other countries together with the arrival of Muslim immigrants there. In European countries various models relative to immigrants operate: (1) assimilation (rejection of native cultures and acceptance of the values of the society into which they are injected); (2) integration (the mixing of cultures is provided for, but in essence there is assimilation, which is deferred for a certain period); (3) entry of an immigrant into society with all of its cultural peculiarities when subordination is required to the generally-accepted norms in the State of sojourn.[44] It is impossible to transport a legal system and the territory on which it functions, but it is essential to respect all legal systems (religious and secular).

[44] N. Rouland, Историческое введение в право [Historical Introduction to Law], transl. from the French (2005), p. 553.

ABSTRACT FORMS OF STATEHOOD

At first glance religion was solely the basis for forming the Muslim legal system in the past. In fact the sources of any statehood and legal system is the *socium*, the community, which is transformed on the basis thereof. Religion, which takes possession of the consciousness of the members of such a community, predetermines the rules of behaviour that a formed as a result of repetition and objectification of social circumstances. The forming and functioning of religious-legal norms occur in close connection with social possibilities of their realization by the participants of these relations, for example, by members of the Muslim community.

In this context it is advisable to recall the view relating to the form of statehood set out by the Russian scholar Cheshkov[45] and developed by the Ukrainian scholar Oborotov.[46] They classify statehood as an abstraction of the type "civilization", "society", or "labour" and understood by statehood a State in its relation to the *socium*. Cheshkov singled out three forms of statehood which developed in the course of civilization: monadal, reflective, and self-sufficient. Oborotov added to the list the pluralist form of statehood where man is allotted a central place.

Monadal statehood is called form-formation, which developed on the basis of the community and therefore is characteristic for the period of the origin of civilization (States of antiquity and early Middle Ages). Reflective statehood is deemed to be a form-formation which arose on the basis of two types of community which dissolved (antiquity and Germanic). Unlike the diversity of monadal statehood, reflective statehood was embodied in a single form of being – the nation-State – and became the first form-formation of the political State, a special (autonomous) form of social being/consciousness. Self-sufficient statehood was expressed in the form of dominance of the State over the *socium*, which is characteristic of totalitarian regimes. In denying reflective statehood or the State in general as a work of society, the self-sufficient statehood attempts to place the State above society, which led to a dead-end situation, exit from which became not simple for a society.

If the above view as to the forms of statehood are used, one may recognize that the basis for the development of the Muslim (and also the Hindu and

[45] M. Cheshkov, «Государственность как атрибут цивилизации: кризис, угасание или возрождение» [Statehood as an Attribute of Civilization: Crisis, Extinction or Renaissance], Мировая экономика и международные отношения [World Economy and International Relations], no. 1 (1993), pp. 30-32.

[46] Iu. N. Oborotov, [The Contemporary State: Foundations of Theory] (Odessa, 1998), pp. 94-95.

Jewish) legal system became monadal statehood, which originated in the Muslim (or Hindu or Jewish) community with the multiplicity of mutual links thereof. The Muslim legal system was formed in a certain *socium* which developed within its own boundaries rules of behaviour proposed in religious sources and combined with traditional norms of customary law, the *adat*. The Muslim legal system expressed and incorporated the entire legal organization of the Muslim community within certain State boundaries. The State supported and developed the Muslim legal system through the interpretation by jurists (fakirs) of religious texts. The *socium*, the character of the dynamics of the public attitude, determined the domination of certain sources or forms of law (especially the extent of the preservation of Muslim law), the similarity and differences in the structure of law, legal institutions, legal culture, and so on.

One may state that the genesis and formation of Muslim law within the community differs from the modern legal systems of Muslim States. These distinctions are expressed in a specific monadal statehood of the Muslim legal system, which was reborn over the centuries not without the influence of the State.

Any society is not a closed system of certain relations but an organism which constantly develops. The States acts as a factor which promotes the improvement thereof and organizes this by means of the effectuation of direct legal regulation of various processes therein. This quality of social development naturally requires constant renewal of law and each of its systems, particular legal systems to a varying extent experiencing changes depending upon their links with social processes.

If the fundamental bases of Muslim law still remain constant since the tenth century, when they were formed in Arabia, the legal system of the Muslim countries formed on the basis of their statehood has proved to be dynamic, especially during the second half of the nineteenth and the twentieth centuries. During this period the system of law, legal consciousness, and legal activity which reflect to a certain extent a generalization of legal reality, experienced the influence of secular legal systems of the Romano-Germanic and Anglo-American types. This is normal not least because not only Muslims live in the Arab East.

The inheritance of elements of Muslim law are embodied in the most recent forms of law-creation, application of law, legal protection and defense, and the like. In modern Iran the Council of Guardians of the Constitution operates (twelve members), the basis duty of which is verification of draft laws for conformity to Muslim (Islamic) law and in the event divergences are identified with the shariat, they send the draft laws for reworking. In essence, Muslim law acts as a certain form of constitutional justice which is filled with traditional religious content. The highest measure of the constitutionality of a legislative act is not the constitution of the State or international human rights standards, as is typical for civilized secular States, but Muslim law, the shariat.

The Muslim legal system (if it is studied not through the use of universal abstractions and generalizations, but cultural and historical specifics) was structured on the basis of a profound unity of religious-legal regulation of social relations. Today one may hardly assert that there are "parallel" legal systems in Muslim States. Their existence may be recognized only in the first group of States in the aforesaid classification of Muslim countries.

The structure of legal systems in complex federal States of the Arab East has no special differences with States having a federal structure in Western Europe and other continental regions. In Muslim federal States one observes the same hierarchical co-subordination of the legal system of the federation and the legal system of a municipal formation. Thus the Kurdistan Region (usually called by Kurds "Southern Kurdistan") was endowed in the federated Iraq under the 2005 Constitution with the right to have a constitution, legislative parliament, government, and own armed formations, which testifies to the statehood thereof as a subject of the Federation and consequently about the presence of an own legal system.

Statehood in its broad understanding as the aggregate of relations in a self-sufficient, self-governing, autonomous *socium* is a turning point for the legitimate and legal development of a legal system. The maturing of these relations occurs thus: they are born in a community at the stage of forming statehood; they are transformed into a community of formed States; they return to a municipal formation.

GLOBALISM AND SUPRANATIONALITY

The existence of a large number of legal systems and the trends of their configuration in the future are not exhaustive by State and municipal formations. Under conditions of globalization the highest level of their formation becomes the inter-State level. Globalism in law, if we regard this as a movement towards universality, finds reflection in international legal cooperation and inter-State integration, international agreements and obligations, harmonization of national system of legislation and unification of norms of law, maintenance of international legal order, priority of general humanitarian values, and so on. In the supranational organization-power aspect globalism finds itself in the creation of inter-State communities, which in Europe are the Council of Europe and the European Union, whose legal systems operate on the basis of statehood (close to a confederation or even a federation)[47] with their own specific indicia – general and special. To the category of general indicia one may relegate: (1) functioning within limits which have been determined by the constitutive document in accordance with international norms and principles (general and regional); (2) eliciting will through subjects of international law; (3) basing activity on a system of norms objectified in external forms of law – normative legal act, normative-legal treaty, judicial precedent, and others.

The special indicia of the legal systems of the Council of Europe and the European Union include also: (1) different level of encompassing social life on the European continent; (2) dissimilarity of systems of political and legal structures, with whose assistance: (a) the executive general organs of these communities exercise a regulatory-organizing and protective-defensive influence on relations between States and societies; (b) citizens of these States react to the activities of executive organs – support or condemn, activize or limit (for example, the failure to support the draft constitution of the European Union by the French population at a referendum). Whereas the European Court for Human Rights operates in the Council of Europe and forms European standards in the domain of human rights protection, the European Union differs from the Council of Europe not so much in the activity of the European Court of Justice as in the multi-tiered system of law (primary, secondary, tertiary) objectified in such sources or forms as constitutive treaties, regulations, directives, judicial precedents, and so on. The European Union is characterized by a high level of legal unification, legislative harmonization, effective means of normative-legal integration, and most important – by recognition of the priority of norms of this community over norms of law of the States-parties in the event conflicts arise between them.[48] These and other peculiarities (development of norm-creative function, elaboration of procedures for norm-creation based on international principles; direct operation and supremacy of European law relative to national law of States-parties, and so on) testify to the high level of self-government of the European Union and the branching out of the legal system of the European Union.

[47] The view exists that the European Union is a supranational organization of power of the federated type which by form and content is close to the model of a "federation of sovereign States". See V. I. Salo, Внутренние функции государства в условиях членства в Европейском Союзе [Internal Functions of the State Under Conditions of Membership in the European Union] (Kharkov, 2008), p. 4 (abstract diss. kand. iurid. nauk).

[48] L. Luts, «Источники права Европейского Союза: общетеоретические аспекты» [Sources of Law of the European Union: General Theoretical Aspects], in Проблемы создания государства и защита прав человека в Украине [Problems of the Creation of the State and Protection of Human Rights in Ukraine] (Lviv, 2004), pp. 470-472 (Materials of X Regional Scientific-Practical Conference (5-6 February 2004)).

One should take into account that the European Union is a specific inter-State association which includes the Communities. The last by their legal nature are also inter-State organizations and forms of inter-State cooperation in the sphere of foreign policy. They have expanded legal personality in comparison with the curtailed legal personality of the European Union and consequently may claim to have their own legal systems which are part of the legal system of the European Union (especially this was observed in retrospect – before the formation of the European Union).

It is understandable that the correlation and interaction of international law and the legal systems has special importance in conditions of globalization when the process is occurring of an expansion of economic, cultural, legal, and other links, duties, and dependencies from the local to the general and *vice versa*, irrespective of spatial boundaries, including State boundaries.[49] Intensification of the interaction between the legal systems of the world leads to such intertwining that they acquire a new quality. Globalization inevitably will further the formation of a global social system where several levels of legal systems will function: (1) national, which is a complex of interconnected phenomena in the sphere of national jurisdiction of a State (regulated by municipal law); (2) inter-State as a complex of interlinked phenomena in relations between States; (3) transnational (international contractual) – between private persons on questions which are not regulated either by domestic or by international law, but are regulated on the principle "all is permitted which is not expressly prohibited by law"; (4) supranational, as a complex of interlinked phenomena which operate in the sphere of supranational jurisdiction since they create global problems and interests of mankind. The qualitative unity between them may form a global legal system.[50] In this connection it is appropriate to quote Afanasev: "Complex, multi-tiered systems will rule the future world, not necessarily even State systems, in which such factors that regulate mutual relations in various spheres and ensure general stability, such as law and morality, may prove to be not in the last place".[51]

[49] Глобализация и развитие законодательства (очерки) [Globalization and the Development of Legislation (Essays)] (2004), p. 136.

[50] See O. A. Lvova, Трансформация правовой системы России в период глобализации (вопросы теории и практики) [Transformation of the Legal System of Russia in the Period of Globalization (Questions of Theory and Practice)] (Ulianovsk, 2003), pp. 3-4 (abstract diss. kand. iurid. nauk).

[51] Iu. N. Afanasev, «Опасная Россия» [Dangerous Russia], in Iu. N. Afanasev, Традиция самовластия сегодня [Tradition of Despotism Today] (2001).

COMPLEX FORMATION OF LAW-STATEHOOD

In summing up, it is necessary to point to the advisability of involving in an analysis of legal system the category of "law-statehood", having regard to its potential as a basis for the development of a legal system. Law-statehood is a complex formation which rests on the aggregate of contacts, mutual relations, mutual influences between a person, society, and the State through law, when law fulfills its regulatory-organizational and protective-defensive functions. Law-statehood which gives impetus to the development of a legal system, is possible in a human community (or *socium*) which is relatively autonomous, self-governing, and formally (to the necessary extent) self-sufficient politically and legally.

Thanks to autonomy and diversity, openness and tolerance, national legal systems based on own law-statehood, create the obvious prerequisites both for splitting law in space (legal systems of municipal formations) and for aggregating it (legal systems of inter-State communities), as a result of which they change the municipal and world infrastructure.

Attention must be drawn to one of the distinctive features of law-statehood – State sovereignty is not an indicator thereof. It also does not determine the existence of the legal system since legal order is inherent to any of them (world order is comprised of the interaction of such legal orders). Subjects of a federation, political (or legislative) entities within regional States, and other State-similar formations also do not have State sovereignty. Those States have sovereignty within whose territorial boundaries these State-similar, regional formations are situated. Therefore, the functioning of a legal system of a separate country is limited by the territory on which States exercise their sovereignty. Within a sovereign country several legal systems may coexist besides the general legal system of the State.

However, the supremacy of State power on the territory of a country and independence in international relations is increasingly being limited by international law. This is connected with the formation of transnational societies not under the control of a State; the formation of international and inter-State (regional-continental) communities and commonwealths; the activization of activity of international governmental and nongovernmental organizations and institutions; and also the decentralization within a State in connection with the expanded rights of its regions. Therefore, the modern understanding of sovereignty does not exclude the possibility and necessity of a democratic limitation by States of their sovereign rights in the interests of resolving problems of the world society by joint efforts and in the interests of many States.[52] Inter-State legal systems which arise on the basis of law-statehood of several *sociums* enjoy the sovereign rights of the States which are delegated to them.

CONCLUSIONS

The ultimate position may be as follows: the diversity of legal systems (States, inter-State and municipal formations) for which law-statehood is the basis is not precluded by the fact that in comparative law the legal systems of States (or *sociums* thereof) act, numbering more than 200 in the world.[53] The specific dimensions of legal systems are: (1) legal dimension – characterized by the presence and operation of legal means and other phenomena which form the structure thereof; (2) territorial dimension – sovereignty within a determined space representing a kind of "jurisdictional zone" within whose limits law has the highest legal force, is capable of influencing social relations, and occupies a priority place relative to other social regulators; (3) temporal dimension (chronosphere) having temporal, chronological parameters (genesis, formation, transformation, contemporary functioning, or otherwise: "the moment of time, duration, simultaneity, repetition, intensiveness, rhythm, and continuity").[54]

The accent should be placed on the fates of legal systems in the process of globalization. The unification trends underlying globalism should not cede distinctiveness of each legal system of the world, devalue them. It is vital that globalization not undermine the foundations not only of cultural pluralism, but of legal pluralism, when the boundaries between legal families and legal systems that underpin the universality of types of cultures and civilizations will be wiped away.[55]

The process of forming European and international legal space must be structured on a consensual basis, having regard to the will or interests of the peoples of all States which are or who wish to enter them. Under these conditions the responsibility of law is enhanced in modern States. First, law should ensure the gradual democratic development of a socially-orientated society, limit the monopoly of the State to power, curtail the usurpation

52 Note 49 above, p. 142.

53 Naturally when one speaks about the legal systems of the world, one has in view the legal systems of States and not the legal systems of inter-State communities or municipal formations.

54 V. F. Martynov, Параметричкеские и структурные характеристики правовой системы современной России: теоретико-методологический анализ [Parametric and Structural Characteristics of Legal System of Modern Russia: Theoretical-Methodological Analysis] (Spb., 2005), p. 109 (abstract diss. doctor iurid.nauk).

55 A. I. Kovler, Антропология права [Anthropology of Law] (2002), pp. 4-5.

of power, and ensure pluralism (political, economic, ideological). Second, with the development of international legal cooperation of States as a global aim which is reflected in the integration of ties, mutual relations, and rules of behaviour when their diversity increases, law must fulfill the role of a means of bringing order, of being a positive influence on the progress of socio-cultural interaction between all legal systems – inter-State, State, and municipal as parts of one another and bring to each of them qualitative change.

The Concepts of 'Jus' and 'Lex": Historical and Legal Linguistic Aspects

R. A. ROMASHOV*

This contribution imposes special burdens upon the translator because there are no English equivalents for the variety of Russian terms for law. We use the Latin "jus" [право] and "lex" [закон] to distinguish between право and закон respectively throughout the article and indicate in square brackets the Russian versions of certain English equivalents that we have chosen – WEB.

The correlation of "jus" and "lex" is among the eternal topics of scientific and theoretical discussions. Herein we consider this problem not from the general philosophical standpoint, but more concrete legal historical and legal linguistic positions, and in doing so the principal method being used is the method of comparative law analysis that enables various approaches to be juxtaposed for an understanding of the aforesaid phenomena both in historical retrospective and in modern Russian and western European jurisprudence.

CORRELATION OF LEX AND JUSTICE [ПРАВДА] IN ANCIENT AND MEDIEVAL RUS

An excursion into the history of the formation of the words "jus" and "lex" enables one to say that from the outset the word "lex" was used to designate the objective system of regulatory-protective norms. The word "jus"

* доктор юридических наук, professor. Meritorious Figure of Science of the Russian Federation; Head, Chair of Theory of Law and State, St. Petersburg University of the Ministry of Internal Affairs of Russia; author of numerous books on legal theory and legal conflictology.

appeared in the Russian legal language only at the end of the seventeenth and beginning of the eighteenth centuries as a result of the transformation of the word "justice" [правда]. It should be noted that the understanding of "justice" [правда] in the Ancient Russian State and Medieval Rus differed materially from the modern understanding. Whereas at present "justice" [правда] is a synonym for "truth" (the antipode of lie), in Ancient and Medieval Rus the word "justice" [правда] described an act of princely law-creation.[1] Functionally, the word justice [правда] represented in its first four letters the instrument of "rule" (which in Russian has the same four letters) used by the ruler (which word in Russian also has the same four letters) in order to realize own powers of authority. As a result the word "justice" [правда] was the formalized will of the lord. Consequently, "justice" [правда] could not exist distinct from the will of the lord.[2]

A consideration of the correlation of the terms "justice" [правда] and "lex" in ancient Russian law, in our view, it is advisable to undertake in the context of a comparative analysis of the concepts "lex" and "custom" [обычай].

In the view of Sergeevich, "custom" and "lex" in Ancient and Medieval Rus represented identical categories. "Our first chronicler", Sergeevich wrote, "mentions not only the 'laws of the fathers', but also the 'customs of the fathers'. The words "lex" and "customs" he substituted for one another. The legends coming from the fathers he without distinction calls customs and laws. These laws and customs have for him the same source: the 'activity of the fathers'".[3] Thus, unlike the "justice" [правда] representing the result of princely law-creation and being a type of proto-legislative (in the modern understanding of the words "lex" and "legislation") normative legal acts, the "lex russica" were examples of legal customs "applied in individual instances by virtue of the agreed persuasion of persons needing to be subjected to them".[4]

[1] It should be noted that specialists consider the Russkaia Pravda to be a digest of princely laws, the sources of which are norms of customary law, princely charters, and individual decrees. See M. B. Sverdlov, От Закона Русского к Русской Правде [From Lex Russica to the Russkaia Pravda] (1988), p. 4.

[2] Here and hereinafter the materials have been used which were published in R. A. Romashev, «Русское право: закон, правда, указ (из истории отечественного правосознания)» [Russian Law: Lex, Truth, Edict (From the History of Russian Legal Consciousness)], in V. G. Grafskii (ed.), Наш трудный путь к праву: Материалы философско-правовых чтений памяти академика В. С. Нерсесянца [Our Difficult Path to Law: Materials of Philosophical and Legal Readings in Memory of Academician V. S. Nersesiants] (2006), pp. 347-354.

[3] V. I. Sergeevich, Лекции и исследования по древней истории русского права [Lectures and Studies on the Ancient History of Russian Law], ed. and preface V. A. Tomsinov (2004), p. 10.

[4] Ibid., p. 2.

In Sergeevich's opinion, "customary law arises under the impact of two forces. First, the individual consciousness of the material interests of man, under the influence of which a particular means is determined for his actions. This is the principle of self-determination (autonomy). Underlying it is personal interest, personal discretion as to what should be under given conditions but not an abstract idea of "justice" [правда] or equity. But self-determination in and of itself does not create customary law. If the actions of personal will of different persons are identical in identical instances and a significant mass thereof accumulates, a second force arises convincing all who know about the existence of a certain form of actions, a certain practice – to so act. This is the inert force of usage. A form of action chosen by some, always more energetic, people becomes a general norm, a custom, thanks to the fact that others form the habit, more or less passively, to act so. Some practice passes into a general custom because by means of the passive imitation the actions of progressive people form the conviction of the need to act thus and not otherwise. A custom proceeds not from a general, but from individual persuasion that become more or less general. We say "more or less" because the persuasion of each performing a custom in the truth, the equity, and the reasonableness of the grounds thereof are not needed for the operation of the custom. Only general persuasion is needed of the need to act according to predominant practice. On this condition people will subject themselves to the custom although personally some of them may not be correspondingly persuaded. "A general custom is the Tsar's edict", says the Russian proverb, that is, a custom also is binding, also binds the will, as does an edict".[5]

Thus, Russian lex (custom) and Russian "justice" [правда] (edict of the lord) have underlying them an individual will-power. However, the most important distinguishing indicator of lex (custom) is the objectivity thereof. Having arisen as a result of the forming of individual wills and subsequent transmission from the generation of fathers to the generation of children, lex (custom) is binding upon rulers and those ruled. Unlike lex, "justice" [правда] emanates from the lord (Grand Prince) who, being the creator of "justice" [правда], is thereby elevated above it and accordingly is not under the control nor accountable to the "justice" [правда] issued by him. "The King is not subordinate to the power of any human laws, and no one may judge or punish him", Iurii Krizhanich wrote in his treatise *Politica*. "Two bridles restrain the king and remind him of his duty; these are "justice" [правда] and respect for commandments of God and shame before the

[5] Ibid. p. 6.

people".[6] Thus, unlike lex (custom) which exerts its regulatory-protective impact only so long as the most active representatives of the socium live in accordance with customary norms, the lord's "justice" [правда] from the outset assumes the existence of two normative standards: the "justice" [правда] of the lord and "justice" [правда] for the lord. The last, as was said above, comes down to divine will and own conscience.

Having determined how in Ancient and Medieval Rus the concepts of "justice" [правда] and "lex" correlated, we turn to analyze the socio-legal essence of lex itself.

In the ancient Russian language two works, "lex" and "pokon" [покон] were used as identical. However, in our view, although having the same root and mutually connected, these words have a different meaning. We shall try to substantiate this thesis. The word "kon" is the root for "lex" and *pokon*. "Kon" means limit, boundary, and some beginning, or determined place, within known boundaries.[7]

The preposition "za", which prefixes the Russian word for "lex", with the accusative case expresses sensitively the anticipated limit of movement (or behavior going beyond the limits of the normal; ship concealed beyond the horizon line; sun concealed behind a cloud).

The preposition "*po*" (transliterated) has a somewhat different meaning and designated the direction of movement for a contemplated purpose (to go for mushrooms (or for water), bound for the grave, etc.).

The "za" used together as a prefix imparts to the word a limiting meaning and thereby establishes the obvious, or assumed "za" *prêt* (prohibition) against the commission of particular actions. The existence of a prohibition automatically conditions both the presence of a special authorization to overcome it or a previously determined punishment for unsanctioned overcoming.

The prefix "po", unlike "za", imparts to the word an encouraging meaning "Occasion (po|vod) to act in some way". In so doing the encouragement itself is not an obligation and is secured not by compulsion (or chastisement) but by stimulating (or incentive) measures.[8]

6 Iu. Krizhanich, «Политика» [Politics] (1997); cited from G. Iu. Semigin (ed.), Антология мировой правовой мысли [Anthology of World Legal Thought] (1999), IV, p. 265.

7 Sergeevich, note 3 above,l p. 11; N. G. Komlev, «Закон, правило и норма в языке» [Law, Rule, and Norm in Language], in P. A. Rachkova and V. S. Maneshina (eds.), Проблема закона в общественных науках [Problem of Law in the Social Sciences] (1989), p. 140.

8 The view expressed by us differs cardinally from the position of Sergeevich, who suggested that "lex and pokon is the order to which man *must* subordinate himself in his actions". Only lex has the feature of being binding, whereas pokon is characterized by incentive (empowerment) properties and by virtue of which does not give rise to a subject having duties to perform and punishment connected with a refusal to perform.

Thus, the words "lex" and "*pokon*" in the ancient Russian language reflected two functional meanings of law – restrictive and, accordingly, authorization-prohibitory, and incentive, empowering. In this understanding jus-lex signified the establishment of determined limits restricting the freedom of behavior of individual and collective subjects. In turn, jus-pokon acted as a scale of freedom of behavior-powers. Custom, being a form of law in Ancient and Medieval Rus, simultaneously fulfilled also the functions of lex (limitation of right) and pokon (powers).

The gradual squeezing out of customary law (lex russica) from the mechanism of legal regulation formed in the Russian State occurred under the influence of intensifying the socio-legal significance of edict law (princely law) within the framework of which the transformation of grand princely "justice" [правда] into Tsarist (and subsequently, imperial) edicts was not of a material, but merely a formal-content nature. The head of State – lord (irrespective of what the post was called) throughout the entire history of the Russian State acted as the supreme legislator. The reduction of lex to the formalized will of the lord signified a qualitative change of the meaning of this category. Lex lost the quality of being an essential, universal, and material link with the phenomena of objective reality (in such capacity it acted with regard to customary law) and acquired the meaning of a rule, method, means established by a subject for determined purposes and bearing the imprint of a secondary phenomenon containing the characteristics of an object by the mind of man.[9]

In summarizing the above, one may single out two stages of perception of the correlation of jus and lex in the history of Russian political and legal thought of the pre-imperial period.

At the first stage there occurred a differentiation of customary (lex russica) and edict (princely "justice" [правда]) law. At this stage the word lex (or pokon) is used to designate customary law as the basic source of the ancient Russian legal system. At the base of custom as a source of law is the legal tradition (law of the fathers) transmitted from generation to generation. In turn, the "justice" [правда] is a systematized and codified normative act, the basis of the creation of which are both norms of customary law and the prerogatives of the prince in the sphere of administrative norm-creation and court procedure. "Justice" [правда] unlike custom (people's law) is an edict (lord's) law. The lord (prince) himself, acting as law-creator, in the legal sense is not subordinate to "justice" [правда], having elevated himself above it and used it as an instrument of rule. Thus, initially two forms of law co-exist in the individual and social consciousness: jus – lex russica

[9] Komlev, note 7 above, p. 140.

– customary law formed within the framework of and by means of legal tradition, and jus – "justice" [правда] – the will of the prince expressed in lex. It is "justice" [правда] combining the principal features of a normative legal act (special procedure for working out and adoption, documentary consolidation, attributiveness and structuredness, ensuring by a system of State guarantees and measures of legal responsibility) that in closest to the modern understanding of lex.

At the second stage of law genesis customary law is pushed out by princely (edict) law. The understanding of lex is reduced to the will of the lord formalized and ensured by State compulsion.[10] In so doing the lord himself is a legally non-responsible subject, accountable in his law-creation and law-realization activity only to God and own conscience.

CORRELATION OF LEX AND LEGISLATIVE ACTS [УЗАКОНЕНИЕ] IN THE RUSSIAN EMPIRE

The forming of the Russian Empire is one of the major stages in the history of Russian statehood. The official status of empire Russia received in 1721 after the Senate proclaimed Peter I to be the All-Russian Emperor and Father of the Fatherland.[11]

Completion of the process of absolutization of monarchical power meant the final confirmation of edict law of the lord, which received the official name "lex". The "main reason which conditioned the dominance of lex as a source of law … lay in the fact that the sole subject of legislative power became the autocratic sovereign whose will created lex".[12]

In acquiring the status of lex, however, the will of the sovereign must have certain legal forms. In his study of the theory of lex, Tikhomirov said that "lex in the material sense is regarded as an act of State power containing legal norms of a general character, and lex in the formal sense encompasses any acts issued by the legislative agency irrespective of the

[10] Hence the definition of jus as the will of the State (or more precisely, the lord) embodied in a lex.

[11] An interesting detail is that a decision of the Senate in practice meant recognition of the divinity of the Emperor, in whose person were miraculously combined the Father of the Fatherland and his son – captain-bombadier Petr Mikhailov.

[12] V. M. Latkin, Учебник истории русского права периода империи (XVIII-XIX вв.) [Textbook of History of Russian Law of the Period of Empire (XXVIII-XIX Centuries)], ed. with preface of V. A. Tomsinov (2004), p. 3.

character of the norms contained therein".[13] Any act issued at the highest State level should be regarded as a lex of the Russian State.[14]

One cannot agree with this assertion. The question arises: are the concepts of "lex" and "legislative act" identical categories? We believe not. Having left for the moment the problem of to what extent edict law in principle has the right to be called lex, attention should be drawn to the fact that legislative power in the process of functioning has issued decrees of both a normative and non-normative character called by the general term "legislative act" [узаконение]. Consequently, within the system of imperial law legislative acts [узаконение] and lex should be differentiated.

In speaking about the system of legislative acts [узаконение], the following are usually distinguished:

1. edicts – acts of the highest legal force containing norms of a generally-significant character. One may name such significant acts as the Edict on Founding he Provinces and Listing of Cities Therein of 1711; Edict on Founding the Ruling Senate and the Personnel Thereof of 1714; the Edict on Fiskals and Their Posts and Actions of 1721; Edict on the Post of Procurator General of 1724, and others.
2. statutes (or articles) – acts containing norms of law regulating the organization and activity of an individual department, or determining the procedure for legal regulation in a determined sphere of social relations. For example, the Military Articles (or Statute) of 1716, Naval Statute of 1720; Bill of Exchange Statute of 1729; Statute of Decorum of 1728, and others.
3. reglaments, institutions, formations – documents whose norms regulated the procedure for the organization and activity of State institutions. As examples there may be named the General Reglament of 1720; reglaments of individual colleges of 1719 to 1721; Establishment of Provinces of 1775; Formation of the State Council of 1810; Formation of Ministries of 1802 and 1811; and others.[15]

13 Iu.A. Tikhomirov, Теория закона [Theory of Lex] (1982), p. 14.

14 A similar view is traditional to a considerable extent. The question of the division of lex into types was raised for the first time in the Nakaz of Catherine II by the codification commission ("Nakaz on police headquarters"), which created a structural section in the Statute on headquarters. The Nakaz contains an article "On the entry in police headquarters and announcement in the city of legislative acts, institutions, and edicts issued by autocratic authority". See Российское законодательства X-XX веков [Russian Legislation of the X-XX Centuries] (1987), V, p. 336. Latkin gives a characterization of the said acts of State power, noting that legislative acts are "those provisions which may not be changed at any time and may not be greater. Institutions are the order for all cases".

15 See G. V. Vernadskii, История права [History of Law] (1999), p. 107; Note 14 above, IV and V.

Manifestos and instruments occupied a special place in the system of legislative acts [узаконение] of the Russian Empire.

Traditionally in legal doctrine the manifesto is characterized as a declarative act containing specialized norms (as a rule, norms-purposes and norms-principles). However, such a characterization applied to manifestos adopted in Imperial Russia does not, in our view, reflect in full the functional load of this type of legislative act [узаконение]. It seems that it is desirable to separate out two types of manifestos: doctrinal manifestos and preambular manifestos.

A doctrinal manifesto fulfilled the same functions which State doctrine performs at present, that is, determined the most significant orientations of State policies in a determined sphere of social activity. To the category of doctrinal manifestos may be relegated the Manifesto on giving freedom and liberty to the nobility of 1762 and the 1905 Manifesto on the Improvement of State Order.

A preambular manifesto had no autonomous importance and was used as the introduction to a respective document. Thus, the Formation of the State Council in 1811 is in structure two acts in one, consisting of a Manifesto and the Formation itself. The Manifesto identifies the reasons which caused the creation of the State Council, consolidated the basic principles for its activity, and determined the subject-matter of the jurisdiction of the agency being formed.

Instruments performed the function of acts of an allocation character. In particular, the Letters Patent for rights, liberties, and privileges of the Russian nobility of 1785 confirmed the basic provisions of the 1762 Manifesto and in significant degree multiplied the privileges of representatives of the estate of the nobility. The instrument for rights and privileges to cities of the Russian Empire of 1785 regulated the organization and activity of the agencies of city self-government introduced.[16]

In summary, one may conclude that within the system of Imperial legislation the words "legislative act" [узаконение] and "lex" were regarded as synonymous. The concept of lex was used as a generalized name for all acts of highest State power. In the Statute on Decorum it was noted that "The Administration of Decorum shall not seek performance from people under the lex so long as the lex is not promulgated".[17] Thus, lex was to a great degree abstract and logical, and not a formal legal construction. However, in the imperial period there was awareness of the distinction between concepts of lex and an administrative regulation. In particular,

[16] Note 14 above, V, p. 67.
[17] Ibid., p. 336.

permanent and provisional edicts were differentiated. The first were understood as those "which were issued for all years in decreeing on some matter" and the second were provisional regulations (in modern parlance – acts of law-application".[18] Accordingly, only permanent (normative) edicts should be considered to be lex. Efforts were undertaken to delimit lex and administrative regulations (subordinate acts). In the draft Statute on State Lex, M. M. Speranskii noted: "Positive lex is nothing more than a limitation of the natural freedom of man. With respect to freedom lex may be divided into two main classes. In the first should be placed those decrees which introduce a change with respect to State forces or in relations of private people between themselves. In the second those which without introducing any material change establish only the way of performing the first. To the first appertain in the strict sense an interpretation of lex, whereas the second comprises statutes and institutions. The first should comprise the subject-matter of the legislative estate, and the second appertain to the action of executive power".[19]

However, the terminological delimitation of lex and administrative regulations was of a deeply speculative character. In practice no differences were made between the various types of acts of highest State authority. One reason for such indifference was the fact that Russian "legal terminology never distinguished by special definiteness and stability, and that is why the particular name under which lex was issued was not linked always with definite content and often practice itself used certain terms in very different meanings".[20]

CORRELATION OF "JUS", "LEX", LEGISLATIVE ACT IN THE SOVIET POLITICAL AND LEGAL SYSTEM

The 1917 October Revolution is traditionally regarded as a factor which transformed the Russian State-law system. The commencement of the Revolution was marked by an armed State coup – an act relegated to the gravest types of crimes for all times and in all States. However, having triumphed in armed resistance, the new power became the sole and by virtue of this legal political force effectuating the functions of public administration of Russia and its people. Naturally in order to administer a normative system was essential. The system of Soviet law became such a system in whose structure the institute of Soviet legislation occupied the

18 Latkin, note 12 above, p. 4.
19 Cited from ibid., pp. 5-6.
20 Ibid., p. 16.

place of the basic instrumental element. The understanding of jus in Soviet legal reality was formed under the impact of two basic principles:

- priority of Party dogmas over legal;
- class nature of jus.

In reducing jus to an instrument of class rule, the new power undermined a tradition of many centuries under which ethical limitations were placed on the legal system irrespective of whether they were apparent or real. Having taken this view, the Bolsheviks construed jus as a continuation of political power. The formula "revolutionary expediency equals revolutionary legality" expressed the recognition by the new regime of only those legal norms which served the interests of the Revolution.[21]

The right to control the court and to interfere in human fate began to be a tragic problem since the issue of the moral responsibility of the judge lost any reality. Tens of thousands of death sentences were signed for "enemies of the revolution" by an unshaking hand by the judges of various judicial agencies guided in their activity by no normative legal act whatsoever (the acts of the old regime did not operate, and there simply were no new ones), but by proletarian flair. The lack of a legally established list of crimes led the administration of justice by analogy of jus through the subjective legal consciousness of persons who controlled the "vigilante court". "The introduction of analogy is completely justified by the socialist legal consciousness", wrote Cheltsov-Bebutov. "If one sees in society (in the ideal) a labor unity determining the common supreme aim, the concept of a criminal code disappears as a charter of freedom of the individual person. The common good is a common lex which must be comprehended by and close to everyone. Any harmful act (or failure to act) obstructing progress is a crime".[22]

Having regard to the aforesaid, one may single out the following basic features characterizing the State legal system in the early years of Soviet power: jus was assigned purely a service role; the issue of legality (as a public law regime restricting both individual freedom and as State will) was not raised at all; the freedom of administrator and judges to deviate from the requirements of normative-legal acts for reasons of advisability was emphasized; decentralization was permitted (and in some instances encouraged) of law-creation, when judges on site decided who to judge

[21] E. Huskey, Российская адвокатура и советское государство [Russian Advokatura and Soviet State] (1993), p. 32; id, *Russian Lawyers and the Soviet State: The Origins and Development of the Soviet Bar, 1917-1939* (1986), p. 36.

[22] M. A. Cheltsov-Bebutov, Социалистическое правосознание и уголовное право революции [Socialist Legal Consciousness and Criminal Law of the Revolution] (Kharkov, 1924), pp. 67-68.

and for what; and, finally, and most important – in the interval of time here considered the absolute priority of a political viewpoint over legal was recognized by State authorities.

As Nenovski wrote, in this period the State as sovereign power in a certain sense merged with the dictatorship of the proletariat and emerged as an instrument thereof. "No lex stand above it, no supreme abstract natural law principles which might bind it absolutely. No lex may bind the expression of will of the ruling classes. Any lex, including constitutional, may at any time be changed or repealed if the requirements of class domination give rise to this necessity".[23]

Identifying the State with the dictatorship of the ruling class had a dual aim. First, in essence representatives of the "enemy" classes were declared to be outside lex, virtually deprived of civil rights by Soviet power. Second, the legal non-responsibility of the State, failure to accept abstract natural law principles, meant that the ruling class was in complete dependence on the will of the dictatorship, which used its powers not according to lex, but in accordance with the interests of the Revolution.

The next step of the development of the Soviet legal system may be conditionally called the stage of the strengthening of Soviet legality. This stage was characterized by the following principal features:

1. law-creation in the localities was deemed to be inadmissible;
2. the central (federal) authorities attacked a generally-binding character to normative legal acts;
3. severe legal sanctions were provided for a violation of decrets or for the inaccurate execution of directives provided for by them. In this period the concept of "jus" and "lex" begins to be regarded as identical since the will of the State embodied in lex is jus.

As a result if the exclusion of a nihilistic attitude towards written law by the ideas of Vyshinskii, in whose opinion "under socialist legality achieves the peak of its development" and represents a digest of precise socialist laws which enjoy authority from justice workers and the entire population as a whole,[24] a system of totalitarian legality formed in Russia and was strengthened in which supposedly mutually-exclusive positions got on with one another: on one hand, a denial of traditional legal values (declared to be bourgeois and, by virtue of this, false) and, on the other hand, planting of the principle of the general bindingness of lex. Just as in jus of the imperial period, the understanding of lex was unequivocal.

[23] N. Nenovski, Единство и взаимодействие государства и права [Unity and Interaction of State and Law] (1982), p. 108.

[24] A. Ia. Vyshinskii, «Революционная законность и наши задачи» [Revolutionary Legality and Our Tasks], Правда [Pravda], 28 June 1932.

The term "lex" in the USSR came to be used not only in the general (as in the Empire), but in a specific sense.[25] In speaking about the types of laws in the USSR, one may name: *lex* (1938 on Citizenship of the USSR; 1938 on the Procedure for the Ratification and Denunciation of International Treaties; 1951 On the Defense of Peace; and others); *fundamental principles of legislation and court proceedings* (1958 Fundamental Principles of Legislation on Court Organization of the USSR, Union and Autonomous Republics; 1958 Fundamental Principles of Criminal Procedure of the USSR and Union Republics); *codes* (1961 Air Code of the USSR; 1964 USSR Customs Code; and others); *edicts* (1954 On the State Bank of the USSR; on Making Changes in the Depiction of the State Arms of the USSR; 1955 On Termination of the State of War between the USSR and Germany; 1961 On Confirmation of the Air Code of the USSR; 1940 On Provisional Application of Criminal, Civil, and Labor Legislation of the RSFSR on the Territory of the Lithuanian, Latvian, and Estonian SSR; 1940 On the Provisional Application of Codes of the Ukrainian SSR on the Territory of the Moldovian SSR, and others); *statutes* (1960 On Protection of the State Boundary of the USSR; 1966 On Procuracy Supervision in the USSR; 1969 On Preliminary Confinement Under Guard); *decrees* (1965 On Travel Free of Charge of School Children Living in Rural Locality; 1967 On the Procedure for the Introduction into Operation the USSR Law "On Universal Military Duty"; 1965 On the Procedure for Elections of District (or City) People's Courts; and others); *charters* (1975 Charter of Garrison and Guard Services of the USSR Armed Forces; 1975 Disciplinary Charter of the Armed Forces of the USSR, and others).

An analysis of the content of the enumerated legislative acts enables one to speak about their diversity being conditioned by a rather eroded status of the documents adopted by legislative power, and this in turn made the structuring of the block of legislation more difficult. The absence of a precise and logically consistent conception of a legislative act often led to the fact that various types of documents were adopted with regard to the same subject-matter of legal regulation.[26] The explanation of this situation lies, in our view, in the fact that at all stages of the origin and development of the Soviet State jus and lex were accorded a purely service role – as instruments of State administration. There was virtually no difference what an act was called when issued by legislative power since the legislative

[25] The word "lex" begins to be used for the names of normative legal acts commencing in 1938.

[26] Traditionally the procedure for the introduction of laws of the USSR into operation was established by respective edicts; however, the procedure for introducing the Law of the USSR "On Universal Military Duty" was established in 1967 by decree.

power itself (Presidium of the USSR Supreme Soviet) was such only nominally and principal power was concentrated with representatives of the highest link of the Party-economic nomenclature and it is they who were the *de facto* legislators of the country of Soviets. A similar correlation of formal and real power was especially clear during the Great Fatherland War of 1941 to 1945.

During the critical situation which formed in the Soviet Union at the end of June and early July 1941 a decision was taken to create an extraordinary agency of State power – the State Defense Committee (SDC).

In the newly created agency were concentrated the entire plenitude of power in the State. In accordance with the decree adopted, all citizens, as well as all Party, soviet, komsomol, and military agencies, were obliged to unconditionally fulfill the decisions and regulations of the SDC.

The SDC operated in the period from 30 June 1941 to 4 September 1945. Throughout this period the SDC adopted 9,971 documents. The SDC occupied the highest position in the structure of State power, in essence combining the functions of Party, soviet, and economic direction of the USSR.[27]

Against the background of the creation of a single agency of the State in which State power was absolutized, an intensification of the personal dictatorial power of I. V. Stalin occurred. On 10 July 1941 Stalin headed the Headquarters of the High Command, on 19 July took the post of People's Commissar for Defense, and on 8 August 1941 became the Supreme Commander in Chief.

The mechanism of absolute power of the Soviet State excluded the division of powers with anyone else. Stalin took the most significant decisions personally or they were obligatorily agreed with him.

During wartime, the formal procedure for law-creation was not complied with, within the framework of which the normative acts highest in legal force were adopted by the Presidium of the USSR Supreme Soviet. During the war years the functional status of this agency was minimized and to a great extent was of a formal character.[28] The SDC and Stalin personally had the real law-creation functions. In the period here considered an unwritten procedure, albeit rather precise and based on its own kind of State-law

[27] See R. A. Romashov and A. G. Tishchenko, «Политико-правовая природа и структуно-функциональные особенности государственной власти в СССР в условиях Великой Отечественной Войны» [Politico-Legal Nature and Structural-Functional Peculiarities of State Power in the USSR in Conditions of the Great Fatherland War], in V. P. Salnikov, R. A Romashov, and N. S. Nizhnik (eds.), Государство. Право. Война: 60-летие Великой Победы [State, Law, War: 60-Anniversary of the Great Victory] (Spb., 2005), pp. 255-268.

[28] Three sessions of the Supreme Soviet of the USSR were held during the four years of war: June 1942, February 1944, and April 1945.

tradition, for drafting and adopting documents regulating the major issues in the spheres of military, economic, and political life of the USSR was formed and, in essence, real State laws appeared.

This example rather persuasively demonstrates the minimization of the actual significance for State power (exercised, as noted, by the higher Party-economic nomenclature) of the legislative agencies themselves and the acts which they issue being laws not in essence, but in form. As regards the real laws of the Soviet State, Party directives at all stages of Soviet construction determined the basic orientations of State policy in all spheres of social activity, including in the sphere of legislation.

CORRELATION OF CONCEPTS "JUS" AND "LEX" IN THE MODERN RUSSIAN LEGAL LEXICON

Lex in the modern Russian legal language is understood in several senses:

- as the name of a normative legal act having the highest legal force in comparison with other normative legal acts (federal law in the sense of the Federal Law "On State Secrecy") or a law of a subject of the federation);
- as a collective concept designating the aggregate of sources of jus – normative legal acts regulating a particular sphere of legal regulation (federal law in the sense of legislation: Article 120(1) of the 1993 Constitution of the Russian Federation: "Judges … shall be subordinate only … to a federal law"; or Criminal Code of the Russian Federation – criminal lex and so on). In this context the concept "lex" is identical with the concept "legislation".

Jus is understood in the following contexts:

- jus as legal culture (legal life, legal reality);
- jus as a normative system, including the norms of positive (newly created) and natural (objectively formed and discovered in the process of socio-legal development) jus;
- jus as a branch (or sphere) of legal regulation (criminal jus, civil jus, administrative jus, international jus, jus of human rights, and so on);
- jus as the aggregate of powers and obligations of a person (subjective jus);
- jus as a value characteristic (jus/non-jus lex, rule of jus State).

In speaking about the correlation of the concepts "jus" and "lex", one should have the following approaches in view.

First, these concepts are perceived as identical categories. In this instance the terms "positive jus" and "legislation" are used. And in other instances they have in view administrative systems through which the most significant social relations are ordered and protected in a centralized manner.

Second, lex is perceived as an element of a system of formal-juridical sources of jus – a type of normative legal act.

Third, jus and lex correlate as a substantive substance and legal form. This understanding of the said categories predetermines the issues as to whether lex may be non-jus and whether jus may exist without being expressed in lex (in the sense of in legislation). Attempts at an unequivocal answer to these questions are known to be unpromising and qualified, above all by the fact that under some circumstances we perceive the words "jus" and "lex" as identical categories and in others, these words are juxtaposed. As a rule, the juxtaposition is based on a rather primitive logic in accordance with which lex may be good (jus) or bad (non-jus), but jus in any event acts as an immutable (from the standpoint of social value) measure of good and justness.[29]

This approach is to a great extent typical of theology, appealing to Divine grace, rather than to jurisprudence, the basis of which is not so much categories of the struggle of good against evil (sins against virtue) as the principles of the adversariality of the positions of the parties, each of which insists on own rightness.[30] Laws (in the sense of legislative acts) are written, adopted, and applied by living people, and consequently conversations about the jus/non-jus nature of laws assumes the existence/absence of a legal culture in the legislator, law-applier, and law-executor. But in this understanding the word "lex" loses its initial sense – objectiveness.[31] If

[29] In the context of such an understanding the existence of mutually-exclusive positions is entirely possible. A violation of the lex of a State is a crime entailing punishment for the violation of a specific lex. Execution of the lex of a State if this lex is non-jus (unjust, inhumane, etc.) is a crime entailing punishment for lex-abiding from wrongful behavior. The second variant is possible only if the system of legislation declared to be non-jus has ceased to exist. Fascist criminals were condemned not because they violated the lex of their State, but because the State which they served lost the war. Otherwise, the situation would be the mirror opposite, with the only difference that the places of the accused would be occupied by representatives of the anti-Hitler coalition.

[30] In this instance one should recall the meaning of the word "jus" as a direction of movement. This direction may be put by way of an order "Who there steps to the right? Left! Left! Left!" – V. V. Mayakovsky, Левый марш [Left March], and may be chosen autonomously ("Each chooses his own path, which may be right or not") – R. A. Romashov, "I leave as it begins to rain …"). If the right of choice belongs to the subject, he realizes this as it seems correct to him; whereas if the right of others, consequently, the other rules (in the sense of direction of activity) are perceived as mediated by an own category of rightness.

[31] If lex is regarded as objective jus, it must have the following qualities: lex is generally binding irrespective of participating in the working out thereof and adoption by a specific subject; lex is considered to be true (correct, jus) irrespective of the subjective valuation of its provisions by individual persons; lex is realized both in the event of law-abiding and illegal behavior of a subject.

we call lex that which in essence subjectively depends upon the will of a specific person (or group of people), this is not lex in the proper sense, but an established rule of behavior (through individual or collective expression of will) which depending on the circumstances may be executed by he to whom it is addressed or not. In the context we should conduct ourselves not by the law as such, but by an edict (or charter)[32] – the aggregate of rules of behavior secured by guarantees and sanctions on the part of the center of publicness adopting the respective document.[33]

In summary, the following conclusion should be drawn. A mixing occurs in the modern Russian legal language of linguistic (vocal) and substantial (or material, substantive) load of the terms "jus" and "lex". Depending on the circumstances, these words are used in different meanings, which ultimately affects the insolubility of the problem of their correlation. It seems that to mitigate the sharpness of the discussion one may reduce the load of these terms in the future and thereafter compare only categories of the same order. In speaking about jus, one should distinguish objective jus (law operating with respect to subjects irrespective of their will) and subjective (jus on a claim determined by the will of a subject), jus as a unified system (Russian law), and jus as a branch element of the system (criminal law, civil law, administrative law), national jus as a product of municipal activity and international jus, positive (created by norm-creative activity) and natural (existing independently of legal formalization and State sanctioning) jus. When using the word "lex", one should distinguish the meaning of lex as an objective positive jus (judges are subordinate to a federal lex), source of branch regulation (criminal lex), type of normative legal acts (together with the word "lex" to designate the "laws of the Russian Federation" also use such words as "charter", "code", and "edict").

As noted above, in and of itself such vocabulary diversity, gently put, does not further the perception of lex as an act of the highest legal force

[32] It is supposed that from the outset the words "charter" and "edict" were of a practically identical character and acted as the personified expression of will of the sovereign (edict of the sovereign) with the difference merely that the charter (from the word "established" – finally consolidated) was unequivocally imperative, and the edict (indication of variants of the possible, ought, inadmissible behavior) contained a certain dispositiveness connected with the choice of possible means and methods of realization of a prescription of the authorities. There is another point of view which hold that the charter (from the word "mouth", symbolizing a certain primary, initial point of birth of the respective information). In turn, "edict" in substance to a greater degree is orientated towards a method of bringing the necessary information to the addressee.

[33] An edict (or charter) may have the status of lex as a document possessing the highest legal force. For example, the Military Charter has the force of lex in the sphere of military service, and the basic law for the majority of subjects of the Russian Federation is the charter of the subject; edicts of the President of the Russian Federation are endowed under certain circumstances with the legal force of federal laws.

since the possibility exists of endowing other normative acts with the force of a lex, which automatically reduces the legal authority of the word "lex" itself.[34]

CORRELATION OF CONCEPTS "JUS" AND "LEX" IN LANGUAGES OF THE ENGLISH AND ROMANO-GERMANIC GROUPS

For foreign jurisprudence the problem of the correlation of jus and lex is not so topical, above all because these concepts are signified by different words in the language, which enables the meaning load to be avoided and the passions reduced materially around the discussion of so significant a problem for Russian specialists.

In the English legal language the words "law" and "right" are used in completely different senses which preclude their being identified as synonyms. Law is an integral category including a diversity of approaches to public law, legislation as a whole, branch legislation, that is, everything that in the Russian language is relegated to objective (with respect to a specific subject) jus. Right is a subjective right in its various forms and manifestations which also concerns the names of a type of normative-legal act adopted by the parliament, the word "statute" being used.[35] That which is translated into the Russian language as statute law should more precisely be called charter [уставное] norm-creation. These categories, by virtue of their being on various levels, cannot be understood one through the other, and this means they do not enter into a contradiction of meaning. One may speak about how much law expressed in a statute adopted by parliament and legislation corresponds to natural law; however, this is a problem of the correlation of meanings, but not of categories.

The correlation of "jus" and "lex" in the French language has a clearly expressed correlation with the English tradition. In order to designate objective jus (lex in the proper sense) the word "loi" is used. Natural law is translated as "loi de la nature" (literally a lex of nature or natural lex). The word "droit" (jus) is used to designate branches and spheres of legal regulation (droit international – international law), and also to designate a subjective right (droit de vote – right of vote). It seems that "droit" is part of loi as a normative system. As regards the designation of acts of parliamentary norm-creation, two words are used: "loi" (lex) and "code".

34 The contempt for the perception of lex in the Russian socio-legal tradition is reflected in the proverb: "Lex is a shaft that turned somewhere and then left".

35 Translated into the Russian language as statutory law, but would be called more precisely charter norm-creation.

Thus, consideration of "loi – lex" as a product of official norm-creation (codified or uncodified) is combined with the perception thereof as "loi" – a system of objective jus formed from positive jus based on legislation and natural jus based on the "loi de la nature". Unlike the English language, in the French language the word "statut" is used to designate acts of corporative norm-creation (charters of social organizations, commercial organizations, and so on) which under no circumstances may be regarded as lex.

As regards the correlation of the concepts "jus" and "lex" in the German language, it is in essence the same as the Russian legal-linguistic tradition. In the German language the word "jus" is translated as "Recht", and the term "legality" also is conveyed by this word (although, in our view, it would be more precise to speak about legal order); the same is true in the Russian language. Recht is used in a rather broad sense to designate jus in general – national and international law, branch, and subjective law. Lex in German is Gesetz. As in both the Russian and French languages, Gesetz is used to designate lex in the sense of objective law and for the name of acts of federal legislation and legislation of the länder. The word "Statut" is used similarly to the French tradition – for the names of sources of corporate law which are derivative with respect to Gesetz.

On the basis of the above analysis, one may conclude that the problem of the correlation of the concepts "jus" and "lex" are key to determining the type of legal understanding. An unequivocal resolution of this problem is not possible. Consequently, it makes no sense to attempt to work out such a resolution. However, one may agree about the content of the concepts designated by the said words within a determined language field so as to subsequently avoid internal contradictions about the logical (philosophical) and practical (formal-juridical) constructions arranged.

Philosophical Problems Of Legal Comparativistics

A. D. TIKHOMIROV*

PROBLEMS OF UNDERSTANDING COMPARATIVE LAW IN THE CONTEXT OF THE PHILOSOPHY OF SCIENCE

Many comparatists have devoted their studies to an understanding of comparative law which enables this problem not to be illuminated separately but, resting on their results, to attempt to demonstrate the dynamics of the changes in the understanding of comparative law in the context of the philosophy of science, to systematize them in historical (temporal), national (spatial, geographical), and theoretical aspects.

Before the early twentieth century, when science had originated in its classical understanding as objective, verifiable, and true scientific knowledge, when this knowledge had only just come into being and increased in volume and not only in scientific form, it was important to single out and separate scientific knowledge from other previously dominant forms of worldview (religions, practices). Therefore, comparative law is not regarded as a science, but as comparative legal scientific studies distinct from extra-scientific and pre-scientific comparative studies of law.

By the end of the nineteenth and beginning of the twentieth centuries the amount of comparative legal studies, to which in priority were relegated the study and description of foreign law for practical purposes, conditioned the need for their systematization and ordering in a form peculiar to the science of that time – a scientific discipline, the basis of which was subject-matter conditioned by a method corresponding to it, and also the purposes and tasks of science and the need and social significance of the organization of scientific knowledge and studies.

* доктор юридических наук, профессор. Chair of the Theory of State and Law, Kiev National University of Internal Affairs.

Whereas earlier the principal comparative legal studies were undertaken for extra-scientific purposes, with the formation of science and its organizational or institutional forms within the framework thereof, comparative legal studies were organized and a division thereof occurred into scientific studies having scientific or practical importance. Those studies which were directed towards the systematization and ordering of scientific knowledge met the requirements of comparative law proper as a science and consequently were developed by individual scholars as a result of their initiative. The institutes which then existed, being financed basically by the State or privately, conducted research directed towards making provision for State needs.

A new form of organizing the cooperation of comparatists-scholars not only within a single country but different countries of Europe arose from the time of holding the First International Congress of Comparative Law. The significance of this Congress lay in the fact that scholars who belonged primarily to the French school expressed the view that it was necessary to recognize comparative law as an autonomous science.

At a certain period of time this orientation of the development of comparative law, not being the sole one, became dominant with respect to alternative approaches. Its priority to a great extent was conditioned by the idea of creating a "universal" or "world" law on the basis of the comparative study of national legal orders. But the foundation of comparative law comprised not attempts to elaborate an autonomous science, but of the comparative legal studies themselves in their practical orientation. To this testifies the fact that in the periods of world wars and the adoption of national codes, when the practical significance of the comparative study of foreign law diminished, the development of these studies also fell even though the scientific needs for an autonomous science remained unchanged. Therefore, the aspiration to organize comparative-legal studies in the form of an autonomous science did not receive extensive recognition or dissemination either among scholars or among national schools.

After the Second World War, the pragmatic orientation of comparative legal studies again began to dominate in many European countries, affected by the emergence of a "critical theory of comparative law" and an understanding of comparative law as a method of research; consequently, not a disciplinary, but a methodological form of the organization became dominant.

However, the existence of bourgeois and socialist law affected the need for the manifestation of material distinctions, which was possible primarily in a theoretical context. Consequently, in socialist countries to a certain extent an understanding of comparative law as a science was reanimated and attempts made for the conceptualization thereof.

With the growth of national-liberation movements and the acquisition of independence by the former colonies, the need for comparative legal studies became more urgent in those countries, both bourgeois and socialist, although the purposes and orientation thereof were different. Whereas for bourgeois countries it was essential to retain their influence, and for socialist countries to expand theirs, for the countries which acquired independence, self-determined themselves, it was necessary to combine local customs with the law of the metropolitan retained, international law, and the law of their own State.

Given the differences of culture and ideologies, the aspiration to bring order to national legal orders on an international scale (as at the beginning of the twentieth century) lost its importance, but the role of methods provision and the organization of comparative legal studies increased.

At the end of the twentieth and beginning of the twenty-first centuries, changes are occurring in the understanding of the science itself; its nonuniversality is acknowledged, the limitedness of phenomena to a certain sphere, the need to take into account other forms of worldview, which has found its completed embodiment in post-modernism. The modern development of science is orientated towards interdisciplinarity, problems, a multiplicity of theories and paradigms, pluralism of methodologies, and the incidentalness and alternativeness of social development. Also to be noted is the status of crisis in science and the searches for a way out from this. By its content science is regarded as a multiplicity of various phenomena: a scientific discipline, field of research, vanguard of science, social institution, phenomenon of culture, and so on.

The discussion of a particular generalized understanding of comparative law under these conditions loses its scientific importance, and the diversity and investigation of the peculiarities of particular components acquires greater significance, a study of comparative law as a scientific discipline only as one of the forms of organizing respective scientific knowledge and research. The lack of a generally-recognized conceptualization, a dominant theory of law, differences in national legal orders, and the like facilitate this.

It should be noted that during the second half of the twentieth century the sociology and philosophy of science, the science of science, began actively to develop and is elaborating a modern understanding of science and the paths of its development. Therefore, under conditions of a change of the subject-matter field of comparative legal studies, their scientific grounds, forms of organization, role, and significance in legal development, the impression of comparative law merely as a science, method or science and method is not responsive to the modern interpretation of science and the place and role of comparative legal studies.

Comparative studies are not the prerogative of merely legal science, and therefore those trends should be taken into account which exist in other socio-humanitarian sciences and also other forms of worldview, practice, and the direct life of the subjects of law.

The same is observed in the geographical (or spatial) dimension of considering the origin and dissemination of particular approaches to a comprehension of comparative law. Without doubt various approaches of scholars to an understanding thereof existed and do exist within any national school, and therefore one may speak only about the domination of a particular approach most widely shared by scholars engaged in comparative legal studies. Without assuming here the task of a detailed exegesis of this problem, we note that in the geography of comparative law there is more pluralism, multiplicity, and diversity of understanding manifested affected by the language, culture, and legal orders of a particular country or region. There is even greater diversity of opinions among scholars belong to different civilizations in which science and law occupy a place and play a role different from the situation in the countries of European civilization.

Having regard to historical and geographical pluralism in the understanding of comparative law, the possibility of its existence as a "universal" or "world" science would seem to be exaggerated. If comparative law has not formed in this guise an aspiration towards universality during the era of modernism, even more doubtful is the existence thereof in such form during the era of post-modernism, for which multiplicity, pluralism, incidentalness, and so on are characteristic.

It would be more advisable to speak about comparative law as a "world" science in the context of those forms of its organization such as international cooperation, dialogue, and polylogue of scholars of various countries, in the course of which in a specific historical situation common approaches are achieved and solutions of urgent problems of world and national legal and cultural development. The origin of the common in comparative law refers to the diverse approaches, opinions, and views on the establishment of the common in real cooperation and interaction of scholars, and not some previously established theories, conceptions, or doctrines. To be sure, in such interaction scholars may at a certain time and in some countries be dominated by particular approaches, but none had or have a "universal" character.

A "world" science does not exist outside national sciences; it is a result of their interaction, polylogue. The task also may be put in national legal science of thinking over problems of the development of mankind, civilization, or region, but this does not transform a national school of science into an international science; it becomes such in the cooperation with scholars and sciences of other countries and continents as a result of their interaction, finding compromise decisions, and so on. The national diversity of science may be thought over and understood as the result of such joint scientific activity analogously and variously.

Pluralism in an understanding of comparative law also is dominant in the theoretical perception thereof (outside time and space). The theoretical contemplation is most often used by scholars who have studied comparative law research and obtained knowledge as a result.

A distinctive feature of this approach is the constructing of a determined theoretical model and study of the properties of comparative law on the basis of "placing" this model against the reality of comparative law studies. The attempts at such conceptualization in history and modern times testify more to the inadvisability, difficulties, or impossibilities of the effectuation thereof than to the unity achieved in an understanding of comparative law. In addition, any theoretical model (or conceptualization) is created or constructed on the base of empirical studies or on base theoretical postulates or axioms. An understanding of comparative law as a science, method, or other scientific phenomenon requires structures and substantiations of the respective models, proceeding from positions accepted in science, and not only among scholar-comparatists. The nature of comparative law influences only the distinctive features, the distinctiveness of these models and their differences from models accepted in other sciences.

Another form of theorizing in comparative law is the generalization of existing comparative law studies and their results. Whereas the first approach is based on the use of deduction, the second is based on induction. The first path has been typical for the conceptualization of comparative law in the past, which is linked with the objective difficulties of the study and generalization of comparative law studies undertaken in various countries (language barriers, inaccessibility of many respective materials, significant amounts of comparative law studies, and others).

However, modern informational resources and respective technologies are materially enhancing the possibilities of the inductive approach to the conceptualization of comparative law orientated towards the study of the mass of studies which in some measure or form are relevant to a comparison in the sphere of legal reality, the structurization thereof, a determination of the interlinkages of structural elements and combinations thereof, to forming on this basis a conceptual apparatus and theoretical constructions (similar to the approach used by Rheinstein).[1]

[1] M. Rheinstein, «Предмет и задачи сравнительного правоведения» [Subject-Matter and Tasks of Comparative Law], in V. A. Tumanov (ed.), Очерки сравнительного права [Essays on Comparative Law] (1981), pp. 90-95.

Therefore, under the inductive approach to investigating comparative law one should avoid the dominant trend filling "comparative Law" or "comparative jurisprudence" with some sort of arbitrarily taken content and undertake the opposite operation – study the sphere of comparative legal research and then designate the elements thereof, parts, or fragment, and also it as a whole with respective terms.

On this level it seems advisable to:

- separate out and describe the "space" within whose limits various comparative law studies existed and exist (theoretical, methodological, comparative, contrastive, descriptive);
- determine the criteria for separating out and investigating the distinctions from other such "spaces", establish the entry thereof as parts of larger "spaces" and structure it on various grounds;
- analyze the common and distinctive properties of the levels and elements thereof, clarify (or typologize) them, and determine the character of interlinkages;
- separate out the necessary and sufficient characteristics thereof, formulate definitions, and designate terms, ensuring that they are not contradictory and are contrastive.

The separating out and description of the "space" of the existence of comparative legal studies in correlation with other similar "spaces" is possible within such frameworks (or limits, "coordinates", understandings): juridical – legal – extra-legal; scientific – practical – cognitive (worldview); professional – nonprofessional; monist – integrative (synthetic) – pluralist; methodological – subject-matter (content); national – civilized – world; general – special – unique; out-lived (obsolete, lost significance, forgotten) – successive (traditional) – new; concrete – abstract; theoretical –empirical; positivist – social – cultural; basic – necessary – sufficient – not basic; contradictory (opposite) – supplementary.

Recognition of the non-dominance of one point of view of scholars over another is the primary grounds for such an approach, and the necessity thereof, substantiation, reality as determined systems of scientific knowledge reflecting its own subject-matter and obtained by a determined means. And they should be evaluated only within the limits of their "coordinates".

This interpretation logically leads to a pluralistic understanding of the problem above, the diversity of forms of its manifestation and exposition thereof by scholars, as well as the correlation of various scientific structures along principles of dialogicality (polyphonism), supplementarity, tolerance, and others.

A consideration of comparative law in the aspect of integration, interdisciplinarity, and problems of the sciences, and also within the coordinates of object-subject-matter-problem, the correlation thereof with the fact that in legal reality something new has emerged that has become dominant and how this is reflected in jurisprudence and by which sciences, shows that legal reality is not "concealed" by "subject-matter" existing and structured on the grounds of both legal and non-juridical scientific disciplines. Therefore a number of new sciences are emerging which reflect new domains of a changing legal reality (for example, the science of tax law, the science of customs law, and so on), separated out from some base sciences of integrated (or synthesized) with others, or, on the contrary, separated out from several on the basis of separating out a synthesized subject-matter (for example, the subject-matter of legal linguistics is separated out both from legal and linguistic sciences on the basis of their intersecting, synthesis).

The differentiation and subject-matter of juridical scientific disciplines has led to fractionalization, fragmentation, "dispersion" of scientific knowledge about the integral, inter-connected world, which creates the need to recognize the integration of scientific knowledge, conduct inter-disciplinary research, develop comparative and other similar sciences as the dominant trends in the change of scientific legal knowledge.

Comparative law is being directed to a certain extent towards the resolution of this problem (overcoming the fractionalization of scientific knowledge); however, it is not the sole science in this field of scientific research. Such orientations of inter-disciplinary and other integrative studies as legal globalistics, legal transitology, legal regionalistics, legal futurology, legal geography, legal country studies, research in the spheres of transnational and world law, law of mankind, and others are emerging and beginning to develop. Common to these sciences is the study not only of national law, but also other law equal to or higher than national law (law of other countries, associations thereof, legal realities of continents, mankind, their future, and so on). They have not only a philosophical or theoretical nature, but also an empirical, pragmatic orientation, and the theoretical component of the last has an applied significance and relates to theories of average level.

All these various approaches to an understanding of comparative law truly exist in comparativistic science, and comparative studies are being carried out in accordance with them and on their basis and their results are used in science, education, and practice. On the other hand, the aspiration and claims to a solely correct determination of the nature, place, and role of comparative law cannot be deemed to be well-founded, either historically, or by the modern state of legal science, or by the developmental trends. Therefore a single (generally-recognized) understanding has been lacking, is lacking, and should be lacking because there are no grounds today that this will be otherwise in the near future.

The theoretical and methodological problems of research of comparative law set out merely in part identify the diversity of views, the difficulties and unresolved issues, which exist in understanding them. However, even so fragmentary an account testifies to the unpromising resolution thereof only within the framework of traditions which have formed. Under the new geopolitical, worldview, economic, and other conditions at the post-neoclassical stage of development of science, another interpretation of comparative law should be formed.

JURIDICAL COMPARATIVISTICS AS MODERN STAGE OF THE DEVELOPMENT OF COMPARATIVE LAW

In light of the above, one possible way out from this rather "deadend" situation may be juridical comparativistics, understood as a variety of comparativistics – a new stage in the development of inter-disciplinary comparative studies in the humanities.

The possibility of such an understanding of the modern stage of the development of comparative law, while not "closed" to changes and "open" to the understanding being formed, enables the development of comparative research of law on another basis to be predicted to a certain extent.

The distinctive features of juridical comparativistics are not conditioned by the use of the term "comparativistics", which recently has been extensively employed in scientific literature, but by the modern world understanding based on pluralism (diversity, globalization, spontaneity, incidentalness) of the world, national, social, humanitarian, and legal development. In this connection it seem optimal to set out in the study of the science aspect, certain properties of juridical comparativistics which affirm not only the need for another approach with regard to the traditional one, but also the general which is inherent in juridical comparativistics and other understanding of comparative law, and also those problems which should be studied in the future.

Among the basic distinctive features of juridical comparativistics is that an understanding thereof is reflected, on one hand, in the continuation and, on the other, the expansion and other interpretation of those provisions of understanding comparative law which were elaborated in the works of scholar-comparatists who interpreted it not as a science or methods, but as a science and method (A. Tille, A. Saidov, M. Marchenko, Iu. Tikhomirov, and others). By virtue of this legal comparativistics is not reducible either to one of the existing understandings thereof since the pluralism of its interpretations is reflected. Therefore, it encompasses science and method, methodological and substantive knowledge, a scientific discipline and "cutting edge of science", traditional notions and existing innovations, the study of foreign law and identification of extra-national processes.

Juridical comparativistics is a method and a science, and a science on method, and inter-disciplinary studies within the legal sciences, and between them and non-juridical sciences. Ultimately, it reflects the pluralism of the sciences on law and interconnected phenomena on the basis of one of the general-scientific methods and means of worldview – a comparative one.

Having an inter-disciplinary nature, juridical comparativistics emphasizes the need for recognition of the urgency of the problem structuring of sciences, a search for the subject-matter of comparative studies not only on the level of subject-matter of special and branch legal sciences or the theory of law, history of State and law, but in the entire range of the existence of legal reality: from the legal order of the world, law of mankind (universal law), up to the legal space of social groups and lives of a specific subject of law.

Juridical comparativistics is characterized not only by the integration and differentiation of sciences (or scientific studies) of a comparative orientation, their disciplinary nature and problem nature, separation and combining, but also the synthesis of scientific studies, practice, other forms of worldview, and direct life of the person.

The subject-matter field of juridical comparativistics is not confined only to legal systems, which by their nature are one of the forms of reflecting legal reality, but encompasses the last to its full extent, but within a determined radius – through investigation of the general and different therein and the correlation thereof with other realities (cultural, economic, social, virtual, and so on). The principal limitation is investigation not of one object or property, the state of legal realities of countries, States, cultures, traditions, including both comparable and noncomparable, that is "same", "other", and "different". On the level of the science of science, the problem field of research, the disciplinary space of science – are the general scientific concepts which reflect the field, sphere, space in which the search for phenomena or properties is carried out or may be or should be carried out that are within or may be within the subject-matter of the science.

The methodological foundation of juridical comparativistics, unlike traditionally understood comparative jurisprudence (or comparative law), is not only the comparative method, but also the contrastive, systemic, functional axiological, synergetic, historical, and a number of other methods which are combined in the comparative approach.

This understanding is based on the fact that the comparative method is not only one of the simplest and universal methods of thought and means of practical, daily, and other cognition, but also a general-scientific method requiring special knowledge having a complex structure. In juridical comparativistics it is understood not only as a method of comparison, but as an arsenal of mutually-linked methods of research of "more than one" object (constrative, analogy, and so on), that is, as the comparative approach. In this event questions arise as to whether all the methods of science may be classified according to the criterion of one – not one object in comparativistics (pluralist) and monist, to distinguish those methods which are within the comparative approach from those which are not and which may not be within it? Moreover, if one takes into account that in the comparative approach objects are investigated initially one by one, naturally non-comparative methods may be used with whose assistance, in particular, objective facts are separated out from reality and scientific facts, results of research, the ordering thereof, systematization, and so on are described.

To other distinctive features of juridical comparativistics may be relegated the consideration of legal reality in time as the comparative history of law,[2] in space as the comparative geography of law, the orientation thereof in contrasting law and other social regulators, differentiation of comparative legal studies with regard to their effectuation and use of results achieved in science, practice, and the immediate life of subjects, and also in legal and other sciences, in one of the countries being compared, or in a third country. In addition, recognition of the importance of the position of the researcher-comparatist himself is of material significance (choice of determined method, criteria of comparison, general theory used, and so on).

This leads to the subject-matter of juridical comparativistics, which is pluralist – disciplinary, inter-disciplinary, extra-disciplinary, extra-scientific in character. A new field is thereby formed, a new sphere of knowledge, a new system of legal knowledge in general, and also non-juridical, integrated with political, economic, social, and other sciences. Accordingly, they should reflect also the new comparative reality as a community and the distinction between legal and other realities of various countries and continents.

Since the comparative represents a certain cross-cut of more than one legal reality, there are grounds to consider the comparative aspect of the

[2] K. Zweigert and H. Kötz, Введение в сравнительное правоведение в сфере частного права [Introduction to Comparative Law in the Sphere of Private Law] (1998), I, pp. 18-19.

entire structure of legal sciences and respectively separate out, by analogy with respective non-juridical or legal disciplines, a comparative philosophy, sociology, and psychology of law (comparative legal psychology), theory and history of law, history of political and legal doctrines, legal linguistics, legal geography (country studies), legal pedagogy, and so on. In considering the integrative (inter-disciplinary) nature of juridical comparativistics, it is essential to take into account the fact that, in addition to the existing, in the long-term new similar inter-disciplinary subject-matter and problem fields of scientific research may emerge (disciplines).

Thus, one of the arguments of opponents of recognizing comparative law as an autonomous legal discipline with which one must concur is the lack of a single conception thereof either in the past or at present, to which the diversity of understanding of comparative law, theories of law, legal realities of countries, associations thereof, and so on testify. Therefore if it makes sense to speak about such a conception, this may be worked out on the basis of the principles of diversity of the legal works, pluralism of legal understanding and social regulation, and integrity on the principles of dialogue, interaction, mutual-supplementation, synergy, and other similar grounds, among which the principle of comparativism should specially be singled out.

A pluralist understanding of comparative law is based on recognizing the scientific significance of "one", "other", and "different": science and method; study of foreign law and own comparison; historical (temporal) and geographical (spatial) parameters of legal reality; the theoretical and empirical comprehension, scientific and extra-scientific, and so on.

PHILOSOPHY OF COMPARATIVISM

In a civilized context the ideas of post-modernism topical today in which much that is "fresh" and "significant" do not correlate in a number of aspects with those values and norms which are inherent in and comprise the foundation of other non-European cultures.[3] On this level, the new worldview of European civilization has remained only its worldview, and only of some of the countries.

Unlike European civilization, for which revolutions and fundamental transformations are inherent, the countries of Asia and the Near East, especially China, Japan, South Korea, and India, are more traditional and stable. They do not directly receive the values of the West, but assimilate

[3] A. S. Timoshchuk, Ведийская культура [Vedic Culture: Essence and Metamorphoses] (Vladimir, 2002).

them, adapt them to their distinctive inherent traditions and cultures. The philosophy, religion, and cultural traditions of these countries differ from the ideas of post-modernism.

In the context of the worldview sources of comparativism, which is manifest at different levels and in various forms of comprehension of and attitudes towards the world, it, at the intersection of philosophy and legal reality, may be represented as the philosophy of comparativism, comparative philosophy, legal comparativism, the comparativeness of law, the philosophy of legal comparativism, and the comparative philosophy of law. Each of these manifestations of comparativism is a modification thereof relative to the common and the distinctive in the diversity of correlations of philosophy and law.

The philosophy of comparativism is a form of comprehension whose distinctiveness lies in the primarily rational cognition and interpretation of the work and the world of law as one of its components based on the position that the world cannot be comprehended by any single philosophical system, but only the aggregate thereof, the common and the difference between them being established not by a theoretical scheme inherent in a particular philosophical position, but in the result of their real dialogue or adialogue. Therefore, the philosophy of comparativism cannot be reduced to one of the existing philosophies; it is simultaneously phenomenology, hermeneutics, pragmatism, structuralism, but distinct from all of them and from each of them individually.

Modifying the concept of "family similarity" proposed by Ludwig Wittgenstein (1889-1951), one may say that the philosophy of comparativism reflects not only "family similarity", but "family difference", the absence thereof, and also the common and the different in "family similarity" and "family difference", identity, parallelism, analogousness, the contrasting thereof, emphasizing their relativity.

The philosophy of comparativism does not reduce to individual philosophical systems just as it does not reduce to comparative philosophy, comparative politology, comparative economic systems, comparative law, and others. It, on one hand, is an integration and differentiation thereof that "enters" or penetrates into them as the philosophical basis thereof and, unlike them, acts with regard to them as the "other", linking and distinguishing them with regard to comparative "quality" and, on the other hand – is merely one of many existing philosophical approaches.

The philosophy of comparativism as not only comparative philosophy is orientated not to cognition and understanding of philosophical cultures and traditions, but to cognition, philosophical comprehension, of various worldviews of various subjects and in various parts of the planet; comparative philosophy is a component, a part, thereof, a means of thinking. The philosophy of comparativism is the philosophy of combining and differentiating diversity and unity; it encompasses comparative philosophy, but does not limit it.

The philosophy of comparativism as philosophical knowledge is based on a determined methodology and in this status is similar to many other philosophical systems, traditions, currents. As in the case of other philosophical systems, the philosophy of comparativism, in even greater measure, has its own methodology, the basis of which is the comparative approach and comparative method. The dominating methodological orientation of both comparativism and the philosophy of comparativism is more orientated towards understanding them primarily in the context of a means of thought and attitude towards the world, a means of philosophizing rather than subject-matter knowledge.

A distinctive feature of comparative philosophizing is the comprehension and perception of the world, in particular the world of law, through the prism of categories "one – other – different" in their post-modernistic interpretation.

The correlation traditional in the dialectic of the universal, general, special, and unique was form in the era of modernism, classical and neoclassical periods of the development of rationalism. In the idealistic and materialistic dialectic the point of departure was namely unity – the "spirit" of Hegel, the "matter" of Engels; therefore the general interlinkage of phenomena was actualized. However, if the accent is moved from unity to diversity, difference, the interpretation of these categories also changes. The universality of the interlinkage of phenomena in post-modernist philosophy is formed through contrasting – the universality of differences of phenomena, and in the philosophy of comparativism – as relativity (the non-universality of a common link and non-universality of a common divergence) of the common and the different – everything is not interlinked, all phenomena have a common and differences since the common exists relative to the different, and *vice versa*.

The reflection of the common through the concept of "world", "universal", "unified", "identical", and divergence through the concept of "unrepeatable", "unique", "distinctive", "incomparable" in turn affects the identification of the common and the differences of these concepts. The concepts "universal", "common", "special", "sole", and "unique", which are categories of the dialectic, have been investigated in detail in the literature of philosophy[4] and are used in scientific studies at various levels

4 See G. L. Tulchinskii and M. N. Epshtein (eds.), Проективный философский словарь [Projective Philosophical Dictionary] (Spb., 2000).

of complexity and subject-matter. In using the experience of philosophical comprehension and adaptation of these categories in relation to the distinctive features of socio-humanitarian, including legal, sciences, one may separate out such methodological positions which have significance for the philosophy of comparativism, reguliatology, and juridical comparativistics (or legal comparatology).

1. The categories of common and different are, in turn, common and different with other categories of the dialectic – essence and phenomenon, abstract and concrete, necessary and incidental, and also the laws thereof: transition of quantitative changes into qualitative, unity and the struggle of opposites, negation of the negation.
2. The forming of these categories commences in the sources of philosophical thought connected with the origin of abstract cognition. The problems of understanding these categories arose in ancient philosophy (Parmenides, Socrates, Plato, Aristotle) when comprehending the relation of thought to the sensitively perceived multitude of various phenomena, was analyzed in mediaeval philosophy, by German classical idealism (Hegel), and Marxist philosophy (Marx, Engels, Lenin). In modern methodological studies the problem of the common, special, and unique has become the basis for the study of the theoretical and empirical, ideal and real, abstract and concrete, typologies, classifications, and so on.
3. The categories of the common and the different reflect the dialectical unity of ontological and gnosiological aspects since they as concepts reflect the properties of reality and, embodied in theoretical thought, become a regulator of behavior (axiological aspect), reality, and change thereof.
4. The common and the different characterize stability and changeability, equality and inequality, similarity and distinction, identity and non-identity, repetition and nonrepetition, continuity and noncontinuity of properties, links, relations, and trends of development of various states of one or different objects. Therein is manifest the uniqueness and universality of the common and the different.
5. Discussions with regard to the reality of the separate did not arise when they took place in the past regarding the reality of the common and continue to this day, especially within the framework of modernism and post-modernism, phenomenology and hermeneutics, and so on. One of the solutions to this problem modern investigators see in the problem of virtual reality. In the sphere of law this is embodied in the context of discussions

about the *a priori* nature of the common in the theory of natural or religious law and *a posteriori* – in comparative law.

6. The problem of the correlation of the common and the different is significant for a study of the historical development of legal reality, including comparative study. The failure to resolve this problem is traced through the different understanding of the historical process as unique, local, or common.

Dialectical materialism proceeded from the unity of the common, special, and unique, and post-modernism – from the different as the foundation of worldbuilding, and comparativism – from the mutual reinforcement of unique and difference of the unique, special and common, avoiding thereby the juxtaposition and absolutization of the common and the different.

One ideal of the philosophy of comparativism is not only the common or the different, commensurability and incommensurability, but their proportional correlation, since with an increase of the common the different becomes smaller, and *vice versa*. An increase of the common (or reduction of the different) increased the commensurateness and reduces the non-commensurateness, and an increase of the different – *vice versa*. Thus, one may speak not only about the commonness or difference of phenomena, but also the degree of their commonness – difference, the relativity of commonness or difference. If comparative law is orientated towards a search for the common in the different, in the philosophy of comparativism it is augmented by a search for the differences both in the common and in the different since the different itself (by definition) interrupts the link with the other different. The philosophy of comparativism thereby affirms that the common also is different as is all other, but the different also is common.

The philosophy of comparativism is orientated towards a comprehension of the relativity of necessary and incidentalness, possibility and reality, commensurateness and non-commensurateness, constancy and changeability. Commensurateness and non-commensurateness in particular are considered through the concept of "other" and "different". The "other" is a concept which reflects the modern reading of the traditional philosophical concept "my – other" (G. Hegel), which became the result of the synthesis of the ideas of dialogue inherent in neoclassical philosophizing within the framework of existential psychoanalysis, philosophical anthropology, hermeneutics, and other trends.[5]

[5] M. Buber, Два образа веры [Two Forms of Faith], transl. G. S. Pomerants (1995); T. P. Lifintseva, Философия диалога Мартина Бубера [Philosophy of Dialogue of Martin Buber] (1999).

This concept became one of the basic ones in post-neoclassical philosophy (philosophy of late post-modernism) within the limits of the communications approach to philosophical studies. Basing himself on the ideas of "being – with" of Heidegger, "being with another" of Jean-Paul Sartre, "being – one – with – another" of Binswanger, relations of "I – Thou" instead of "I – it" of Buber, the concept of "other" reflects the need for another in order to know the peculiarities of one's own being. It, according to Sartre, means "to be seen by another" since the dialogue form of the correlation "one" and "other" is manifest in their mutual transitions which predetermine the similarity with traditional concepts of the Chinese philosophy "tsi-zhan" and "lei", which presuppose their own co-relation and self-determination through the "other".[6] On the contrary, the concept of "different" fixes not the "with", but the absence of dialogue of one and the other, the absence of "one" in the "other", their different qualitative definitude where the "other" becomes "different" – noncomparable.

The interpretation of the triad "one – other – different" in comparativism has certain distinctive features:

First, the dichotomy "one – other" allows the commensurateness of various objects on the principle of conformity, the possibility of the quantitative study within the limits of certain common qualities, fixation of the presence of similar qualities (the common), that is, all that is inherent to comparison in its traditional understanding.

Second, the dichotomy "one(other) – different" is directed towards identifying the non-commensurateness of objects and their correlation to the principle of supplementarity (N. Bohr), reflects the possibility not of comparison, but of contrast (juxtaposition), the fixation of various qualities, the ontological tribute of the different as the opposite.

Third, the triad "one – other – different" enables objects to be imagined, fixed, and studied in relations of commensurateness – non-commensurateness, which is inherent to comparative research, unlike comparative studies orientated only towards commensurateness, which introduces into scientific research the identification and study of the non-comparable as unique and juxtaposed, essential for the integral perception and reflection of the world.

Fourth, the failure to accept in comparative studies only relations of "commensurateness" or "non-commensurateness" fixes the principle of relativity – their dependence upon aspects, coordinates, grounds, and parameters of study.

[6] M. A. Mozheiko and D. V. Maiboroda, «Другой» [The Other], in Постмодернизм: Энциклопедия [Post-Modernism: Encyclopedia] (Minsk, 2001), pp. 250-251.

An important aspect of the philosophy of comparativism is eliciting the "dynamics" of the common and the different, the methodological basis of which may be dialogue,[7] polylogue, "polyphony", and their juxtaposition. In this situation the common is illuminated as derivative from the interaction of the different; the common is manifested in the dialogue of the different when the absence of the common is a manifestation of the absence of dialogue, that is, adialogue. Dialogue leads to the origin of the common and a change in the process of dialogue of the different, and therefore the more dialogue, the more common and the less different, and *vice versa*. Nonetheless, dialogue not only furthers the origin and respectively the identification of the common in the different, but an awareness of the different relative to the common. By such means adialogue is not only the presence of the different, but the absence of the common. The dialogue nature of the common and the different makes possible the transition to their changeability, their mutual transitions and mutual changes, that is, to a comprehension of the common and the different in the coordinates of time and space.

The forms of cognition of the world are as diverse as is the world, and therefore a universal and true philosophy (theory, conception, doctrine), of the world is lacking. Moreover, each of the existing forms of cognition of the world (philosophy, science, religion, mythology, practical and daily cognition) reflect and understand the world by means and methods inherent thereto, form as a result distinctive pictures of the world which become regulators of behavior and thought of their adherents and through the last participate in the transformation of the world.

The forms of cognition and understanding of the world may correspond or not to reality, as a consequence of which the diversity of these correlations contain simulators (Jean Baudrillard), "virtual reality", and so on. The real world is diverse, it acquires the common in cognition but the cognition itself is reality, part of the world, which cognisizes, understands, and transforms diverse forms of behavior and thought of various subjects, and not only

[7] Iu. M. Oborotov, Традиції та новації у правовому розвитку [Traditions and Innovations in Legal Development] (Odessa, 2001), pp. 95-103; I. L. Chestnov, «Общее и особенное в праве» [The General and Special in Law], in Государство и право на рубеже веков [State and Law at the Turn of Centuries] (Spb.., 2000), pp. 33-35; Chestnov, Общество и юриспруденция на исходе второго тысячеления [Society and Jurisprudence at the End of the Second Millennium] (1999); Chestnov, Принцип диалога в современной теории права (проблемы правопонимания) [The Principle of Dialogue in the Contemporary Theory of Law (Problems of Legal Understanding)] (Spb., 2002); Chestnov, «Ддиалогическая онтология права в ситуации постмодерна» [Dialogical Ontology of Law in the Post-Modern Situation], Правоведение [Jurisprudence], no. 3 (2001), pp. 45-52.' Chestnov, «Правопонимание в эпоху постмодерна»]Legal Understanding in the Post-Modern Era], Правоведение [Jurisprudence], no. 2 (2002), pp. 4-16.

philosophers, scholars, religious figures, politicians, and representatives of other elites who merely determine in certain spheres and aspects (or cross-cuts) the orientation of these processes.

Proceeding from this, the diversity of the daily life of all people, associations thereof, processes and mechanisms for the transmission, perception, and embodiment of various forms of cognition and understanding of the world by sundry subjects have significance for the philosophy of comparativism. Therefore, for example, the directly perceived legal reality in the philosophy of comparativism, on one hand, is inconstant and diverse, exists in the form of various legal phenomena and events which have individual, unrepeatable properties, are limited in space and time, and are characterized by uniqueness. On the other hand, on this level of sensitive perception one observes not only the differentiation, but also the interconnection of legal phenomena and the fixing of their properties, community.

In the anthropological context[8] the orientation to "I – one", "other", and "different" advanced man to the forefront, who thinks, communes, acts and in whose life all other phenomena are manifest, are effectuated which are the result of his thought and behavior. Moreover, man and his life are the subject-matter of all forms of cognition, understanding, and practice. Everything in this world relates to man, how he relates to everything. The philosophy of comparativism is oriented not towards the perception of man and his life as "I" and "my life" (an isolated person, an abstraction), but towards a perception of man as "I" who am inextricably linked with "other" and "different", his being as "with" (Heidegger) in his "daily life".

This aspect of the philosophy of comparativism may be investigated in the context of the philosophical contemplation of life. The concept "life" is inherent to the neo-classical type of philosophizing, in particular the "philosophy of life" in which the content thereof and methodological burden are linked with an understanding of the inextricability of subject and object, the "presence" of the subject in knowledge about the "object"; the aspiration by various means to express the internal activeness, spontaneity, self-organization, and self-development of the being of the subject; the presence in the being of the subject not only of the rational, but of the irrational, cognitive and non-cognitive, investigated and guessed with the aid of intuition, the psyche of the subject, the normative and non-normative, and so on.[9] "Life is a reality in which one lives, one resides,

[8] S. I. Maksimov, Правовая реальность: опыт философского осмысления [Legal Reality: Experiment of Philosophical Contemplation] (Kharkov, 2002).

[9] A. I. Demidov, «Политико-правовая жизнь: ненормативный аспект» [Politico-Legal Life: Non-Normative Aspect], Правовая политика и правовая жизнь [Legal Policy and

that is, it always belongs to someone, always is someone's life. Life is a ... means of existence in the world of the subject of activity, cognition, evaluation, survival, thought".[10]

PHILOSOPHY OF LEGAL COMPARATIVISM

The common and the different in the diversity of forms of being of law condition the common and the different in the gnosiological discourse about the sphere of the "intersection" of comparativism and law as forms of the cognition of law, and of law as cognition. This problem hereinafrter may be investigated within the conception of the gnosiology of law advanced by Kozlovskii.[11]

Thus, the philosophy of comparativism, just as comparativism proper, does not represent a new philosophical conception of subject-matter, but is recognition of a multiplicity of philosophical systems which reflect the diversity of the world, a contemplation of the "universal, general, different, and unique" between them, a result of the presence-absence of their interaction (dialogue or adialogue). Therefore, the philosophy of comparativism, being methodological by nature and a means of philosophizing, is based on the principles of the primacy of the diversity of the world, a denial of the absolutization of universality and uniqueness, relativity and supplementarity, determinativeness and spontaneity, chaos and order, and, in adapting itself to certain subject-matter, acquires distinctive qualities. Thus, the multiplicity of the "common and different" between the philosophy of comparativism and the legal sphere of social life, legal reality, may be contemplated and concretized through the concept of legal comparativism and the comparativeness of law.

Legal comparativism and, respectively, the philosophy of legal comparativism reflect the distinctive features of comparativism in the worldview and philosophical contemplation of legal reality or, in other words, perception, contemplation, and relations through the category "common and different" to law in its temporal, spatial, ontological, gnosiological, axiological, and other aspects.

Legal Life], no. 3 (2002), pp. 18-25.

10 I. D. Nevvazhai, «Понятие правовой жизни: философские основания» [Concept of Legal Life: Philosophical Grounds], in Политическая и правовая жизнь: Федеративные и региональные аспекты [Political and Legal Life: Federative and Regional Aspects] (2001), pp. 23-35.

11 A. A. Kozlovskii, Гносеологічна природа права (філософсько-правовий аналіз) [Gnosiology of the Nature of Law (Philosophical-Legal Analysis)] (Kiev, 2000) (abstract of diss. doctor iurid. nauk); id, Право як пізнання: Вступ до гносеології права [Law as Cognition: Introduction to the Gnosiology of Law] (Chernovets, 1999).

Legal comparativism as worldview contemplation of legal reality encompasses the diversity of views towards law in unity and difference with knowledge, convictions, value orientations, and ideals inherent to various social subjects, in various countries, and at various times, law being reflected in unity and difference with other socio-cultural phenomena.

The philosophy of legal comparativism as, above all, the theoretical nucleus thereof represents the comparativeness of the philosophy of law which may not be confined only to a comparative approach to philosophical systems of the contemplation of law which inhere in the comparative philosophy of law, but encompass that comparativeness which is peculiar to each of them and in which the comparativeness of legal reality as their subject-matter finds its interpretation. If the comparativeness of law reflects the uniqueness of its comparative nature, the philosophy of legal comparativism is its ontology, gnosiology, axiology, anthropology, and so on.

The distinction with respect to previous interpretations, the correlations of unity and diversity, lie in the fact that legal comparativism introduces relations of equality and inequality.[12] The use of these categories, on one hand, fixes the link with this general philosophical principle (comparativism), and, on the other, is an individual manifestation thereof since it is supplemented by these categories. In addition, the introduction of relations of equality-inequality makes possible the consideration of the cyclicity of their mutual transformations, that is, the dominance of the diversity relating to unity, the equality of diversity and unity, the dominance of unity relative to diversity, and a new cycle again commences with the dominance of diversity. If an orientation towards the pluralism of law, towards the unity of the diverse and equality in legal reality, is inherent in post-modernism, and in modernism towards universality, the diversity of the and inequality (hierarchy) of legal reality, then legal comparativism includes their extreme and intermediate stages of mutual transformation, which may be interpreted as equality-inequality of diversity and unity, which meets the modern state of the world of law, its cognition and understanding. Moreover, monism, in recognizing the

[12] N. A. Berdyaev, «Философия неравенства: Письма к недругам по социальной философии» [Philosophical Inequality: Letters to Opponents in Social Philosophy], in N. A. Berdyaev, Русское зарубежье: Из истории социальной и правовой мысли [Russia Abroad: From the History of Social and Legal Thought] (Leningrad, 1991), pp. 7-242; K. K. Zhol', Философия и социология права [Philosophy and Sociology of Law] (Kiev, 2000); Zhol', Язык как практическое сознание (философский анализ) [Language as Practical Consciousness (Philosophical Analysis)] (Kiev, 1990); V. I. Zhukov, Компаративистика в современной социологии: методологические и методические подходы [Comparativistics in Modern Sociology: Methodological and Methods Approaches] (2003).

existence of diversity, singles out the unity as the principal, and pluralism, on the contrary, in acknowledging the unity, sees the basis in diversity.

Legal comparativism, while retaining a link with legal monism and pluralism, is based on their indissolubility in the form of equality and inequality, relating to their normal state not dominance, the more so elimination of one or the other, but their equality, interaction, mutual transformation, and so on. They exist in equality not as such, but as interchangeable, inter-conditioned forms thereof. Equality and inequality may in their correlation form harmonious and disharmonious, optimal or non-optimal correlations, combinations, may be comparable, resonant, form an ensemble, or *vice versa*. The recognition of diversity of the unity and unity of the diverse is not only inherent to legal comparativism, but also the equality and inequality of the diversity and the unity.

Legal comparativism is commensurability, co-subordination, pluralism, and monism. The path of its development is the path to the harmony of life in which equality or inequality have dominated. Harmony is a link, consent, proportionality, the order of parts of the whole, coordination, reflects the correlation not of the "or", but of the "and", and also symmetry, beauty. Law in comparativism may be regarded as the harmony of relations which precludes disharmony – anti-law, violation of law. Legal rules are a "musical score", and life of functioning law is a "resonant melody", the "song of life" (B. Kistiakovskii).

Law reflects the harmoniousness of equality and inequality in life, anti-law – disharmony. If this proposition is interpreted through the category of chaos and order, then their "link" may be represented as the dominance of chaos over order – the equality of chaos and order – the dominance of order over chaos. Then a system in equilibrium is that in which order and chaos are in equilibrium, that is, equal. Having accentuated attention not on the internal states of law as a system, but on the correlation thereof with the socio-cultural milieu, one may speak about the equality and inequality of chaos and order in the milieu of law, and also equality and inequality of chaos and order in the interaction of law and milieu.

However, the relations of equality – inequality, harmoniousness – disharmony, commensurability – incommensurability comprise only individual aspects of the manifestation of comparativness in legal reality and the contemplation thereof. To other aspects should be relegated relations investigated in detail in the philosophy of law of freedom – arbitrariness, possibility – reality, necessity – incidentalness, compulsion – voluntariness, justness – unjustness, values – anti-values, subjective

– objective, material – ideal,[13] and others. Therefore the essence of the comparativeness of law constitutes the diversity of the common and different thereof, which has a distinctive configuration in each of the legal realities of countries, civilizations, world religions, sociums, man, and in their uniqueness acts as the "different" with respect to the dominant social regulators.

Relations of equality, tolerance, patience, justness, freedom, "humanness", which comprise the content of the comparativeness of law not only have been developed in fundamental works,[14] theories of law,[15] but also been officially recognized at the international and national levels. Without dwelling on their manifestations in the law of Ukraine, since they have been considered in detail in a number of monographs,[16] it should be noted that the recognition of the diversity of countries, cultures, and

[13] V. S. Nersesiants, Философия права [Philosophy of Law] (1997); O. O. Bandura, S. A. Bublik, and M. L. Zainchkovskii, Філософія права [Philosophy of Law] (Kiev, 2000); O. G. Danilian, L. D. Bairachna, and S. I. Maksimov, Філософія права [Philosophy of Law] (Kiev, 2005); Leger Raymond, Великие правовые системы современности: сравнительно-правовой подход [Great Legal Systems of Modern Times: Comparative Law Approach] (2009).

[14] O. O. Bandura, Єдність цінностей та істини в праві [Unity of Values and Truth in Law] (Kiev, 2000); E. V. Burlai, «Право в естетичному вимірі (до постановки питання)» [Law in Aesthetic Measure (On Raising the Question)], in Проблеми філософії права [Problems of Philosophy of Law] (Kiev, 2004), II; Kozlovskii (1999), note 11 above; S. I. Maksimov, «Толерантность как черта правосознания» [Tolerance as Feature of Legal Consciousness], in Толерантность как культурная универсалия [Tolerance as a Cultural Universal] (Kharkov, 1996), pp. 59-60; id, «Справедливість як основна правова цінність» [Justness as Basic Legal Value], Вістнік Университету внутп. справ. [Herald of University of Internal Affairs], no. 12 (2000), pp. 268-273; Iu. M. Oborotov, Традиції та новації у правовому розвитку [Traditions and Innovations in Legal Development] (Odessa, 2001); M. P. Orzikh, Человеческое измерение права: доктринальная ретроспектива и современная постановка проблемы [Human Measure of Law: Doctrinal Retrospective and Modern Posing of Problem], in Iu. S. Shemshuchenko (ed.), Антологія української юридичної думки [Anthology of Ukrainian Legal Thought], vol. 9; Iu. S. Shemshuchenko and V. F. Pogorilko (eds.), Юридична наука незалежної України [Legal Science of Independent Ukraine] (Kiev, 2005), pp. 85-99.

[15] S. N. Egorov, Аксиоматические основы теории права [Axiomatic Foundations of Theory of Law] (St. Petersburg, 2001); V. M. Kravtsev, Типи праворозуміння як методології основних філософсько-правових дискурсів [Types of Legal Reasoning as Methodology of Basic Philosophical-Legal Discourse] (Kiev, 2003) (abstract diss. kand. iurid. nauk); A. V. Poliakov, Общая теория права: проблемы интерпретации в контексте коммуникативного подхода [General Theory of Law: Problems of Interpretation in Context of Communicative Approach] (Spb., 2004); A. V. Ptushenko, Системная парадигма права [Systems Paradigm of Law] (2004); Сравнительное правоведение: наука, методология, учебная дпсциплина [Comparative Law: Science, Methodology, Instructional Discipline] (Krasnoiarsk, 2008).

[16] A. M. Kolodii, Конституція і розвиток принципів права України (методичні питання) [Constitution and Development of Principles of Law of Ukraine (Methodological Questions)] (Kiev, 2000) (abstract of diss. doktor iurid. nauk).

civilizations is the dominant trend in international law and in the activities of the United Nations and other international organizations.

This process was to a great extent initiated by the collapse of the colonial system and origin of new States as subjects of international law. In the Declaration on the Granting of Independence to Colonial Countries and Peoples adopted as a United Nations General Assembly Resolution 1514 (XV) on 14 December 1960 the aspiration of all previously dependent peoples for freedom is noted and the obstruction thereof is a threat to peace.

The orientation of mankind towards cooperation between States was elaborated and clarified in the Declaration on the Principles of International Law Concerning Friendly Relations and Cooperation Between States in accordance with the Charter of the United Nations, confirmed by United Nations General Assembly Resolution 2625 (XXVI) on 24 October 1970. It accentuated the principles of equality, freedom, sovereignty, justice, refraining from the threat or use of force, and good-faith fulfillment of duties. The aspiration of the United Nations to overcome intolerance of the "different" is consolidated in the Declaration on the Elimination of All Forms of Intolerance and Discrimination on the Basis of Religion or Belief, confirmed by United Nations General Assembly Resolution 36/55 on 25 November 1981 and the Declaration of the Rights of Persons Belonging to National or Ethnic, Religious, or Linguistic Minorities, adopted by United Nations General Assembly Resolution 47/135 on 18 December 1992.

The end of the twentieth and beginning of the twenty-first centuries was marked by increased attention to the pluralism of cultures and the forming of a world order, in particular in the context of globalization. This concerns the cultures of the world which are retarded as the combining of value purposes, worldviews, traditions, types of behavior and ways of life based on the principles of freedom, justness, democracy, tolerance,[17] solidarity, cooperation, pluralism, cultural diversity, dialogue, and mutual understanding at all levels of society and between peoples.[18] In particular, the United Nations Millennium Declaration, confirmed by United Nations General Assembly Resolution 55/2 of 8 September 2000 emphasized that globalization may acquire an all-encompassing and just character only if there are large-scale measures to form a common future based on a common affiliation to mankind in all of its diversity and stressed those fundamental values such as freedom, democracy, equality, solidarity, tolerance, respect for nature, the rule of law, and others.

[17] Declaration on the Principles of Tolerance, confirmed by Resolution 5.61 of the General Conference of UNESCO on 16 November 1995.

[18] Declaration on Culture of Peace and Programme of Action of Culture of Peace, confirmed by United Nations General Assembly Resolution 52/243, of 13 September 1999.

Recognition of the cultural diversity of the peoples of the world permeates other international legal documents[19] in which culture is regarded not only as the aggregate of distinctive spiritual, material, intellectual, and emotional qualities inherent in society or a social group, but in which, in addition to art and literature, it encompasses the way of life, knowing how to live in amity, systems of values, traditions, and beliefs. It is emphasized that although the process of globalization is a challenge to cultural diversity, it also creates conditions for a new dialogue between culture and civilizations on the principles of recognition of: cultural diversity of the common heritage of mankind; the need for a transition from cultural diversity to cultural pluralism – the harmonious coexistence and interaction of cultures; cultural diversity as a factor of development; human rights as a guarantee of cultural diversity, and so on. The globality and interdependence of the world, the need for the effectuation of a global partnership of regions and countries, and the preservation of cultural pluralism have become the principal motive of international legal documents of recent years, which finds affirmation in the Human Development Report 2004: Cultural Liberty in Today's Diverse World and in the Human Development Report 2005: International Cooperation at a Crossroads: Aid, Trade and Security in an Unequal World.

Thus, the principles on which legal comparativism is based reflect the substantive properties of modern legal reality, its comparativeness, and also the developmental trends of the last.

An important orientation of investigating the link between comparativism and law is the study thereof within the context of the concept of "legal life", including: the philosophical bases thereof; methodologies of research, conceptual apparatus, subject-matter of research, and correlation with other legal concepts.[20]

[19] UNESCO Universal Declaration on Cultural Diversity, adopted by the General Conference at its 31st session on 2 November 2001; UNESCO Declaration Concerning the Intentional Destruction of Cultural Heritage, adopted by the General Conference on 17 October 2003.

[20] A. I. Demidov, A. V. Malko, A. Iu. Solomatin, and V. M. Dolgov, Политическая и правовая жизнь модернзирующего общества [Political and Legal Life of Modernizing Society] (2002); N. I. Novikova and V. A. Tishkov (eds.), Закон и жизнь. Юридическая антропология [Law and Life. Legal Anthropology] (2000); A. V. Malko, «Категория «правовая жизнь»: проблемы становления» [Category of "Legal Life": Problem of Origin], Государства и право [State and Law], no. 5 (2001), pp. 5-14; A. V. Malko, A. E. Mikhailov, I. D. Nevvazhai, «Методологические основы исследования правовой жизни общества» [Methodological Foundations of Study of Legal Life of Society], Правовая политика и правовая жизнь [Legal Policy and Legal Life], no. 3 (2002), pp. 5-17; A. E. Mikhailov, «Философские аспекты правовой жизни» [Philosophical Aspects of Legal Life], Правовая политика и правовая жизнь [Legal Policy and Legal Life], no. 1 (2001), pp. 93-100.

The methodological significance of the concept "life" in comparativism is much broader than the concept of "legal life": the concept of life reflects the existence of a subject especially through pluralism, diversity, multiplicity of the lives of people, societies, civilizations, culture, their being in time and space, by group of persons and forms of behavior; life as a concept requires no substantiation, verification, evidence of its reality; it in various aspects and by various means is investigated, reflected, and understood in various forms of worldview (science, religion, mythology, philosophy, art, morals, practical and daily consciousness and unconsciousness); the concept of life is directly linked with the subject, its "being – with", coexistence with other and different subjects; the term "life" is adequately translated into all languages of the world; life is orientated towards an understanding of man in the context of his being, life space, family, collective, group, class, ethnos, which do not exist outside the life of people; in philosophy and science life is reflected through the concept "reality", "validity", "being", "system", "order", "superstructure", "sphere", which in essence are specific means or forms of an understanding thereof inherent in philosophical systems and scientific approaches; life is diverse, different, ultimately not cognizable, and therefore, unlike its reflection in concepts, it also contains the uncognizable.

Thus, for comparativism, comparative studies, the point of departure and ultimate aim is the study of life and man in all the diversity of their manifestations and forms in sundry civilizations, culture, countries, and worldviews. Under this understanding of life and man in correlation with comparativism and necessity of a real polylogue of cultures (or civilizations), they may become a domain of search for the common in real life and not only in philosophy, religion, and others.

CONCLUSIONS

Since the philosophy of comparativism stands between the philosophy of modernism and the philosophy of pluralism, between the philosophy of the "identical" inherent to the era of the modern and the philosophy of the "difference" inherent to the era of post-modernism, comparativism may be relegated to "post-modernism", which assimilates both modernism and post-modernism.

The philosophy of comparativism as philosophical contemplation of comparativism is the philosophical basis of comparativistics – the sphere of interdisciplinary studies which are based on a comparative approach, which conditions the further study thereof but already in this quality.

Thus, in the context of pluralism of cultures, of the "nonuniversality" of post-modernism, the locality and cultural conditionality of any theoretical schemes, recognition of the diversity of worldviews, the establishment of the common and the different between them in the process of their real interaction, the origin and arising of comparativism is not a consequence of any individual philosophy, but a result of the presence – absence of the interaction of various philosophical systems.

The philosophy of comparativism is primarily a rational way of eliminating the absolutization of universality and uniqueness, determination and spontaneity, chaos and order, is based on their relativity, supplementarity, cyclicity, and incidentalness of mutual transformations and through them optimizes, harmonizes modernism and post-modernism, contemplates the world as pluralistic, multi-dimensional, multi-polar through the diversity of forms of cognition adequate to its nature and cultural distinctiveness of the subject of cognition.

Contemplation of the philosophy of comparativism through the category of the common and the different, proportionality, necessity and incidentalness, constancy and changeability, and others, and also in the context of the philosophy of "identical" and "different", makes it possible to suggest an own interpretation of the philosophy of comparativism on the basis of recognition of the fundmentalness of the dialectic of the category "one – other – different".

The diversity of the "common and different" between the philosophy of comparativism and the legal sphere of social life is summarized by the concepts of legal comparativism and the comparativeness of law. The last, having as common for them the distinctive features of the emergence of comparativism in law, are different aspects of "dialogue" and "adialogue". Whereas legal comparativism reflects the distinctive features of comparativism as a worldview and forms of philosophical contemplation of legal reality, the "general and different" – social and legal, then comparativeness of law – as the uniqueness of its comparative nature and as the distinctiveness of law as a form of comparative cognition, that is, that comparative which has an exclusively legal nature, is supplementary, does not reduce to other manifestations of comparativism.

In the ontological aspect legal comparativism reflects the existence of law as an element of social being, and comparativeness of law – its comparative content: equality – inequality, possibility – reality, necessity – incidentalness, freedom – arbitrariness, power – voluntariness, and so on. The unique configuration of these elements is inherent solely to law, which in this event acts as the "different" with regard to social phenomena.

The gnosiological discourse of the contemplation of pluralism of the correlations of comparativism and the legal sphere is pre-determined by the multiplicity of forms of the cognition of law and of law as forms of cognition, and axiological – by the multiplicity of legal values and the values of law, legal assessments, their being conditioned by the diversity of legal cultures and also by anti-values, then as an anthropological "cross-section" – pluralism of subjects of law, countries, and civilizations, multiplicity of forms of the subjectivization of ontology, gnosiology, and axiology of comparativism and legal reality.

Social Naturalism As A Methodological Principle Of Comparative Law And Legal Globalistics

A. N. KOSTENKO*

THEORY OF "NATURALISTIC JURISPRUDENCE"

What people understand by law depends on how they will use it. To be sure, an incorrect understanding leads to incorrect use and, respectively, the better the understanding, the better the use. If, for example, in modern Ukraine there are sufficient indicia which testify to shortcomings in law-use, this means, from our standpoint, that shortcomings also exist in law-understanding.

It is evident that some basic question of jurisprudence should exist on the resolution of which an understanding of law depends in general.

In our view one may conclude, having closely considered the history of jurisprudence, that the basic question of jurisprudence should be formulated as follows: "Law – is it a creation of nature or of people? And if both, then what role does nature and what role do people have in the co-creation of law?" This question determines all other questions which emerge in jurisprudence: how it is decided, all others are then decided. There are sufficient grounds to believe, in particular, that the basic question of jurisprudence was properly decided by the creators of Roman law since the last also today astonish by their perfection.

A close consideration of the history of the development of jurisprudence enables one to note that the progress of law always occurred thanks to

* доктор юридических наук, professor. Academician of the Academy of Legal Sciences of Ukraine; Meritorious Figure of Science and Technology of Ukraine.

"naturalist" jurists, that is jurists who propagated the ideology of natural law. Among these are Domitius Ulpianus (c. 160-228 A.D.), Marcus Tullius Cicero (106-43 B.C.), Hugo Grotius (1583-1645), Samuel Pufendorf (1632-1694), John Locke (1632-1704), Herbert Spencer (1820-1903), C. de Montesquieu (1689-1755), Thomas Jefferson (1743-1826), and others.

Proceeding from this, the present writer proposed at a Scientific-Practical Conference "Legal System of Ukraine: Theory and Practice", held at Kiev from 7-8 October 1993, to commence the renaissance in Ukraine of the idea of natural law on a new methodological foundation – on the basis of the principle of social naturalism.[1] Later studies by us affirmed the prospects for this approach based on the principle of social naturalism.[2]

The need for a renaissance in Ukraine of the idea of natural law is predetermined by the fact that it has the properties to "cure" law of the illness which is called "legal voluntarism" and is manifest, in particular, in

1 See O. M. Kostenko, «Принцип натуралізму в юридичній науці і кримінології» [Principle of Naturalism in Legal Science and Criminology], in Правова система України: теорія и практика [Legal System of Ukraine: Theory and Practice] (Kiev, 1993), pp. 390-392.

2 See Kostenko, «Трикутник долі» [Triangular Below], Віче [Eye], no. 6 (1993), pp. 91-99; «Принципи «універсальної конституції» природи» [Principle of a 'Universal Constitution' of Nature], Трибуна [Tribune], no. 8-9 (1993), pp. 15-16; «Справедливість кримінального закону як передумова ефективності його застосування» [Justness of Criminal Law as Prerequisite for Effectiveness of Application Thereof], Закогнодавство: проблеми ефективності [Legislation: Problems of Effectiveness] (Kiev, 1995), pp. 146-162; «Концепція природного права і законодавство» [Conception of Natural Law and Legislation], Правова держава [Rule of Law State], no. 7 (1996), pp. 77-84; «Наказание в системе средств борьбі с преступностью» [Punishment in the System of Means of Struggle against Criminality], in Уголовное наказание [Criminal Punishment] (Kiev-Donetsk, 1997), pp. 76-101; «Зашморг на злочинність» [Noose for Criminality], Віче [Eye], no. 7 (1997), pp. 118-125; «Конститиція і правова культура громадян: що головніше» [Constitution and Legal Culture of Citizens: What is Primary?] in Державно-правова реформа в Україні [State Law Reform in Ukraine] (Kiev, 1997), pp. 64-66; «Культура і закон» [Culture and Law], Правова держава [Rule of Law State], no. 9 (1998), pp. 130-136; «Розвиток кримінального права в незалежній Україні» [Development of Criminal Law in Independent Ukraine], in Iu. S. Shemshuchenko (ed.), Державотворення і правотворення в Україні: досвід, проблеми, перспективи [State Creation and Law-Creation in Ukraine: Experience, Problems, Prospects] (Kiev, 2001), pp. 562-576; «Основне питання правознавства: пошуки сучасного рішення» [Basic Questions of Law: Searches for Modern Solutions], in Ерліхівський збірник [Erlikhiv Collection], no. 3 (Cherniv, 2002), pp. 5-10; «Європейська юридична освіта (концептуальний підхід)» [European Legal Education (Conceptual Approach), Часопис Київського університету права [Journal of Kiev University of Law], no. 1 (2003), pp. 75-79; «Природні і людські фактори у праві (Дослідження з позиції соціального натуралізму)» [Natural and Human Factors in Law (Studies from the Position of Social Naturalism)], Вісник Національної академії наук України [Herald of National Academy of Sciences of Ukraine], no. 8 (2005), pp. 25-35; «Соціальний натуралізм – світогляд майбутнього» [Social Naturalism – World Outlook of the Future], Вісник Національної академії наук України [Herald of National Academy of Sciences], no. 10 (2006), pp. 33-39; «Універсальний натуралізм – підгрунтя наукової культури нового типу» [Universal Naturalism – Basis of Scientific Culture of New Type], Вісник Національної академії наук України [Herald of National Academy of Sciences of Ukraine, no. 10 (2007), pp. 37-43, and others.

legislative willfulness. Therefore in the history of the development of law the idea of natural law always was used as a means of overcoming legal voluntarism.

In order to properly understand the role of the idea of natural law in overcoming legal voluntarism, one must correctly define what law is. In our view, this should be done with the assistance of the so-called principle of social naturalism,[3] or, as it also may be called, the "principal of social naturalness" or the "principle of the naturalness of the social". According to it, social phenomena can never be considered beyond the limits of the operation of the laws of Mother Nature and, *vice versa*, they need to be regarded as those which are no less natural than physical and biological, and more natural because they are the highest form of the development of nature.

The principle of social naturalism arises from the idea of the natural integrity of the world, according to which everything material in the world should exist according to the laws of Nature. The idea of natural integrity of the world is grounds for structuring a general theory of universal naturalism, in accordance with which Mother Nature is the Supreme Legislator for everything material for all time, including for social phenomena. The existence in the integral world of a *socium* as part thereof, in turn, is the basis for structuring a special (partial) theory of social naturalism.

Therefore the dualist formula "nature and society" is a dramatic mistake since the dangerous illusion is created that society is beyond the limits of nature and it is thus denied that society also is nature, but another nature than physical or biological. Social naturalism, in creating "new eyes", makes it possible to see that there exist not two natures – physical and biological – but three – physical, biological, and social. And this "third nature" (that is, social) does not sink below the first two but, on the contrary, rises above them as the highest and exists according to its own natural laws inherent to it. According to the special theory of social naturalism, social phenomena are not outside nature, but recognition of their being natural does not mean

[3] For details on the principle of social naturalism, see, for example, O. M. Kostenko, Зашморг, note 2 above; id, Принцип соціального натуралізму в правознавстві [Principle of Social Naturalism in Law], Часопис Київського університету права [Journal of Kiev University of Law], no. 1 (2001), pp. 19-21; id, in Ерліхівський збірник [Erlikhiv Collection], note 2 above; id, «Основне питання правознавства з позиції соціального натуралізму» [Basic Questions of Law from the Positions of Social Naturalism], Проблеми філософії права [Problems of the Philosophy of Law] (2003), I, pp. 72-79; id, «Культура и закон – у протидіої злу» [Culture and Law : On Counteracting Evil] (Kiev, 2008); id, Проблема № 1 сучасної цивілізації (в українському контекст) [Problem No. 1 for a Modern Civilization (in the Ukrainian Context)] (Cherkassy, 2008).

the "physicalization" or the "biologization" of social phenomena, as may appear at first glance.

The so-called "basic question of jurisprudence" may be resolved with the assistance of the principle of social naturalism underlying the special theory of social naturalism which enables there to be determined anew what in the phenomenon of law is from Mother Nature, and what – from the will and consciousness of People. According to this principle, the "basic question of jurisprudence" is resolved as follows: "Law [jus] is the laws of Mother Nature according to which People should live in social life, being cognizant thereof and reflected in the form of legislation". This formula removes the problem of the juxtaposition in jurisprudence of the conceptions of "natural law" and "positive law", enabling one to understand that these conceptions in fact merely express two inter-connected aspects of the same phenomenon – law. The following proposition also arises from the principle of social naturalism: "Mother Nature allows to Man all that meets her laws, and prohibits that which is contrary to them".

One should have in view that the nature of each thing is mutable; it may either develop or degrade (that is, evolution occurs, involution, or other metamorphoses). The laws of nature also change under which a thing exists while in a particular natural state. The nature of man, for example, in childhood is rather different than in old-age. Consequently, in childhood a person should live under some laws of nature, and in advanced age, according to others. In other words, what is natural for a child may be unnatural for a person of advanced years.

As regards, for example, a comparison of an animal and a person, what is natural for an animal may be unnatural for a person, and *vice versa*.

It follows from the principle of social naturalism (or the principle of social naturalness) that two forms of reality exist: natural, that is, that which is responsive to the laws of nature, and unnatural, that is, that which does not correspond to the laws of nature. Good deeds exist in social reality which are natural phenomena, and crimes, which are unnatural phenomena. In biological reality, for example, the state of health exists which is a natural phenomenon and a state of illness, which is an unnatural phenomenon. Therefore, theories which "dwell" at the point of reality – so-called theories of "social realism" – are unproductive, and therefore they do not distinguish natural phenomena of social reality (that is, phenomena which are a social norm) and unnatural phenomena of social reality (that is, social pathologies), considering them eclectically. Thanks to this, they open doors for voluntarism and utopianism. The theory of social realism differs from the theory of social naturalism here presented. Only with the assistance of the principle of social naturalism may one adequately explain the phenomenon of social reality. The theory of "social realism" confines itself to declaring the reality of particular phenomena without uncovering their natural or unnatural essence and not providing criteria for this essence to be identified. They offer no criteria especially for distinguishing good from evil, limiting themselves to recognizing the reality thereof.

According to the principle of social naturalism, the criterion of good and evil is the naturalness or unnaturalness of a particular social phenomenon. Good is that which accords with the laws of nature, and evil is that which is contrary thereto. Good is a manifestation of the *socium* of man, that is, the state of coordination of the will and consciousness of man with the laws of social nature, and evil is the manifestation of a sociopathy of man, that is, a state of the lack of coordination of the will and consciousness of man with the laws of social nature. Either is a phenomenon of social reality, but there are different realities – natural reality, that is one which accords with the laws of social nature, and unnatural reality, that is, which does not correspond to the laws of social nature. The practical significance of a theory which leads to such a division lies in the fact that it gives answers to the question: what are social pathologies and how they may be counteracted thanks to social progress.

Under the principle of social naturalism societies and all societal phenomena, including law, exist not dispute the biological nature of man and not to suppress his biological instincts, as Freud believed, but, on the contrary, they exist thanks to the biological nature of man and to ensure the freedom of the emergence of biological instincts in accordance with the laws of Mother Nature.

Proceeding from the principle of social naturalism, law is a social norm of the laws of nature and especially of natural laws of social life. If this is so, then law as a social phenomenon has two aspects: (1) natural content; (2) social form. In other words, law in reality should be natural in content and social in form.

With the assistance of the principle of social naturalism one may come to the view that the concept "natural law" should be regarded as a means for depicting the first aspect of law, namely the natural content of law; and the concept "positive law" to depict the second aspect of law, namely, the social form of law. Therefore, in our view, it is not correct to juxtapose "positive law" and "natural law", but to contrast them as two inseparable aspects of the same social phenomenon – law. Consequently, in accordance with the principle of social naturalism there exist not "natural law" and "positive law" as two phenomena juxtaposed to one another, but a single phenomenon – law, which has two inseparable aspects: "natural" and "positive".

It is thus possible, in our view, to eliminate the dispute as to whether "positive law" or "natural law" is true, and also to resolve other controversial issues relative to the interpretation of these concepts and the essence of law itself.

According to the conception of law set out, ignoring the "natural aspect" of law leads to legal voluntarism, and ignoring the "positive aspect" of law leads to legal disorder (anarchy). The most perfect is that law in which the "natural aspect" (that is, the natural content of law) is best embodied in the "positive aspect" (that is, in the social form of law – legislation). Ignoring the "natural aspect" of law leads to so-called "juridical positivism". "Juridical positivism" makes the legal culture of man unnecessary and thereby opens the possibility to various forms of abuse of law, that is, willfulness concealed by the "fig leaf" of a law. If legislation is not based on the laws of natural law, it may "legalize" any willfulness, for example, recognize black to be white.

In accordance with the principle of social naturalism, the basic question of jurisprudence may be resolved as follows: nature plays the role of the creation of laws which we call the "laws of nature" in the formation of jus, and people impart to the "laws of nature" a social form, called "legislation" or "normative legal acts".

Proceeding from this resolution of the basic question of jurisprudence, law may be defined as follows: law is based on the laws of nature embodied in the form of normative legal acts, an institute of ensuring social order favorable for the normal (natural) existence of people in society. This resolution of the basic question of jurisprudence is the foundation for building a new theory of jurisprudence – the theory of "naturalist jurisprudence" set out by this writer in his books.[4]

The doctrine of human rights also should be based on the principle of social naturalism. What natural grounds exist for human rights?

Here one should have in view the following. Today, with the growing degree of human freedom a special danger for mankind is the crisis of social culture of people, which includes political, economic, legal, and moral culture. One consequence of this crisis is the spread in society of willfulness and illusions manifest especially in the form of abuse of right, legislation, and democracy. One may now observe such phenomena as the abuse of human rights.

Willfulness and illusions manifest in the form of abuse of human rights are a genuine threat to modern democracy. These abuses facilitate especially the incorrect (or obsolete) notions concerning the essence of human rights. The evolution of our concepts of the essence of human rights is the law of societal development which is urgent for us as a challenge of

[4] Kostenko, note 3 above (2008).

modern times. The answer to this challenge must become the search for a new and better doctrine which would preclude interpreting human rights from the standpoint of willfulness and illusions.

The active demand of persons having a so-called non-traditional sexual orientation for the legalization of single-sex marriages under the banner of struggle for human rights should be deemed to be an abuse of human rights. The same might be said about feminists, who construe human rights in the form of the "equalization" of women and men. This also relates to those entrepreneurs who exploit hired workers and justify this by the human right to freedom of entrepreneurship. And is the dissemination by a journalist of information obtained by him using his status for mercenary purposes not an abuse of the human right to freedom of speech?

In order to find criteria enabling the rights and pseudo-rights of a person to be distinguished, one must decide the so-called "basic question" of the human rights doctrine. It is evident that society in the modern world which is armed by the most progressive social doctrine, including the doctrine of human rights, will be the most progressive, and this means more competitive.

Proceeding from the principle of social naturalism, the "basic question" of the doctrine of human rights should be formulated as follows: "Human rights are a work of Mother Nature, or the will and consciousness of people, or one or the other?" This question should be resolved by basing oneself on the laws of the so-called "Natural Constitution of Man", which is the embodiment of the idea of the naturalness of the social, including human, designated by the term "social naturalism".

The "Natural Constitution of Man" may be as follows:

LAWS OF NATURAL CONSTITUTION OF MAN

1. Nature – the Mother of everything material – nonliving, living, and human, and the Supreme Legislator for everything material for all time.
2. Man – this is material born by the development of the nonliving into the living, and living into human, each of which exists according to its own laws given by Mother Nature for it, forming in man "three strata": physical, biological, and social.
3. Mother Nature placed in Man as a "three-strata substance" the will and consciousness for adapt Him to laws which she gave for Him.
4. Man is allowed by Mother Nature all that corresponds to Her laws and is not allowed that which does not correspond to them. Proceeding from this, the "golden rule" of behavior of Man is formulated so: "Live in amity with the laws of Mother Nature!", and the criterion of truth for Man is thus: "All is true for Man that agrees with the laws of Mother Nature,

and untrue is all that which does not agree with them". The concept of humanity should be interpreted thus: "All that is natural is humane, that is, agrees with the laws of Mother Nature, and all that does not agree with them is inhumane".
5. In following the laws of Mother Nature, Man creates good, and in violating them, creates evil.
6. Will not agreed with the laws of Mother Nature is in a state of willfulness, and consciousness not agreed with the laws of Mother Nature is in a state of illusions, forming a complex of willfulness and illusions. Evil is the manifestation of this complex, and good is the manifestation of the complex of will and consciousness agreed with the laws of Mother Nature.
7. The coordination of will and consciousness of Man with the physical, biological, and social laws of Mother Nature form the culture of Man, determining His life according to the following formula: "What is the culture of Man – also is His life!".
8. The Freedom of Man is the possibility to manifest his will and consciousness in accordance with the laws of Mother Nature, that is, to live culturally. Without culture, freedom is a manifestation of willfulness and illusions.
9. The Security of Man in the world is the protection of His physical, biological, and social freedom, that is, the possibility to live according to the physical, biological, and social laws of Mother Nature.
10. Human Rights are his freedom protected in society by consolidation in legislation embodying the laws of Mother Nature.

Thus, proceeding from the principle of social naturalism, human rights have been determined by the laws of nature which should be embodied in legislation – the freedom of man, ensuring his security against any willfulness, that is, the possibility to live in amity with Mother Nature. This definition of the concept of human rights is the basis of the naturalist doctrine of human rights.

Proceeding from the "Natural Constitution of Man", the criterion for the differentiation of rights and pseudo-rights of man can be determined as: "naturalness – anti-naturalness": human rights are rights corresponding to the laws of Mother Nature, and the "rights" of man not corresponding to these laws are pseudo-rights. According to this criterion, one should define concepts of human rights based on willfulness and illusions manifest in the form of various abuses. The requirement of the legalization of single-sex marriages, and the "equalization" of men and women, and the exploitation by an entrepreneur of hired workers, and the dissemination by a journalist for mercenary purposes of information obtained with the use of his status – all these should be defined as abuse of human rights, proceeding from the criterion that such behavior is anti-naturalness, that is, contrary to the laws of Mother Nature. The criterion "naturalness – anti-naturalness" should apply in all instances when determining human rights.

In accordance with the "Natural Constitution of Man", human rights may be divided into three types: (1) physical; (2) biological; (3) social. The physical rights of man are the freedom to live according to the laws of the physical form of nature. For example, the freedom of man to move in space. The biological rights of man are the freedom to live according to the laws of the biological form of nature. For example: sexual freedom. The social rights of man are the freedom to live according to the laws of the social form of nature. For example: the freedom of entrepreneurship. The conformity to the laws of these "three natures" also should serve as the criterion of truth for our concepts about human rights.

One of the fundamental rights of man is the right to justness, arising from the following law of social nature: "Each person receives in society for participation in its life that which should belong to him according to the natural laws of this society". An infringement against this human right is corruption which, being a manifestation of willfulness and illusions, is a violation of the said law of social nature. Also an infringement against this human right is a social policy which does not distinguish between "good" people and "bad" people, that is, people living in harmony with the laws of social nature and people living not in harmony with those laws. Indeed, even the ancient Greek philosopher Aristophanes (c. 448-385 BC) asserted that States perish when they cease to distinguish between people good and bad. Such a social policy is anti-naturalness and therefore fatal. The warning of Aristophanes is germane today. On the basis of the symptom formulated by Aristophanes one may diagnose society and predict: if there are "bad people" in society, that is, people whose will and consciousness are not in accord with natural laws of social life, will prove to be in a better position that "good people", that is, people living according to these laws, such a society is sick and in the absence of proper treatment the prediction for it is unfavorable.

The following problems should be resolved similarly: "Is the division of a people into an 'elite" and a 'mass' a norm?" From the standpoint of the "Natural Constitution of Man", such a division is a norm of social life if it occurs according to the laws of social nature, that is, the criterion of social (or political, economic, legal and moral) culture of people. People with a higher social culture form the "elite" of the people whose natural role is to "pull" the remaining part of the people along the path of social progress, and the remainder of the people form the "mass" whose natural role is to be "pulled" by the "elite". There is no obstacle to the realization of human rights in this. On the contrary, this facilitates their realization. The same may be said about dividing people into rich and poor, if this division occurs by natural means, that is, not as the result of the manifestation of willfulness and illusions of people, but according to natural laws of the economy, especially the law of economic competition. The division of people into rich and poor as a result of the exploitation of man by man is anti-naturalness, and this means violates human rights, because this is contrary to natural laws of the economy. A normal economy is one in which the exploitation of man by man is squeezed out by the development of economic competition in free market conditions – a radical means against exploitation (and not revolution, as Karl Marx suggested).

The doctrine of human rights so presented based on the "Natural Constitution of Man" enables the challenges of the new days to be adequately met, especially such urgent issues as the "social differentiation of people and human rights", "competition between people and human rights", "sexual differentiation of people and human rights"; and so on. Is the division of people into an "elite" and "mass", into "competitive" and "non-competitive", into male and female, an obstacle to the realization of human rights? To these and similar questions from the standpoint of the doctrine of human rights here formulated the answer should be: all that is in accord with the laws of social nature may not be an obstacle to the realization of human rights, and all that is not in accord with them – is such an obstacle. Moreover, one should recognize that which does obstruct the realization of human rights, the social "equalization" of people, that is, the artificial removal of difference between the "elite" and the "mass", competitive and non-competitive people, men and women, because this is "pseudo-equality", contrary to the laws of social nature.

In accordance with the Natural Constitution of Man, natural equality – unlike anti-naturalness "pseudo-equality" – in an adequate attitude towards the "elite" as an elite, and not to the "mass", to the "mass" as the "mass", and not to the "elite", to the competitive as to the competitive, to the non-competitive as to the non-competitive, to men as to men, and not to women, and to women as to women, and not to men. The "adequateness of the attitude" means that, for example, the equality of men and women lies in the fact that men do not cease to be men, and women, to be women. Therefore, natural equality (unlike pseudo-equality) is determined by the following formula "equality through adequateness"; in other words, an adequate attitude towards various people also is a manifestation of the "principle of natural equality". An identical attitude towards various people is pseudo-equality, that is, social "equalization", which opens the possibility of abuse of human rights.

This doctrine, based on the criterion of naturalness, guards against voluntarism and utopianism in understanding human rights, which in reality is anti-naturalness. It offers an unequivocal reply to the question whether this "right" appertains to human rights as a "human right" in a single-sex marriage, or the "human right" to consume narcotics: these are anti-naturalness "human rights", that is, pseudo-rights.

From the principle of social naturalism it also follows that human rights may be ensured with the assistance of the formula which is expressed thus: "Social culture of citizens plus legislation"; or thus: "With culture in the mind and with law in the hands!", understanding culture as a measure of the coordination of will and consciousness of people with the laws of nature. The attempts to ensure human rights otherwise are manifestations of voluntarism and utopianism.

According to the principle of social naturalism, the determining factor in ensuring human rights in modern Europe is the social culture of citizens of European countries, and not legislation on human rights in and of itself. This legislation is merely an instrument in the hands of people who use it in accordance with their social culture. Therefore, the hope that human rights may be ensured only by improving legislation on human rights is chimerical – this is one of the legal illusions. Without the development of social culture of citizens it is impossible to ensure human rights by any manipulations of legislation.

This is how the "basic question of jurisprudence" is resolved, and how the "basic question" in every branch of jurisprudence should be resolved.

For example, the "basic question of civil jurisprudence" may be formulated thus: "Is civil law a creation of Mother Nature or People, or both?" According to the principle of social naturalism, the reply should be the following: "Civil law is certain laws of Mother Nature embodied by People in the form of civil legislation which should be applied in order to bring order to the private sphere of social life with the assistance of the expression of will of citizens". Hence, a civil violation is a manifestation of willfulness which consists of a violation of natural laws of the social life of people embodied by People in the form of civil legislation.

The "basic question of criminal jurisprudence" may be similarly formulated: "Is criminal law the creation of Mother Nature or People, or both?" Proceeding from the principle of social naturalism, the reply should be: "Criminal law is certain laws of Mother Nature to which People should impart the form of criminal legislation to be applied in bring order to the public sphere of social life with the assistance of power". Hence, a criminal violation is a manifestation of willfulness consisting in a violation of natural (that is, given by Mother Nature) laws of social life of people to which People have imparted the form of criminal legislation.

Social nature compels people to adopt those legislative acts which better or worse reflect its laws, including the laws of natural law. An act must be recognized in criminal legislation as a crime only if it violates the laws of social nature, that is, is anti-naturalness. The willful deprivation of life of another person is deemed to be a crime because this act is anti-naturalness, that is, violates natural laws of the social life of people. The willful taking possession of another's property (theft) is deemed to be a crime because this act is anti-naturalness. The same should be said about rape, evading the payment of taxes, receiving a bribe, and so on.

Any act which is recognized in criminal legislation to be a crime should meet this criterion. If it does not do so, this means the legislator has erred in having recognized it as a crime. The same rule concerns any other legislative norm which determines a civil violation, administrative violation, and so on. Any legislative norm must be established on a natural basis – the laws of social nature: is this a norm of civil, criminal, constitutional legislation or any other norm? In order to ensure the principle of naturalness of jurisprudence an adequate theory is essential. In our view, the theory of "naturalistic jurisprudence" based on the idea of social naturalism is such.

The means of resolving the "basic question of jurisprudence" proposed above with the assistance of the principle of social naturalism enables one not only to determine what law is, but also what the antipode is, that is, what is non-law. According to the principle of social naturalism, non-law, that is, the antipode of law, is the manifestation of the special state of the will of a person which is called willfulness in the form of an act violating the laws of social nature to which the form of legislation or other normative legal acts is imparted. From this one may conclude that any violation – or crime, or administrative offense, violation of the Constitution or norms of civil and international law – is nothing other than a manifestation of the special state of the will of a person – willfulness.

In turn, from the definition of a violation as a manifestation of human willfulness the prospect is opened for the definition that the culture of people, especially social culture, is the radical means for counteracting willfulness. And this means that it is become possible anew to determine the role of the social culture of people in counteracting a violation and in ensuring social order. We have elaborated a cultural-legal conception of ensuring social order on the basis of the formula: "culture + legislation".

The resolution of the basic question of jurisprudence suggested above assumes, in our view, that the role of legal doctrine in jurisprudence will be enhanced. Only with the assistance of legal doctrine may one properly ensure the "natural aspect" of law because it is an instrument of cognition of natural laws of social life, in accordance with which legislative acts should be drafted. The role of doctrinal interpretation in law also is to be enhanced in this connection since only with the assistance of he who applies legislation can and should the "natural" content be discovered on which law is based. Thanks to this, jurisprudence may become a real science, and not an apology for the legal voluntarism of the legislator or, on the contrary, a critique of legislation from the standpoint of the legal voluntarism of jurists.

Without identifying the "natural aspect" of law one cannot get around the legislator, but also judicial practice, especially constitutional proceedings during which the conformity of a particular legislative act to the Constitution is decided. It is impossible to establish the constitutionality or unconstitutionality of a legislative act without identifying its conformity or nonconformity to the laws of natural law. Upon close consideration it also turns out that the European Court for Human Rights, just as any international court, also cannot avoid recourse to the laws of natural law.

The modern crisis of law in Ukraine to which the well-known state of legal order attests is a manifestation of the crisis of social (including legal) culture of citizens. And this is a consequence of the fact that Ukrainian legal science is in a state which makes it incapable of playing a culturizing role in society. This may be avoided when it begins to concern itself with that to which Hugo Grotius (1583-1645) and later David Emile Durkheim (1858-1917) appealed – a study of the "natural aspect" of law – and not confine itself merely to the study of texts of legislative acts as one of the components of the "positive aspect" of law. Here one should note that legal practice, inasmuch as this is a manifestation of the will of people and of the legislator, should be relegated (just as legislation) to the "positive aspect" of law.

Therefore the study of legal practice, just as the study of texts of legislative acts, does not create legal science unless it is linked with the study of the "natural aspect" of law, namely natural laws of the life of people in society.

Consequently, in departing from the "natural-positive" formula set out above for resolving the basic question of jurisprudence, legal science should be "natural-positive". Therefore, one may say that with the assistance of the theory of social naturalism a new jurisprudence is being created – "naturalistic jurisprudence", that is, a jurisprudence based on the principle of social naturalism.

PRINCIPLE OF SOCIAL NATURALISM IN COMPARATIVE LAW

One of the major means for ensuring the progress of jurisprudence is so-called "comparative law". Comparative law is a term designating comparative studies in law, that is, juristic studies, the method for conducting which is the comparison of legal phenomena of various countries or various periods. In our view the phenomenon which we today call "comparative law" or "legal comparativistics" is a special procedure (or process) of law (that is, cognition on the science on law) based on the method of comparing legal phenomena, that is manifest in the form of comparing legal phenomena. An outstanding contribution to the development of comparative law as a means of scientific provision for the process of the globalization of jurisprudence was made especially by Hugo Grotius in his fundamental work *On the Law of War and Peace* (1625), first published in the Latin language. Upon close examination it seems that he compared legal phenomena of various countries and times based on the idea of the naturalness of law. This demonstrates that reliance on the principle of social naturalism as a modern form of the development of the idea of natural law is a condition of the further development of comparative law.

Proceeding from the principle of social naturalism, the "basic question of comparative law" may be formulated as follows: "Should the criterion for the comparison of legal phenomena be sought in the laws of nature or drawn from the will and consciousness of people?" Or, in other words, "What should be chosen as the criterion for the comparison of legal phenomena: their conformity to the laws of nature or to the will and consciousness of people?" Depending on how this basic question is answered, all remaining issues are resolved.

For a proper understanding of the essence of comparative law one should proceed from a conception of comparison as a method of scientific cognition drawn from the general theory of universal naturalism and, accordingly, from the special theory of social naturalism. In our view, in comparing different things, that is, which differ by their nature, between themselves, we are cognizing, strictly speaking, the distinction between the manifestation in comparable things of one and the same, namely, laws of nature in accordance with which these things must exist. The measure of coordination of each of the comparable things with these laws of nature also is the criterion for comparison which imparts sense to this.

The comparison of various phenomena without contrasting each of them individually with the common "denominator" for them will lead to false conclusions. Thus, one must distinguish true and false comparison.

Therefore, by proceeding from the principle of social naturalism, one may formulate the rule of comparison of social phenomena: "To compare different social phenomena between themselves means to compare them according to the criterion to what extent does the existence of each of them correspond to the laws of social nature". Comparison without recourse to this criterion is like comparing, for example, a fish and a bird and concluding that a fish is an "incorrect" bird, and a bird is an "incorrect" fish, and therefore the fish should be rectified by adding wings and a beak, and the bird should be rectified by adding gills. Such a conclusion may be reached when comparing men and women without the said criterion, and so on.

In accordance with the principle of social naturalism, comparison on the cognition of social phenomena, including legal, may be true – if this is so-called "natural" comparison; that is, comparison with the use of the criterion to what extent the existence of comparable social phenomena corresponds to the laws of social nature, or false – if this is so-called "positive" comparison, that is, comparison without the use of the said criterion.

Comparative law cannot be truly scientific, and this means, true, if the investigator does not use for the comparison of legal phenomena the correctly chosen criterion. In and of itself comparison in comparative law is, in our view, the identification of the extent to which each of the legal phenomena being compared accords with the natural laws of social life of people, especially with the laws of natural law. In other words, to compare legal phenomena is possible only according to the criterion of the extent of agreement of each of them with these laws. Only such comparison makes sense. Comparison according to other criteria makes no sense. For example, the establishment, when comparing the legislation of Denmark and the legislation of Ukraine, of the fact that the first legalizes single-sex marriages and the second does not, makes no sense. This is so-called "positive comparison". So-called "natural" comparison makes sense when it is elicited that the legislation of Ukraine, in not legalizing single-sex marriages, is in accord with the laws of natural law, and the legislation of Denmark is not.

The foregoing enables one to say that the principle of social naturalism may and should become the methodological principle of comparative law ensuring the progress of jurisprudence.

PRINCIPLE OF SOCIAL NATURALISM IN LEGAL GLOBALISTICS

With each passing day it becomes more evident that the globalization of modern life of people is a process in accord with the laws of societal development. Jurisprudence, just as any other attribute of society, cannot be outside this process. For mankind to adequately react to the process of globalization it is necessary to cognize the laws of societal development inherent in globalization. The science on the laws of societal development of globalization by which people should be guided in social practice is called legal globalistics.

In and of itself the new phenomenon of the globalization of jurisprudence creates for mankind, including for Ukraine, problems whose resolution requires a new methodological instrument. In other words, life requires from the investigator new ideas with whose assistance these problems might be resolved. And here it is appropriate to recall the rather penetrating observation of Christian Johann Heinrich Heine (1797-1856), who noted that "each era, in acquiring new ideas, receives new eyes". The modern era in the development of jurisprudence is generating an urgent requirement for "new eyes" which would enable us to discover phenomena still unknown and the laws of societal development of the "world" of jurisprudence, would make it possible to penetrate more deeply into the secrets of its nature. Cognition of nature of modern jurisprudence is essential in order to resolve those problems which arise in connection with its globalization, including globalization problems inherent in Ukrainian jurisprudence.

It is evident that legal globalistics, just as any other sphere of science, must commence with the resolution of the so-called "basic question". On the resolution of the "basic question of legal globalistics" depends how all other questions of this science will be resolved. It seems that the "basic question of legal globalistics" may be formulated as follows: "Is the globalization of jurisprudence a natural phenomenon or a product of the will and consciousness of people, or one both?" According to the principle of social naturalism, the reply to this question should be: "Globalization of jurisprudence is a phenomenon of social nature consisting of the manifestation of the will and consciousness of people who should act according to natural laws given by social nature for this phenomenon".

Proceeding from this, in order to react adequately to the challenges connected with globalization of jurisprudence studies must be conducted in law directed the cognition of those laws of social nature under which this globalization exists. The methodological principle of such studies should be, in our view, the principle of social naturalism embodied in the theory of "naturalistic jurisprudence".

Thanks to this one will succeed in resolving the following problems which the globalization process as put to legal globalistics:

- the criterion for distinguishing good and evil;
- the criterion of truth, equity, and humanity (especially in the administration of justice);
- the globalist concept of legal and illegal;
- the new conception of law according to which law is defined under the formula "legal culture of citizens plus legislation";
- the globalist legal concept of human security;
- the globalist concept of human rights;

- the conception of the equality of State and citizen before law and court;
- the new conception of democracy based on the social culture of citizens (conception of "cultural democracy");
- the problem of disassociating the legal equality of people from "equalization";
- the conception of abuse of right;
- the criterion for distinguishing entrepreneurship from pseudo-entrepreneurship;
- the globalist legal conceptual vision of single-sex marriages;
- the conception of ensuring the procedural symmetry of accusation and defense in criminal justice;
- the globalist concept of crime;
- the globalist concept of guilt;
- the globalist concept of terrorism;
- the globalist legal concept of corruption;
- the globalist legal concept of exploitation of man by man;
- the globalist legal concept of pornography, and others.

According to the principle of social naturalism, social progress occurs through so-called "naturalization" of social phenomena, including jurisprudence. This naturalization consists of all social phenomena (being products of the will and consciousness of people) increasingly should be coordinated by people with the laws of social nature. This is the law of social progress, which emanates from the principle of social naturalism. The globalization of jurisprudence as a manifestation of progress should be based on "juridical naturalization". Hence it follows that the task of legal globalistics is to assist with the introduction into social practice of the formula "the globalization of jurisprudence should occur by means of its naturalization, that is, the bringing into concordance of national jurisprudences with the laws of nature of the social life of people".

One should note in developing the conception of "juridical naturalization" that the globalization of jurisprudence puts to national jurisprudences (including the jurisprudence of Ukraine) the requirement to follow the formula: "only that may be deemed to be illegal which is anti-naturalness, that is, that which is contrary to the laws of social nature", which is based on the principle of social naturalism. Ignoring this formula leads to the dissemination in society of legal willfulness and legal illusions manifest in abuses of right and in self-isolation of national jurisprudence in world space contrary to the natural process of globalization.

An important problem of legal globalistics is determining the laws of societal development and corresponding developmental trends of national jurisprudence in conditions of globalization. Globalization should not be understood as voluntary or compulsory reception of national jurisprudence of another's legislation or the implementation of international legal acts. Globalization of jurisprudence is that developments of national jurisprudences which consists of their approximation to a "common denominator" peculiar to all nations that may be determined only with the assistance of the principle of social naturalism. According to this principle, such a globalizing "common denominator" for all national jurisprudences is the natural laws of social life of people which should be cognized by people and embodied by them in the form of national legislation.

It is evident that it would be more correct to assert that the process of globalization of jurisprudence commenced from the moment of the emergence of jurisprudence itself. It is especially evident that this process began during the stormy spread of Roman law in the world. It should be stressed that underlying the ideology of Roman law is the idea of natural law elaborated by the ancient Greeks. It is clear that thanks to this idea Roman law could become fundamental for the development of the globalization of jurisprudence. This fact lays the grounds for asserting that the principle of social naturalism, being a new form of the development of the idea of natural law, may and should become the foundation for the modern development of the process of globalization of jurisprudence.

The principle of social naturalism is the "key" underlying the theory of "naturalistic jurisprudence" which makes it possible to resolve anew other problems of legal science.

CONCLUSIONS

On the basis of the foregoing, the following conclusions may be drawn:

1. The principle of social naturalism (in other words, the "principle of social naturalness" or "principle of naturalness of the social") is a means suitable for resolving any humanitarian and social problems, including problems of jurisprudence.
2. According to the principle of social naturalism, any social evil is a manifestation of a complex of willfulness and illusions of man violating natural laws of the social life of people on which social order is based. A crime is an evil infringing against the social order, and therefore responsibility for it is established by criminal legislation.
3. The struggle of good against evil is the struggle of naturalness against anti-naturalness. Depending on what triumphs in society, progress or regression will occur therein.
4. In accordance with the principle of social naturalism, law may be defined as an institute for ensuring social order based on the laws

of social nature refracted by people in the form of legislation (or normative legal acts).

5. That legislation which most fully reflects the laws of social nature, in particular the laws of natural law, is the most perfect. Every person has the right given by Mother Nature to demand the repeal of any legislative act on the grounds that it is contrary to natural laws of the social life of people (especially, laws of natural law).
6. Proceeding from this, any violation, including a crime, is a violation of the law of social nature embodied in the form of legislation.
7. Any violation of the laws of social nature is a manifestation of willfulness, and this means that any violation, including a crime, should be regarded as a manifestation of human willfulness. A violation (including a crime) is a real phenomenon, but anti-natural.
8. Human rights have been determined by the laws of social nature and they must be embodied in legislation in force – the freedom of man ensuring to him security against any willfulness, that is, the possibility to live in harmony with Mother Nature.
9. A criminal is a person whose will is in a state of willfulness, and consciousness in a state of illusion, forming a so-called complex of willfulness and illusions that emerged in the form of the commission of a crime. This definition affects any offender, that is, persons who violate norms of constitutional, administrative, civil, or any other law. The state of defeatism of a man by the complex of willfulness and illusions is called sociopathy.
10. In view of the fact that the measure of concordance of the will of man with the laws of nature may be defined as the culture of man the following conclusion should be drawn: the most effective means of counteracting human willfulness manifest in the form of violations and, in particular, crimes is the culture of people, including the social culture of citizens, which includes the legal culture of citizens. This gives grounds for the creation of the cultural-legal conception of ensuring social order. In accordance with this conception the problems of jurisprudence should be resolved by being guided by the principle "Culture – the mother of order!".
11. The basis of a rule-of-law State and legal order should be deemed to be the legal culture of citizens, which is a component of their social culture. Hence follows the idea that legislation is merely an instrument which "works" as people apply it, being guided by their legal culture. The so-called instrumental conception of legislation

should be founded on this idea. Laws in any society "work" as the social culture of citizens directs them.

12. Justness, proceeding from the principle of social naturalism, may be defined as the conformity of the manifestations of the will of people to the laws of social nature, and especially to the laws of natural law.
13. The legal behavior of people is defined by their legal culture, and not by legislation. Normative-legal acts are merely a means for: (a) determining what behavior is legal and which is non-legal; and (b) social reaction against the legal and non-legal behavior of people.
14. The so-called principle of the "rule of law" lies in the fact that law should be "supreme" as the laws of social nature embodied in legislation (that is, laws of natural law). This principle, as the norm of social life, may be ensured only when there is proper legal culture of citizens, proceeding from the fact that this culture is higher than any constitutions, codes, and laws.
15. Resolution of the "basic question of jurisprudence" with the assistance of the principle of social naturalism gives grounds to believe that an interpretation of legislation is nothing more than eliciting its natural content. Ignoring this content leads to the "positive" aspect of law becoming an instrument suitable for legal voluntarism, especially for abuses of legislation.
16. Freedom of man in society is his independence from any willfulness, thanks to which he has the possibility to live according to the laws of social nature. A man having freedom, that is, the possibility to manifest his will and consciousness, may do anything that is advantageous to him but only that behavior is normal which is responsible to the laws of nature and especially to the laws of social nature.
17. Thanks to freedom, man has the possibility not to subject himself to anyone if this someone does something contrary to the laws of Mother Nature. The power of Mother Nature is the highest power over man, and any other (including State power) only insofar as it embodies the laws of Mother Nature. This also concerns authority. Mother Nature must be deemed to be the highest authority for man. Other people or human formations have authority insofar as they embody the laws of Mother Nature.
18. The security of man in society is the protection of his freedom to live under the laws of social nature against any manifestations of human willfulness.
19. The criterion of truth in legal science should be deemed not to be legal practice, but the natural laws of the social life of people.

20. The progress of law as a means of ensuring social order is impossible without cognition of the laws of natural law. Therefore, one should in priority elaborate a doctrinal Code of Laws of Natural Law, the basis of which should be the works of the creators of Roman law. It should include laws of natural law discovered by doctrinal means, which should be embodied in legislation.
21. Comparative law is the procedure (or process) of cognition of legal phenomena by means of the comparison of the extent of the conformity of legislative acts of various countries or various times to the natural laws of the social life of people, including the laws of natural law.
22. The globalization of jurisprudence is the process which consists of the approximation of all national jurisprudences to a "common denominator" – to the natural laws of the social life of people (especially to the laws of natural law).

The foregoing provide grounds for the following: the "natural-positive" approach to legal science which follows from the resolution proposed above to the basic question of jurisprudence with the assistance of the principle of social naturalism opens new prospects for resolving questions arising in all branches of law.

The principle of social naturalism, being the foundation for structuring the theory of "naturalistic jurisprudence", may become, in particular, the methodological principle of comparative law and legal globalistics.

Consequently, the progress of jurisprudence may and should ensure a methodology based on the principle of social naturalism.

Classification of European Systems of Private Law

E. O. KHARITONOV* AND O. I. KHARITONOVA**

The idea of comparative law as a means of investigating foreign law with a view to analyzing and improving one's own law was formed long ago. The noted French comparatist, René David, noted that comparative law has existed since ancient times.[1]

But only the emergence of the notion of comparison in law may be traced from times long past. One may hardly regard any instance of the influence of another's law on one's own (borrowing, reception, acculturation, and so on), as some authors do,[2] as evidence of the existence of comparative law. In our view the science of comparativistics in Europe could not appear earlier than when national systems of law began to be formed, that is, at the end of the eighteenth century. Prior to then one may only speak about the principles of historical comparativistics – the study of Greek, Roman, and Graeco-Roman law in comparison with others, including local systems of law.

There are more grounds to believe that as a domain of legal science comparative law was formed only in the nineteenth century and expanded throughout the twentieth century, which, viewed from this angle, might be called the "century of comparativistics". Comparative law research grew significantly after the Second World War when the European

* доктор юридических наук, Professor. Head of Chair of Civil Law, Odessa National Legal Academy; author of numerous works on Roman private law and comparative law.
** доктор юридических наук, Professor. Head of Chair of Entrepreneurial and Commercial Law, Odessa National Legal Academy.

1 R. David, Основные правовые системы современности [Principal Legal Systems of the Modern Day (Comparative Law)] (1967), p. 25.

2 M. N. Marchenko, Сравнительное правоведение: Общая часть [Comparative Law. General Part] (2001), pp. 16-42.

Communities were formed and international cooperation was intensified and institutionalized.

During recent decades a number of works by Ukrainian scholars appeared, as well as specialists on post-Soviet States. The overwhelming majority are either summary works or devoted to the comparative investigation of individual institutions and branches of public law.

As regards private law, here Ukrainian comparatists have been less active. Against the background of numerous foreign studies,[3] this situation is depressing. It is explained by the fact that for a long time the category "private law" was not recognized by Soviet legal doctrine, the reason for which was not only Lenin's statement in a Letter to D. I. Kurskii that "we have nothing private in the domain of economic management", but also the assessment by Soviet jurists of private (civil) law as the "natural law of the bourgeoisie".[4] Post-Soviet jurisprudence is overcoming this antipathetic attitude, as a consequence of which the number of works in this field is so far insignificant and reference is made, as a rule, not to "private" but to "civil" or to civil and trade law.[5]

CONCEPT AND ESSENCE OF PRIVATE LAW

Therefore it is advisable to consider the problem of the classification of European legal systems in the sphere of private law. One should begin by defining the concept and essence of private law. It is more convenient to do this by using the classical dichotomy "private law – public law". One must have in view in so doing that this construction to some degree is conditional and intended to establish the principal foundations of regulating a particular group of social relations.

One also must take into account the undesirability of simplifying when defining these concepts and establishing differences between private and public law. Most often such simplifications are linked with identifying law

[3] See, for example, K. Zweigert and H. Kötz, Введение в сравнительное правоведение в сфере частного права [Introduction to Comparative Law in the Sphere of Private Law] (1998), H. Koch, U. Magnus, and W. von Mohrenfels, Международное частное право и сравнительное правоведение [International Private Law and Comparative Law] (2001); G. Eörsi, *Comparative Civil (Private) Law* (1979); R. David, *Traité elémentaire de droit civl compare* (1950).

[4] See, for example: M. Reisner, Право. Наше право. Чужое право. Общее право [Law. Our Law. Other's Law. Common Law] (1925), p. 165.

[5] See Основные институты гражданского права зарубежных стран. Сравнительно-правовое исследование [Basic Institutes of Civil Law of Foreign Countries. Comparative Law Study] (1999); N. G. Eliseev, Гражданское процессуальное право зарубежных стран: источники, судоустройство, подсудность [Civil Procedure Law of Foreign Countries: Sources, Court Organization, Jurisdiction] (2000).

and legislation. As a result, one may encounter the assertion: since any law is a public phenomenon, private law exists only within the framework of public law.[6]

Nonetheless, "law" and "legislation" are not identical concepts. The concept of "law" is broader and multi-faceted. It is an element of a socio-political system, social consciousness, constituent element of the spiritual world of man and his worldview. The concept "norms of law" encompassed all generally binding norms which exist in society (including those which are based on the prescriptions of natural law) and cannot be reduced merely to the aggregate of normative acts issued by State agencies. Therefore, a particular branch of law does not automatically become public law by reason of the regulation of relations by legislative acts.

When dividing law into private and public a danger of another simplification exists – the rather general (superficial) characterization of each of these branches. Sometimes when defining public and private law one confines oneself to quoting the abridged view of Ulpian which appeared in Justinian's Digest: "… public law is that which concerns the status of the Roman State, and private which relates to the advantage of individual persons".[7]

However, Ulpian wrote not about the division of Roman law into branches, but that the "… study of Roman law is divided into two parts: public and private law" (D.1.1.1.2). Therefore he gave the definition of these parts in simplified form, being guided by instructional, methodological and other purposes.

If one circumvents this standard to assess the distinctiveness of private and public law, it proves to be plainly insufficient, to which the Romanists V. M. Khvostov and I. A. Pokrovskii drew attention in their works in the early twentieth century. Thus, clarifications are necessary. When characterizing public law it is not sufficient to merely indicate that it concerns the interests of the State in general. One must also take into account that one of the defining features of public law is the imperative method of regulating respective relations for which, in particular, there are characteristic: a sharp configuration of the limits of possible behavior of subjects; establishment of prescription for participants of legal relations to

[6] V. K. Mamutov, «До питання про поняття приватного права» [On the Question of the Concept of Private Law], Вісник Академії правових наук України [Herald of Academy of Legal Sciences of Ukraine], no. 2 (1999), pp. 58-61.

[7] See, for example, I. Plavich, «Исследование проблемы соотношения частного и публичного права» [Study of the Problem of the Correlation of Private and Public Law], Актуальні проблеми політики [Urgent Problems of Policy] (Odessa, 1999), V, p. 185.

act in a determined manner; use of the prohibition of certain actions, and so on.

One should also take into account that in essence public law is, on one hand, a supranational system having as subject-matter not only municipal but also inter-State relations (this also concerns private law) and, on the other, it is a continuation of the social phenomenon of public power with all the positive and negative possibilities of the last.

With regard to the above, one may define public law as the aggregate of legal norms which comprise a special functional-structural system which for the purpose of the regulation and protection of social interests with the aid of norms of primarily an imperative character regulates relations with the participation of the State and also between subjects which are figurants of the state or in relations of power and subordination.

The characteristic features of private law are: recognition of the priority of interests of the individual (private) person, in other words, the "sovereignty of the individual"; the legal equality of participants of the respective relations; initiative of the parties when establishing legal relations; choice of rules of behavior not expressly prohibited by legislation; suit procedure for protecting the interests of subjects in a court, and so on. To a significant extent these features are determined by the essence of private law as that part of objective law through whose respective institutes the natural "law of freedom" is realized.[8]

To this should be added that the character of these relations is not changed by their being sanctioned by the State since in the ideal variation the laws of a State should be responsive to the prescriptions of natural law, and in the real variant if this is not met, then one should aspire to this (if, to be sure, one refers to a civil society and a rule-of-law State).

Having regard to the foregoing, private law may be defined as the aggregate of rules and norms which affect determination of the status and protection of the interests of individual persons who are not figurants of the State, are not in relations of power-subordination to one another, and who equally and freely establish rights and duties in relations which arise at their initiative.

One must also draw attention to the fact that private law is not the same as the concept of "civil law", just as public law cannot be identified with constitutional, administrative, or other law. Constitutional, civil, labor, criminal, administrative, financial, and other law comprise the system of national law. Their essence and content are affected by general principles

[8] S. S. Alekseev, Самое святое, что есть у Бога на земле. Иммануил Кант и проблемы права в современную эпоху [Most Sacred of What God Has on Earth. Immanuel Kant and the Problem of Law in the Modern Era] (1998), p. 185.

and national traditions of law. Private law together with public forms a single general (supranational) system of law which is an integral part of civilization (or culture). On the basis of this understanding the essence of private and public law may be defined as their significance for the regulation of particular relations with the participation of private persons, the State, figurants of the State, and so on.

Here we encounter an interesting and rather typical situation: depending on which group of relations is taken for analysis, one may speak about the existence of public or private elements in their regulation. This is linked with the fact that the category "private law" and "public law" are summary concepts which are applied to designate a certain type of normative blocks which regulate various relations with the assistance of sundry means and methods.

As regards real relations when particular types of activity are effectuated, they are subject to regulation on the principles of private or public law, depending upon their specific content.[9]

CLASSIFICATION OF PRIVATE LAW SYSTEMS

Having regard to the said basic moments, we may pass on to consider the classification of systems of private law, which is among the most complex in the sphere that is of interest to us. This is of theoretical and practical interest since the criteria on the basis of which we distinguish systems of law ultimately depend not only on self-identification, a search for their place in world or European legal space, but the choice of orientators to improve the legal system, respective system of legislation, and practice of the application thereof.

The absence of an awareness of the importance of these orientators leads to an eclectic chaotic system of law and divergences when adopting legal decisions of principle. Ukraine already has suffered for a decade with civil legislation which was created and develops in dependence on ideological doctrines, the degree of influence of a particular group of jurists, and recourse to particular legal models.

This has a general appearance: a "repudiation of private law" is proclaimed but in doing so the German civil code is used; all law is declared to be an "opium for the people", but all property relations fall into the sphere of economic law; all economic turnover is regulated by

[9] See E. O. Kharitonov and O. I. Kharitonova, «До питання про значення диходотії 'приватне право – публічне право'» [On the Significance of the Dichotomy 'Private Law – Public Law'], Вісник Академії правових наук України [Herald of Academy of Legal Sciences of Ukraine], no. 2 (2000), pp. 83-89.

"civil law" which is virtually undistinguishable from economic law in its previous version.

Thus, the first problem which should be resolved in Ukraine or any other State is the creation of a conception of own civil law having regard to its place in the general system of private law. In addition, the problem exists of choosing a model for imitation in the process of law-creation work.

To be sure, the existence of this problem in some measure is evidence of the penetration of democratic principles into the sphere of law-creation. In Ukraine for many years this issue did not arise since the Civil (just as any other) Code of the RSFSR serves as the "irreproachable model" and orientator, and in the 1960s all-union models were established – the Fundamental Principles of Legislation of the USSR and Union Republics. During the mid-1930s the problem was not entirely eliminated since the 1936 "Stalin Constitution" from the outset made provision for the adoption of all-union codes. Drafts of such acts were even worked out, including a Civil Code of the USSR, but the situation changed, the competence of the union republics was enlarged, although the limits thereof were rather precisely established by the said Fundamental Principles of legislation.

After the dissolution of the USSR, the former union republics faced the problem of creating a legal doctrine and forming a conception of law in individual branches, and then a conception of law-creation, in priority in the sphere of trade (or civil) circulation. Here it turned out that to choose a single model was not so simple. An urgent avalanche of borrowing (or more precisely – pulling out) of legal resolutions from the legislative acts of various, primarily European, countries – the German Civil Code, French legislation, English and American law. The Civil Code of the Netherlands exerted significant influence on the draft Civil Code of Ukraine.

It seemed there was nothing bad in this. But the lack of self-identification of an own system of law, especially civil, and conception of law-creation led to inconsistent and contradictory decisions. Although the draughtsmen of the Civil Code of Ukraine did enormous work and created a virtually perfect variant of this major legislative act, it was not adopted for so long, at least in its initial version, because it was not responsive to the traditions of the national system of civil (private) law and accordingly to the legal consciousness, understanding of law, which had formed over the centuries.

This does not mean we always should look back to the past. But without having regard to the tradition of private law, to the systems of civil law which had formed, the formation of a new system is not possible.

These reflections at first glance do not directly relate to the question here considered. But they cast doubt on the widely shared view that one may avoid classifications of systems of private law without "excessive" theoretical structures since an operational practice of law-creation should have primacy of place. The aforementioned sad experience of Soviet and post-Soviet law testifies to what such an approach may lead.

It should be noted that attempts to classify world and European systems of law, including civil law, were made in the early twentieth century. The criteria were various. It was proposed to classify legal systems within the Romano, Germanic, Anglo-Saxon, Slavonic, and Islamic legal families (Adhémar Esmein, 1848-1913). Having regard to the ambiguity of criteria, this approach was criticized and later various grounds for classification were named: the various role of sources of law which made it possible to separate out the continental European, Anglo-American, and Islamic legal families (Henri Lévy-Ullmann, 1870-1947), national indicia, according to which the Indo-European,[10] Semitic, and Mongol legal families were singled out, and also the law of uncivilized peoples (Georges Sauser-Hall, 1884-1966); a genetic indicator – the influence of international legal customs, Roman and canon law, and modern democratic traditions (Enrique Martinez Paz, 1882-1952); and on substantive criteria it was proposed to identify seven legal families: French, German, Scandinavian, English, Russian, Islamic, and Hindu (Pierre Arminjon (1869-19?), Boris Nolde (1876-1948), and Martin Wolff, 1872-1953).

In the course of time the number of criteria multiplied and the classifications became more complex. Adolf F. Schnitzer (1889-1989) proposed a classification on the basis of the criterion of "great civilizations", separating out the legal family of uncivilized peoples; the legal family of ancient civilizations of the Mediterranean and the Far East; the Euro-American law which encompassed the Romanist, Germanic, Slavonic, and Anglo-American law; religious law (Jewish, Christian, Islamic), and the law of the Afro-Asian peoples.[11]

René David (1906-1991) identified five legal families on ideological and technical legal criteria: western law, Soviet law, Islamic law, Hindu law, and Chinese law; however, later the classification was modernized: Romano-Germanic law, common law, socialist law, and other systems (Islamic law, Jewish law, and others).[12]

Åke Malmström (1905-1985) proposed a classification which was based on the nature of the sources of law. This gave him occasion to single out the western (Euro-American) group, which includes the French, Scandinavian, German, and English families, and also the Latin American legal family

[10] The Indo-European family was divided into subgroups: Hindu, Iranian, Celtic, Graeco-Latin, German, Anglo-Saxon, and Lettish-Slavonic.

[11] A. F. Schnitzer, *Vergleichends Rechtslehre* (2d ed., 1963), p. 133ff.

[12] R. David and C. Jauffret-Spinosi, Основные правовые системы современности [Principal Legal Systems of Modern Times] (1996), pp. 20-28.

and Common Law family. The socialist, Asian, and African (nonsocialist) systems of law comprised a special group.

It should be noted that for a long time comparativistics did not draw the attention, or very nearly so, of researchers from the socialist countries. Only in 1979 did the work of the Hungarian jurist, Gyula Eörsi, appear devoted to comparison in civil (private) law. Based on the postulates of Marxism-Leninism, he chose as the criterion for classification the character of production relations, especially, relations of ownership. The class approach enabled him to single out two types, or two systems, of law – capitalist and socialist. In turn, the legal systems of European countries of "capitalist law" were divided into four groups, depending upon the time and character of transition from feudal to capitalist production relations (early, later, radical-revolutionary, and so on).[13]

Critically analyzing the proposed conceptions from the standpoint of the well-foundedness of a classification of private law systems, Zweigert and Kötz supported the position of Arminjon, Nolde, and Wolff, emphasizing that the refusal to use all external criteria is justified because the rational classification of modern legal families needs an investigation of their content. However, Zweigert and Kötz drew attention to the fact that when applying the theory of legal families it was essential to recall the possible divergences in the sources of origin of legal systems which are being investigated. These sources may be various for the law of ownership, contract, obligations, and others.

It was justly observed that comparative law studies should be distinguished which depend little on the "whimsy of the legislator", as sometimes happens with positive material, acquiring its own assessment in the comparison and classification of legal systems into legal families and the own formation of the last, which to a significant degree is conditioned by time and constantly experiences the influence of law-creation activity and other factors.

Ultimately, the conclusion was drawn that the classification of legal families and the criteria which determine their affiliation to them of individual legal systems depend upon historical development and those changes which are occurring in the world: "This means that the comparative history of law, or so-called 'vertical' comparative law, studies various legal families which have receded into the past and are distinguished from one another depending upon the era

[13] For a survey, see Zweigert and Kötz, note 3 above, pp. 100-102.

which is being considered, whereas 'pure' comparative law studies those legal families which contain merely modern 'living' legal orders".[14]

In order to eliminate the shortcomings of other classifications it was proposed to take into account the style of a legal system. The factors which determine style in the theory of legal families, in the view of Zweigert and Kötz, are: (1) the historical origin and development of a legal system; (2) the dominant doctrine of legal thought and specific nature thereof; (3) legal institutions which are distinctive; (4) sources of law and methods of interpreting them; (5) ideological factors. On this basis Zweigert and Kötz grouped all national legal systems into eight legal families: (1) Romanist; (2) Germanic; (3) Scandinavian; (4) Common Law; (5) socialist law; (6) law of countries of the Far East; (7) Islamic law; and (8) Hindu law.[15]

Despite the detailed nature of this classification, it can hardly be irreproachable, partly because the unity and consistency of the criteria have not been observed to the end. Moreover, doubts arise as to the correctness of legal institutes being among the distinctive elements of style. It seems to us that the selection of such institutes which are inherent to a particular system are very subjective and a certain institute is far from always typical within the legal family for all legal systems which might be relegated to it.

As regards the classification of legal systems in Ukrainian comparative legal studies, despite the excessively optimistic statements that "according to Ukrainian legal thought all national legal systems are grouped into these legal families: Anglo-Saxon legal family, Romano-Germanic legal family, Muslim law, and Slavonic legal family",[16] there is far from unanimity on this "thought". Regrettably, there are no references to specific works in the assertion on the unity of Ukrainian comparative legal studies where such a classification[17] is proposed, which complicates the discussion, but in any event one may assume that this is the author's position to which any objections should be addressed.

[14] Ibid., p. 106.

[15] Ibid., pp. 108, 117.

[16] N. M. Onyshchenko, «Правові системи сучасності. Порівняльне дослідження національних правових систем» [Legal Systems of Modern Times. Comparative Study of National Legal Systems], Держава і право [State and Law], VII (2000), p. 8.

[17] Further statements give reason to suggest that reference is being made to a somewhat updated classification by Esmein, which in the West is considered to be obsolete but has a certain popularity among Russian scholars, especially insofar as "Slavonic law" is mentioned. See V. N. Siniukov, in N. I. Matuzov and A. V. Malko (eds.), Теория государства и права: курс лекций [Theory of State and Law: Cours of Lectures] (1997), pp. 171-181.

A NEW APPROACH TO CLASSIFYING PRIVATE LAW SYSTEMS

Without absolutizing the significance of classification of private law systems and not dwelling therefore in detail on the virtues and shortcomings of the various variants, we propose to consider a somewhat different approach to private law systems, having placed stress on the need to take into account certain circumstances. First, the essence of the phenomenon of law itself and its affiliation to a category such as "civilization" should be taken into account. Second, attention should be drawn to the advisability of differentiating the classification of legal systems in general and systems of private law separately, since these may not coincide. Third, one should avoid efforts at a single universal classification of private law systems (and of legal systems in general), bearing in mind that we refer to a phenomenon which exists in various temporal and spatial dimensions. Finally, one must review the system of criteria to find which exerts decisive influence on the development of national legal systems or a certain aggregate thereof. We dwell on these issues in more detail.

[1]. As regards the linkage of the categories "civilization" and "law", it is the influence of this factor on classification that interests us. Without dwelling on various approaches to the definition of law, which is a multi-dimensional concept, we refer only to the need to reject a simplified materialist approach according to which law is merely the ideological superstructure of the material base of a certain type of production relations, together with which it is born, changes, and then dies away.

More justified is an understanding of law as an element of civilization. Since the last category plays a noticeable role in the context of this article, we dwell on its definition in greater detail. Although this concept itself figures in scholarly studies from the seventeenth century, profound studies were undertaken only during the last two centuries. A somewhat simplified understanding of "civilization" acquired currency in the nineteenth century. This term designated a third stage in the development of human culture which had been preceded by two others – the era of savageness and the era of barbarism. In the view of Engels, civilization "... is that stage of the development of society in which there is a division of labor, an exchange between individual persons which follows, and good production, which combines these two processes, achieving full flower and effecting a revolution in all society".[18]

[18] F. Engels, Происхождение семьи, частной собственности и государства [Origin of the Family, Private Ownership and the State] (1975), p. 195.

Although this definition of civilization is sometimes encountered even now, by the early nineteenth century an understanding of civilization as a more complex category was widespread which could not be reduced to an understanding of it as merely an individual stage in the development of mankind. Attention was drawn especially to the fact that one should speak not about a "civilization", but about "civilizations", since this concept exists in the plural.[19] Gradually, the various meanings of a definition of civilization were recognized[20] and the fact that a distinction must be made between world and local civilizations.

World civilizations are a stage in the history of mankind which are characterized by a certain level of needs, abilities, knowledge, skills, and interests of man, technological and ecological means of production, system of political and social relations, level of development of the spiritual reproduction (or regeneration); in essence we refer to a long-term (many centuries) historical cycle. A change of world civilizations reflects the gradual movement of the historical process, the self-development of mankind.

Local civilizations express cultural-historical, ethnic, ethical, religious, economic and geographical peculiarities of an individual country, group of countries, and etnoses which share a common fate; they reflect the rhythm of the general historical progress, which proves to be its epicenter and is remote from it. Each local civilization has its own outline, its own rhythm, more or less synchronized with the rhythm of world civilizations.[21] Civilizations are not static forms. They are dynamic formations of the evolutionary type. They are not only incapable of being in a state of repose, but they cannot arbitrarily alter the direction of their gradual movement. By taking into account the presence of various approaches to defining the concept of "civilization"[22] it is necessary to identify the essence of law as an element of culture.

Civilization (or culture) of mankind as a whole may be schematically regarded as a cut pyramid which has five levels: the first is man (or family); the second is the technological means of production; the third is the ecological means of production; the fourth is the socio-political system; and the fifth is social consciousness (spiritual world). Law is regarded as an element of the socio-political system of society.[23]

19 L. Febvre (1878-1956), Бои за историю [Battles for History] (1989), pp. 263-281.

20 K. S. Gadzhiev, Геополитика [Geopolitics] (1997), pp. 41-45.

21 Iu. Iakovets, История цивилизаций [History of Civilizations] (1995), pp. 53-54.

22 On other approaches to defining the concept of "civilization", see, for example, I. B. Orlova, Евразийская цивилизация [Eurasian Civilization] (1995), pp. 21-26.

23 Iakovets, note 21 above, pp. 60-69.

Nonetheless, this approach simplifies the role of law and its significance in the system of values (or culture) of mankind. Ensuring the existence and functioning of society as a complex dynamic system is merely one of the orientations of normative regulation which law performs (although here its socio-political properties are manifest).

If law is evaluated as a phenomenon of civilization as a whole, one must take into account that it is deemed to be a bearer of the highest principles determining the values of civilization, to realize the historical purpose of society connected with the affirmation of the powers within it and the potential of reason and high humane principles.

It should thus be acknowledged that the essence of the phenomenon of law as a phenomenon which reflects the requirements of civilization is not confined merely to the fact that law normatively objectifies and realizes these requirements, but also is a factor of individual self-expression of the person, creativity, the accumulation thereof, self-growth.[24] Law belongs not only to the elements of the socio-political system, but also is an element of social consciousness comprising the spiritual world of man and his worldview.

It should be taken into account that law arises inextricably linked with religion; then is gathers ever more socio-political weight and requires philosophical and professional legal contemplation and substantiation; ultimately, at the time of its highest flourishing, it becomes an element of social and individual consciousness, while retaining its genetic link with religion, which plays the role of a certain genetic worldview code. Thus classifications of law must inevitably be influenced by the link with the category of "civilization". Obviously, each local civilization will have its own law. We call this the "tradition of law".

In turn, the tradition of law may be divided into several legal families or a single certain tradition may be one certain legal family. Suppose that the western European legal tradition is divided into the Anglo-Saxon, Romanist, and Germanic (central European) legal families. The eastern European tradition of private law encompasses a precisely expressed orthodox eastern European legal family and a somewhat eclectic central-east European legal family.

[2]. It should be noted that the classification of legal systems as such and the classification of private law systems may not coincide. This is linked with a different concept of law and the different weight of private law in sundry

[24] S. S. Alekseev, Право: азбука – теория – философия: опыт комплексного исследования [Law: Alphabet – Theory – Philosophy: Experiment of an Integrated Study] (1999), pp. 200, 219, 221, 224.

civilizations. In the eastern, traditional, and other civilizations private law does not play a notable role. The respective norms regulate not so much the legal status of the private individual as trade turnover. Therefore, one speaks not so much about private law as civil law, which determines the mutual relations of participants of civil (or trade) relations.

Having regard to this circumstance it is advisable to concentrate on classifications of systems of private law in Europe since in other traditions one encounters not private, but civil, law.

[3]. As noted, one should refrain from efforts in the direction of a single universal classification of systems of private law (and legal systems in general), having in the that we refer to a phenomenon which exists at various temporal and spatial dimensions. A general structure of law should be devised which is based on the existence of various national systems of law. The hierarchy of elements, in our view, should look as follows:

The first link of the classification is the "tradition of law", which in this event may be treated as the aggregate of legal values, categories, institutes, and norms that throughout the centuries have consciously been passed from generation to generation. Since the common European tradition of law is divided into eastern and western, the preceding analysis requires the construction "East – West".

The essence thereof consists of singling out the two mainlines of socio-historical development. The "East" or the "Orient" is characterized by such features as: (1) absolute primacy of collective, social, and State interests over individual ones; (2) significant statization of economic life and the absence of underdevelopment of the institute of private ownership; (3) despotic (in some instances, theocratic) type of power (socio-political monism); (4) egalitarian and regulation social ethic; (5) ethical-normative and social-legislative function of religion (inherent to all eastern confessions – Judaism, Islam, Buddhism, Confucianism, Russian Orthodoxy, and so on).

For the "West" or the "Occident" there are characteristic: (1) powerful institute of private ownership, which plays a decisive role in economic life based on market principles; (2) socio-political pluralism, separation of powers, self-government, secular nature of power; (3) competitive and personalistic social ethic; (4) separation of religion from State institutions, relative autonomy of the church, and others.

These two concepts characterize a number of distinctions which affirm the differences between western and eastern Europe by geographical coordinates, according to which Poland, for example, may be relegated to the "East" and distribution by worldview, culture, organization of society, and so on – having regard to everything that comprises in aggregate a civilization. Thus, the western tradition of law is those legal values, categories, and institutes which immanently are peculiar to the western

European local civilization based on the worldview, culture, and mentality of the western world.

By Eastern tradition of law we understand the legal values, categories, and institutes which are inherent in eastern European civilization that unite countries within the so-called "Byzantine community of nations" or now are heirs to the "Spirit of Byzantium".

As regards the Western tradition of law, there are inherent to it: (1) a relatively precise boundary between legal and other institutions. This means, in particular, that although politics and morality may determine law, they are not treated as law itself, as occurs in some other cultures; (2) the management of legal institutions is assigned to a special body of people who engage in legal activity on a professional basis; (3) these specialists have special legal education; (4) the sum of legal knowledge received by specialists is in dialectical unity with the legal institutions; (5) law is perceived as an integral system, and "organism", which develops over time across the centuries and from generation to generation; (6) the vitality of the system of law is based on the confidence of society in the long-term nature of law; (7) the development of law is not only an adaptation from the old to the new. Law does not simply continue, but has a history; (8) the historicity of law is linked with an awareness of its advantages over political authority; (9) the coexistence and competition within a single society of various jurisdictions. This pluralism makes the virtues of a law necessary and possible.

The principal features of the Eastern tradition of law may be defined as follows: (1) the limited nature of the worldview foundations of law, as a rule, to Christian teachings in their Orthodox interpretation; (2) an inclination towards treating law as positive law whose content is conditioned not so much by natural prescriptions as by the needs of society that ultimately the State knows best (monarch, dictator, ruler) and embodies them in norms of laws; (3) the organization and conducting of law-creation, systematization, research, and other work in the sphere of law at the initiative of "from above"; (4) the limited nature of the creative search for and, as a result, loss of authority and significance of jurisprudence; (5) trend towards limiting the "excessive" expansion of private-law regulation and the aspiration to ensure maximum possible control and interference of the State with respect to private persons. As a result, private law is here "diluted" by public-law norms and often treated as "economic" or something akin; (6) an insufficiently precise demarcation between legal institutes and institutions, on one hand, and State institutions of another type (for example, administrative and management institutions) on the other; (7) lack of theoretical substantiation and officially recognized conception of the succession of law in general and of private law especially within a single

State or civilization. As a result of this phenomena such as the reception of law occurs in latent forms and has a limited and inconsistent nature; (8) accentuation of attention primarily not on rights, but on the duties of participants of civil-law relations.

On the basis of the views set out above on local and world civilizations, it is advisable to distinguish between local and general systems of private law. Proceeding from this one may single out two local systems or traditions of the private law of Europe: (1) Western European; and (2) Eastern European (Byzantine). However, one should bear in mind that both systems as "subsidiary" with regard to the "mother" system – Roman private law, which is an element of an ancient civilization personifying the highest achievements of ancient law. Their "kinship" relations are manifest especially in the emergence of the reception of Roman law which imparts to it the character of universality, worldwideness.

Therefore, it is suggested that Roman private law by its "civilized" nature is not merely an element of Antiquity (as, for example, ancient Greek law), but the common system of European private law which is responsive to the previous spiral of world civilization. The new common system is now being formed as the unified law of Europe.

Thus we are concerned with three systems or traditions of private law of Europe which exist in two strata: (1)) Roman private law as the "mother" element of a past civilization – a universal, common law, the predecessor of later systems of European law; (2) Western European and Eastern European traditions of private law – "subsidiary" relative to Roman and which continue to develop now.

It should be noted that the "civilization" criterion in this understanding is externally close to the ideological criterion proposed by René David, who relegated to ideology in this context the reflection of religious and philosophical notions of a particular society and its political, economic, and social structure. However, civilization, as noted above, is a broader concept which encompasses not only spiritual, but also material, aspects of the life of society and its being and mentality, and so on. This makes possible to take into account more fully the factors which form the system of law, especially private, and the specific nature of its existence.

However, separating out the systems of private law in accordance with world and local civilizations is obviously insufficient since within each of them subsystems (legal families) exist which have peculiarities in the understanding of law, formation of the normative mass, ensuring legal order, and so on. These peculiarities in aggregate or in total form the criterion for the classification of families of private law. To such criteria there belong in our view: (1) the tradition of law characteristic for the particular country or civilization; (2) the peculiarities of worldview within the limits of a tradition and then the conception of the mutual relations of the State and the private person; (3) the character of sources (or factors of forming) of law having regard to the extent of the influence of Roman private law; (4) the character of the sources as forms of law.

In order to classify systems of private law we should identify preliminarily the concept of "sources of law" which, as will be shown below, is one of the defining indicia of such a classification. One should bear in mind that the term "sources of law" may be used in several meanings. Most widely used is an understanding of a source of law as a factor which gives birth to law and as forms of a legal norm.[25] As regards sources of private law as factors or elements which in the process of their interaction form the aggregate (or phenomenon, category) of a new quality, to them should be relegated natural law, national systems of law, conflicts norms, and international agreements.

Since private law is a supranational system of law which has as its basis so-called "universal humanitarian values", its principal sources are norms of natural law which create its distinctive legal foundation. These norms encompass the natural inalienable rights of man. They are fixed in the 1948 Declaration of the Rights of Man, the 1950 European Convention on the Protection of Human Rights, and other analogous international acts. The right to personal life, the right to private ownership, and others are relegated to such norms.

It should be emphasized that these rights belong to sources of private law not because they have been consolidated in international legal acts, but, on the contrary, they are inalienable natural rights of man and condition the need for creating respective acts.

Another source of private law is the norms of national systems of law. In every country (civilization, etnos, and others) there exist views about the nature of the status of the individual, a separate person in society, and the possibility and procedure for defending the rights thereof. Although these norms are based on certain common notions about the freedom of the individual, being passed through a specific local or national consciousness they acquire an ideological tinge, or hue, and then influence the content of private law with the assistance of conflicts norms.

Yet another source of private law is international treaties concerning the legal status of private persons which after ratification by parliaments become norms of national law. It should be noted that although when such

[25] Some authors do not distinguish these concepts. See Plavich, «Понятие, сущность и истоки частного права» [Concept, Essence, and Sources of Private Law], Актуальні проблеми політики: Збірник наукових праць [Urgent Questions of Policy: Collection of Scholarly Works] (Odessa, 2000), VIII, p. 181.

treaties are concluded norms of natural law are taken into account and national traditional of law too; norms of a new quality are created as a consequence of reaching a certain compromise.

Thus, the system of sources of private law looks as follows: (1) natural law as the principal foundation; (2) national legal institutes, branches of law which determine the legal status of the individual, the private person; (3) conflicts norms which are a compromise of various national traditions, solutions, and so on. To this list should be added Roman private law as an ideological paradigm or distinctive benchmark of European systems of private law. As regards the sources of private law as forms of its existence, treaties, customs (including judicial practice), legislation, and precedents (judicial and administrative) appertain thereto.

CIVIL-LAW SYSTEMS

Having regard to these factors, civil-law systems also may be singled out: Romanist, Anglo-Saxon, Central European (Germanic), Central-East European, Eastern European, Muslim, Far Eastern, African. Since only the first five of the said systems are "private law" in essence, we confine ourselves hereinafter to setting out only the characteristic peculiarities of the last.

Romanist Family of Private Law. A precise division of law into private and public, where private law is regarded as that which concerns only the interests of private, legally equal persons, and public law serves the interests of society and the State as a whole, is characteristic of this family. Private law, in turn, is regarded as consisting of two parts: civil law (regulates relations between citizens) and trade law (regulates relations between entrepreneurs).

Codification acts are typical for this system of private law: the most noteworthy are the French Code civil of 1804 (Code Napoleon) and Commercial Code of 1809.

The reception of ideas, basic principles, and institutes of Roman privat4 law is characteristic for the Romanist system. The structure of civil codes is borrowed from Roman law and taking into account this structure the textbooks of law in ancient Rome are called "Institutes", including basic sections (institutes) on: persons, things, and means of acquiring things (obligations).

Central European (Germanic) Family of Private Law. As for the Romanist system, this system is characterized by a demarcation between public-law and private-law interests, a dualism of private law, and the existence of acts of codification, the most important of which are the Austrian Civil Code, 1896 German Civil Code, and Swiss Civil Code.

Rather material differences exist between them. These include: a significant weight of public-law elements in regulating relations between private persons; a different approach in principle in determining the structure of civil law. Unlike the system of institutes for structuring civil law (especially the civil codes), the German civil law has as its basis the so-called "Pandectian system", which is the product of the creation of mediaeval German glossators (commentators on Roman law). Accordingly, the German Civil Code consists of five parts (or books): General Part, Law of Obligations, Law of Things, Family Law, Inheritance Law.

The reception of Roman private law exerted a significant influence on the Germanic system of private law which especially occurred in the Middle Ages in the form of the study of and commentary on Roman primary sources, and also in the form of the direct application of norms of Roman law by courts.

Anglo-Saxon Family of Private Law. The Common Law underlies this system (the result of the activity of the royal courts), law of equity (formed from decisions of the court of chancery), and statutory law (includes acts adopted by Parliament). The absence of acts of codification of civil legislation is characteristic. They were replaced by laws on special issues and by judicial practice, which comprises the law of precedent.

The law of precedent materialized in the form of systematized collections of decisions of the courts of higher instances whose application is obligatory in analogous cases. Therefore, precedents are sources of law. The concept of the Anglo-Saxon system of civil law is determined by the leading significance of the law of precedent: the absence of a symmetrical finished system of legislative acts is compensated for by the generalization of individual precedents and the forming of legal norms on the basis of specific cases.

Although in civilist literature the view exists that the Anglo-Saxon system avoided the reception of Roman private law, this is not so. Roman law influenced this system of civil law, but in a special form: it borrowed the methodology of law-creation of Roman jurists, especially the praetors, who compiled norms on the basis of practice and according to its needs.

Eastern European Family of Private Law. The absence of a precise division of law into private and public is typical of this system. This concerns not only the period of existence of so-called socialist law, but virtually the entire history of the development of law in countries of this group. The influence of public-law elements is strongly felt in the civil law, the granting of privileges to State institutions and respectively a limitation (up to the complete elimination thereof) of the right of private ownership.

Codes are, as a rule, the sources of civil law. However, they are accompanied by an enormous number of subordinate acts which often change and augment civil codes and other acts of codification. The system of structuring civil codes is close to the Pandectian but with certain variations (for example, family law is outside the sphere of civil-law regulation, but author's right is within it, and so on).

The weakness of legal traditions and a feeling for law (legal consciousness) is characteristic of jurisprudence, which over time leads to the dominance in the regulation of commercial or civil turnover of so-called organizational-legal means.

Byzantine (Graeco-Roman) law had a noteworthy influence on the structure and content of this system of law, the direct or obscured reception of which occurred in countries of this group.

Central-Eastern European Family of Private Law. This family of private law was formed on the basis of local law but under the influence of the Romanist and Germanic legal families, as a consequence of which there are a number of distinctive features. The presence of civil codes and the dominance of legislative acts over judicial practice are characteristic. In the majority of instances the structure of codes gravitates towards the Pandectian system, but without fully replicating the last (as a rule, family relations are not within the sphere of the civil code).

This system of law has a rather stable legal tradition: law is regarded as one of the fundamental supports of society. However, unlike Western European systems of law, there is no sharp division here between public and private, and the civil law has material public-law elements.

A noteworthy role in forming this system of civil law is played by the intermediating nature of the reception of Roman law. This occurred here by borrowing a number of ideas and decisions from the legislation of Western European countries, where this process was based on the study and analysis of primary sources and the mastery thus of the "spirit of Roman law".

CONCLUSIONS

These families of the private law of Europe may be separated out: Romanist, Germanic (Central European), Anglo-Saxon, Central-Eastern European, Eastern European. The first three were formed in the western tradition of law; the last in the eastern tradition, and the Central-Eastern European experienced the influence of both traditions.

As regards the distinctive features of the Ukrainian tradition of private law, we observe merely that it is conditioned by historical, geopolitical, and cultural distinctive features of Ukrainian State construction. A noteworthy role was played by the fact that a significant part of its history Ukraine devoted to the choice of a civilized orientation between "East" and "West". Therefore, sometimes Ukraine is characterized as a "country of boundaries" which simultaneously experienced several influences: from the west – the European tradition; from the east – the Russian tradition; from the south – the near Eastern tradition. As a consequence a certain balance between competing forces historically was established back in the Middle Ages, Ukraine between politically divided between Poland and Muscovy, and culturally between West and East.

Ultimately, this affected the material scale of the impact of the Graeco-Byzantine East on the spiritual tradition and of the Latin West on the socio-political structures of Ukraine. The cultural space of Ukraine is a synthesis between West and West (V. Lipinskii), and Ukraine itself is described as a European State but one constantly in a state of worldview reflex. In the religious sphere this made Ukraine a classic country of the Uniate tradition, in the sphere of culture this was expressed in the style of so-called Ukrainian baroque which combined the Byzantine and western traditions, and in the sphere of law this led to a certain compilationness and sometimes to eclecticism.

Especially noticeable was the fractionalization of Ukrainian culture into two branches (eastern and western) and its impact on the formation of the tradition of private law. The distinctions between the Ukrainians of the Dniepr Ukraine and of Galicia exist not only in language, psychology, and religious confessions, but also on the level of legal consciousness.[26] In Western Ukraine the tradition of private law reflects the sensitive influence of the West, whereas in Eastern Ukraine the Eastern European tradition is more noticeable. These influences give rise to the complexity of the forming of private law in Ukraine at the contemporary stage. The interaction and sometimes the juxtaposition of Western and Eastern legal traditions are expressed in the inconsistent attitude of society to the division of law into private and public, the resistance of some jurists to recognition of the existence of private law, the gravitation of the State towards paternalism in private-law relations, to the rejection of incorporating family law into civil law, and others.

[26] I. Vaskovich, «Правосвідомість та її вплив на менталітет українського народу» [Legal Consciousness and its Influence on the Mentality of the Ukrainian People], Право України [Law of Ukraine], no. 6 (1998), p. 110.

These distinctive features of the Ukrainian tradition of private law have materially influenced the formation of the conception of civil law in Ukraine. The last, having experienced the substantial impact of the Central European (Germanic) and Eastern European views on civilistics, made the civil law of modern Ukraine in essence a classical model of the legal system of the Central-Eastern European family of private law.

Convergence of Romano-Germanic and Anglo-Saxon Law

M. N. MARCHENKO*

GENERAL AND SPECIAL IN ROMANO-GERMANIC AND ANGLO-SAXON LAW

In speaking about the convergence of Romano-Germanic and Anglo-Saxon law, about their development in the direction of a gradual approximation, it is necessary to draw attention to what lies at the base of this approximation. Namely – the *similarity of the foundation on which these legal families are structured and function, the similarity of their bases.*

During the 1980s, western specialists pointed to the fact that despite the existing distinctions between the Romano-Germanic (continental) and Anglo-Saxon (Common) law, they are united chiefly by the fact that they and the national legal systems comprising them are structured on a common foundation, which is the "western bourgeois-democratic foundation".[1]

Attention has been drawn to the fundamental similarity of the legal families herein considered by many western authors in the most recent period up to the present, especially when in view of the more active interaction of the United Kingdom – a member of the European Union and bearer of the traditions of the Common Law with other States who are members of the European Union and bearers of the traditions of continental law at full maturity – the question was put relative to their legal systems, and on the regional level – relative to these legal families not only

* доктор юридических наук, профессор. Meritorious Public Figure of Science of Russian Federation; Professor, Moscow State University; author of numerous works on comparative law and legal theory.

[1] J. H. Merryman and D. S. Clark, *Comparative Law: Western European and Latin American Legal Systems* (1978), p. 210.

on the plane of their community and similarity, but of their unification and integration.

Although previously in a number of scholarly studies devoted to the interlinkage and interaction of Romano-Germanic and Anglo-Saxon law significant attention is placed not only, and in certain works even not so much on their community and similarity, as on their "fundamental" distinction from one another,[2] nonetheless the view is predominant in western doctrine of recent years that the existing differences between the legal families here considered is rather a matter of form than content.

As the noted English judge, Lord Goff of Chieveley, noted in his lectures on the future of the Common Law delivered at the British Institute of International and Comparative Law, my personal academic experience and my observations say that the "major differences between the common law and what we may broadly call the civil law are to be found rather in the form than in the substance of our law ...".[3]

An analogous view relating to the similarity and difference of the legal families here considered, and likewise all western legal systems, is shared, albeit for entirely different reasons – reasons of an ideological nature – by Soviet legal scholars, who believed that the significant differences, as a general rule contradictions in essence and content, occur only between socialist and capitalist law. As regards differences existing within capitalist law itself, they concern merely the form thereof and not the essence and content thereof.[4]

This at first glance rather ideological conclusion is affirmed in significant measure by many western specialists discussing the similarities of the legal families here considered and the national legal systems forming them by virtue of their having arisen and developed on the base of "types of society rather close to one another", by virtue of the "common or rather similar process of their historical development", a "common or rather similar religion", and also other "rather similar aspects" of social and State life.[5]

By "common or rather similar" bases of the Romano-Germanic and Anglo-Saxon law should be understood a uni-type – market, capitalist economy on whose base arises and develops corresponding to it and adequately reflecting it not only a social, political, ideological, but also a

[2] R. Caenegem, "Civil Law and Common Law: The Twain That Seldom Met", *Droit Anglo-Saxon et Droit Continental. Confrontation or Harmonisation?* (1995), p. 3.

[3] Lord Robert Goff of Chieveley, "The Future of the Common Law", *International and Comparative Law Quarterly*, XLVI (1997), p. 746.

[4] For details, see M. N. Marchenko, Правовые системы современного мира [Legal Systems of the Modern World] (2001), pp. 206-241.

[5] M. Bogdan, *Comparative Law* (1993), pp. 68-83; R. Cooke, "The Road Ahead for the Common Law", *International and Comparative Law Quarterly*, LIII (2004), pp. 273-286.

legal milieu in the form of national legal systems and the legal families here considered.

Since the terms "capitalist", "capitalism", and so on with regard to a market economy, and likewise with respect to other "market" phenomena, institutes, and institutions in Russian literature have been artificially removed from circulation and are being replaced by others far from adequate but "better-sounding" terms such as "civilized", "post-industrial", and so on, one must explain that in western political and sociological sciences capitalism is understood to be a system or structure under which: (a) "ownership to land and the basic means of production belong to individuals, joint-stock societies, and corporations"; (b) free competition has as its "express purpose the obtaining of profit by the owner"; (c) the achievement of a "high level of specialization in production, and also in the financial sphere of activity"; (d) an intensification of the "concentration of capital" occurs and the rapid growth of "powerful national and transnational corporations"; (e) State control is established and maintained over the activity of business, and so on.[6]

Together with uni-type economic bases as common indicia and features of Romano-Germanic and Anglo-Saxon law uni-type socio-political (uni-type social and political system), ideological (liberal and neoliberal ideas and conceptions), and civilizational, or more specifically – culturological foundations – also act in significant part to condition them.

When we speak about common civilizational bases of the legal families here considered, we have in view that general-social milieu in the broadest sense associated with various components and phenomena of social life, such as "religion, painting, architecture, morals and customs" and others,[7] within the limits and under the impact of which these legal families arose and developed. This is western civilization, which not only gave birth to State-legal systems similar in foundation, but also exerted enormous influence on other civilizations existing in parallel and which arose within their framework of State-legal systems.

Western, and likewise all other civilizations which conditioned the existence and functioning of respective types of States, and together with them – legal systems and legal families, arose long before the emergence of these States and, as historical experience demonstrates, continue to exist a rather lengthy period after the departure of the last from the arena of active life, after their disappearance.

[6] *Dictionary of Sociology and Related Sciences* (1988), p. 32; *Webster's New Universal International Unabridged Dictionary* (1993), p. 269.

[7] A. Toynbee, Цивилизация перед судом истории [Civilization Before the Court of History] (1995), p. 133.

States, the English historian Toynbee wrote on this occasion, "are inclined to a short life and sudden deaths: Western civilization to which we relate with you may exist centuries after the United Kingdom or the United States disappear from the political map of the world, just as older contemporaries disappeared – the Venetian Republic and the Austro-Hungarian Empire".[8]

The situation is similar with national legal systems engendered on a common civilization basis, including the Romano-Germanic and Anglo-Saxon legal families.[9]

In speaking about the civilization base common to these legal families as a complex and multi-component phenomenon, we must have in view one of the most important, if not the most important element thereof, the culture of society in general and legal culture in particular.

Legal culture as part of Western civilization is that common direct base on which both the respective national legal systems arise and develop and the legal families which they form.

Acting in the guise of the "aggregate of all positive components of legal activity in the real functioning thereof embodying the achievements of legal thought, legal technique, and practice", legal culture, as Salnikov noted rightly, "permeates" all law, legal consciousness, legal relations forming the legal order in society, and also law-creation, law-application, and all other legal activity".[10]

Legal culture as part of general culture of a particular human community creating together with it a determined musical, linguistic, and other culture, affects decisively the essence, content, nature, and character not only of various legal systems, but the legal families formed on the basis thereof.[11]

It follows from this, in particular, that the Greco-Roman or Muslim civilization, according to Toynbee's classification,[12] in creating a respective legal culture, thereby affects through it the emergence not only of similar municipal legal systems in their basic parameters, but also the legal families combining them. This relates also fully to all other civilization formations

[8] Ibid., p. 134.

[9] See H. P. Glenn, *Legal Traditions of the World* (3d ed., 2007).

[10] V. P. Salnikov, «Правовая культура» [Legal Culture], in M. N. Marchenko (ed.), Общая теория государства и права [General Theory of State and Law] (2d ed., 2002), III, p. 362.

[11] J. Gibson and G. Caldeira, "The Legal Cultures of Europe", *Law and Society Review*, no. 1 (1996), pp. 57-59; L. Cohen-Tanugi, "Legal Cultures Compared: The American and the French and the German", in V. Gessner, A. Hofland, and C. Varga (eds.), *European Legal Culture* (1996), pp. 269-275; A. Watson, *Legal History and Common Law for Europe: Misery, Reality, Imagination* (2001), pp. 101-176.

[12] Toynbee, note 7 above, pp. 99-101.

and legal cultures, not excluding, *inter alia*, the presently existing western phenomena.

To be sure, in speaking about the community and conditionality of the Romano-Germanic and Anglo-Saxon law of western legal culture, this phenomenon (or community) and process (or conditionality) should not be absolutized, and western legal culture should not be regarded as some mono-culture.

Being a certain type of legal culture in which the similarity of the legal phenomena being investigated is decisively predetermined with regard to parameters of essence and content, western legal culture being at the same time a homogeneous phenomenon and concept with respect to legal cultures of various countries respectively relegated to countries of Romano-Germanic and Anglo-Saxon law, which are generic phenomena and concepts, a priori contains the potential possibility of their differentiation at a minimum according to formal (secondary) indicia.

In recognizing, for example, freedom of speech in essence and significance for a civil society as a manifestation of the community of Romano-Germanic and Anglo-Saxon law, each legal family at the same time demonstrates its special attitude towards this phenomenon in form.

This is manifest, in particular, in the fact that representatives of Romano-Germanic law are Europeans who from the outset regarded and regard "this liberty and right", as scholarly sources and social practice testify, as nothing other than "in the context of many other rights and freedoms of the same order" and as an attribute of democracy, which may be limited without prejudice for civil society "under the most different circumstances".[13]

In contrast to this perception of freedom of speech as some ordinary phenomenon, representatives of Anglo-Saxon law – the Americans – attach to this phenomenon an exceptional role, considering the freedom of speech and "all directly related rights" to be subject to no limitation, to be "primary rights".[14]

The similarity and community in the main part of Romano-Germanic and Anglo-Saxon law – in the essence and content thereof, on one hand, and the distinctiveness thereof (different) in the secondary part – in the technical-legal and other formal (non-principle) respect – on the other, is rather precisely manifest not only in the example cited of freedom of speech, which in Romano-Germanic law is regarded as some routine

[13] H. Schwartz, "Defamation and Democracy", *Parker School Journal of East European Law*, no. 2 (1996), p. 217.

[14] Ibid.

phenomenon, and in the Common Law system, especially American, the right is fetishized, as also in many other instances.

This relates entirely, for example, to the liberal (or market) values underlying the legal families here considered, their socio-political (protection of the interests of the well off and powers that be in priority) and formal-legal (regulation of social relations) targeted aims, to the internal structure of Romano-Germanic and Anglo-Saxon law and external forms of their expression (sources), to the principal tasks and functions of the legal families here considered, and others.[15]

Speaking about the similarity and community of Romano-Germanic and Anglo-Saxon law primarily and their secondary differences one must not fail to acknowledge the substantiation of the thesis uttered in western doctrine that the general and the special in the legal families here considered is not only two sides of the same coin, but that they continue and augment one another.[16]

The community of Romano-Germanic and Anglo-Saxon law is the logic of their historical development that inevitably assumes simultaneously their distinctive features since otherwise it is difficult to explain their relatively autonomous, separate existence, and the more so – their active functioning. This is one aspect. The other is that the presence of distinctive features of the legal families being considered testifies to the fact that only community, similiarity, but not unity exists between them, that they are in essence systems relatively isolated from one another but are not a monosystem, not a single organic system.

WHAT FACTORS EXERT A POSITIVE INFLUENCE ON THE PROCESS OF CONVERGENCE OF ROMANO-GERMANIC AND ANGLO-SAXON LAW AND WHICH OBSTRUCT THEIR APPROXIMATION?

In responding to this question one should, it seems, direct attention to the fact that within each group of factors facilitating or, on the contrary, obstructing the approximation of the legal families here considered the basic, primary, and derivative, secondary factors should be singled out.

As primary factors facilitating the process of the convergence of Romano-Germanic and Anglo-Saxon law one should point to the general – in the form of a uni-type economy, social and political structure of society,

[15] P. Legrand, "European Legal Systems are Not Converging", *International and Comparative Law Quarterly*, XLV (1996), pp. 52-68; Glenn, note 9 above, pp. 126-212.
[16] Bogdan, note 5 above, pp. 68-70.

uni-type of State mechanism, legal culture, and other components similar to them in character and potential orientation – that unite these legal families.

In turn, as primary factors obstructing the approximation of Romano-Germanic and Anglo-Saxon law one must single out and consider the special – in the form of historical and national traditions, customs, particular to each legal family and other phenomena, institutes, and institutions similar to them in nature – which separate these legal families.

The primary factors are that base which not only establishes the essence, internal structure, and content of each of the legal families here considered, but also predetermines the character and developmental trend of relations between them.

As regards secondary factors, they, being derivative from the primary, express, or more precisely reflect, the base potential in the Romano-Germanic and Anglo-Saxon legal families, as well as the trends for their approximation and their divergence.

Among the secondary factors – elements facilitating the approximation of the legal families here considered – should be single out those which are manifest at the regional level of interlinkage and interaction of the Romano-Germanic and Anglo-Saxon law.

To be sure, secondary factors facilitating the approximation of these legal families are inextricably linked with the primary factors and are manifest to some extent also on the global level – at the level of legal families as a whole and on the local level – individual national legal systems. This occurs, for example, in the legal system of the United States, where the legal system of the State of Louisiana, being by nature and character a Romano-Germanic phenomenon, is directly linked with an Anglo-Saxon phenomenon, which is a legal system of the American federation.

However, the most prominent character of the impact of secondary factors facilitating the approximation of the Romano-Germanic and Anglo-Saxon law, just as these factors themselves, is manifest at the regional level, in particular on the level of the European Union.

One such factor at this level is the membership of the United Kingdom – the primogenitor of Anglo-Saxon law – in the European Union, within which are States whose legal systems are built on the principles and traditions of Romano-Germanic law.

Being in close connection and intraction with each other in the process of the fulfillment, in essence, of identical technical-legal and socio-political functions,[17] these legal families exert constant influence on each other. The Common Law system exerts direct influence through the law of the United

[17] See A. I. Ogus, *Regulation: Legal Form and Economic Theory* (1994), pp. 338-341.

Kingdom on Romano-Germanic law. In turn, the last through the same channels of a regional level exerts a reverse impact on Anglo-Saxon law.

In doctrinal writings it is not accepted to raise and discuss the degree of influence on one another at the regional level, at least, within the framework of the European Union, of the legal families here considered, although there undoubtedly seems, proceeding from an analysis of the legal foundation, to be the fact of the primary impact of general-European (continental) Romano-Germanic law on the British common (Anglo-Saxon) law.

There is nothing surprising in that, as Beatson noted in his article, soon after the accession of the United Kingdom to the European Union "English law increasingly looks to European law and European Community and European Union law".[18] The author adds that the influence of European continental law on the English Common Law in time not only is not weakening, but, on the contrary, is growing as its develops and improves, testified to, in particular, by the numerous decisions of a number of institutions of the European Union "proceeding from the traditions of Romano-Germanic continental law" and directly affecting, *inter alia*, the English Common Law.

As legal regulation expands effectuated with the assistance of norms contained in acts of institutions of the European Union, the process of the "Europeanization" of English law is gathering pace, the process of the "penetration" and adaptation of many norms and institutes of general European (continental) law in the system of Anglo-Saxon (Common) law.[19]

As a result thereof, and also under the impact of a number of other factors, in the view of certain specialists "English law is gradually becoming less English"[20] on the practical and theoretical levels. In so doing one must bear in mind the fact that the membership of the United Kingdom in the European Union is increasingly telling not only on law-creation and law-application activity of the respective British agencies, but also on the traditional concept of the British legal establishment, especially, constitutional law.[21]

The fact is that, whereas previously in English legal theory the view dominated of the undoubted primacy of an unwritten constitution in comparison with a written one, since the entry of the United Kingdom into the European Union under the impact of general-European law and its principles and various general theoretical provisions, the situation

18 J. Beatson, "Has the Common Law a Future?", *Cambridge Law Journal*, LVI (1997), p. 292.
19 Ibid.
20 Cooke, note 5 above, p. 273.
21 V. Bogdanor (ed.), *The British Constitution in the Twentieth Century* (2003), p. 663.

has changed significantly. In English jurisprudence, the experts state, a noticeable advance in views is noticeable, both in the form of a constitutional act and on constitutionalism. With regard to the form of a constitutional act the "improvement" is noted from an unwritten to a "quasi-written" constitution within the country[22] and to a written constitutional act without, within the limits of the European Union.

As regards constitutionalism as a phenomenon and concepts concerning it, here significant changes also have occurred, especially after the adoption in the United Kingdom in 1998 of the Human Rights Act limiting the "sovereignty of Parliament" and expanding the prerogatives of judicial power in the sphere of "constitutional control".[23]

Various "internal and external forces", it says in special studies in this connection, changed to a significant extent the English concept not only of a constitution, but of constitutionalism, bringing it closer to the general-European continental notion.[24]

As factors bringing the English conception of constitutional phenomena closer to the general-European, continental perception and thereby Anglo-Saxon law closer, albeit one iota, to Romano-Germanic, not only membership of the United Kingdom in the European Union is named, but also globalization, or more precisely, the "global economy", regionalization, Europeanization, understood as the unification, harmonization, and integration of legal systems of the members of the European Union, including the Common Law system of England, mixed legal system of Scotland, and other similar factors.[25]

Great significance among the factors facilitating the approximation of Romano-Germanic and Anglo-Saxon law in western, primarily American, doctrine is attached to the phenomenon of the Americanization, or reception of American law, Common Law in character, in European continental law.[26] In calling the reception of American law an enormous influence after the Second World War on European law, and in a number of instances in the law of other regions of the world, the authors greatly exaggerate the significance of this phenomenon, even drawing a parallel between the

[22] D. Jenkins, "From Unwritten to Written: Transformation in the British Common-Law Constitution", *Vanderbilt Journal of Transnational Law*, XXXVI (2003), pp. 865-867.

[23] For details, see Marchenko, Судебное правотворчество и судейское право [Judicial Law-Creation and Judge's Law] (2007), pp. 336-350.

[24] J. Alder, *General Principles of Constitutional and Administrative Law* (2004), pp. 139-141.

[25] Ch. Joerges, "Europeanization as Process: Thoughts on the Europeanization of Private Law", *European Public Law*, no. 1 (2005), pp. 63-84; J. Napolitano, "Towards a European Legal Order for Services of General Economic Interest", *European Public Law*, no. 4 (2005), pp. 565-581.

[26] W. Wiegand, "The Reception of American Law in Europe", *American Journal of Comparative Law*, XXXIX (1991), pp. 229-248.

reception of American and the reception of Roman law: "The process of the reception of American law, as in the case of all other reception procedures", note western jurists, "is comprised of a number of interdependent factors. On this regard, the parallel between the reception of American Law and that of *ius commune* in the Middle Ages is significant".[27]

Greatly exaggerating the influence of American law on European in the postwar, and the more so in subsequent periods, and without any grounds, equating the "Americanization" of European law to the reception of Roman law, specialists nonetheless are right that the Common Law in the person of the American legal system exerted a certain influence on the Romano-Germanic in the person of general-European continental law.

This influence told on those branches, sub-branches, and institutes of law which augment the content of private law.[28] Among them are civil, commercial, corporate, and other components of the system of European law.

Together with the influence on European legislation and on the practice of law-creation, law-application, and law enforcement activities of European States, whose legal systems are relegated to the Romano-Germanic family, the reception of American law to some extent affected European legal theory. In the view of some authors, "virtually all the major and long-term changes which occurred in the postwar period in European private law and its theory had their beginning in America".[29]

Reference is made to "new business conceptions" concerning "new contractual concepts in the economy"[30] connected with leasing, factoring, franchising, secrecy of bank deposits, protection of rights of an owner and consumer rights, private-law torts, and others.[31]

The basic principles and prerequisites for intensive Americanization of European law in the postwar period were, first, in the distinctive universalization of American private law enabling its various institutes to be extensively used within Anglo-Saxon and Romano-Germanic law. Second, the economic and political dominance of the United States in the western world during the postwar years enabled them to disseminate their influence in the legal sphere. Third, the extensive use and introduction of the English language in the postwar years in day-to-day and professional life of many countries of Western Europe created the conditions for the

27 Ibid., p. 246.

28 Wiegand, *Studien zur Rechtsanwendungslehre der Rezeptionszeit* (1977); R. Sturner, *Die Rezeption U.S.—americanischen Rechts in der Bundesrepublik Deutschland* (1989).

29 P. Cruz, *A Modern Approach to Comparative Law* (1993), p. 335.

30 Ibid., pp. 335-336.

31 Wiegand, note 26 above, pp. 235-247.

use of American "makings" not only in the domain of technology, but also in law. Fourth, the European law students studying in universities of the United States who upon completing their studies "occupied key positions in European academic institutions, large banks, law firms, and private business" enabled them to carry over American knowledge in the domain of law and practical experience into European law.[32]

It should be added that American and transnational corporations have played and continue to play a rather important role in the "Americanization" of European and continental, indeed the entire Romano-Germanic law.[33]

In addition to the aforesaid factors enabling the approximation of Romano-Germanic and Anglo-Saxon law and the growing development of economic, socio-political, and other links between countries and convergence, other primary and secondary factors are considered in doctrinal writings.

Without analyzing these factors, it should be noted that in aggregate they ensure the stable and targeted development of Romano-Germanic and Anglo-Saxon law towards their constant mutual permeation and the formation on this basis of a qualitatively-new block of law. There is no doubt that, proceeding from the experience of the socio-political and legal development of western countries, the factors facilitating the development of the processes of convergence of the legal families here considered will in the foreseeable future at least play a dominant role in determining the character of relations between Romano-Germanic and Anglo-Saxon law.

However, their role and significance should not be exaggerated or absolutized. As practice shows, together with factors facilitating approximation and, in the long-term, possibly the complete merger of the Romano-Germanic and Anglo-Saxon law, there exist numerous economic, socio-political, psychological, ideological, and other factors which not only do not facilitate, but in some instances even, on the contrary, obstruct the approximation thereof.

Nor should it be overlooked that law – laws, legal systems, and legal families, exist not by themselves, isolated or divorced from economic, social, and other systems. They arise and function not other than as a reflection of their essence and as a kind of legal superstructure above the said systems. It follows from this that the factors obstructing the approximation of Romano-Germanic and Anglo-Saxon law are rooted not only and even not

[32] Cruz, note 29 above, p. 335.

[33] I. Ia. Kiselev, Транснациональные корпорации и буржуазное трудовое право [Transnational Corporations and Bourgeois Labor Law] (1985), pp. 46-183; J. Trochon, "Challenges Facing Multinational Corporations: A Legal Perspective", *International Business Law Journal*, no. 8 (2003), pp. 847-854.

so much in legal as in the economic, socio-political, and others spheres of life of western society and also in the respective interests embodied in each of them.

Where the interests of the ruling strata and States which are bearers of the traditions of the legal families here considered are similar, factors operate directed towards the approximation of these blocks of law. On the contrary, where these interests diverge, factors emerge obstructing their approximation.

One such factor is called, especially in doctrinal writings, the "political"[34] factor, whose essence lies in the coinciding or diverging of political interests.

One may, for example, assert with assurance that whereas in the postwar period the political interests of the United States – the bearer of the traditions of the Common Law – and the countries of continental Western Europe – the adherents of Romano-Germanic law – coincided to the same extent in their economic interests so that Americanization affected in significant degree not only European private, but also public law – constitutional, administrative, criminal, and other respective branches.

However, this did not happen since the path of the "Americanization" of this sector of European law and, accordingly, the process of approximation of the legal families here considered pursued various political and other related interests of the parties participating in this process.

The political and other interests of the parties not coinciding with one another act as those factors which not only do not promote, but most often obstruct the harmonization and integration of different legal systems and legal families, including Romano-Germanic and Anglo-Saxon law.

Naturally, these interests in and of themselves are not the only or, moreover, even primary factors obstructing the approximation of different national legal systems forming Romano-Germanic and Anglo-Saxon law or even those legal families. Together with these rather subjective and in this sense derivative, secondary factors, there exist a number of others more profound and more significant from the standpoint of impact on the system of relations of Romano-Germanic and Anglo-Saxon law analogous in orientation to factors having an objective character.

We refer to such factors that, on one hand, determine the nature of particular laws arising in each individual country and, on the other, the character of national legal systems and the legal families forming them.

34 Merryman, On the Convergence and Divergence of the Civil Law and the Common Law, p. 213.

"Laws", Montesquieu (1689-1755) wrote in the mid-eighteenth century in his noted work *The Spirit of Laws*, "should be adapted in such a manner to the people for whom they are made". It is essential" he said, that "they should be relative to the nature and principle of the actual, or intended government", and relative to the "climate, whether hot or cold, of each country, to the quality of the soil, to its situation and bigness, to the manner of living of the natives ... degree of liberty which the constitution will bear; to the religion of the inhabitants, to their inclinations, riches, number, commerce, manners, and customs". Finally, the author summed up, "they have relations amongst themselves, as also with their origin, with the object of the legislator, and with the order of things on which they are established".[35]

Proceeding from this, laws and the system of legislation and system of law of one country together with them, may not be identical to the respective legal phenomena of another country. As a consequence, some legal families formed on their basis may not be fully-fledged copies of other legal families.

This relates in full not only to heterogeneous legal families, such as Muslim and Jewish law, but also to legal families close in nature and character, which the Romano-Germanic and Anglo-Saxon law represent.[36]

Being structured and functioning on the same level in principle, a uni-type economic, socio-political, ideological, and other bases and accumulating for this reason rather many general indicia and features, each of these legal families cannot at the same time, as a reflection of different "properties of people" and "physical properties" of each country, fail to contain a mass of distinctive features separating these legal families from one another.

The last may act as various forms and manifestations such as, for example, the distinctive features of the internal structure of individual legal systems and legal families; the distinctive features of legal culture and legal consciousness; the distinctive features of historical and national traditions; the distinctive features of legal customs existing within the families here considered and others.[37]

In addition, the distinctive features of Romano-Germanic and Anglo-Saxon law may be manifest and are manifest also in their ideologies

[35] Charles Louis de Secondat Montesquieu, *The Spirit of the Laws* (Dublin, 1751), p. 8.

[36] M. Chesterman, "Contempt: In the Common Law, But Not the Civil Law", *International and Comparative Law Quarterly*, XLVI (1997), pp. 521-560.

[37] Merryman, note 34 above, pp. 223-227; Cooke, note 5 above, pp. 274-276; E. Blankenburg, "Patterns of Legal Culture: The Netherlands Compared to Neighboring Germany", *American Journal of Comparative Law*, XLVI (1998), pp. 1-42; J. H. Baker, "Why the History of English Law Has Not Been Finished?", *Cambridge Law Journal*, LIX (2000), pp. 63-84.

and various postulates augmenting this ideology, which are regarded as something ordinary within one legal family but are not perceived by representatives of another. For example, provisions as follows are customary and differ for the system of Anglo-Saxon law: "legislation is that which the legislator (or parliament) says, and legally-significant legislation is that which the court has said"; "on the practical level the legal significance of a parliamentary act primarily comes down to a determination of its force by a higher court"; "an authoritative statement concerning the legal force of a law is the sole prerogative (function) of the court", and so on.[38] However, these propositions are not fully or are not at all perceived within the system of Romano-Germanic law.

The situation is analogous with certain postulates comprising the content of the ideology of Romano-Germanic law. Being common and generally-recognized in the Romano-Germanic legal family, they are not perceived and do not find support in Anglo-Saxon law.

Despite the fact, for example, that the number of laws in the United Kingdom in recent years has significantly grown in comparison with precedents by reason of intensive national and general European law-creation, they all the same, as specialists note, continue psychologically to be perceived by many jurists concerned with Anglo-Saxon law, despite the "Romano-Germanic tradition, as having primacy of place in the system of sources of law "as an exception from the rules rather than as a rule itself".[39]

The distinctive features of the ideology of Romano-Germanic and Anglo-Saxon law, together with other distinctive features of these legal families, often act as factors not only restraining, but also obstructing, approximation by various routes, including by way of harmonization and possible subsequent integration.

BY WHAT MEANS AND IN WHAT FORMS IS THE PROCESS OF CONVERGENCE OF ROMANO-GERMANIC AND ANGLO-SAXON LAW MANIFEST?

As there is evolution of Romano-Germanic and Anglo-Saxon law in the direction of their approximation as systems having uni-type economic, political, ideological, and other foundations, throughout the entire space of their interlinkage and inter-action numerous and various forms of the manifestation of this approximation may be traced. However, they are most precisely manifest on the European continent, where Romano-Germanic

38 F. Bennion, *Understanding Common Law Legislation: Drafting and Interpretation* (2001), pp. 201-202.

39 Beatson, note 18 above, p. 229.

law in the person of its bearers – the majority of countries of the European Union – are situated in constant and direct linkage with the Common, Anglo-Saxon law in the person of its traditional bearer and member of the European Union – the United Kingdom.[40]

The process of approximation (or convergence) of the legal families here considered is developing by what means and in what forms? In replying to this question, one should note the reflection and manifestation of the process of the convergence of the forms or sources of Romano-Germanic and Anglo-Saxon law.

In western doctrinal writings the issue of the approximation (or convergence), more precisely, the harmonization, of sources of the legal families here considered has long since been within the purview of specialists. The principal reason is not only and not even so much that the manifestation of the process of convergence of Romano-Germanic and Anglo-Saxon law, and likewise certain other evidence of this process, lies at the surface and is evident to the untrained eye, as that the sources of law and the state and character of their correlation plays a key role in the process of the development of each of the legal families here considered and in their interlinkage and interaction.

In directing attention to the approximation of sources of Romano-Germanic and Anglo-Saxon law in general and to their harmonization in particular, scholars not without reason point out that this process is not effectuated in and of itself, but under the impact of processes of economic, social, and other integration which exerts direct influence not only on the development of national legal systems and legal families, but also on the evolution of the respective sources of law.[41]

Harmonization of the last also is affected, in the view of specialists, by those processes occurring on the European continent but influencing Romano-Germanic and Anglo-Saxon law as a whole, as the Europeanization of the legal sphere connected with the gradual squeezing out of national law from the legal field of the European Union and, consequently, of its sources and the replacement thereof by all-European legal institutes,[42] the creation of a "new European legal order" that is "more advanced than the

[40] See M. Sheridan and J. Cameron, *EC Legal Systems: An Introductory Guide* (1992); E. Denza, "Two Legal Orders: Divergent or Convergent?", *International and Comparative Law Quarterly*, XLVIII (1999), pp. 257-284; Joerges, note 25 above.

[41] A. Wilts, "Europeanization and Means of Interest Representation by National Business Associations", *European Journal of Industrial Relations*, no. 3 (2001), pp. 269-270.

[42] K. Mortelmans, "The Relationship between the Treaty Rules and Community Measures for the Establishment and Functioning of the Internal Market – towards a Concordance Rule", *Common Market Law Review*, no. 39 (2002), pp. 1307-1310.

global (world) legal order",[43] requiring both the adoption of new legislative acts and a certain unification of legal forms, among others.

It should be noted that the harmonization of sources of Romano-Germanic and Anglo-Saxon law, just as the convergence of these families itself, proceeds on the basis of its being an objective phenomenon conditioned chiefly by such processes objective in nature and character as globalization and regionalization. This does, however, not preclude subjective interference and impact on the process of the harmonization of sources of law caused by practical necessity.

The objective character of harmonization just as subjective interference of the purpose of influencing this process concerns not only individual but also the entire system of sources of law as a whole, including normative legal acts, judicial precedents, customs, international legal treaties, general principles of law, and legal doctrines.

To be sure, laws as the principal sources of Romano-Germanic law and judicial precedents as the leading sources of Anglo-Saxon law are always at the forefront of this process.

In singling them out, it should be noted that Russian jurists – theoreticians and practitioners – and some foreign authors engaged in comparative law, have formed the firm view of a law not only as the chief and dominating source, but as the sole source of Romano-Germanic law and, respectively, the exclusive affiliation of judicial precedent to Anglo-Saxon law.[44]

This position, especially with respect to the exclusive affiliation of judicial precedent to Anglo-Saxon law, was justified to some extent and had a certain basis "yesterday", before the comparatively tempestuous development in the world of the processes of globalization and regionalization during the second half of the twentieth century exerted significant influence on the process of European integration, including legal. However, it has completely lost its foundation "today" when the European Union functions as a relatively integral formation resting to a significant degree on the legal culture and institutes which gave birth to it and being by its nature and character affiliated not only to Romano-Germanic but also to Anglo-Saxon law.

Speaking with respect to judicial precedent, and to judicial law-creation at the early stages of the development of Romano-Germanic law, one

[43] Napolitano, note 25 above, p. 581.

[44] See Ch. Kourilsky, A. Rácz, and H. Schäffer (eds.), *The Sources of Law: A Comparative Empirical Study* (1982); R. White, *The English Legal System in Action: The Administration of Justice* (1999); P. Craig, "Constitutional Foundations, the Rule of Law and Supremacy", *Public Law* (Spring 2003); *International Encyclopedia of Laws. Civil Procedure* (2004), II.

cannot fail to note the fact known to specialists in foreign State and law and to comparative lawyers that in this legal family, unlike Anglo-Saxon law where judicial precedent was recognized as a source of law throughout its entire history, there was not consistency in the perception thereof.

Depending on the stages of development of Romano-Germanic law, the spectrum of opinion and social practice concerning judicial law-creation and judicial precedent as a source of law varied in different periods from full recognition thereof to categorical denial thereof.[45] This diversity of views and approaches to resolving the problems of the place and role of judicial precedent as a source of law within the system of other sources of law was noted not only at the level of the entire block of law from which the Romano-Germanic legal family later formed, but within individual national legal systems.[46]

To be persuaded of this, suffice it to recall, for example, that in France whose legal system comprises the heart of Romano-Germanic law, for various reasons from the seventeenth century up to the French Revolution of 1789-94, according to many specialists, case law was extensively "used even more than in England in this period", whereas after the Revolution an official prohibition was placed on judicial law-creation and even the free interpretation of the Code Napoleon and other legislative acts.[47]

The situation was analogous with the legislation of Austria, which in about the same period as the legislation of France, actually recognized in its legal system judicial acts (or precedents) containing general norms as sources of law, and commencing from 1811, when the civil code was introduced into operation, placed on this recognition and on judicial law-creation itself a semi-official prohibition. The Law of 1811 (§12, ABGD) expressly provided that "judge-made law shall not be a source with respect to the Austrian legal order" and that here the principle operates under which "judicial decisions with respect to specific cases do not create a general norm would might be applied in analogous instances".[48]

Similar issues concerning periods of rise and fall of judicial law-creation and judge-made law at various stages of the development of Romano-Germanic law arose not only with respect to the legal system of Austria or France, but also the legislation of other countries from whose legal systems the Romano-Germanic legal family emanates.[49]

[45] For details, see Marchenko, note 23 above, pp. 235-249.

[46] Caenegem, *European Law in the Past and the Future: Unity and Diversity Over Two Millennia* (2003).

[47] John P. Dawson, *The Oracles of the Law* (1968); Glenn, note 9 above, p. 126.

[48] Kourilsky, note 44 above, p. 32.

[49] E. Vrij, "Equity in Holland v. Equity in Australia: A Comparative Essay on the Place and Administration of Equity in Civil Law and Common Law Jurisdictions", *The ELSA Law*

They arose, in particular with respect to the legal system of Denmark, in which previously, according to historical materials, until the second half of the seventeenth century or, more precisely, until the Rules of 1672 permitted "in especially complex instances the deviation of a court from the strict letter of the law" and the "periodic use of judicial precedent", and then such a "deviation" was limited by a simple formula – "the court and precedent created by it do not make law";[50] with respect to the legal system of Norway, where just as in the legal systems of other countries of Romano-Germanic law, at various periods of its development sundry assessments were noted of the significance of judicial law-creation and where traditionally beginning from 1907 – from the adoption of the Sales Act 1907 – "legal" decisions of courts rendered on the basis of "usages" formed as a result of numerous repetition – "series of preceding judicial decisions in analogous cases",[51] and others were recognized.

Having in view fluctuations – "rise and fall" in the perception of judicial precedent as a source of law at early stages of the development of the Romano-Germanic legal family – and having regard to the inconsistency of the proponents of a particular legal family with respect to this legal phenomenon, it is possible to say that precedent in the period considered was most significant and even a sole source only in Anglo-Saxon law, unlike Romano-Germanic law, where a law has analogous significance.

However, an affirmation of this type will not correspond to reality, bearing in mind the difficult incontestable fact that in recent decades under the impact of globalization and regionalization processes and, as a consequence, legal and other integration, judicial precedent lost its former unilateral exceptionalness and became the heritage of both Anglo-Saxon and Romano-Germanic law.

From an episodically recognized source of law in earlier stages of development of the Romano-Germanic legal family, judicial precedent has now actually become a generally-recognized normative-legal phenomenon. The overwhelming majority of countries of the Romano-Germanic law use judicial precedent as a source of law actually and some of them consolidate it also legally.

In confirmation of what has been said one may cite the Civil Code of Switzerland, in force from 1912. Article 1 of the Preliminary Chapter of the legislative act, providing that "law must be applied in all instances in strict conformity with the letter and spirit of the provisions contained

---

Review, no. 2 (1996), pp. 45-51.

[50] St. Iuul, "The Danish Supreme Court Through 300 Years", *Scandinavian Studies in Law*, VI (1962), pp. 172-173.

[51] Kourilsky, note 44 above, p. 212.

therein", precisely consolidates the procedure for not only law-application, but also law-creative activity of courts. According to this Article, if when considering a specific case "there are no legislative provisions might apply in this instance, the judge should render a decision in accordance with existing customary law".[52] And in the absence of the last, he should act "in accordance with those norms of law which he himself would establish if had to act as legislator".[53] In so doing, the law emphasizes, the judge "should be guided by recognized legal doctrine and by judicial precedent".[54]

At present, a clearly expressed trend towards the actual,[55] and partly legal, recognition of precedent as a source of law is noticeable, not only at the level of national legal systems, but on the scale of all-European law, more precisely – the law of the European Union.

A shining example of the last is the activity of the European Court of Justice (ECJ), engaged not only in law-application, but also in law-creative activity, the result of which is judicial precedent.

Being the principal judicial institution of the European Union, the ECJ adopts act having a precedential character containing a general norm or provision (or principle) which should be taken into account by all judicial organs of the European Union when considering cases linked in some measure with the decision of the ECJ.[56]

One should recognize as this type of act emanating from the ECJ and having a precedential character the acts of interpretation and judicial control over the conformity of decisions adopted by various European Union institutions and members of the EU to the provisions contained in the constitutive and treaty acts and in all-European legislation formed on their basis.

These acts of the ECJ are imperative, uncontestable, and generally-binding upon European and national institutions and, to a certain extent, national courts of members of the European Union. This is conditioned, on one hand, by the undoubted priority of the law of the European Union with respect to the national law of EU members in the event conflicts

52 *The Swiss Civil Code* (1976), I, Article 1.

53 Ibid.

54 Ibid.

55 B. A. Gomard, "Programme of Legal Policy of Judge-Made Law", *Scandinavian Studies in Law*, XXXII (1988), pp. 14-17; R. A. Alexy, *Theory of Legal Argumentations* (1989), pp. 274-276; C. Green-Gonas, "The Scandinavian Legal System: An Introduction", *Comparative Juridical Review*, XXVII (1990), pp. 11-15; Ch. Dadomo and S. Farran, *The French Legal System* (1993), pp. 40-43.

56 L. Brown and T. Kennedy, *The Court of Justice of the European Communities* (2000); Gr. De Burca and J. Weiler (eds.), *The European Court of Justice* (2000); B. Nascim-Bene, "The European Court of Justice and the Powers of the Italian Antitrust Authority: The CIF Case", *European Public Law*, X (2004).

arise,[57] and, on the other, the complete monopoly of the ECJ to give a final interpretation of the constitutional (in the sense of fundamental) acts of the European Union and accordingly to decide the issue of the legal validity (or constitutionality) of decisions adopted by various EU institutions.

In enjoying a monopoly in this domain, the ECJ in pursuance of its mission also orientates national courts to act in the direction of taking measures for the uniform understanding and application of law of the European Union by various institutions of the member States.

According to the practice which has formed in those instances when there is no interpretation of the ECJ with respect to a particular European act to be applied within the framework of the jurisdiction of a national court and the possibility of preliminary recourse to the ECJ for such an interpretation has lapsed, national courts in cases of urgency "should declare legally invalid the actions of national institutions applying the European act which, it is assumed, has no legal force", that is, is not constitutional.[58] In such instances national court also may "undertake other appropriate provisional measures, referring in so doing to the particular legally valid European act".[59]

Together with the said acts of the ECJ having a precedential character, one should point to other analogous acts, such as the preliminary rulings or rulings of the ECJ which it renders in the event of the legal validity of a particular European act or conformity of acts emanating from national institutions of members of the European Union to European legislation.[60]

In essence preliminary rulings are nothing other than acts of interpretation, more precisely a variety thereof, which the ECJ gives with regard to a preliminary application on the part of a particular national court.

By virtue of the fact that in conformity with legislation in force and practice "each national court is regarded simultaneously as part of the European court", all national courts "from the lowest judicial instance – judge conciliateur – to the highest – constitutional court" are endowed with powers to apply to the ECJ for a preliminary ruling in all instances when during the consideration of a specific case connected with the application of norms of European law doubts arise as to the constitutionality of a particular European act or the need for its interpretation.[61]

57 J. Shaw, *Law of the European Union* (2000), p. 419.
58 Ibid.
59 R. V. Secretary of State for Transport Ex P. Factortame Ltd. (1991) 1 A.C. 603 ECJ.
60 Shaw, note 57 above, pp. 397-418.
61 M. Cappelletti, *The Judicial Process in Comparative Perspective* (1989), p. 366.

These, just as all other, provisions relating to the precedential character of decisions of the ECJ concern naturally not only judicial and other institutions of countries of Romano-Germanic law, but also all institutions of the United Kingdom – the progenitor of Anglo-Saxon law.

It is stressed in western legal doctrine in this connection that the English courts, just as the courts of other members of the European Union, "must respect decisions of the European Court of Justice"[62] and treat them as "precedent when considering respective cases".[63]

The expansion and consolidation of precedent as a source of law "on a permanent basis" not only in the system of Anglo-Saxon, but also the Romano-Germanic legal family shows, *inter alia,* that at present there is occurring if not unification between these legal families, then at least a clearly expressed approximation.

The essence of the matter does not change the fact that the precedent being created by European structures, especially the ECJ, differs to a certain extent from classical precedent existing in the system of Anglo-Saxon law in general and English law in particular.

One such distinctive feature of judicial precedent being created by the ECJ lies in the fact that by virtue of the absence of a hierarchy of judicial agencies in the European Union, there is no sharp link and duty for national courts to follow decisions of the ECJ, and also in the absence of a precise distinction between such important structural components of precedent as *ratio decidendi* and *obiter dictum*.[64]

Unlike the system of Common Law, where the presence of the *ratio decidendi* in a judicial decision enables courts to be strictly bound in the future when deciding analogous cases, the law of the European Union does not officially recognize the doctrine of "binding" precedent. For this reason the distinction between *obiter dictum* by the ECJ in the process of considering a case and the *ratio decidendi* "to a great extent is erased and loses its initial significance and meaning".[65]

An important distinctive feature of a decision of the ECJ regarded as a precedent is that it has, by virtue of consolidated circumstances formed legislatively, a final character with regard to issues concerning European law "not subject to doubt, appeal, or review".

[62] J. Brown and A. Jacobs, *The European Court of Justice* (1994), Chapter 16.

[63] P. Birks (ed.), *English Private Law* (2000), I, p. 37.

[64] In English doctrinal writings it is noted that the "problem of distinguishing *ratio decidendi* from *obiter dictum* is a very old one". R. Cross, Прецедент в английском праве [Precedent in English Law], ed. F. M. Reshetnikov (1985), p. 57.

[65] A. Arnull, *The European Union and its Court of Justice* (1999), p. 529.

This distinctive feature of precedential decisions of the ECJ, *inter alia,* is conditioned by the fact that within the European Union the lack of a hierarchy of courts to a significant extent "is compensated for" by the hierarchy of legal systems. According to legislatively consolidated provisions, legal theory, and practice, despite the fact that European law is applied in a "compulsory procedure through national courts and tribunals of members of the European Union", it has absolute priority over national law.[66]

The substantiated conclusion follows from this that the priority of one legal system as a whole over the others inevitably predetermines the priority character of mutual relations of their individual components, including precedential decisions of the ECJ concerning issues of European law.

It is no accident in such members of the European Union as England where officially – formally and actually – precedent is recognized as one of the leading sources of law, proceeding from the priority of European law over national, the distinctive hierarchy of precedents is arranged in which the precedential character of precedents of the ECJ is given a leading role. The ECJ, it is stated in doctrinal writings, rendered a final verdict with regard to all questions concerning European law and the "precedent created by them is binding upon all national courts of members of the European Union".[67]

In addition to the foregoing the exist other distinctive features of precedential acts of Romano-Germanic law in comparison with similar acts in Anglo-Saxon law. However, they do not cast doubt on the fact that the consolidation "on a permanent basis" of precedent in the system of Romano-Germanic law acts as one of the manifestation of the approximation thereof with Anglo-Saxon law.

The state of affairs is analogous with respect to other sources of law of the legal families here considered, such as a law or statute, which being the principal source of Romano-Germanic law, strengthened its influence in the postwar period in a number of countries of Anglo-Saxon laws and plays an inestimable role in them at present;[68] legal and non-legal custom, which as studies show has significantly increased its significance in the second half of the twentieth century in various legal families, especially in

66 A. Barah, "The Court of Justice of the European Communities", in Sh. Shetreet (ed.), *The Role of Courts in Society* (1988), pp. 391-394.

67 P. Redmond and P. Shears, *General Principles of English Law* (1993), p. 29.

68 J. Bell, *French Constitutional Law* (1994); P. Hay, *Law of the United States* (2002); P. Leyland and T. Woods, *Textbook on Administrative Law* (2002); Bogdanor, note 21 above; and others.

the sphere of private law – commercial, civil, and others, and plays in them a more noticeable role in comparison with the prewar period.[69]

The expansion of the sphere of application of these and other sources of law in various legal families testifies not only to their community, but to the distinctive nature of the process of development of the legal families here considered in the direction of their unification and harmonization.

To this testify other paths of their development and the forms of manifestation. One such path of the development and forms of manifestation of the process of convergence of Romano-Germanic and Anglo-Saxon law is the intensification of the similarity of their structures and content. This is expressed especially in the expansion of old and emergence in both legal families, or more precisely – the forming of their national legal systems – of new branches, sub-branches, and institutes of law such as, for example, corporative law, information law, internet law, and also regional (within the European Union) constitutional, customs, labor, and other branches and sub-branches of public and private law.

The strengthening of the similarity of structure and content of the legal families here considered also is expressed in the establishment and dissemination throughout the national legal systems within the European Union of "universal" labor and other standards;[70] and in addition – in the expansion of the block of law concerning such relatively new rights and freedoms of man and citizen as the third generation rights – collective rights, right to development,[71] and social rights, which in European law are a "conglomerate" of continental and Common Law and are regarded simultaneously in national cross-section as well as in the context of regionalization and globalization.[72]

To go on. The strengthening of the structure and content of Romano-Germanic and Anglo-Saxon law is manifest in the expansion and deepening in the national legal systems forming these legal families of the practice of judicial supervision and control over the conformity of laws applied and adopted to the letter and spirit of the constitution in force.

[69] G. Burca and B. Witte (eds.), *Social Rights in Europe* (2005); *Social Protection in the European Social Charter* (2000); *The Protection of Fundamental Social Rights in Europe Through the European Social Charter* (2001).

[70] J. Servais, "Universal Labor Standards and National Cultures", *Comparative Labor Law and Policy Journal*, no. 1 (2004), pp. 35-49.

[71] S. Marks, "The Human Right to Development Between Rhetoric and Reality", *Harvard Human Rights Journal*, XVII (2004), pp. 137-167; P. Alston, "Making Space for New Human Rights: The Case of the Right to Development", *Harvard Humanitarian Rights Year Book* (1988), pp. 3-20.

[72] Burca and Witte, note 69 above, and other sources in note 69.

A striking example of the strengthening of the similarity of legal families in this respect is the expansion of the practice in the State-law mechanism of the United Kingdom after the adoption in 1998 of the Human Rights Act by Parliament.

The fact is that until the emergence of this Act supervisory activity of the English court traditionally was confined only to the sphere of the adoption and application of administrative acts, whereas now it extends also to statutes. "A significant part of judicial supervision, if not all of it", it is stated in English doctrinal writings, has at present noticeably shifted from administrative law to constitutional".[73] Judicial supervision concerns especially statutes affecting particular human rights.

In accordance with the Human Rights Act (Article 4[2]), the courts of the United Kingdom are empowered to "make appropriate declarations" and, more precisely – recommendations in all instances when a particular law or subordinate act, in their view, does not conform to the provisions of the European Convention or to the Human Rights Act.[74] Although Parliament may not agree with the opinion of the court, it is binding upon all civil servants, who have a duty to strictly follow all the prescriptions of this Act.[75]

Expansion of the practice of judicial control in the United Kingdom, a Common Law country with an unwritten constitution, is noted by western specialists as is the respective declaration of the English courts, "rather similar to what which happens in democracies with written constitutions securing the rights of citizens against interference from State institutions and officials".[76]

Simultaneously, this is one of the manifestations of the growing similarity between Romano-Germanic law, represented as "democracies with a written constitution"[77] and Anglo-Saxon law in the person of the United Kingdom – a "democracy with an unwritten constitution".

Finally, the strengthening of the similarity of the structure and content of the legal families here considered, in addition to the noted manifestations,

[73] J. Jowell, "Beyond the Rule of Law: Towards Constitutional Judicial Review", *Public Law* (Winter 2000), p. 672.

[74] B. Markesinis (ed.), *The Impact of the Human Rights Bill on English Law* (1999), pp. 21-28.

[75] R. Stevens, "Government and Judiciary", in Bogdanor, note 21 above, pp. 333-365.

[76] Jowell, note 73 above, p. 671.

[77] It should be noted, however, that the institution of judicial supervision over the conformity of acts of Parliament to the constitution in force does not exist in all "democracies" of Romano-Germanic law with a written constitution. In Finland, for example, in the view of specialists there exists only the so-called "quasi-legal institution watching over compliance with the constitution". J. Pöyhönen (ed.), *An Introduction to Finnish Law* (1993), p. 31. Also see §58, Constitution of Finland, in Конституции государств Европейского Союза [Constitutions of States of the European Union] (1999), p. 622.

cannot fail to be seen as a growing universalization and expansion of the sphere of the application of general principles of their structure and functioning.

We refer, in particular, to the principles extended within the framework of the law of the European Union to the Common Law and continental law (the principle of the priority of "law ensuring the existence of the European Union" with respect to national law; the principle of the "legal equality" of provisions contained in the constitutive treaty acts of the European Union) and the "general principles of law of the European Union" (the principle of strict conformity to "primary law" of the European Union consisting of the system of norms contained in the constitutive treaties of the European Union, amendments to them, and other acts of "secondary law" acting as the aggregate of norms contained in the acts emanating from various organs of the European Union).[78]

The importance of these general principles for all member States of the European Union, including the United Kingdom, lies in the fact that they, as specialists confirm, being principles different by their nature and character ("horizontal" and "vertical" institutional principles, "subsidiary", and others),[79] are regarded together with the constitutive treaties and "secondary law" as the "third type of sources of European law"; that they are recognized by the ECJ, the highest judicial instance of the European Union; and that these principles act as rather significant regulators of social relations existing, on one hand, between various institutions of the European Union and, on the other, between European institutions and institutions of members of the European Union.[80]

Together with the general principles arising on a European basis – against the "common field" of Romano-Germanic and Anglo-Saxon law, the growing similarity of these legal families is illustrated by the transformation, or more precisely, the mutual transition in adapted form to new conditions of the principles of one legal family into the other.

The dissemination of a number of principles of "classical precedential law" may serve as one of the examples of this joint process from traditionally Anglo-Saxon law to Romano-Germanic law. We have in view not only principles concerning ordinary, sometimes called "positive" precedent, that is, corresponding to all the canons of the Common Law, but also

[78] T. Hartley, "International Law and the Law of European Union: A Reassessment", *British Year Book of International Law* (2002), pp. 3-19; K. Lenarets and M. Desomer, "Towards a Hierarchy of Legal Acts in the European Union? Simplification of Legal Instruments and Procedures", *European Law Journal*, no. 6 (2005), pp. 745-765.

[79] F. Snyder (ed.), *Europeanisation of Law: The Legal Effects of European Integration* (2000), pp. 83-97.

[80] Ibid., pp. 83-86.

principles of so-called "incorrect", or "wrong" precedent,[81] in accordance with which precedent loses legal force and is not applied, especially in all those instances when "actual social conditions" and the "respective legal principles" have radically changed in comparison with that period when the precedent was formed or when the precedent "on the practical level is recognized to be unworkable".[82]

This is one aspect. Another, as an example of the growing similarity of the legal families here examined from this standpoint, is the more extensive dissemination in Anglo-Saxon law and other legal families together with it of the principle of the "supremacy of law", historically orientated towards the statute as the principal source of Romano-Germanic law and only in part the leading source of Anglo-Saxon law.

In western legal theory and law-application practice the principle of the "rule of law" is in the view of specialists an "integral part of the legal culture of the West" and called upon to the maximum extent to "ensure human rights and defend the individual against the State",[83] has many meanings and interpretations distinguishing one meaning from another.

The Anglo-Saxon "rule of law" and the Romano-Germanic "Rechtsstaat", "État du droit", or "estado de derecho" are not simply a different linguistic expression of the same phenomenon designated in Russian translation as the "dominance of law". These are a different vision of this phenomenon with distinctive nuances of understanding and, respectively, interpretation.[84]

Whereas the Anglo-Saxon understanding and interpretation of the phrase "rule of law" is associated with the supremacy of the Court in the system of State agencies and accordingly the irreproachable legal force of the acts issued by them, the Romano-Germanic version of the "rule of law", the so-called positivist doctrine of the "rule of law", emanates from the sovereignty of parliament and the supremacy of lex.[85]

Traditionally, the Anglo-Saxon treatment of the principle "rule of law" is stressed in the studies of western authors and ultimately reduces to the establishment of a constitutional order under which the "court, and not the

[81] B. Harris, "Final Appellate Courts Overruling Their Own 'Wrong' Precedents: the Ongoing Search for Principle", *Law Quarterly Review*, CXVIII (2002), pp. 408-412.

[82] See Lewis v. AH. General Jamaica (2001). 2 A.C. 50, at p. 89.

[83] M. Kuhne, "Rule of Law Put to the Test: The Case of Judicial Rule-Making by Agreement", *Netherlands International Law Review*, no. 1 (2004), p. 78.

[84] See J. McCormick, "Supranational Challenges to Rule of Law: The Case of the European Union", in D. Dyzenhaus (ed.), *Recrafting the Rule of Law: The Limits of Legal Order* (1999), pp. 267-273.

[85] R. Ekins, "Judicial Supremacy and the Rule of Law", *Law Quarterly Review*, CXIX (2003), pp. 127-151.

legislature, would have the powers of the final, in accordance with other fundamental principles of the Common Law, decision of the question as to what is law and what is not".[86]

However, the traditional Romano-Germanic treatment of the "rule of law" principle appeals to that legal order when the legislature with the "semi-autonomous" status of the national court and its "attitude of respect for the sovereignty of parliament" in the ultimate variant would decide all fundamental questions of law.[87]

At present, as studies indicate, together with the expansion of the sphere of application of precedent and dissemination of a number of principles of classical precedential law to Romano-Germanic law, the counter process is proceeding of the dissemination and adaptation of the Romano-Germanic variant of the "rule of law" to Anglo-Saxon law.[88]

This is shown, *inter alia*, not only by the community of the legal families here considered, but the ever growing approximation as the processes of globalization and regionalization continue, the evolution of these legal families in the direction of their further unification and harmonization.

Other evidence of their approximation exists together with the aforesaid paths and forms of manifestation of the process of convergence of Romano-Germanic and Anglo-Saxon law.

One should point out as such, for example, the intensification of attention in both legal families during the last half-century not only to law-creation and law-application, but also to the interpretation of legal acts.

To be sure, in each legal family as before certain distinctive features of this process are preserved. It is no accident in this connection that it is frequently emphasized with regard to Anglo-Saxon law especially that in the process of interpreting statutes in each country belonging to a particular legal family "the court inevitably must be guided by the principles of the Common Law".[89]

However, at present for both legal families provisions are becoming more common and alike, according to which "law is nothing other than the result (or consequence, or matter) of the interpretation of legal acts";[90] "the

[86] Ekins, ibid., p. 127; also see *The Constitution, Morals and Rights* (1996), pp. 627-630; T. Allan, *Constitutional Justice: A Liberal Theory of the Rule of Law* (2001), pp. 21-25.

[87] See J. Campbell, *The Theory of Ethical Positivism* (1996), pp. 3-18; McCormick, note 84 above, pp. 267-269; Ekins, note 85 above, pp. 146-151.

[88] A. Harding, "Global Doctrine and Local Knowledge: Law in South East Asia", *International and Comparative Law Quarterly*, LI (2002), pp. 35-53.

[89] Bennion, note 38 above, p. 5.

[90] R. Dworkin, "Law As Interpretation", in A. Arnio and D. MacCormick (eds.), *Legal Reasoning* (1992), p. 528.

real legislature is not he who first wrote and adopted a law, but he who construed it"; and so on.[91]

Besides the foregoing, the process of convergence of Romano-Germanic and Anglo-Saxon law is shown in other respects: expansion of the sphere of codified legislation not only in continental, but also in the Common Law; approximation of basic postulates of State-law ideology of the legal families here considered; more extensive use of the branch, and together with it – public law and private law classification of normative material in various legal systems and legal families, and so on.

Each of these and other similar manifestations of the process of convergence of Romano-Germanic and Anglo-Saxon law have great significance for the study of these legal families and therefore requires individual consideration.

[91] R. Coomaraswamy, "Toward an Engaged Judiciary", in *The Role of Judiciary in Plural Societies* (1997), p. 3.

Religious Legal Systems: Features And Classifications

D. V. LUKIANOV*

Religious legal systems are among the most interesting but under-researched phenomena in western legal science. The greatest attention is devoted to religious law as one of the historical forms of law in studies of legal history. The general theoretical, comparative, and branch aspects remain insufficiently examined. The reasons lie in the processes of secularization and the declining role of religion in the life of modern western society, the recognition in the majority of democratic countries of the principle of separation of church from State, the complexity of the subject-matter of research, the inadequacy of objective information for scientific analysis, and sometimes a misunderstanding of the differences in the civilization of societies structured on other principles.

Nonetheless, we believe the view that the influence of religion, and correspondingly of religious law, is declining in the world to be mistaken. During the last thirty years the number of Muslims in the world has tripled. Whereas in 1973 the number of Muslims was about 500 million, this figure has increased to 1.5 billion.[1] Data from The Pew Forum on Religion and Public Life (United States) indicate that 1.57 billion people in the world profess Islam, that is, every fourth inhabitant of this Planet is Muslim.[2] These trends extend to western countries. Sociologists in Europe say there are 38 million Muslims. The largest number of people in Europe who profess Islam are in Russia – 16 million. About six million live in France; four million in Germany, two million in the United Kingdom, and one

* кандидат юридических наук, Docent, Head of Section for Planning and Coordinating Legal Research, National Academy of Legal Sciences of Ukraine; Docent, Chair of Theory of State and Law, Yaroslav the Wise National Legal Academy of Ukraine (Kharkov).

1 Europe will become Muslim in 50 Years // www.islam.az/modules/sections/index

2 See ukrbiznes.com/news/education/61807.

million in Italy, Spain, and the Netherlands. There are approximately 7 million in the United States.

Ignoring the interests of such a numerous social group in Europe is impossible. The lack of theoretical studies leads in practice to numerous socio-cultural and legal conflicts. Among the conflicts are those relating to wearing the hijab and the paranja, the images and caricatures of the Prophet Mohammed, demands of Muslims that the shariat court be legalized, and others. The initiative of the Archbishop of Canterburgy, Rowan Williams, testifies to the seriousness of the problem, an initiative later supported by the Prime Minister of the United Kingdom, who declared that the introduction of certain norms of the shariat into British legislation is inevitable.

The number of adherents to other world religions also is growing, albeit at a slower rate. The number of Christians in the world exceeded two billion persons, and the number of adherents to Judaism – one billion.[3] The total number of believers of the three largest world religions is 4.5 billion persons of the nearly 7 billion inhabitants of the earth.

Thus, under conditions of world globalization and the increased number of persons in all western countries professing various religions, the need is growing to investigate their distinctive features, including religious legal systems and the correlation between them and with national legal systems of individual States.

RELIGIOUS SYSTEMS ON THE LEGAL MAP OF THE WORLD

Before passing on to an analysis of religious legal systems, it is essential to determine what the legal map of the modern world looks like, what legal systems comprise it.

The distinctive features and types of various legal systems have not received sufficient illumination in science. The most widely-shared approach is that all legal systems are national ones, and the entire legal map of the modern world is defined as the aggregate of these national systems. However, this approach is an unjustified simplification of the diversity of legal systems. Even David noted that in the modern world each State has its own law, but it happens that several competing legal systems sometimes operate in a single country. Non-State communities may also have their own law, and international law exists separately.

No doubt national legal systems are the most numerous in the world. There are 192 members of the United Nations at present (only the Vatican is not a United Nations member among the generally-recognized States),

[3] Major Religions of the World Ranked by Number of Adherents // www.adherents.com

each of which has its own legal system. However, one must bear in mind the so-called unrecognized or partially recognized States (Taiwan, Northern Cyprus, and others, more than ten in total). These formations actually have all the features of a State, including their own national legal system, although they are not recognized by the international community. Some territories may be temporarily dependent on other States or international organizations (so-called territories with a transitional legal regime). There are now more than twenty non-autonomous territories under the external administration of the United Kingdom, United States, France, and New Zealand. The Palestine National Autonomy is a clear example of a territory with a transitional regime. All these territories, although not having sovereignty, have their own national legal systems.[4]

An interesting phenomenon is the existence in some countries of several legal systems which coexist within a single national system but are sufficiently autonomous to be considered as individual legal systems. A typical example is the structure of the legal system of the United States, where within a unified federal system there are the legal systems of fifty states. In individual instances they may be structured on different principles (for example, the legal system of Quebec in Canada, Scotland in the United Kingdom). To distinguish them from national legal systems we propose to call them sub-national legal systems in the present article. Thus, there exist more than 200 national and sub-national legal systems in the modern world.

Furthermore, national legal systems exist which extend to the social systems of several States. Some of the sub-types are inter-State legal systems formed by individual States according to international agreements – for example, the legal system of the European Union.

The existence of religious legal systems which also have a supranational character and enormous number of distinctive features is a separate legal phenomenon that remains largely untouched by western legal science. On the legal map of the world it is essential to differentiate national, sub-national, and supranational (international and religious) legal systems that exist and compete with one another.

CLASSIFICATION OF LEGAL SYSTEMS

The investigation and comparison of such a multi-tiered phenomenon as a legal system on a world scale is a complex undertaking. Classification is

[4] V. V. Oksamytnyi, "Legal Systems of the Modern World: Problems of Identification", *The Journal of Comparative Law*, V (2010), p. 41-64.

used to make diverse legal systems more accessible for scientific analysis and to determine their place among other legal systems. The system of distributing subject-matter, phenomena, or concepts into classes, groups, and so on pursuant to common indicia or properties is called classification. However, certain Ukrainian comparatists (O. F. Skakun, L. A. Luts) suggest that, together with classification, the methodological potential of typologies be used. The majority of investigators, though, do not distinguish between classification and typologies as individual means of scientific research.

The history of the classification of legal systems dates back more than a century. The problem of the classification of legal systems was defined as one of the priority orientations for comparative studies at the First International Congress of Comparative Law held in 1900 at Paris. The conference participants had no precise concept of the methods for classifying legal systems and acted mostly through intuition; singling out the French, German, Anglo-American, Slavic, and Muslim legal families. Georges Sauser-Hall (1884-1966) suggested, using the nationality criterion, that the following families be singled out: Indo-European, Semitic, Mongol, and the law of uncivilized peoples.[5] During the 50th anniversary of the French society of comparative law in 1919, the participants limited the classification to three families: French, Anglo-American, and Muslim.[6]

During the second half of the twentieth century, two principal orientations in the classification of legal systems enjoyed wide currency. The first was embodied in David's classification, which suggested the notion of a trichotomy – the three principal legal families: Anglo-American, Romano-Germanic, and socialist on the basis of two criteria – legal technique and similarity of philosophical, political, and economic principles. All other legal systems he combined under the name "other types of social system and law", among which were Muslim, Hindu, and Judaic law, as well as the legal systems of Africa and the Far East.[7]

The representatives of the second orientation, Zweigert and Kötz, added to the classification of Arminjon, Nolde, and Wolff by suggesting "legal style" as a criterion for classification, consisting of five factors: origin and evolution of legal systems, distinctiveness of legal thought, specific legal institutes, nature of sources of law and the means of interpreting them, and ideological factors. On this basis they singled out eight legal families:

5 K. Zweigert and H. Kötz, *Introduction to Comparative Law*, transl. Tony Weir (3d ed.; 1998).
6 A.Kh. Saidov, *Comparative Law*, transl. W. E. Butler (2003).
7 R. David and C. Jauffret-Spinosi, Основные правовые системы современности [Major Legal Systems of the World], transl. V. A. Tumanov (1999), p. 25.

Romano, Germanic, Anglo-American, socialist, Scandinavian, Far Eastern, Islamic, and Hindu.[8]

Modern Russian and Ukrainian authors also use these basic classifications to some extent. Tikhomirov distinguishes between the continental (Romano-Germanic) legal family, the Common Law family, the socialist legal family, the family of a moral-religious orientation, and also northern European and Latin American law and nomadic legal families.[9] Saidov identifies the following legal families: Common Law, Romano-Germanic, Scandinavian, Latin American, socialist, Muslim, Hindu, customary (African), and Far Eastern.[10] Marchenko investigates the two more widespread and "influential" legal families – Anglo-Saxon and Romano-Germanic, together with the socialist and post-socialist, Judaic, and Muslim.[11]

Skakun points to the following types (or families) of legal systems: Romano-Germanic, Anglo-American, mixed, religious, traditional, and socialist.[12] Zaichuk and Onishchenko examine the Romano-Germannic, Anglo-Saxon, socialist, and family of traditional law.[13] Luts distinguishes among the following types of modern legal systems: Romano-Germanic, Anglo-American, mixed (with sub-types: dualist: Scandinavian and Latin American; religious-community: Muslim, Hindu; traditional philosophical: Japanese, Chinese, customary-community.[14] Bekhruz considers the Romano-Germanic, Anglo-American, Far Eastern, and customary law families, and individual legal systems: Muslim, Hindu, and post-Soviet.[15]

The central issue for any classification is the criteria it uses to make determinations. Throughout the development of comparative law: the role of sources of law (Levy-Ullman), nationality (Sauser-Hall), the content of law (Arminjon, Nolde, and Wolff), the specific features of production relations (Eörsi), ideological and technical legal criteria (David), legal style (Zweigert), and so on.

[8] K. Zweigert and H. Kötz, Введение в сравнительное правоведение в сфере частного права [Introduction to Comparative Law in the Sphere of Private Law] (1998), I, p. 117.

[9] Iu. A. Tikhomirov, Курс сравнительного правоведения [Cours of Comparative Law] (1996), pp. 112-140.

[10] Saidov, *Comparative Law*, transl. W. E. Butler (2003).

[11] M. N. Marchenko, Правовые системы современного мира [Legal Systems of the Modern World] (2008).

[12] O. F. Skakun, Теорія держави і права [Theory of State and Law (Encyclopedic Cours)] (Kharkov, 2006), pp. 310-312.

[13] O. V. Zaichuk and N. N. Onishchenko (eds.), Теорія держави і права: Академічний курс [Theory of State and Law. Academic Cours] (2006), pp. 567-609.

[14] L. A. Luts, Типологізація сучасних правових систем світу [Typologies of Modern Legal Systems of the World] (2007), p. 12.

[15] Kh. Bekhruz, Вступ до порівняльного правознавства [Introduction to Comparative Law] (Odessa, 2002).

Comparatists so far have not agreed with regard to many issues of classifying legal systems: whether it is essential to use only legal criteria or possibly others; should there be one or several criteria; should the criteria have an objective nature or is the subjective approach of the comparatist possible?

Having regard to the fact that legal systems that are being classified, in this author's view the legal criteria for classification should be the principal ones. A legal system is a complex formation consisting of many elements which need to be analyzed in order to determine which of them may criteria for classification. The primary element of any legal system is law, around which all other elements of the system are formed. Therefore, sometimes they even determine that law exists, is formed and functions in the form of a legal system.[16] But this is far from a unified structural component. All legal phenomena of a certain society relate to its structure: legislation, legal institutions, legal practice, realization of law, application of law, rights, freedoms, and duties of citizens, legal relations, legal culture, legality and legal order, and so on.

For the convenience of analysis, all elements of a legal system are grouped into several sub-systems:

1. institutional components: aggregate of all subjects of law (individual and collective, State and non-State);
2. normative components: aggregate of principles and norms of law which regulate relations between subjects of law, rules of law-creation, and system of recognized sources of law;
3. ideological components: aggregate of views on law and other legal phenomena which are divided into legal psychology, legal ideology, and legal culture;
4. functional components: process of the realization of law and law-application, judicial and other legal practice.

Are all these elements of a legal system of equal significance? May any of them be a criterion for the classification of legal systems? In our view a simple classification may be structured on any of the elements of the legal system. Taking into account that the classification is a logical and relational process, the criteria may change depending upon the aims of the researcher. Saidov writes on this occasion that geographic spheres may underlie a classification; it may have a historical (diachronic) or logical (synchronic) nature; it may be conducted at the level of the entire legal system or individual domains of law. Hence the possibility in principle

[16] Tikhomirov, Курс сравнительного правоведения [Cours of Comparative Law] (1996), p. 5.

of multiple classifications structured on the basis of various criteria and for various purposes.[17] Various classifications do not exclude one another, but reinforce, assist in investigating more soundly the similarities and differences between legal systems. This is especially vital under conditions of the convergence of legal systems, which is actively underway in the world.[18]

Can any group of legal systems be considered to be a family? We believe that the division into legal families is a special process of distributing legal systems on the basis not of any criteria, but only the most important and significant. Thus we refer to the organization of legal systems by typologies and determine the basic and most widespread types.

The methodology of selecting elements of a legal system as criteria for classification may be an evaluation of their influence on the development of the entire system, and investigation of their mutual linkage from the standpoint of "cause – consequence". In our view the ideological component – legal consciousness and legal culture of society – should become the principal criteria for typologies classifying legal systems into legal families. The primacy of legal consciousness over all other elements of the legal system is stressed by many legal philosophers. Maksimov characterizes legal consciousness as the most important element of legal reality.[19] In Ilin's view, legal consciousness is a necessary element of the genesis, functioning, and development of law present in the processes of the creation, application, and compliance with law. It is a direct source of the legal order and all legal phenomena.[20]

Law as a social phenomenon is thus a consequence of the forming of a certain legal consciousness in society. Legal ideology and legal psychology both play an important role at the same time. The form of all other phenomena of a legal system – legal norms and the system thereof, sources of law, distinctive features of law-application, and so on are a consequence of the determined legal consciousness of society. However, the application of such a complex and multi-faceted phenomenon as the criterion for classification may give rise to certain complexities during

[17] Saidov, *Comparative Law*, transl. W. E. Butler (2003).

[18] See M. N. Marchenko, Конвергенция романо-германского и англо-американского права [Convergence of Romano-Germanic and Anglo-American Law] (Kiev, 2007).

[19] S. I. Maksimov, Правовая реальность: опыт философского осмысления [Legal Reality: Attempt at Philosophical Speculation] (Kharkov, 2002), p. 253.

[20] I. A. Ilin, Путь к очевидности [Path to the Obvious] (1993), p. 247; also see Ilin, «О сущности правосознания» [On the Essence of Legal Consciousness], in id, Общее учение о праве и государстве [General Doctrine on State and Law] (2006), pp. 180-508. Ilin's thought is belatedly becoming accessible to the English reader. See his capital work: Ilin, *The Philosophy of Hegel as a Doctrine of the Concreteness of God and Humanity*, transl. P. T. Grier (2010-2011). 2 vols.

the research. Therefore, in some instances other additional criteria may be used which, on one hand, should clearly reflect the specific nature of legal consciousness of a particular society and, on the other, be simple, instrumental, and convenient for comparison. One of the most convenient criteria on this place is sources of law. Marchenko stressed that the specific nature of the understanding of law in various legal systems is reflected in significance measure in the sources of law.[21]

Another issue on which there is no unanimity among comparatists is whether extra-legal factors can be criteria for classifying legal families? Among the first to substantiate this need using the example of the socialist family was David. He wrote that Soviet law undoubtedly has similarities with the Romanist system on the basis of legal indicia: terminology, structure, conception of norms of law, and so on. But to cross the boundary into a socialist State was to enter a new world where such questions as democracy, elections, parliament, trade union, ownership, contract, and arbitration acquire a different content. The reasons for this he rightly considered to be entirely different philosophical, political, and economic reasons underlying a socialist society. The legal system is a subsystem of the social system, side by side with other subsystems thereof – political, economic, religious, and others which exert a material external impact upon its development. Therefore phenomena nonlegal in essence may be important additional criteria for the classification of legal systems into families.

Each of the aforesaid classifications (or typologies) is not perfected, including the classification of such under-researched legal systems as religious and traditional. First, the said classifications are incomplete since they do not encompass all legal systems. David himself observed that his trichotomy embraced only one-fifth of the planet. Only two systems of religious law were investigated: Muslim (Islam) and Hindu – far from a complete list of legal systems of a religious type. Second, sometimes legal systems are combined which have nothing in common or even have opposite feature. We have in mind the widespread unification into a single classification of legal systems of the religious and traditional types. Third, the aforesaid classifications defy logic: one cannot consider individual religious systems, for example, Muslim law, as a legal family – they do not combine different legal systems.

Together with the generally-recognized families of Romano-Germanic and Anglo-American law one must separate out two additional individual families (or types) – religious and traditional law. The principal criteria for

[21] Marchenko, Источники права [Sources of Law] (2005), p. 13.

separating each type are the material distinctions in their understanding of law by following rather precisely the distinctions with regard to an instrumental criterion – sources of law.

We have consequently single out four legal families: Romano-Germanic, Anglo-American, religious, and traditional which represent four universal types of law and encompass the entire legal map of the modern world. All legal systems of certain States, State-similar formations, or other social subjects are formed under the influence of one of the principal types or law or combinations thereof.

DISTINCTIVE FEATURES OF RELIGIOUS LEGAL SYSTEMS

In our view, four legal systems may be classified as a religious legal family: Muslim, Hindu, Judaic, and Canon law. The legal systems of the religious type have been combined by us into a single legal family through the ascertainment of the following common features:

Inextricable link with religion. Each legal system within this legal family is part of a certain religion – Islam, Hinduism, Judaism, Christianity. The norms of law are based on religious conceptions and beliefs, as a consequence of which legal and religious norms are closely intertwined and often coincide. In these systems there is no sharp differentiation of norms of law from other social norms, especially religious. This correlation of law and religion is pre-determined by several factors. First, the common origin and coincidence of the sources of law and sources of religion. Divine revelation is the source of law and religion respectively according to the fundamental principles of the faith. Religious tenets which determine the relationship of man to God are simultaneously legal and religious norms.

Second, the strict duty of a person to adhere not only to religious prescriptions, but to legal laws since their violation is no less than a grave sin arises from the unity of religious and legal norms. Third, law and religion are unified by a single system for the application of all norms. The same organs and persons who decide issues relating to religious relations also decide issues connected with legal relations – property disputes, labor relations, conflicts relating to purchase and sale, and so on. Religious law claims, unlike secular, the role of universal regulator of all social relations.

Perception of law as result of Divine Revelation and not as consequence of rational activity of man and State. In accordance with the theo-centric concept of the world, the will of God is always the source of law which determined the boundaries of the permissible and the prohibited, the rights and duties of all subjects. For example, according to Islam, the Koran – the holy book of Muslims – was given by Allah to mankind through the Prophet Mohammed. Law is granted once and forever, and therefore the task of man in such a system is merely to correctly be conscious of and interpret divine norms. No single person, no social groups, and not the State may claim the role of law-creator. In this aspect religious legal systems are formed on an absolutely opposite principle in comparison with western legal systems – the Romano-Germanic and Anglo-American, which recognize the law of only one of the existing social institutes which arises and develops under the influence of objective laws of societal development and the State.

The reasonableness and rationality are deemed by man to be obligatory requirements for norms of law in western society. If one assesses reality, and not church dogmas, it must be acknowledged that the content of the norms of religious law has changed in the course of history. This happened primarily by means of a new interpretation of sacred texts by religious figures. Nonetheless, such religions, both Christianity and Judaism, have acknowledged their right to create new norms of law provided that these are not contrary to the principles of the respective faith.

Personal character of the operation of law. This means that law based on religion extends its operation not to a determined territory, but individually to a specific religious community. This is one of the cardinal distinctions between religious and national systems of law, the last extending their operation on the territorial principle to all persons within the boundaries of a State and extraterritorially to their citizens beyond the limits of the State. Religious legal systems extend their operation only to persons who profess a specific religion irrespective of where they live territorially. This leads to a competition of norms of national and religious law and sometimes to conflicts between them. The effort to convict an emigrant from Morocco on the territory of Spain by nonlegal shariat court for extramarital relations, which are prohibited by Muslim law, is well-known.[22] If a person repudiates his religion, he leaves the sphere of operation of this legal system, that is, the law does not extend to nonbelievers and atheists.

Recognition of social value of law. In all religions the idea of a law pleasing to God is present. It is deemed to be an essential element of a just social structure. David noted that two types of principles exist by which nonwestern countries are guided. One recognized the great value of law, but law itself is understood differently from the west, whereas others cast aside the very idea of law and believe that social relations should be regulated by other means. The first group embraces countries of the

[22] www.cripo.com.ua

Muslim, Hindu, and Judaic law; the second group includes countries of the Far East, Africa, and Madagascar.[23]

This is one of the principal features which precludes combining within a single family the religious and traditional legal systems. For comparison we take the views of the founder of the principal philosophical doctrine of China – Confucius – who reacted with distrust to the idea of regulating social relations with the use of law and of laws: "If the people are to be guided with the assistance of laws and maintain order with the assistance of punishments, the people will seek to evade and will not experience shame. If the people are to be guided with the assistance of good deeds and maintain order with the assistance of ritual, the people will know shame and reform themselves".[24]

Confucianism did not approve of the judicial protection of the subjective rights of citizens. For ethical considerations, even if some interest of a person was affected, this did not give to him the moral right to apply at once to a court. A civic-minded citizen should autonomously choose to settle a conflict by means of compromises and partial concessions. He who applied to a court or publicly accused another was considered to be a person not properly brought up, lacking modesty and readiness to seek reconciliation in the interests of social peace.

Nonrecognition of principle of formal equality of human rights. Unlike western legal systems, for example, the Romano-Germanic and Anglo-American, in which this principle is recognized to be universal, religious legal systems endow a person with a different legal status – rights and duties depend upon affiliation to a specific group distinguished according to various criteria – gender, nationality, religion, or social. The classical example is the caste distinctions in India which are recognized and protected by Hindu law. The caste is characterized as a social community or group within Indian society, a community by birth, succession, endogamy, closed to outsiders, which traditionally is specialized according to nature of economic activity or group of occupations with a clearly expressed caste consciousness whose place is stipulated in a complex Indian social hierarchy.[25]

Relations within a caste and with members of other castes are regulated by social norms of behavior. Respectively they are divided into four groups by historical tradition: Brahmins (initially the caste of the clergy), Kshatriya (warriors), Vastriya (merchants), and Huiti (servants and artisans). Outside

[23] David and Jauffret-Spinosi, Основные правовые системы современности [Major Legal Systems of the World], transl. V. A. Tumanov (1999), p. 25.
[24] Ibid.
[25] M. K. Kudriavtsev, Кастовая система в Индии [Caste System in India] (1992), p. 4.

this division is the caste of "untouchables" who occupied the lowest place in the social hierarchy. It is actually outside the sphere of regulation of Hindu law, which affects the system only on matters of limitation of legal capacity. Transition from one caste to another is not permitted. A sharp hierarchical order was established between the castes. The principle of the purity of the caste, on the degree of which depended its place in the hierarchy, was the basis thereof. The purity of a caste should remain unsullied, and therefore contacts should never be established with members of lower castes.

Numerous norms were elaborated on the basis of this principle, which prohibited marriage with members of lower castes or to take food in their presence and even to approach them.[26] These norms were applied by the courts of India until 1949. For example, a court deemed a marriage between representatives of different castes to be invalid, and the children born of such a marriage to be illegitimate. According to the 1950 Constitution of India, all legislative norms were abolished by which affiliation to castes had respective legal consequences for their members. Despite attempts of the State to change the rules of behavior in this sphere, the majority of Hindus – primarily village inhabitants (who represent 80% of the population) – continue to live while adhering to the ancient principles of caste division.

Prohibitions, duties, and sanctions for nonperformance predominate in the system of religious norms. In all religious systems primacy is accorded to prohibitive norms and obligations to those who are empowered. The relationship of members of a religious community to God and to the laws and teachings thereof, to religious rituals, to the State, social institutions, and to other members of the community and nonbelievers is so consolidated. For example, in emphasizing attention to this feature, an Israeli scholar described Judaic law as a complex of all-encompassing duties which regulate all aspects of Jewish life.[27]

The religious legal duties consolidated in Muslim law order the believer to perform actions determined to be appropriate from the standpoint of Islam and refrain from those not appropriate. The Koran, for example, prescribed that a Muslim be sensitive to the helpless and weak, honorably enter into commercial matters, not bribe a judge, not engage in usury, and not gamble. For a violation of many norms of religious law punishments are provided for at once, and sometimes rather severe ones – death penalty, amputation, beating with rods, and so on. For example, for theft the Koran prescribes the cutting off of hands. Subjective rights of the individual,

[26] Zweigert and Kötz, Введение в сравнительное правоведение в сфере частного права [Introduction to Comparative Law in the Sphere of Private Law] (1998), I, p. 462-463.
[27] Z. Falk, "Jewish Law", in J. D. M. Derrett, *Introduction to Legal Systems* (1968), p. 28.

unlike in western legal systems, have not found extensive consolidation in religious law.

TRADITIONAL LEGAL SYSTEMS

A traditional legal system combines two sub-types of legal systems – the States of the Far East and the countries of Africa. To the Far Eastern subsystem belong the legal systems of China and Japan, as well as certain other countries which developed under their influence – Mongolia, Korea, Malaysia, Indonesia, Myanmar (before 1989, Burma). More than forty States belong to the second subsystem, located on the African continent, and Madagascar. The traditional legal systems are a phenomenon absolutely dissimilar from the religious systems, and therefore combined by us into a separate legal family by reason of the following distinctive features.

Custom as leading source of law. Unlike the legal systems of the west which have acknowledged the leading role of the State in the creation of norms of law (by legislative or judicial activity) and religious systems, priority is accorded to society itself in forming norms of law in traditional legal systems. For many centuries norms of customary law based on traditions and moral and ethical conceptions of the people are the foundation of legal regulation in these countries. Custom, which is a rule of behavior that became habitual as a consequence of repeated application over an extended period of time, regulated virtually all aspects of the life of society.

Negative attitude towards legislation. Legislation as a source of law was considered to be a phenomenon unnatural for society. The negative attitude of the population towards legislative law, formed over many centuries, served as the cause of future consequences. In the twentieth century, after the extensive reception of western law and a significant turn in the development of legislation and codification, the situation arose when a large portion of the population constantly continued to ignore these norms of law. Real social relations, just as previously, were regulated on the basis of traditional norms.

Ignoring of State structures in the process of realizing norms of law. The recognition of customary law and ignoring of legislative law is responsible for distinctive features in the process of implementing norms of law, especially in the consideration of legal disputes. For centuries these norms were secured for the most part not by State structures, including courts, but by self-governing social structures and social pressure on offenders. People avoided turning to courts for the protection of their rights. The great majority of disputes were decided in the process of conciliation procedures through the mediation of respected members of society on the basis of customary law norms.

Weak development of legal infrastructure. For hundreds of years these countries had no legal professions – judges, procurators, advokats, notaries, and so on, since educational institutions did not exist for their training, nor legal science, nor law schools, nor outstanding legal scholars who had a command of legal knowledge.

CONCLUSIONS

The number of members of the three great world religions has grown significantly during the past century. Changes in the social structure of the leading States of the world make reforms inevitable in the legal sphere. Ignoring the necessity of reform is fraught with social tension and numerous conflicts on ideological and religious grounds. The world processes of globalization affecting the legal sphere are leading to a gradual convergence of the principal legal systems and the mutual penetration of individual norms, institutions, and branches of law belonging to different legal systems.

As a result of the typologization on the basis of the criteria proposed by us, four legal families – Romano-Germanic, Anglo-American, religious, and traditional represent four universal types of law and encompass the entire legal map of the contemporary world. All legal systems of determined States, State-similar formations, or other social subjects have been formed under the influence of one of these basic types of law or combination thereof.

Religious legal systems act as a separate legal phenomenon on the legal map of the world and are relegated to the category of supranational legal systems. The widely-accepted combining of religious and traditional legal systems into a single legal family is erroneous. A comparative analysis of their characteristic indicia shows that there are significantly more material distinctions between them than similarities. The combining of religious legal systems – Muslim, Hindu, Judaic, and canon law – into a single legal family on the basis of the commonality of their major characteristics, as argued here, is the correct approach.

Canon Law in the Modern Legal System of Society

A. S. SMYKALIN* AND V. P. MOTREVICH**

The new political realities of today require a reconsideration of an important system – the spiritual-cultural. Under Soviet power the church was subjected to legal discrimination and deprived of the rights of a juridical person. Consequently, church organizations could not be subjects of civil-law relations. The church was separate from the State, and school from church. The law faculties ceased the teaching of canon law.

As a result, there occurred the artificial separation of an entire branch of legislation from the legal system of society. It continued thus for seventy long years. The exclusion of the course of Canon Law from the instructional syllabi of institutions of higher legal education led to paradoxes. In studying the monuments of medieval Russian legislation, for example, the Russkaia Pravda, we do not find a single article establishing responsibility for sexual crimes since they all were addressed in the Kormchaia kniga [Book of the Pilot]. Norms of Canon Law were never studied in Soviet institutions of higher legal education. And this is typical for subsequent Russian legislation.

It seems the situation may be changing. But gaps and conflicts exist in modern Russian legislation in the relations between church and State which lead to undesirable exacerbations between secular and church authorities. An ignorance is evident of Canon Law, which represents an entire cultural stratum in the history of Russia and has a specific normative base.

The authority of the church has grown in the new democratic State – the Russian Federation – although the principle of the separation of church and

* доктор юридических наук, профессор. Head of the Chair of History of State and Law, Urals State Legal Academy (Ekaterinburg)

** доктор исторических наук, профессор. Chair of History of State and Law, Urals State Legal Academy

State has been retained (Article 14, 1993 Russian Constitution). Now the church is not only a central for the spiritual renaissance of the nation, but actively takes part in social life and, willy-nilly, even a convinced atheist has to take this into account.

A number of important laws have been adopted in the last decade concerning the spiritual-cultural sphere of society. Among them: federal laws on counteracting extremist activity (2002);[1] on alternative civilian service (2002);[2] on objects of cultural heritage (or monuments of the history of culture) of peoples of the Russian Federation (2002).[3] Amendments were made to the labor,[4] land,[5] and tax codes.[6] Requests of religious organizations and citizens were taken into account to ensure freedom of conscience n other codes: penal, criminal, and administrative legislation. All this testifies that a profound rethinking is underway of the rights to freedom of conscience. Therefore, the study of such an important branch of the modern legal system of society, as is Canon Law, is essential.

Legal science (jurisprudence) is the aggregate of constitutional and legal sciences which differ from one another in degree of abstraction and specialization. The principal content of jurisprudence by volume and orientation forms specific, special legal sciences devoted to individual branches of law, elements or aspects of the State, political system of society (civil law, criminal law, theory of State administration, doctrines on political parties, and others). This definition is uncontested. But in order to analyze this matter scrupulously and in detail, a historical excursus made be undertaken into the not so remote past of the Russian State.

Before 1917 virtually all law faculties of universities offered a course on Russian Canon Law. Suffice it to say that of the eleven law faculties of universities, it was offered at ten. The course was given by historians of law, jurists, theologians, and secular professors. Among them were noted scholars such as M. F. Vladimirskii-Budanov (1838-1916), V. O. Kliuchevskii (1841-1911), V. N. Latkin (1858-1927), A. S. Pavlov, N. S. Suvorov (1848-1909), and others. From 1917 to 1940 this course was not offered in the historical and legal institutions of higher education. Only in 1940 did S. V. Iushkov's (1888-1952) textbook appear (also a former historian of Canon Law) under the title История государства и права [History of State and Law of the USSR]; it went through several editions.

1 СЗ РФ (2002), no. 30, item 3031, as amended.
2 СЗ РФ (2002), no. 30, item 3030, as amended.
3 СЗ РФ (2002), no. 26, item 2519, as amended.
4 W. E. Butler (ed. & transl.), *Labour Code of the Russian Federation* (London, 2002).
5 W. E. Butler (ed. & transl.), *Russia & The Republics: Legal Materials* (looseleaf service; 2006-).
6 W. E. Butler (ed. & transl.), *Tax Code of the Russian Federation* (Moscow, 2004).

Iushkov undoubtedly understood that it was impossible to transmit the entire history of the State and law of peoples who previously inhabited the territory of the USSR by excluding such an important section as "Russian Canon Law", that is, to separate "blood from the flesh". Therefore, using various means (for example, not referring to books of canon laws), he succeeded in relating on the pages of his textbook marriage and family relations, sexual crimes, religious and secular principles of criminal law norms, and other issues regulated by the church.

Under conditions of Bolshevist propaganda and open persecution of the church, this was not entirely safe. And Iushkov more than once was criticized for his textbook, being labeled in February 1958 a "liberal kadet" on the pages of *Литературная газета* [Literary Newspaper]. Subsequent textbooks on the history of Russian State and law omitted a section on Russian Canon Law. Such an important stratum of the history of the development of society encompassing marriage and family relations and some civil-law and criminal-law relations as Russian Canon Law was excluded from the general history of the Russian State.

And today too church or canon law is not studied as part of Russian jurisprudence. In the nineteenth and twentieth centuries it was studied in the law faculties not only in Russia, but also in Europe. The outstanding cleric and Metropolitan of Moscow, Platon (Levshin) (1737-1812), was behind the origins of the course "Canon Law" in Russia. In 1776 he gave an Instruction to the Moscow Slavonic-Graeco-Latin Theological Academy to read and gloss the Kormchaia kniga [Book of the Pilot] – one of the sources of Canon Law.[7]

Canon law in 1835 began to be taught in law faculties. In that period it was called church jurisprudence. The new University Statute adopted in 1863 furthered the development of canon law as an instructional discipline. Special chairs emerged in law faculties, and the teaching was moved from the theological to the legal stratum. As Varias noted: "... This gave an impulse to the emergence of fundamental studies in virtually all the basic sections of canon law. The training of new scientific cadres capable of investigating church and legal phenomena not only from a theological or historical, but primarily from a legal point of view became urgent".[8]

At the turn of the nineteenth and twentieth centuries, the first textbooks and systematic treatises appeared.[9] The coming of the Bolsheviks to power

[7] M. Varias, «Церковное право (исторический очерк)» [Canon Law (Historical Survey)], Российская юстиция [Russian Justice], no. 8 (1997).

[8] Ibid.

[9] See N. S. Suvorov, Курс церковного права [Cours of Canon Law] (Iaroslavl, 1889-1890). 2 vols.; A. S. Pavlov, Курс церковного права [Cours of Canon Law] (Sergiev Posad, 1902);

and persecutions of the church slowed down the studies of canon law. In accordance with Marxist-Leninist postulates about the separation of church from State and of school from church, the teaching of canon law in secular educational institutions was terminated.

In the early 1920s canon law studies moved to the west. The Russian Law Faculty was created in Prague, where canon law was taught by Professors S. N. Bulgakov (1871-1944) and G. V. Florovskii (1893-1979). Later a similar educational institution for Russian clergy opened in Paris.

Only in the early postwar years was the teaching of canon law renewed at the Moscow Theological Academy. The Professor of Theology, Archpriest Vladislav Tsypin, has done much to contribute to and develop canon law. In 1992 he published the first course of lectures in this discipline for more than eighty years. His work on canon law has since been republished several times. Interest in this rarity was such that despite a large print-run, the textbook was sold out within several days. A great service of the author is that he uses the works of the classics of legal thought and for the first time addresses the concept of the subject-matter, the method of the treatise, and the relations with other branches of law in the general system of legal norms.

CANON LAW AS A BRANCH OF LAW

A controversial issues presently exists in legal science. Is canon law an autonomous branch of law or not? If yes, such place should it occupy in the system of other branches of law. Also controversial is the question of its classification under the principle of the distinction between private and public law used in secular legislation. The view that canon law is a branch of private law is most widely accepted.

In defense of this position it is said that religion is a matter of conscience, a private affair, and not a State duty. But private law regulates the relations of private persons. In confirmation one may cite the Federal Law of 26 September 1997 "On the Freedom of Conscience and on Religious Associations", where it is noted that the State shall not interfere in the determination by a citizen of his attitude towards religion and religious affiliation" (Article 4).[10]

An analysis of the 1993 Russian Constitution (Article 28) also enables one to conclude that issues of religion are the personal affair of each citizen, a matter of conscience for each. However, not all students of canon law

I. S. Berdnikov, Краткий курс церковного права [Concise Cours of Canon Law] (Kazan, 1903). 2 vols.

10 Transl. in W. E. Butler, *Russian Public Law* (2d ed.; 2009), pp. 122-137.

share this position. Opponents refer to the historical situation. In Ancient Rome, for example, religion was identified with State interests. Roman emperors believed it their duty to support religion. They looked after the state of temples, established the calendar of holidays, and distributed funds for the maintenance of heathen priests.

The trend in the direction of canon law and the law of the State growing persisted in the Byzantine era. The entire history of the Russian State testifies to the continuation of this trend. Russian monarchs were not inclined to be in opposition to the church and were forced to support it, understanding that religion is the sole solidifying foundation of society. Therefore, proponents of singling out canon law as a branch of public law advanced as an argument that the aggregate externally of canon norms depended upon the will of State power and fell within the system of civil law.

There was a third, centrist, view. A number of authors believe that canon law cannot be relegated to either private or public law. As an example they cite the catholic West. The initial treatment assumed basic laws binding upon the Universal Church; the second, legislative acts operating in local churches.[11] We share this view and believe that Canon Law is an autonomous branch of law within the system of legal norms having its own specific object.

Historical sources also point to the legal norms of Canon Law. In one of the books of the Pentateuch, where there is yet no division into civil, family, and criminal law, a detailed list is given of acts considered to be a crime by the ancient Jews and the punishments provided for these crimes.

Crime: a violation of religious prohibitions. Punishment: death.

Crime: intentional homicide, theft of a fellow tribesman and sale thereof into slavery; beating of father or mother; backbiting against father or mother; failure to watch over an ox given to butting if this entailed the death of a person. Punishment for crimes in this section has the clearly expressed nature of blood vengeance; however, at the wish of the relatives the victim may pay a fine.

Crime: sorcery; bestiality; worshipping other gods; profanement of the Sabbath; adultery; sodomy; and incest; rape of a betrothed maiden; causing bodily injury. Punishment: maiming (causing of equal bodily injury, principle of "eye for an eye, tooth for a tooth"); beating with rods of not more than 40 blows; cutting off the hands of a women who seized a male by the sexual organ.

[11] S. Potanina, «Церковное право – самостоятельная отрасль права» [Canon Law – Autonomous Branch of Law], Российская юстиция [Russian Justice], no. 12 (1999).

Crime: evasion from worshipping in the temple; crimes against morality. Punishment: exile.

Crime: causing temporary injury, murder of a slave; beating a pregnant woman which entail a miscarriage; maiming caused to another's slave (for maiming by the master of his own slave the last is subject to being released). Punishment: fine.

Crime: death of a slave from an animal given to butting; perishing of another's animal from failure to supervise during the construction of a house; perishing of another's domestic animal through the fault of an animal given to butting; theft of livestock; theft of property; damaging of crops; burning of crops; seduction and rape of maiden not betrothed; false testimony. Punishment: sale as a slave.

It should be noted that even in those days such concepts as intent, negligence, and neglect were used and had legal significance.[12] In the view of a number of authors public criminal law owes its origins to religious sources. At this earliest stage of the development of judicial power there is no division between legislative and executive authority, but the principles of a future criminal procedure are being formed. The norms of Canon Law were thus the foundation for the creation of secular norms of material and procedural legislation.

Russian jurists and philosophers drew attention to the inextricable link between Canon Law and secular legislation. N. M. Korkunov (1853-1904) saw in law the external order of human relations. Another great representative of the Russian formal school, the religious philosopher Prince E. N. Trubetskoi believed that: "law is external freedom provided and limited by a norm".[13]

This is not contrary to an understanding and definition of Canon Law. Canon Law, as the external clothing of church life, Pavlov, the author of a pre-revolutionary treatise on canon law wrote, of course must correspond to the internal essence and vital purpose of the church itself. However, the pre-revolutionary researchers emphasized the distinction between the very nature and tasks of the church and State. The church by its nature and purpose is completely distinct from the State, which has come to be considered as the primary (if not exclusive) sphere of the formation of law in pure form. Hence the question arises: is the formal concept of law in the generally-accepted meaning of this word applicable to canon law?

[12] E. Myslovskii, «Религиозно-светские начала уголовно-правовых норм» [Religious-Secular Origins of Criminal Law Norms], *Российская юстиция* [Russian Justice], no. 4 (1997).

[13] E. N. Trubetskoi, *Лекции по энциклопедии права* [Lectures on the Encyclopedia of Law] (1913), p. 30.

In Pavlov's view, the reply may only be affirmative, albeit with certain limitations. First, "Canon law in the objective sense is the external order of a special social organism embodying a determined and essential vital purpose ...".[14] This purpose relates solely to the internal spiritual life of man to which only religion, and not law, may extend its operation. Nonetheless, if this purpose combines people into a special organized union and places them in certain external relations with one another, all the conditions necessary for the formation of law are present.

Second, the norms of this law as an imperative for external activity of the members of the church with respect to one another and to the entire church are as different from the moral prescriptions of the Christian religion as law in general differs from morality: the first relates to the external actions of members of church society, and the last to the internal motives for these actions.

A canon-law norm, for example, determines a certain punishment for a proved link with another's wife, calling this link adultery; and a religious-moral law points to the internal aspect of this crime and says: "But I say unto you, That whosever looketh on a woman to lust after her hath committed adultery with her already in his heart" (Matthew 5:28).

Third, in canon laws, as social laws, the same boundaries for the activities of individual members of church society are established as are necessary in the legal order in general, and a violation of these boundaries is accompanied by the same reaction. Thus, the character of compulsion is inherent in canon law just as in any other branch of law. To be sure, the church itself cannot compel physically as the State compels for the execution of its laws. Nonetheless, it has its own nature of chastisement, with the assistance of which it operates against its individual members who violate the general order of church life.

In the view of Archpriest Tsypin, "the character of compulsion also in inherent in canon law, but the measures of compulsion applicable by the church authorities are decisively different from those which State authorities apply. The church is not empowered by its Founder physically to compel with force; only the State has this lawful monopoly".[15]

Unlike the criminal law sanctions of the State whose penitentiary tasks are of a preventive nature, the church regards crimes as an illness of the soul, and the purpose of a sanction is, first and foremost, to treat and heal

[14] A. S. Pavlov, Курс церковного права заслуженного профессора Московского университета А. С. Павлова, читанный в 1900-1902 гг. [Cours of Canon Law of Emeritus Professor of Moscow University A. S. Pavlov Delivered in 1900-1902] (Spb., 2002), p. 12.

[15] Tsypin, Курс церковного права: Учебное пособие [Cours of Canon Law: Instructional Manual] (Klin, 2002), p. 15.

the soul of the sinner. Therefore, the death penalty provided for by the criminal codes of a number of countries testifies to a departure from the principle of healing the soul of the criminal and is not approved by the church.

The church and State have their own individual spheres of operation, their own special means, and in principle are not dependent upon one another. There are domains, to be sure, where an overlapping of church and State occurs. The moral state of society, for example. Here the State and the church bear an identical responsibility. A more profound study of the legal mechanism of interaction in this sphere may assist canon law, whose place and role, in our view, is still not determined within the system of secular legal disciplines.

We are at present witnesses of the renaissance of Russian Canon Law. This is linked with the growth of general legal culture, an interest in theology and the new place of the church in the life of Russian society. Therefore, newer studies are emerging of the mutual relations of church and State. But whereas the history of the church has been studied well, the theological-legal aspects requires its own philosophical contemplation.

The mutual relations of church and state are best illuminated in their historical, philosophical, and sociological aspects and least well in the legal literature. A branch of law, from the standpoint of the theory of State and law, is the solitary aggregate of legal norms, institutions, regulating homogeneous social relations. Underlying the division of the system of law into branches is the subject-matter and method of legal regulation. It is believed that canon law fully meets these formal requirements. The development of this branch of law will be more successful if scholars of theology are included in these studies together with jurists who are specialists in the theory of State and law. This symbiosis of scholars would help to determine the true place of canon law in the system of legal sciences.

Confessional Law as the Subject of Comparative Research

S. O. SHALIAPIN*

The study of religious law is acquiring greater urgency in modern legal science. Until recently, religious law was perceived as some sort of archaism, legal "exotica", and the subject of study principally by legal historians. However, a narrow historical approach to systems of confessional law can hardly be considered to be scientifically justified since scholars would lose sight of a living, operating element of this law. The contemporary renaissance of religiosity in Eastern Europe, Africa, and Latin America, the enhanced role of confessions as an important factor in social regulation, and the growing conflict of civilizations (according to Huntington)[1] between the Christian west and the world of Islam, on one side, and the world of Islam with the Jewish State, on the other – all of this makes the study of confessional legal systems urgent, systems which have long been on the periphery of legal science.

For the multi-national and semi-confessional post-Soviet States scholarly interest in systems of religious and traditional law has a profoundly practical aspect. The unpreparedness of the scholarly community, the political elite, the legislator, and the law enforcement personnel for perceiving norms of traditional religious law, being a concealed sector of the real legal field (the term belongs to Chernov),[2] and the efforts to replace it with transplants of an "alien" legal field, are fraught with numerous conflicts both purely legal and also of a general social nature.

* кандидат юридических наук, Docent, Head of the Chair of Theory and History of State and Law, Lomonosov Coastal State University (Archangel)

1 S. Huntington, Столкновение цивилизаций [Conflict of Civilizations] (2003).

2 P. V. Chernov, Россия: этногеополитические основы государственности [Russia: Ethno-Geopolitical Foundations of Statehood] (1999), p. 50.

It is interesting to note that an understanding of the significance of religious law in the system of social regulation began in Soviet science, which had a rather specific view of religion as a whole and its role in society, in particular. In 1978 Klochkov wrote that inattention to the correlation of religion and law explained the clear "underassessment of the normative dimension of religion and the lack of a profound analysis of its regulatory function".[3] However, the real possibility for a fully-fledged and objective study of confessional law emerged only in recent decades, which is affirmed by the reanimation of scholarly discussion about the mutual influence of religious and legal norms in legal journals.[4]

A certain neglect of religious law was for a lengthy period not only a distinctive feature of Soviet jurisprudence, but also of western legal science. This was encouraged by the "ethnocentrism" of western society evident in the dominance of the Anglo-Saxon and Romano-Germanic legal families being a mark of civilization and the rejection of any other legal system (the more so, a religious one).[5] A significant portion of western legal scholars drew attention to confessional law after the publication of works by Harold J. Berman (1918-2007) asserting that the "legal systems of countries of the West and all other countries falling under the influence of western law are the secular survivals of religious views and concepts".[6] The crisis of the western system of law was the inspiration for Berman's studies, having been the most universal and free of external influences (including religious) until the end of the twentieth century. Berman's conclusions involved an inevitable reassessment of the role and significance of the western system of law in the work and made the study of religious law dominant in many parts of the world more urgent.

One must also note the important role of comparative legal studies in enhancing scholarly interest in confessional law. The classic work by David rather comprehensively set out the essence and distinctiveness of Muslim and Hindu law, drawing the attention of readers to the fact that the western image of legal thought is not dominant nor uncontested in the modern world.[7] David and Jauffret-Spinosi cautioned too that the systems

[3] V. V. Klochkov, Религия, государство, право [Religion, State, Law] (1978), p. 4.

[4] See, for example, the series of articles in Российская юстиция [Russian Justice} from 1996 to 2001 under the rubric "Law and Religion".

[5] Norbert Rouland, Юридическая антропология [Legal Anthropology] (2000), pp. 20-21.

[6] H. J. Berman, Западная традиция права: эпоха формирования [The Western Tradition of Law: Formative Era] (2d ed.; 1998), p. 166; also see Berman, Вера и закон: примирение религии и права [Faith and Law: Reconciliation of Religion and Law] (1999).

[7] R. David and C. Jauffret-Spinosi, Основные правовые системы современности [Principal Legal Systems of the Modern Day] (1996), p. 308.

of religious law described by them "do not comprise a single family ..., they are alien to one another", and the occasion for combining them in one part of the study was "... merely that they all are based on conceptions different from those which dominate in western countries".[8]

However, despite the warning, a distorted view has been form in the literature of legal theory about some sort of family of religious or even religious-traditional law uniting the aforesaid systems mentioned by David with the system of Judaic law, not described by him, and the legal systems of Africa, China, and Southeast Asia. Such a combination is scientifically unfounded by virtue of the fact that the legal systems united in this "family" do not have uniform sources of law, nor common historical roots. Moreover, if one accepts as a criterion for the crystallization of the said family the dominance of religious norms over the authoritative commands of the State, this criterion is entirely false with respect to the countries of the Far East and Africa.

In modern Russian scholarship the classification of legal systems separating into a single group "canon law systems" has been given currency.[9] A reservation is made in so doing that "canon law systems should be distinguished from religious (or canon) law proper. We can only characterize a legal system as canon law only if the entire State-law structure of the country is build on religious foundations. Otherwise, if canon law acts merely as a regulator of intra-church life, we can speak about canon law, but not about a canon law system".[10]

This position is far from being non-controversial. For example, an answer to the question of the religious foundations of Israel or India as States is not obvious. Only the role of religious law as a significant regulator of the life of society in these States is obvious. If one turns to history, it is unlikely that any of the jurists today doubts the existence, for example, of a system of Judaic religious law even during the absence of a Jewish State over many centuries. To be sure, the degree of correlation of religious law with the generally-binding system of legislation in each State requires clarification and further study. However, it would hardly be justified to place such a criterion as the cornerstone of a comparative classification of legal systems.

The most correct classification in modern comparative studies is that proposed by Osakwe which combines Muslim, Hindu, Jewish, and canon

8 Ibid.

9 I. N. Bartsits, Типология современных правовых систем [Typology of Contemporary Legal Systems] (2000), pp. 5-8.

10 Ibid., p. 7.

(Christian) law into a group of religious legal systems[11] or, to use the term proposed by us – systems of confessional law.[12] One must concur in so doing that this group is "rather eclectic",[13] since the grouping of such heterogeneous religious legal systems may be justified only on the insufficient study thereof by modern legal science.

Having opened the discussion relating to the place of confessional law among other legal systems, David and Jauffret-Spinosi also sowed the seeds of subjectivism by evaluating the place and significance of a particular religious legal system in comparative legal science. The learned French authors consciously did not introduce Jewish Law within the framework of their study purely on the grounds that the sphere of influence of this law was "significantly narrower" than the sphere of influence of other legal systems and families.[14] The rather narrow sphere of the application of Jewish law in the State of Israel is materially augmented by the extensive application of this law by Jewish communities outside Israel, which reduces to "nil" the argument of the learned comparatists for excluding this system from their study. Such criteria as the "narrowness of the sphere of application" might also be advanced for excluding from comparative law research the systems of Christian (Catholic or Orthodox) canon law which the scientific field of comparative legal studies combines. Modern Russian scholars are aware of this and are actively filling such gaps.[15]

The expansion of comparative law research on the systems of confessional law is today as urgent as ever. A theoretical approach which places systems of religious law into one category with the Romano-Germanic and Anglo-Saxon legal families is hardly justified methodologically. As Bergel correctly wrote, "all classifications have a derivative character since … various legal systems are applied and compete within a single State

11 C. Osakwe, Сравнительное правоведение в схемах: общая и особенная части [Comparative Law in Diagrams: General and Special Parts] (2000), p. 27.

12 See S. O. Shaliapin, «Конфессиональное право в цикле историко-правовых дисциплин» [Confessional Law in the Cycle of Historical and Legal Disciplines], in Реформа Российского юридического образования [Reforms of Russian Legal Education] (Spb., 2002), pp. 71-76; id, «Конфессиональное право как предмет изучения» [Confessional Law as a Subject-Matter of Study], in Юридическая география: состояние и перспективы исследования [Legal Geography: State and Prospects for Development] (Ekaterinburg, 2004), pp. 10-12 (Urals Readings in Legal History. All-Russian Scientific Conference. Fourth Session, 16-18 April 2004)

13 J. L. Bergel, Общая теория права [General Theory of Law] (2000), p. 245.

14 R. David, Основные правовые системы современности: сравнительное право [Principal Legal Systems of the World: Comparative Law] (1967), p. 46.

15 See M. N. Marchenko, Правовые системы современного мира [Legal Systems of the Modern World] (2001), pp. 311-394; V. A. Tsypin, Церковное право [Canon Law] (1996); M. Iu. Varias, Краткий курс церковного права: Учебное пособие [Concise Cours of Canon Law: Instructional Manual] (2001).

and, on the contrary, communities of a non-State type also have their own law. Canon (church) law, law based on the Koran, Judaic Law, or the legal system of the Hindus – are the clearest such examples".[16]

The concept of "religious law" which exists in Russian legal science as one of the historical forms of law, together with customary, statute, and the law of precedent[17] does not allow it to be used universally to designate all religious legal systems, each of which has as a source not only sacred texts, but also customs, statutes, and precedents. However, the field for theoretical comparisons of various systems of modern confessional law is a broad one. The classification of sources of religious law, complexes of imperative prohibitions and prescriptions underlying each religious legal system, the structure and content of religious legal and social doctrines elaborated by the greatest confessions of the modern world lend themselves to comparative analysis. Such studies are capable of forming an entire domain of legal comparativistics which allow the legal realities of countries and peoples to be evaluated from more objective positions that are not included (or not wholly included) in the sphere of influence of the two greatest European legal families.

Ultimately, comparative studies in the sphere of confessional law will help identify new "points of contiguity" between various legal systems, both religious and others.

[16] Bergel, note 13 above, p. 244.

[17] Всемирная история государства и права: Энциклопедический словарь [Universal History of State and Law: Encyclopedic Dictionary] (2001), p. 290.

Renaissance of Slavonic Law?

WILLIAM E. BUTLER*

Lafitsky, Vladimir Ilych. Сравнительное правоведение в образах права [Comparative Jurisprudence in the Images of Law]. Moscow, Statut, 2010-2011. 2 vols. 1000 ptd. ISBN 978-5-8354-0653-1

"The comparative method", said the lecturer, "occupies a very large place in the investigations of the laws of social development".[1] With this observation, Feodor Sigel, Professor of Law in the University of Warsaw, commenced what must have been, if not the first, among the earliest series of public lectures on the general subject of Slavonic law in the English-speaking world. The Ilchester Lectures for the year 1900 at the University of Oxford, they happened to coincide that year with the First Congress of Comparative Law held in Paris.

Sigel's works are more easily found under the Russian transliteration of his name, Zigel, Fedor Fedorovich (1845-1921). Born in Novgorod Province, Zigel read law at the University of St. Petersburg (combining his legal studies with Slavonic languages),[2] where one of his classmates, F. F. Martens (1845-1909), became the celebrated international lawyer. In 1872 he defended a magister dissertation on the Zakonnik of Stefan Dushan.[3]The absence of a higher doctorate was no obstacle to Zigel ultimately being appointed *professor ordinarius* at Warsaw University. No one had the range to supervise him. In an internal document held by the Warsaw University, he lamented the complete absence of colleagues who knew Slavonic languages and legal works written in Bulgarian, Polish, Czech and Serbo-

[1] F. Sigel, Lectures on Slavonic Law(London, 1902), p. 1.

[2] The best account of Zigel, based on archival sources, is K. P. Krakovskii, in W. E. Butler and V. A. Tomsinov, *Russian Legal Biography* (2007), I, pp. 391-402.

[3] A major Serbian legal text of the fourteenth century, the Zakonnik has been the subject of considerable research, ably summarized in: Ana Batrićević, "Legal Transplants and the Code of Serbian Tsar Stephan Dushan", in W. E. Butler (ed.), *East European and Russian Yearbook of International and Comparative Law,* II-III (2010), pp. 1-66.

Croatian. When Warsaw University was evacuated in 1915, with its library, to Rostov-on-Don in Russia, he accompanied his colleagues there and remained after the Revolutions of 1917. He died of pneumonia at Rostov in 1921.

Zigel's Ilchester lectures surveyed the principal repositories of Slavonic law: Bulgaria, Serbia, Russia, Bohemia, Poland, and Croatia. Of the two forms of law, customary and statute, the first, he said, prevails throughout all Slavonic history. Even in Russia, he speculated, perhaps three-quarters of the population live "according to their old customs and usages preserved only by tradition" (p. 149). Slavonic law in this respect he believed was nearer to English and American law than to the law of Continental Europe. Slavonic law is, he concluded, the law of an agricultural people.

The history of real property in Orthodox countries can, he averred, be understood only by the relation of the servile classes to the State. The legal rules of Slavonic law are more independent of Roman and canonical law than in Continental Europe. Not being well acquainted with Roman law and its science, the Slavs elaborated their legal rules themselves. While the intellectual influence of foreign ideas was enormous on the Slavs, that influence was confined to ideas alone and not to the legal rules themselves. In the Slavonic world the juridical element was not completely differentiated from the religious, moral, and political ones – which pointed, he suggests, to an earlier development of legal order than in the West (pp. 149-152, Ilchester Lectures).

The present reviewer has not undertaken a thorough inventory of comparative legal classifications of legal systems prior to 1939, but the notion of a Slavonic "family" (whether that word was used or not) of legal systems or "tradition" in law enjoyed currency in some circles.[4] When it disappeared, or was overtaken by the category of socialist legal systems, likewise remains to be documented. Probably "Slavonic law" did not survive the interwar period, at least in the minds of most comparatists, and "socialist legal systems" as an analytical category seems to originate with René David, so far as the popular comparative literature is concerned.

The category of Slavonic law poses some of the conundrums, as a term, that comparative law does. There is no country called "Slavonia" and therefore no positive law which purports to govern all peoples of Slavonic

[4] See, for example, John H. Wigmore, *A Panorama of the World's Legal Systems* (Library ed., 1936), pp. 733-808: "The Slavic race has contributed to the world's human nature some of the most admirable and distinctive traits, -- especially an unquenchable idealism. But no native, pure, and distinctive Slavic legal system ever came to pass" (p. 735). Glenn makes no mention of a Slavic or Slavonic legal tradition. See H. P. Glenn, *Legal Traditions of the World* (3d ed.; 2007).

ethnic affinity. Instead we are dealing with an etnos whose rulers formed sundry entities and allegedly gave expression to Slavonic mores, values, traditions, folkways, and the like. Slavonic law, insofar as expressed in rules, is customary law or is a body of values reflected in particular formulations of State legislation in countries where the Slavonic population is predominant.

The appearance of Professor Lafitskii's monumental treatise on comparative jurisprudence raises anew the issue of Slavonic law in a different and novel context.[5] Lafitskii chooses the expression "jurisprudence" carefully.[6] Images of law are his domain of concern: "Comparative jurisprudence has as ancient a history as the belles-lettres and historical, geographical, and philosophical sciences. It was born together with them, deepening the cognition of law, influencing the merits and shortcomings thereof, revealing the general and the special in the development thereof" (I, p. 12). For him, the origins of comparative jurisprudence lie in the writings of Homer, Herodotus, Thucydides, Plato, Aristotle, Polybius, Strabo, and early works of similar antiquity from China, India, and later the civilizations of the Near and Middle East, Scandinavia, Rus, and western Europe.[7]

The treatise comprises two volumes. The first (429 p.) is devoted to general issues of the history, theory, and methodology of comparative jurisprudence and then to the Christian tradition of law: Slavonic, Romano-Germanic, Common Law, Scandinavian, and Latin American legal families are considered under this rubric and sequence. These collectively form what he calls the "legal community of the Christian tradition of law". He seeks to work from the sources which determined "the spiritual heart", the distinctive features, and ultimately the fates of the major legal systems of the modern world. The Christian tradition is first approached through its foundations, which Lafitskii addresses through the history of the life of Jesus Christ, the teachings of Christ, the early Christian communities,

[5] Lafitskii is Deputy Director of the Institute of Legislation and Comparative Law attached to the Government of the Russian Federation. He foreshadowed the present work in his Поэзия права: страницы правотворчества от древности до наших дней [Poetry of Law: Pages of Law-Creation from Antiquity to the Present] (2003).

[6] Most Russian jurists refer to what in English we call "comparative law" with the expression «сравнительное правоведение», which can be translated as "comparative jurisprudence" and carries the implication, as in German and French, that there is no "comparative law" in the form of natural or positive law. The Lafitskii treatise contains a facing title page in English which uses the title given above.

[7] Lafitskii uses Russian-language sources for all of these writers, the more interesting because the Russian texts do not necessarily coincide in completeness with the English-language versions to which we are accustomed. Sometimes they are considerably longer (more complete?) and based on different manuscripts.

Christianity in the development of State and law, and the embodiment of the images of the Kingdom of God.

He then turns to specific legal families and begins with Slavonic law for "a number of reasons": first, by virtue of the fact that "Christian values find their fullest embodiment in Slavonic law"; second, Slavs are the greatest and, judging by everything, the most ancient etnos of Europe, comprising even today one-third of the inhabitants of Europe; and three, in recent decades Slavonic law is developing at the greatest rate, exerting an ever greater impact on the law of other Christian legal families (I, p. 200).

Although Lafitskii is aware of Zigel's translation of the Zakonnik of Stefan Dushan (I, p. 213), that seems to be the only work by Zigel known to Lafitskii, who otherwise ranges widely in, almost exclusively, Russian-language sources of Slavonic law (as opposed to Polish, Czech, Bulgarian, Serbo-Croatian, etc.). When examining the modern distinctive features of Slavonic law, Lafitskii turns mostly to public law documents, that is, the constitutions of the Slavonic States and, primarily, preambular language: "In describing the features of contemporary Slavonic law, I basically turned to constitutional norms since it is they, despite the multiplicity of unresolved problems, omissions, and oscillations, which determine the path of the development of the legal world of the Slavs" (I, p. 273).

Like Zigel, however, Lafitskii notes the immense continuing influence of customary law: "Customs, traditions, augmenting, changing, or restraining the initiatives of the authorities have great significance" (I, p. 273). Operating in various local, national, or professional communities, these customs, Lafitskii says, form a powerful deep stratum of law which is not under the authority of the rulers. And it is these customs, Lafitskii asserts, which explain the lack of success in the application of many legislative acts in Russia, Ukraine, Bulgaria, Serbia, Poland, and the Czech Republic.

Lafitskii believes the legal language of the Slavs has a noticeable impact upon law. Legal categories such as "State" (государство), "law" (право), "power" (власть), "government" (правительство), "court" (суд), "lex" (закон), "society" (общество) have "in Slavonic law a special content, give rise to distinctive thought patterns not inherent in the bearers of other legal cultures" (I, p. 273). As for Roman law, Lafitskii says that "Slavonic law … has common sources and own history of development. Unlike the legal systems of Italy, Spain, France, Germany, and Austria, there was no noticeable reception of Roman law" (I, p. 273). And although Slavonic law has adopted many legal constructions from Romano-Germanic and the Common Law, they retain their uniqueness.[8] The legal systems, he observes, of Serbia, Croatia, Slovenia, and Bulgaria have not adopted models of private law codification. Poland and the Czech Republic have kept in force civil codes enacted during the socialist era that are closer to the RSFSR Civil Code and not the French and German civil codes. Slavonic law has achieved a balance of public and private interests with respect to ownership, subsoil use, State administration of the economy, and the social sphere that reflects Slavonic values. In matters of codification the Slavonic countries are developing a distinctive legislative style to fully regulate social relations, a style that brings these countries closer to the Common Law jurisdictions than to the Romano-Germanic systems. The judicial style of the Slavonic world is noteworthy for maximum brevity in setting out the circumstances of a case and substantiating positions – an approach that is not characteristic of either the Romano-Germanic or the Common Law families.

Finally, Lafitskii concludes, these features of Slavonic law are manifest irrespective of whether the Slavonic countries are members or not of various regional associations (Commonwealth of Independent States or European Union), differences in profession of faith (Catholic or Orthodox), ideologies, or political direction. Slavonic legal systems belong to a separate, solitary, legal family which is preserving its unity and resisting the "legal colonization" that is implicit in assertions that these legal systems are part of the Romano-Germanic legal family (I, p. 274).

Volume Two (415 p.) is devoted to non-Christian religions and philosophies: Judaic, Islamic, Hindu, Buddhist, Confucian, and Shinto. The penultimate chapter addresses "Comparative Jurisprudence in the Reflection of the Past", which examines common features of traditional legal systems and, in a very interesting essay, the lost world of law. The final chapter is concerned with "Comparative Jurisprudence in the Reflection of the Future", by which Lafitskii means "totalitarian law" and "technocratic law".

Lafitskii's discussion of totalitarian law is a fitting epitaph to that of Slavonic law. He offers two conclusions on this matter: first, the socialist system collapsed not under the assault of external enemies, but under the weight of own contradictions which destroyed its economic, political,

[8] But, contra Batrićević, note 3 above. While emphasizing legal borrowings in the Code ("there is no doubt that these codifications were created under the strong influence of Roman law"), she observes: "... the interaction and the diffusion within the Slavic legal systems themselves, which developed a new legal quality, should be seriously taken into consideration ..." (p. 61). She also notes the influence of Turkish laws, as reflected in terminological modifications in the Serbian language, and speaks of an "overall pan-Slavic diffusion of law" (p. 62).

social, and ideological pillars. Second, the legacy of socialism, despite all predictions, all the same remains. They could not destroy it, and will not be able to do so. Therefore, the task is, insofar as possible, to use the positive aspects of socialism, not forgetting the threat which it conceals within it (II, pp. 400-401).

There has never been a work like this in the Russian language on comparative law. The author's erudition and originality are formidable – new insights, new ideas, new relationships on every page. It is bound to have, and deservedly so, a considerable impact throughout the secular and positivist Commonwealth of Independent States on the dialogue generated by the renaissance of comparative law.

Bibliography

PUBLICATIONS OF THE UKRAINIAN ASSOCIATION OF COMPARATIVE LAW

WILLIAM E. BUTLER

The publications below may be obtained through the Ukrainian Association of Comparative Law. They are not available through ordinary retail book channels. Contact the Learned Secretary, Oleksiy Kresin, at: okresin@gmail.ua

Periodical:

Порівняльно-правові дослідження [Comparative Law Studies]. Kiev, 2005-.

International scholarly journal founded by the V. M. Koretsky Institute of State and Law, National Academy of Sciences of Ukraine, Mariupol State Humanitarian University, Law Faculty of the University of Athens, and the Law Faculty of the University of Thrace. Editor-in-Chief: Academician Iu. S. Shemshuchenko. Executive Editors: O. V. Kresin and Iu. A. Voloshin.

2005: 1 issue; 2006-2010: 2 issues per year. The first issue appeared in October 2005. The journal is issued by the Koretsky Institute of State and Law and the Ukrainian Association of Comparative Law.

Series:

Енциклопедія порівняльного правознавства [Encyclopedia of Comparative Law]:

Established in 2002 at the initiative of O. V. Kresin, the Series contains reference manuals, encyclopedias, and monographs. Five titles have appeared, all in Ukrainian.

[1]. **Kresin, O. V., Kresina, I. O.** (ed.). *Порівняльне правознавство. Порівняльна політологія: Систематичний бібліографічний покажчик* [Comparative Law. Comparative Politology. Systematic Bibliographic Index]. Kiev, V. M. Koretsky Institute of State and Law, National Academy of Sciences of Ukraine, 2002. 312 p.

The first bibliography published in Ukraine on comparative law and comparative politology, it includes books and articles published in Ukraine and abroad. Topics covered include: theory, methodology, and history of comparative law, modern legal system of the world, branch comparative-law disciplines. The materials on comparative politology address the theory and methodologies of political comparative studies, democracy, political and party systems of the world, among others.

[2]. **Kresin, O. V.** (comp.). *Порівняльне правознавство. вітчизняні та зарубіжні спеціалізовані центри дослідження та викладання* [Comparative Law: Ukrainian and Foreign Specialized Centers for Research and Teaching]. Ed. V. N. Denisov. Kiev, V. M. Koretsky Institute of State and Law, National Academy of Sciences of Ukraine, 2005. 192 p.

The first manual in the Ukrainian language devoted to foreign and Ukrainian legal organizations, listing 73 foreign, Ukrainian, and international centers specializing in scientific research, teaching, or practical activities in the sphere of comparative law. Entries contain information about the status of the institution or organization, the purposes and basic orientations of activity, organizational structure and executive personnel, projects, congresses and conferences, publications, and library and electronic resources.

[3]. **Kresin, O. V.** (comp.). *Порівняльне правознавство у системі юридичних наук: проблеми методології: Монографія* [Comparative Law in the System of Legal Sciences: Problems of Methodology]. Ed. Iu. S. Shemshuchenko. Kiev, V. M. Koretsky Institute of State and Law, National Academy of Sciences of Ukraine, 2006. 256 p.

The first Ukrainian monograph to address methodologies of comparative law. The authors examine systemic links, objects and subject-matter of comparative law, and related fields of legal theory, history, philosophy, sociology, and anthropology of law, international private law, and constitutional law.

[4]. **Kresin, O. V.** (ed.). *Видатні компаративісти: Творчий шлях, ідеї, праці* [Pre-Eminent Comparatists: Intellectual Biography, Ideas, Works]. Kiev, V.

M. Koretsky Institute of State and Law, National Academy of Sciences of Ukraine, 2007. 144 p.

Biographical dictionary of leading comparatists from around the world, with bibliographies of principal works and of literature on their careers.

[5]. **Kresin, O. V.** (ed.). *Порівняльне правознавство: Антологія української компаративістики XIX-XX століть* [Comparative Law: Anthology of Ukrainian Comparativistics XIX-XX Centuries]. Kiev, V. M. Koretsky Institute of State and Law, National Academy of Sciences of Ukraine, 2008. 414 p. Casebound. ISBN 978-966-171-002-9

Anthology of works on the methodology of comparative law by Ukrainian legal scholars published between 1836 and 1990, all in the Russian language with the introduction and annotations in Ukrainian. The annotations place the materials within the context of ideas of their time and a bio-bibliography of the author. Completed by data on scholars whose works were used by the authors included in the Anthology.

Академія порівняльного правознавства [Academy of Comparative Law]:

A series of scientific-methods publications intended to further discussion of the most complex and topical issues of comparative law and encourage the teaching of comparative law in institutions of higher legal education. Listed alphabetically by author. All are paperbound in stapled covers.

Bekhruz, Kh. N. Актуализация сравнительно-правовых исследований в эпоху глобализации: Открытая лекция [Actualization of Comparative Law Research in the Era of Globalization: Open Lecture]. Kiev, Odessa, Simferopol, V. M. Koretsky Institute of State and Law, National Academy of Sciences of Ukraine; izd-vo Logos, 2008. 23 p. ISBN 978-966-171-008-4 (No. 13, Series of Scientific-Methods Publications "Academy of Comparative Law")

Bekhruz, Kh. N. Методологические основы сравнительного правоведения: Открытая лекция [Methodological Foundations of Comparative Law: Open Lecture]. Kiev, Simferopol, V. M. Koretsky Institute of State and Law, National Academy of Sciences of Ukraine; izd-vo Logos, 2007. 32 p. 300 ptd. ISBN 978-966-581-880-9 (No. 6, Series of Scientific-Methods Publications "Academy of Comparative Law")

Butler, W. E. Місце пострадянських правових систем на правовій карті світу: Відкрита лекція [The Place of Post-Soviet Legal Systems on the Legal Map of the World: Open Lecture]. Kiev, V. M. Koretsky Institute of State and Law, National Academy of Sciences of Ukraine; Kiev Shevchenko National University; izd-vo Logos, 2009. 20 p. 500 ptd. ISBN 978-966-171-206-4 (No. 19, Series of Scientific-Methods Publications "Academy of Comparative Law")

Butler, W. E. Періодизація і міжнародне право: деялі порівняльні міркування [Periodization and International Law: Some Comparative Reflections]. Kiev – Ivano-Frankivsk, Logos, 2010. 24 p. 300 ptd. (No. 23, Series of Scientific-Methods Publications "Academy of Comparative Law")

Kharitonov, E. O., Kharitonova, O. I. Деякі питання класифікації європейських систем приватного права: Відкрита лекція [Certain Questions of the Classification of European Systems of Private Law]. Kiev, V. M. Koretsky Institute of State and Law, National Academy of Sciences of Ukraine; izd-vo Logos, 2007. 28 p. 300 ptd. ISBN 978-966-581-886-1 (No. 7, Series of Scientific-Methods Publications "Academy of Comparative Law")

Kostenko, A. N. Социальный натурализм как методологический принцип сравнительного правоведения и юридической глобалистики: Открытая лекция [Social Naturalism as Methodological Principle of Comparative Law and Legal Globalistics: Open Lecture]. Kiev, Simferopol, V. M. Koretsky Institute of State and Law, National Academy of Sciences of Ukraine; izd-vo Logos,, 2008. 28 p. ISBN 978-966-171-003-9 (No. 11, Series of Scientific-Methods Publications "Academy of Comparative Law")

Luts, L. A. Типологізація сучасних правових систем світу: Відкрита лекція [Typologization of Modern Legal Systems of the World]. Kiev, Simferopol, V. M. Koretsky Institute of State and Law, National Academy of Sciences of Ukraine; izd-vo Logos, 2007. 23 p. 300 ptd. ISBN 978-966-581-873-1 (No. 3, Series of Scientific-Methods Publications "Academy of Comparative Law")

Marchenko, M. N. Конвергенция романо-германского и англосаксонского права: Открытая лекция [Convergence of Romano-Germanic and Anglo-Saxon Law: Open Lecture]. Kiev, Simferopol, V. M. Koretsky Institute of State and Law, National Academy of Sciences of Ukraine, 2007. 36 p. 300 ptd. ISBN 978-966-581-870-0 (No. 1, Series of Scientific-Methods Publications "Academy of Comparative Law")

Mattei, Ugo. Порівняльне право і критичні правові дослідження: Відкрита лекція [Comparative Law and Critical Legal Studies]. Kiev, V. M. Koretsky Institute of State and Law, National Academy of Sciences of Ukraine; Kiev Shevchenko National University; izd-vo Logos, 2009. 32 p. 500 ptd. ISBN 978-966-171-207-1 (No. 18, Series of Scientific-Methods Publications "Academy of Comparative Law")

Oksamytnyi, V. V. Правовые системы современного мира: проблемы идентификации: Открытая лекция [Legal Systems of the Modern World: Problems of Identification: Open Lecture]. Kiev, Moscow, Simferopol, V. M. Koretsky Institute of State and Law, National Academy of Sciences of Ukraine; izd-vo Logos,, 2008. 36 p. ISBN 978-966-171-004-6 (No. 10, Series of Scientific-Methods Publications "Academy of Comparative Law")

Oksamytnyi, V. V. Сравнительная теория закона и ее место в юридической компаративистике: Открытая лекция [Comparative Theory of Law and Place Thereof in Legal Comparativistics]. Kiev, V. M. Koretsky Institute of State and Law, National Academy of Sciences of Ukraine; Kiev Shevchenko National University; izd-vo Logos, 2009. 32 p. 500 ptd. ISBN 978-966-171-127-2 (No. 16, Series of Scientific-Methods Publications "Academy of Comparative Law")

Romashov, R. A. Проблема соотношения понятий «право» и «закон» в контексте исторического и юридико-лингвистического анализа: Открытая лекция [Problem of Correlation of Concepts "Jus" and "Lex" in the Context of Historical and Legal-Linguistic Analysis: Open Lecture]. Kiev, Simferopol, V. M. Koretsky Institute of State and Law, National Academy of Sciences of Ukraine; izd-vo Logos, 2007. 24 p. 300 ptd. ISBN 978-966-581-871-7 (No. 4, Series of Scientific-Methods Publications "Academy of Comparative Law")

Romashov, R. A. Типология государства в контексте сравнительного правоведения: Открытая лекция [Typology of State in the Context of Comparative Law]. Kiev, V. M. Koretsky Institute of State and Law, National Academy of Sciences of Ukraine; Kiev Shevchenko National University; izd-vo Logos, 2009. 28 p. 500 ptd. ISBN 978-966-171-126-5 (No. 15, Series of Scientific-Methods Publications "Academy of Comparative Law")

Saidov, A. Kh. Религия и международное право: Открытая лекция [Religion and International Law: Open Lecture]. Kiev, Tashkent, Simferopol, V. M. Koretsky Institute of State and Law, National Academy of Sciences of

Ukraine; izd-vo Logos, 2008. 52 p. ISBN 978-966-171-005-3 (No. 9, Series of Scientific-Methods Publications "Academy of Comparative Law")

Saidov, A. Kh. Сравнительное гражданское право как учебная дисциплины [Comparative Civil Law as an Instructional Discipline]. Kiev – Ivano-Frankovsk, Logos, 2010. 24 p. ISBN 978-966-171-255-2 (No. 22, Series of Scientific-Methods Publications "Academy of Comparative Law")

Saidov, A. Kh. Сравнительное правоведение и законотворчество: Открытая лекция [Comparative Law and Law-Creation: Open Lecture]. Kiev, Simferopol, V. M. Koretsky Institute of State and Law, National Academy of Sciences of Ukraine; izd-vo Logos, 2007. 32 p. 300 ptd. ISBN 978-966-581-874-8 (No. 2, Series of Scientific-Methods Publications "Academy of Comparative Law")

Salomatin, A. Iu. Объединяющий потенциал сравнетельного правоведения как науки и учебной дисциплины [Unifying Potential of Comparative Law as Science and Instructional Discipline]. Kiev – Ivano-Frankovsk, Logos, 2010. 22 p. ISBN 978-966-171-246-0 (No. 20, Series of Scientific-Methods Publications "Academy of Comparative Law")

Skakun, O. F. «Загальне порівняльне правознавство» як навчальна дисципліна: досвід і перспективи в Україні ["General Comparative Law" as an Instructional Discipline: Experience and Prospects in Ukraine]. Kiev – Ivano-Frankivsk, Logos, 2010. 20 p. ISBN 978-966-171-253-8 (No. 21, Series of Scientific-Methods Publications "Academy of Comparative Law")

Skakun, O. F. Правова система - держави, суспільства, регіону, світу? (щодо базових категорій порівняльного правознавства): Відкрита лекція [Legal System – State, Society, Region, World?]. Kiev, Kharkov, Simferopol, V. M. Koretsky Institute of State and Law, National Academy of Sciences of Ukraine; izd-vo Logos, 2008. 32 p. ISBN 978-966-171-007-7 (No. 12, Series of Scientific-Methods Publications "Academy of Comparative Law")

Skakun, O. F. Принцип единства логичекского и исторического методов в сравнительном правоведении: Открытая лекция [Principle of Unity of Logical and Historical Method in Comparative Law: Open Lecture]. Kiev, Simferopol, V. M. Koretsky Institute of State and Law, National Academy of Sciences of Ukraine; izd-vo Logos, 2007. 31 p. 300 ptd. ISBN 978-966-581-878-6 (No. 5, Series of Scientific-Methods Publications "Academy of Comparative Law")

Tikhomirov, A. D. Философские проблемы правовой компаративистики: Открытая лекция [Philosophical Problems of Legal Comparativistics: Open Lecture]. Kiev, V. M. Koretsky Institute of State and Law, National Academy of Sciences of Ukraine; Kiev Shevchenko National University; izd-vo Logos, 2009. 32 p. 500 ptd. ISBN 978-966-171-129-6 (No. 17, Series of Scientific-Methods Publications "Academy of Comparative Law")

Tikhomirov, Iu. A. Право: современные границы регулирования: Открытая лекция [Law: Contemporary Boundaries of Regulation: Open Lecture]. Kiev, V. M. Koretsky Institute of State and Law, National Academy of Sciences of Ukraine; Kiev Shevchenko National University; izd-vo Logos, 2009. 18 p. 500 ptd. ISBN 978-966-171-125-8 (No. 14, Series of Scientific-Methods Publications "Academy of Comparative Law")

Tikhomirov, Iu. A. Сравнительное правоведение и интегрирующая роль международного права: Открытая лекция [Comparative Law and Integrating Role of International Law: Open Lecture]. Kiev, Moscow, Simferopol, V. M. Koretsky Institute of State and Law, National Academy of Sciences of Ukraine; izd-vo Logos, 2007. 16 p. ISBN 978-966-171-006-0 (No. 8, Series of Scientific-Methods Publications "Academy of Comparative Law")

Extra-Series Publications:

Kresin, O. V. *Конституція об'єднаної Європи* [Constitution of a United Europe]. Ed. Iu. S. Shemshuchenko. Kiev, V. M. Koretsky Institute of State and Law, National Academy of Sciences of Ukraine, 2005. 116 p.

In Ukrainian language, with bibliography in various languages.

Shemshuchenko, Iu. S., Kresin, O. V. (eds.). *Порівняльне правознавство: сучасний стан і перспективи розвитку: Зб. наукових праць* [Comparative Law: Contemporary State and Prospects for Development: Collection of Scholarly Works]. Kiev, V. M. Koretsky Institute of State and Law, National Academy of Sciences of Ukraine; Tauride National University, Kiev University of Law of National Academy of Sciences of Ukraine, 2006. 432 p.

Collected articles devoted to the General Part of comparative law and to branch comparative law studies. Many of the articles originally were presented at the International Comparative Law

Forum held at Simferopol from 27-29 April 2006. The articles are in English, Russian, and Ukrainian languages.

Shemshuchenko, Iu. S., Guberskii, L. V., Gritsenko, I. S. (eds.). *Порівняльне правознавство: сучасний стан і перспективи розвитку: Зб. статей* [Comparative Law: Contemporary State and Prospects for Development: Collection of Articles]. Comp. O. V. Kresin. Kiev, Logos, 2009. 712 p. 500 ptd.

Collected articles (more than 200) addressing methodologies of comparative law and the classification of modern legal systems, teaching of comparative law, supranational trends in the development of law, and comparative aspects of international and European law. Most articles were presented at the Comparative Law Days held at Kiev from 8-11 April 2009. Authors from Ukraine, Russia, Belarus, Czech Republic, Moldova, Austria, United Kingdom, Azerbaijan, and Kazakhstan. The articles are in English, Russian, and Ukrainian languages.

Shemshuchenko, Iu. S., Gritsenko, I. S., Buchko, M. B. (eds.).. *Порівняльне правознавство: Сучасний стан і перспективи розвитку: Збірник наукових праць* [Comparative Law: Current State and Prospects for Development: Collection of Scientific Works]. Comp. O. V. Kresin. Kiev, V. M. Koretsky Institute of State and Law, National Academy of Sciences of Ukraine, 2010. 520 p. 500 ptd.

151 collected articles addressing the theory and methodology of comparative law, the development of legal systems, comparative studies on the theory and history of State and law, comparative studies in the domain of European and international law, comparative constitutional and municipal law, comparative administrative law, comparative financial law, comparative civil law, comparative criminal law and procedure, among others. Most were presented at the Comparative Law Days held at Yaremche (Ivano-Frankivsk Region) in April 2010. Authors from Ukraine, Russia, Belarus, Hungary, United Kingdom, Kazakhstan, and elsewhere. English, Russian, and Ukrainian summaries of the Proceedings at the Conference.

Shemshuchenko, Iu. S., Gritsenko, I. S., Kresin, O. V. (ed.). *Європейське право та порівняльне правознавство: Збірник статей* [European Law and Comparative Law: Collection of Articles]. Kiev-Chambery, Logos, 2010. 588 p. Casebound. ISBN 978-966-171-267-5. 500 ptd.

54 collected articles presented at a French-Ukrainian Colloquium held a Chambéry and Chamonix, France, from 9-16 January 2010 grouped under the subject-headings of "Comparative Law as an Instrument of Cognition of European Law"; "Law of European Organizations"; "Law of European Countries", and 'European Integration in the Light of Science". Several are in English. Austrian, Hungarian, and Italian comparatists took part together with French and Ukrainian colleagues.

INDEX OF NAMES

Afanasev, Iu. N., 185
Alder, J., 284
Alekseev, S. S., 38-41, 132, 258, 266
Alexy, R. A., 294
Al-Hademi, Abu Said, 177
Allan, T., 302
Alston, P., 298
Ancel, M., 34, 110
Andenas, Mads, 11
Aquinas, Thomas, 101
Arefeva, G. S., 46
Aristotle, 15, 101, 333
Arminjon, P., 37, 261, 262, 307, 308
Arnio, A., 302
Arnull, A., 296

Babaev, V. K., 38, 40, 42, 161
Babich, I.: see Babych, I.
Baburin, S. N., 79
Babych, I., 13, 31
Bairachan, L. D., 228
Baitin, M. I., 161
Baker, J. H., 288
Bakhtin, M. M., 89
Bandura, O. O., 228
Barah, A., 297
Baranov, V. M., 42, 54, 75
Bartsits, I. N., 328
Batrićević, Ana, 331, 335
Baudrillard, Jean, 223
Beatson, J., 283, 289
Bekhruz, Kh., 29, 34, 71, 123-141, 144, 308, 339
Bell, John, 146, 297
Bennion, F., 289, 302
Berdnikov, I. S., 321
Berdyaev, N. A., 226
Bergel, J.-L., 39, 68, 168, 329, 330
Berman, H. J., 67, 72, 131, 132, 327
Bermann, G. A., 34
Biddulph, S., 109
Bigich, O. L., 97
Bingham, T. H., 7
Binswanger, Ludwig, 222
Birks, P., 296
Blankenburg, E., 288
Bogdan, M., 277, 281
Bogdanor, V., 283, 297
Bogdanovskaia, I. Iu., 31
Borgan, M., 41
Brand, O., 94, 105
Brenton, A., 76
Brooks, R., 30
Brown, J., 296
Brown, L. N., 32, 294
Buber, M., 221, 222
Bublik, S. A., 228
Buchko, M. B., 344
Buganova, M. A., 77
Bulgakov, S. N., 321
Burca, Gr. de, 294, 298
Burlai, E. V., 168, 228
Bushev, A. Iu., 146
Butler, W. E., 2, 3-12, 26, 37, 59, 69, 111, 139, 151, 173, 189, 307, 308, 319, 321, 331-345

C., L. S., 31
Caenegem, R., 277, 292
Caldeira, G., 279
Cameron, J., 290
Campbell, J., 302
Canivet, Guy, 11
Cappelletti, M., 295
Carbonnier, J., 135, 167
Carnap, R., 105, 106
Catherine II, Empress of Russia, 195
Chelpanov, G. I., 40
Cheltsov-Bebutov, M. A., 198
Chernokov, A. E., 59, 60, 68, 74, 147

Chernov, P. V., 326
Cheshkov, M., 181
Chesterman, M., 288
Chestnov, I. L., 223
Chetverikov, A. O., 82
Chirkin, V. E., 77
Cicero, M. T., 235
Clark, D. S., 33, 40, 276
Cohen-Tanugi, L., 279
Comte, A., 96
Confucius, 314
Constantinesco, L.-J., 19-21, 31, 38
Cooke, R., 277, 283, 288
Coomaraswamy, R., 303
Cotterell, R., 97
Craig, P., 291
Cross, R., 296
Cruz, P. de, 31, 41, 285, 286

Dadomo, Ch., 294
Dam, Cies van, 11
Damirli, M. A., 84-91, 93, 143
Danilian, O. G., 98
David, R., 5, 23, 37, 41, 42, 55, 59, 64, 110, 255, 256, 261, 305, 307, 308, 311, 314, 327-329, 332
Dawson, John P., 292
Demidov, A. I., 224, 225, 230
Deng Xiaoping, 80
Denisov, A. I., 44
Denisov, V. N., 23, 24, 33, 338
Denza, E., 290
Deriabina, E. M., 146
Derrett, J. D. M., 315
Derrida, J., 100, 101
Descartes, R., 100, 101
Desomer, M., 300
Dolgov, V. M., 230
Dudko, I. G., 55
Dushan, S., 331, 334
Dworkin, R., 302
Dyzenhaus, D., 301

Ebert, K.-H., 38, 41
Egorov, S. N., 228
Ekins, R., 301, 302
Eliseev, N. G., 256
Elster, Jon, 107, 108
Engels, F., 264
Entin, L. M., 67
Eörsi, G., 38, 256, 262, 308
Epshtein, M. N., 219
Esakov, G. A., 146
Esmein, A., 37, 261, 263
Esser, D., 93
Ewald, W., 13, 18, 24, 25, 31, 32

Fairgrieve, D., 11
Faiziev, M. M., 22, 32
Falk, Z., 315
Farran, S., 294
Febvre, L., 265
Fedotova, V. G., 99
Fedtke, J., 11
Feuerbach, P. J. A. von, 17, 20
Fisher, G., 124
Florovskii, G. V., 321
Foelix, J. J. G., 18, 31
Frankenberg, G., 93
Franklin, M., 31
Franko, Ivan, 36
Frolov, I. T., 43
Fulbeck, W., 15

Gadamer, H.-G., 88
Gadzhiev, K. S., 265
Gans, E., 17, 20, 24
Gardner, J. C., 33
Gavrilov, V. V., 55, 83
Gerber, D. J., 93, 98
Gessner, V., 279
Gibson, J., 279
Glasson, E. D., 37
Glenn, H. P., 39, 279, 281, 332

Gödel, Kurt, 102
Goff, Lord Robert, 277
Goiman-Chervoniuk, V. I., 38
Golubeva, L. A., 147
Gomerov, I. A., 162
Gornard, B. A., 294
Grafskii, V. G., 190
Graziadei, M., 95
Grecheno, V. A., 166, 169
Green-Gonas, C., 294
Gresham, Thomas, 99
Griboedov, A. S., 53
Grier, P. T., 310
Gritsenko, I. S., 344
Grosfeld, G., 101
Grotius, H., 17, 235
Guberskii, L. V., 344
Gubskii, E. F., 41, 46
Gutteridge, H. C., 6, 16, 18, 19, 31

Haney, G., 38
Hanifa, Aboe, 71, 177
Harding, A., 302
Harris, B., 301
Hartley, T., 300
Hay, P., 297
Hegel, G. F. W., 16, 20, 24, 26, 30, 31, 221
Heidegger, M., 101, 102, 222
Heine, C. J. H., 249
Henderson, J., 4
Herodotus, 333
Hoeflich, M. H., 31
Hofland, A., 279
Homer, 333
Hug, W., 16, 31, 32
Huntington, S., 326
Huskey, E., 198
Husserl, E., 100
Hyland, R., 25, 26, 32, 96, 105

Iadov, V. A., 44
Iakovets, Iu., 265
Iaremenko, V. V., 46
Iatskevich, A. F., 47
Ikonnikova, G. I., 164
Ilin, I. A., 310
Ishanov, A. I., 22
Iushkov, S. V., 319, 320

Jacobs, A., 296
Jansen, N., 102
Jauffret-Spinosi, C., 42, 59, 110, 261, 307, 314, 327, 329
Jefferson, T., 235
Jenkins, D., 284
Jenks, E., 33
Jesus Christ, 333
Joerges, Ch., 284, 290
Jowell, J., 299
Justinian, Emperor, 257

Kagan, M. S., 44
Kahn-Freund, O., 12
Kalamkarian, R. A., 80
Kamba, W. J., 96
Kant, I., 20, 24, 26, 30, 258
Karpechkina, M. Iu., 173
Kashkin, S. Iu., 67, 82
Kelly, J. M., 30
Kelman, M. S., 161
Kennedy, T., 294
Khabirov, R. F., 124
Kharitonov, E. O., 40, 65, 255-275, 340
Kharitonova, O. I., 40, 65, 255-275, 340
Khvostov, V. M., 257
Kiselev, I. Ia., 112, 146, 286
Kistiakoskii, B., 227
Kliuchevskii, V. O., 319
Klochkov, V. V., 327
Knapp, V., 38, 160
Kniper, R., 116
Koch, H., 59, 256
Kochetov, E. G., 125, 126, 138
Kolodii, A. M., 228

Kolomenskaia, E. V., 99
Kolosov, Iu. M., 80
Kolosova, N. M., 57
Korableva, G. V., 41
Korchevna, L. O., 74
Korelskii, V. M., 162
Koretskiy, V. M., 1, 2, 13, 337-345
Korkunov, N. M., 323
Kornlev, N. G., 192, 193
Korshunov, A. M., 85
Kosach, G., 78
Kostenko, A. N., 234-254, 340
Kostenko, O. M., 235, 236, 239
Kotliar, M., 169
Kötz, H., 5, 10, 30, 31, 37, 38, 41, 64, 92, 93, 95, 97, 100, 105, 110, 160, 216, 256, 262, 263, 307, 308, 315
Kourilsky, Ch., 291-293
Kovler, A. I., 187
Kozlovskii, A. A., 225, 228
Kozyrin, A. N., 146
Krakovskii, K. P., 331
Krasheninnikova, N. A., 39, 153
Krasnianskii, V. E., 38
Kravtsev, V. M., 228
Kresin, O. V., 1, 2, 13-35, 28, 97, 141, 337-339, 343, 344
Kresina, I. O., 338
Krings, E., 158
Krivchikova, E. S., 80
Krizhanich, Iu., 191, 192
Krylova, N. E., 146
Kuchma, L., 169
Kudriavtsev, M. K., 314
Kudriavtsev, V. N., 4
Kuhne, M., 301
Kulchitskii, S., 169
Kultygin, V. P., 124, 127
Kurskii, D. I., 256
Kuznetsov, V. G., 85, 88, 90, 91

Lafitskii, V. I., 6, 145, 331-336
Lambert, E., 133, 137
Latkin, V. M., 194, 195, 197, 319
Lavrov, S. V., 78
Lazareva, T. P., 117
Legrand, P., 94, 95, 97, 100-102, 106, 109, 281
Leibnitz, G. W. von, 15
Lektorskii, V. A., 99, 105
Lenarets, K., 300
Lenin, V. I., 256
Lerminier, J. L. E., 18, 31
Levitt, T., 124
Lévy-Ullman, H., 37, 261, 308
Leyland, P., 297
Liashenko, V. P., 164
Lifintseva, T. P., 221
Lipinskii, V., 274
Locke, J., 235
Lopatka, A., 38
Lotman, Iu. M., 86, 87, 90, 135
Lukashuk, I. I., 119, 133, 138
Lukianov, D. V., 304-317
Lukich, R., 97, 100
Lutchenko, V. A., 41
Luts, L. A., 36-52, 65, 73, 161, 184, 307, 308, 340
Luzin, V., 143
Lvova, O. L., 21, 185
Lysenko, O. M., 13, 28

MacCormick, D., 302
McCormick, J., 301
McLaughlin, P., 107, 108
Magnus, U., 59, 256
Maiboroda, D. V., 222
Maine, Sir H., 15, 18, 25
Makarenko, L. O., 21
Makarova, O. A., 146
Maksimov, S. I., 224, 228, 310
Malinovskii, A. A., 112
Malko, A. V., 147, 230, 263
Malmström, Åke, 261

Mamutov, V. K., 257
Maneshina, V. S., 192
Mantatov, V. V., 85
Mao Tse-tung, 80
Marchenko, N. M., 22, 40, 41, 59, 63, 70, 74, 75, 111, 134, 143, 144, 146, 147, 156, 214, 255, 276-303, 308, 310, 311, 329, 340
Markesinis, B., 11, 299
Marks, S., 298
Martens, F. F., 331
Martynov, V. F., 187
Maslov, P. P., 44
Matiushkin, G. O., 54
Mattei, Ugo, 2, 40, 93, 341
Matthew, Saint, 324
Matuzov, N. I., 159, 161, 163, 263
Mayakovsky, V. V., 203
Mayda, Jaro, 22
Merryman, J. H., 39, 40, 93, 276, 287, 288
Merton, R. K., 103
Metshin, I. R., 77
Michaels, R., 92, 94, 95, 100, 104, 108
Migachev, Iu. I., 80
Mikhailov, A. E., 230
Mirkin, B. G., 44
Mittermaier, C. J. A., 17, 21, 31
Mohammed, Prophet, 312
Montesquieu, C. L. de S., 15, 17, 30, 235, 288
Morozova, L. A., 166
Mortelmans, K., 290
Motrevich, V. P., 318-325
Mozheiko, M. A., 222
Muchnik, I. B., 44
Mukienko, L. N., 173
Munday, R., 94, 95, 97, 101, 106
Murashin, A. G., 161
Myslovskii, E., 323

Nagel, E., 104, 107
Napoleon, 24, 292
Napolitano, J., 284, 291
Nascim-Bene, B., 294
Nenovski, N., 199
Nersesiants, V. S., 166, 190, 228
Nevvazhai, I. D., 225, 230
Newton, Isaac, 99
Nicholson, P., 109
Nizhnik, N. S., 201
Nolde, B. E., 37, 261, 262, 307, 308
Novikova, N. I., 230
Novolodskaia, T. A., 96

Oborotov, Iu. N., 52, 136, 173, 181, 223, 228
Ogus, A. I., 282
Oksamytnyi, V. V., 53-83, 306, 341
Onishchenko, N. M., 21, 74, 147, 163, 263, 308
Onyshchenko, N. M.: see Onishchenko, N. M.
Orlik, Pilip, 52
Orlov, D., 80
Orlova, I. B., 265
Orücü, E., 32, 94, 104
Orzikh, M. P., 228
Osakwe, C., 39, 42, 64, 74, 111, 135, 139, 142, 146, 329
Osminin, B. I., 119
Ovchinnikov, A. I., 90

Palmer, V. V., 34, 35
Pantin, V. I., 127
Patsurkivskii, P. S., 54
Patterson, D., 25, 96
Pavlov, A. S., 319, 320, 323, 324
Paz, E. M., 37, 261
Perevalov, V. D., 161-163
Pérez-Perdomo, R., 39
Peter I, Tsar of Russia, 194
Peteri, Z., 104
Pettit, P., 107
Plastas, A. E., 93, 102

Plato, 102, 333
Platon, Metropolitan, 320
Plavich, I., 257, 270
Pogorilko, V. F., 228
Pokrovskii, I. A., 257
Polenina, S. V., 45, 46
Poliakov, A. V., 228
Polybius, 333
Pollock, Sir F., 13, 15
Pomerants, G. S., 221
Popescu, S., 97
Popondupulo, V. F., 146
Potanina, S., 322
Pound, R., 19
Pöyhönen, J., 299
Prokhorov, A. M., 43, 46
Prokopev, V. P., 154
Prosperini, Ia. Iu., 85
Ptushenko, A. V., 228
Pufendorf, S., 17, 235
Puttfarken, H., 22

Rabel, E., 93, 95, 96, 102
Rabinovich, P. M., 40, 162
Rachkova, P. A., 192
Rácz, A., 291
Radko, T., 163
Rassolov, M., 163
Raymond, L., 228
Redmond, P., 297
Reenan, T. P. van, 30
Rennenkampf, N. K., 14, 15
Reshetnikov, F. M., 296
Reutov, V. P., 58
Reimann, M., 34, 92, 93, 102, 142
Reisner, M., 256
Rheinstein, Max, 41, 97, 99, 211
Richter, M., 30
Rickert, H., 99
Ricoeur, Paul, 84, 86-88
Riles, A., 32, 93
Roberts, John, C. J., 153
Rodière, R., 37, 40
Rogozhin, S. A., 154
Romanov, A. K., 69, 151
Romashov, R. A., 75, 154, 189-206, 341
Rosen, L., 94
Rosenberg, A., 107
Rot, H., 39
Rouland, N., 116, 180, 327
Rozhkova, L. P., 44, 45
Rozin, V. M., 103, 104

Sacco, R., 27, 32, 93
Sadovnikov, V. N., 96
Saidler, G. L., 99
Saidov, A. Kh., 2, 26, 27, 29, 32, 34, 35, 37-40, 42, 59, 74, 83, 93, 111, 112, 139, 144, 146, 160, 214, 307-310, 341, 342
Saidov, R. A., 32
Saleilles, R., 133
Salnikov, V. P., 201, 279
Salo, V. I., 184
Salomatin, A. Iu., 141-158, 147, 154, 157, 230, 342
Samuel, G., 93, 95, 96, 100, 102, 105, 106, 108
Sartre, Jean-Paul, 222
Sauser-Hall, G., 37, 261, 307
Savigny, F., 31
Schäffer, H., 291
Schlesinger, R. B., 24, 40
Schnitzer, A. F., 37, 261
Schwartz, H., 280
Selden, J., 17
Semigin, G. Iu., 192
Semitko, A. P., 39
Serebrennikova, A. V., 146
Serebrova, S. O., 54, 55, 82
Sergeevich, V. I., 190-192
Servais, J., 298
Shaliapin, S. O., 326-330
Shapoval, V. N., 117
Shatilo, I. S., 40

Shaw, J., 295
Shears, P., 297
Shemshuchenko, Iu. S., 1-2, 14, 28, 228, 235, 337, 338, 343, 344
Sheridan, M., 290
Shtatina, M. A., 146
Shtegmaie, V., 101
Shtompka, P., 103
Shumilov, V. M., 128-131
Shvachka, V. Iu., 164
Sigel, F.: see Zigel, F. F.
Silchenko, N. V., 45, 46
Siniukov, V. N., 39, 42, 52, 74, 162, 263
Sjafe'i, Imam, 71
Skakun, O. F., 6, 28, 39, 74, 111, 143, 145, 159-188, 307, 308, 342
Smylakin, A. S., 318-325
Snyder, F., 300
Sober, E., 107
Socrates, 101, 102
Sokuler, Z. A., 100
Spencer, H., 235
Speranskii, M. M., 197
Spipushko, L. M., 46
St. Iuul, 293
Stalev, Zh., 97, 160
Stalin, I. V., 201
Stawecki, T., 42
Steger, M., 123
Stevens, R., 299
Strabo, 333
Sturner, R., 285
Sukiainen, L. R., 153
Sukharev, A. Ia., 76, 79
Suvorov, N. S., 319, 320
Sverdlov, M. B., 190
Syrykh, V. M., 44
Szabo, I., 38, 41, 134

Talapina, E. V., 112, 113
Taranovskii, F. V., 15, 16, 97, 98
Taranovskyi, F. V.: see Taranovskii, F. V.
Tarasov, N. N., 96, 98, 100, 106
Thabit, Ibn Nu'man ibn, 177
Thibault, A. F. J., 17, 24
Thucydides, 333
Tikhomirov, A. D., 13, 28, 35, 111, 112, 207-233, 343
Tikhomirov, Iu. A., 40, 59, 64, 74, 110-122, 128, 129, 142, 145, 146, 195, 214, 308, 309, 343
Tille, A. A., 22, 32, 38, 44, 61, 111, 214
Timoshchuk, A. S., 217
Tishchenko, A. G., 201
Tishkov, V. A., 230
Tkachenko, A. V., 92-109
Tolstik, V. A., 42, 82
Tolstykh, V. L., 154, 156
Tomsinov, V. A., 190, 194, 331
Toporin, B. N., 67
Torkunov, A. V., 125
Toynbee, A. J., 63, 64, 278, 279
Trochon, J., 286
Trubetskoi, E. N., 323
Tsypin, V., 321, 324, 329
Tulchinskii, G. L., 219
Tumanov, V. A., 19, 34, 40, 97, 98, 104, 111, 134, 160, 211, 307, 314
Tumanova, A. S., 157
Tykhomyrov, O. D.: see Tikhimirov, A. D.

Ulpianus, D., 235, 257

Van den Berg, L. W. C., 71
Van Hoecke, M., 98, 100, 105
Varga, C., 279
Varias, M., 320, 329
Vaskovich, I., 274
Vernadskii, G. V., 195
Vico, G. B., 17
Vishniakov, V. G., 80
Vita, A. de, 158
Vladimirskii-Budanov, M. F., 319
Voloshin, Iu. A., 337

Vrij, E., 292
Vyshinskii, A. Ia., 199
Vystorbets, E. A., 117

Wallerstein, I., 124
Watson, Alan, 279
Weber, Max, 84, 99
Weiler, J., 294
Weir, T., 10, 307
White, R., 291
Wiegand, W., 284, 285
Wigmore, John H., 37, 332
Williams, Rowan, 305
Wilts, A., 290
Winczorek, P., 42
Winkler von Mohrenfels, P., 59
Witte, B., 298
Wolff, M., 37, 261, 262, 307
Woods, T., 297
Wright, G. H. von, 99

Zachariae von Lingenthal, K. S., 17, 18, 31
Zaichuk, O. V., 21, 163, 308
Zainchkovskii, M. L., 228
Zaslavskaia, T. I., 44
Zatonskii, V. A., 159, 167
Zazaeva, N. B., 131
Zhidkov, O. A., 38
Zhol', K. K., 226
Zhukov, V. I., 226
Zigel, F. F., 331, 332, 334
Zimmerman, R., 92, 102
Zirk-Sadowski, M., 100
Zweigert, K., 5, 10, 22, 31, 37, 38, 42, 64, 92, 93, 95, 97, 100, 105, 110, 160, 216, 256, 262, 263, 307, 308, 315